FIFTH EDITION

Reading Skills
for
College Students

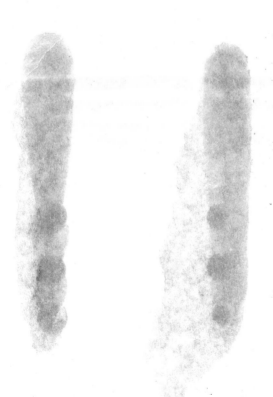

FIFTH EDITION

Reading Skills

for

College Students

Ophelia H. Hancock

Macon State College

Prentice
Hall

Upper Saddle River, New Jersey 07458

Library of Congress Cataloging-in-Publication Data

Hancock, Ophelia H.
    Reading skills for college students / Ophelia H. Hancock. — 5th ed.
      p. cm.
    Includes index.
    ISBN 0–13–022272–0
    1. College readers. 2. Reading (Higher education)—Problems,
    exercises, etc. I. Title.
    PE1122.H34 2001
    428.6—dc21
                                           99–057834
                                            CIP

Editor-in-chief: Leah Jewell
Acquisitions editor: Craig Campanella
Editorial assistant: Joan Polk
Managing editor: Mary Rottino
Production liaison: Fran Russello
Editorial/production supervision: Bruce Hobart (Pine Tree Composition)
Prepress and manufacturing buyer: Ben Smith
Marketing manager: Brandy Dawson
Cover design: Bruce Kenselaar
Cover image: Jane Sterrett/Spots on the Spot

This book was set in $10\frac{1}{2}$/$12\frac{1}{2}$ Palatino by Pine Tree Composition, Inc., and was printed and bound by Hamilton Printing Company. The cover was printed by Phoenix Color Corp.

For permission to use copyrighted material please refer to pp. xiii–xvii which are hereby made part of this copyright page.

Printed in the United States of America

10 9 8 7 6 5 4 3 2 1

ISBN 0-13-022272-0

Prentice-Hall International (UK) Limited, *London*
Prentice-Hall of Australia Pty. Limited, *Sydney*
Prentice-Hall Canada Inc., *Toronto*
Prentice-Hall Hispanoamericana, S.A., *Mexico*
Prentice-Hall of India Private Limited, *New Delhi*
Prentice-Hall of Japan, Inc., *Tokyo*
Pearson Education Asia Pte. Ltd., *Singapore*
Editora Prentice-Hall do Brasil, Ltda., *Rio de Janeiro*

To

CATHERINE

What are little girls made of?
Sugar and spice and all things nice . . .

Contents

PART ONE   READING SKILLS

CONTEXT CLUES   1

To the Instructor

The fifth edition of *Reading Skills for College Students* has the same purpose as the four previous editions—to improve the reading skills of college students and to increase their enjoyment of reading. As technology advances and jobs become more diversified, students need more proficient reading skills in order to be able to select, read, and critically evaluate the abundance of information that is available.

The only changes in the format of the fifth edition is that the graphics, rate, and study skills chapters have changed locations in the book. These skills are now Chapters Ten, Eleven, and Twelve, respectively. The format continues to be flexible so that an instructor can begin on any chapter desired or can omit any chapter or exercise that is not relevant to the needs of individual classes. The exercises in each chapter begin on an easy level and get more difficult as the skill is perfected.

The book is divided into three major parts. Part One, Reading Skills, covers all the basic skills of reading—vocabulary, comprehension, graphics, rate, and study skills—while providing a wealth of interesting, relevant reading material. All paragraphs and passages were selected not only to teach the skill intended but to add to the student's background knowledge as well. Every conceivable kind of questioning is used in the book, from true-false to essay, to prepare students for all the methods of teaching and all types of tests that they will encounter. Each vocabulary and comprehension skill is explained with examples and is then reinforced with exercises using the skill. Chapters One through Nine use words, sentences, paragraphs, and longer passages in appropriate context to teach and strengthen each skill. Chapter Ten, Graphics, covers graphs, charts, tables, and maps. In a reading context, graphics are designed to support information in the text. Therefore, in the exercises in this chapter, the graphics are presented in reading passages rather than in isolation. Chapter Eleven, Rate, stresses phrase reading for ideas, flexibility in rate of reading, and the importance of determining a purpose for reading. The study skills chapter, Chapter Twelve, is an overview of study techniques and test-taking strategies.

Part Two, Reading in the Content Area, contains six chapters: Literature, History, Political Science, Psychology, Biology, and Computer Sciences and Data Processing. Each chapter contains one long passage selected from a college textbook and is followed by a vocabulary and comprehension exercise.

Part Three, Reading Selections, has been changed to include two additional short stories. "A Worn Path" by Eudora Welty has been added and "The Pedestrian" by Ray Bradbury, has returned by popular demand. The selection "One Good Turn," about how machine-made screws brought the world together, has replaced "What's in the Cards?" The short story, "Quality" by John Galsworthy, has been moved to the Inference Tests in the Instructor's Manual. Other tried and true selections in the book were selected from newspapers, magazines, and books to provide a wide variety of reading materials. All of the selections are followed by vocabulary and comprehension exercises and are arranged progressively, regardless of length, from an easy reading level to a more difficult level.

This edition, like the previous editions, provides opportunities throughout the text to practice good writing skills. In addition, the Suggestions for Further Study section at the end of each chapter suggests ways to expand both reading and writing skills.

The *Instructor's Manual with Tests,* containing teaching suggestions for each chapter, and answers to all the exercises in the book, has been expanded to include seven new tests. It has an easy and a hard test on all the skills except the skills of dictionary use, signal words, rate, and study skills, which have only one test each.

Thank you for choosing this edition of *Reading Skills for College Students* for your reading classes. I hope that you enjoy using the textbook and that it will help your students become better readers.

Ophelia H. Hancock

Acknowledgments

I am grateful to Craig Campanella, Maggie Barbieri, Fran Russello, and Joan Polk of Prentice Hall and Bruce Hobart of Pine Tree Composition, Inc., for their patient guidance and expertise in preparing the fifth edition of this textbook. I am indebted to Richard Fuller, Art Institute of Philadelphia; Lois Reeves, University of Great Falls; Jian Zhang, Suffolk Community College; and Della Burt-Bradley, Harold Washington College, all of whom made comments and suggestions that helped shape the content of this edition. A special acknowledgment is due my husband, Jerry Hancock, whose support and help with the manuscript was invaluable.

I would also like to thank the following copyright holders for their permission to quote from their material throughout the book.

Pages 15, 16, 58, 66, 69, 74, 76, 83: Excerpts from Rebecca J. Donatelle and others, *Access to Health,* © 1988, pp. 29, 40, 59, 85, 225, 343, 442. Reprinted by permission of Prentice-Hall, Inc., Upper Saddle River, N.J.

Pages 16, 17, 170, 177: Excerpts from Kotler/Armstrong, *Marketing: An Introduction,* 3rd ed. © 1993, pp. 151, 413, 442, 494. Reprinted by permission of Prentice-Hall, Inc., Upper Saddle River, N.J.

Pages 17, 80, 91–93: Excerpts from Tom McKnight, *Physical Geography—A Landscape*

Appreciation, 4th ed. © 1993, pp. 60, 66, 72–73. Reprinted by permission of Prentice-Hall, Inc., Upper Saddle River, N.J.

Page 18: Excerpt from Gary Kirby and Jeffery Goodpaster, *Thinking*, 1995, p. 244. Reprinted by permission of Prentice-Hall, Inc., Upper Saddle River, N.J.

Pages 19, 20: Excerpts from "A Mississippian Outpost on the Macon Plateau" in the pamphlet, *Ocmulgee*. Reprinted by permission of the National Park Service, Harpers Ferry, W.V.

Pages 45, 47: The key to pronunciation (p. 45) and the dictionary page (p. 47) are used with permission from *Webster's New World Dictionary*, Second College Edition. Copyright © 1984 by Simon & Schuster, Inc.

Page 56: Excerpt from Ruth Lyndeen Memmler and Dena Lin Wood, *The Human Body in Health and Disease*, 5th ed., © 1985 by J.B. Lippincott Company.

Pages 57, 121: Excerpts from Stephen R. Robbins, *Management: Concepts and Applications* 2nd ed., © 1988, pp. 75, 280. Reprinted by permission of Prentice-Hall, Inc., Upper Saddle River, N.J.

Pages 58, 70, 86–87, 120: Excerpts from *The Cousteau Almanac* by Jacques Cousteau. Copyright © 1981 by The Cousteau Society, Inc. Used by permission of Doubleday, a division of Random House.

Pages 60, 63: Excerpts from Necia H. Apfel, *The Moon and Its Exploration*, © 1982 by Franklin Watts Publishers.

Pages 60, 67–68, 104, 119: Excerpts from Ann Ellenson, *Human Relations*, 2nd ed. © 1982, pp. 83, 89, 196, 222–23. Reprinted by permission of Prentice-Hall, Upper Saddle River, N.J.

Pages 61, 111: Excerpts from James Monroe and Bonnie Jackson, *Physical Science: An Inquiry Approach*, copyright 1977, Harper & Row Publishers, Inc.

Pages 56, 61–62, 67, 69, 75, 106, 109: Excerpts from Charles G. Morris, *Psychology: An Introduction*, 4th ed., © 1982, pp. 46, 124, 148, 213, 232, 426. Reprinted by permission of Prentice-Hall, Upper Saddle River, N.J.

Page 77: Excerpt from Charles G. Morris, *Psychology: An Introduction*, 8th ed. © 1993, p. 96. Reprinted by permission of Prentice-Hall, Inc., Upper Saddle River, N.J.

Page 62: Excerpt from Betty Vickers and William J. Vincent, *Swimming*, William C. Brown Company, p. 43.

Pages 63, 68, 105: Reprinted with permission of Macmillan Publishing Company, A Division of Macmillan, Inc., from *Student's Book of College English*, 4th ed., by David Skwire and Frances Chitwood. Copyright © 1985 by Glencoe Publishing Co., Inc.

Pages 64, 70, 89–90: Excerpts from Joseph Machlis, *The Enjoyment of Music*, 4th ed., © 1977 by W. W. Norton & Co. Inc.

Page 64: Excerpt from Thomas Slaymaker and Virginia H. Brown, *Power Volleyball*, © 1976 by W. B. Sanders Co. (CBS), p. 21.

Page 65: Excerpt from "Halley's Comet," in George Fichter, *Comets and Meteors*, © 1982 by Franklin Watts Publishers.

Pages 65, 71, 119: Excerpts from Victor P. Maioriana, *How to Learn and Study in College*, © 1980, pp. 162, 252–253, 280, 283. Reprinted by permission of Prentice-Hall, Upper Saddle River, N.J.

Page 66: Excerpt from *Art: An Introduction*, 3rd edition, by Dale G. Cleaver, Copyright © 1977 by Harcourt Brace Jovanovich, Inc. Reprinted by permission of the publisher.

Pages 67, 72: Excerpts from Dennis J. Sporre, *Perceiving the Arts: An Introduction to the Humanities*, © 1981, pp. 60, 108. Reprinted by permission of Prentice-Hall, Upper Saddle River, N.J.

Pages 72, 76, 77, 118, 120, 121–24: Excerpts from Jordan/Litwack/Hofstadter/Miller/Aaron, *The United States*, Combined 5th ed., © 1982, pp. 55, 56, 117–18, 255, 361, 404, 472, 500–502, 623, 699–700, 826. Reprinted by permission of Prentice-Hall, Upper Saddle River, N.J.

Pages 74, 75, 115: Excerpts from M. Lennier/J. Maker, *Keys to College Success: Reading and*

Study Improvement, © 1980, pp. 10, 88, 151. Reprinted by permission of Prentice-Hall, Upper Saddle River, N.J.

Pages 75, 113: Excerpts from George J. Kertz, *The Nature and Application of Mathematics,* copyright 1979, Goodyear Publishing Division, Scott, Foresman and Company.

Page 81: Excerpts from Eldon D. Enger, *Environmental Science,* © 1983 by Wm. C. Brown Company, Publishers.

Pages 81–82: Excerpt from *The Job Hunt: How to Compete & Win,* by Joseph T. Straub, © 1981 by Prentice-Hall, Upper Saddle River, N.J.

Pages 84–85: Ellen Darion, "Walk, Don't Run," *McCall's,* April 1984, p. 34.

Page 104: Excerpt from Dennis Sporre, *The Creative Impulse: An Introduction to the Arts,* © 1987, p. 15. Reprinted by permission of Prentice-Hall, Upper Saddle River, N.J.

Page 107: Excerpt from David Edwards, *The American Political Experience: An Introduction to Government,* 4th ed., © 1988, pp. 37–38. Reprinted by permission of Prentice-Hall, Inc., Upper Saddle River, N.J.

Page 108: Excerpt from Laird Durham, *100 Careers,* © 1977, p. 6. Reprinted by permission of Prentice-Hall, Upper Saddle River, N.J.

Page 108: Excerpt from Robert Hickok, *Exploring Music,* 3rd ed., © 1979 by Random House, Inc.

Page 110: Excerpts from Clifford T. Morgan, *A Brief Introduction to Psychology,* © 1974 by McGraw-Hill, Inc.

Pages 109, 110, 111, 112, 114: Excerpts from Pasachoff/Pasachoff/Clark/Westermann, *Physical Science Today,* © 1987, pp. 88, 426, 460–61, 480, 509, 523. Reprinted by permission of Prentice-Hall, Inc., Upper Saddle River, N.J.

Page 112: Excerpt from *Psychology: Its Principles and Applications,* 7th ed., by T. L. Engle and Louis Snellgrove, copyright © 1979 by Harcourt Brace Jovanovich, Inc. Reprinted by permission of the publisher.

Pages 76, 105–106, 113: Excerpt from Thomas Devine and Linda Meagher, *Mastering Study Skills: A Student Guide,* © 1989, p. 7, 50–51, 195–96. Reprinted by permission of Prentice-Hall, Inc., Upper Saddle River, N.J.

Page 118: Excerpt from Herman Melville, *Billy Budd and Typee,* © 1962 by Simon & Schuster, Inc.

Page 125: Excerpt from Catherine Marshall, *Christy,* © 1967 by McGraw-Hill, Inc.

Pages 126–27: Excerpt from *The Demon Lover* by Victoria Holt. Copyright © 1982 by Victoria Holt. Used by permission of Doubleday, a division of Random House.

Pages 133–38: Excerpt from Stephen Crane, *The Red Badge of Courage and Selected Prose and Poetry,* © 1968 by Holt, Rinehart, and Winston, Inc.

Pages 128–31: Jay Simpson, *Danny,* 1984 (unpublished). Reprinted with permission of the author.

Page 142: "Fur Coats: Where Do They Come From?" (leaflet). Reprinted by permission of The Humane Society of the United States.

Pages 146–48: "Public Apathy—Highway Killer" (leaflet). Reprinted by permission of the Motor Vehicle Manufacturing Association of the United States, Inc.

Pages 150–52: Larry Fennelly, "Quality of Life Is Much More Than a Job," *Macon Telegraph and News,* Monday, January 31, 1983.

Pages 153–54: George H. Hanford, "SAT Is the Best Way to Test Reasoning Skill," *USA Today,* Tuesday, April 10, 1984, p. 8A. Reprinted with permission of *USA Today.*

Pages 155–57: Ernest L. Bayer, "Why We Need a Test to Replace the SAT," *USA Today,* Tuesday, April 10, 1984, p. 8A. Reprinted with permission of *USA Today.*

Pages 158–59: Becky Constantino, "Should Women Be Allowed in Combat?" *Congressional Quarterly Researcher,* Sept. 25, 1992, p. 849.

Page 159–60: General Robert H. Barrow, "Should Women Be Allowed in Combat?" *Congressional Quarterly Researcher,* Sept. 25, 1992, p. 849.

Page 168, Fig. 10–3: American Cancer Society, *Cancer Facts and Figures—1993*, 1993. Graph, "Allocation of American Cancer Society Funds," page 25. Reprinted courtesy of the American Cancer Society.

Page 169, Fig. 10–4: Larry Long, *Introduction to Computers and Information Processing*, 3rd ed., © 1991, p. 373. Reprinted by permission of Prentice-Hall, Inc., Upper Saddle River, N.J.

Page 173: Map of the Ocmulgee National Monument in the pamphlet "Ocmulgee." Reprinted courtesy of National Park Service.

Pages 174–75: "Technology Is Blamed for Rising Health Costs," *The Macon Telegraph*, Wednesday, June 23, 1993, page 3A. Used by permission of AP/Wide World Photos, Inc.

Page 178–80: Burns/Peltason/Cronin/Magleby, *Government by the People: Basic Version*, 15th ed., © 1993, pp. 421–22. Reprinted by permission of Prentice-Hall, Inc., Upper Saddle River, N.J.

Page 182–83: John J. Macionis, *Sociology*, 4th ed., © 1993, p. 604. Reprinted by permission of Prentice-Hall, Upper Saddle River, N.J.

Pages 184–86: Tom L. McKnight, *Physical Geography: A Landscape Appreciation*, 4th ed., © 1993. Reprinted by permission of Prentice-Hall, Inc., Upper Saddle River, N.J.

Pages 217–27: "Livvie" from *The Wide Net and Other Stories*, copyright 1942 and renewed 1970 by Eudora Welty, reprinted by permission of Harcourt, Inc.

Pages 235–42: Irwin Unger, *These United States: The Questions of Our Past, Volume II*, 5th ed., © 1992, pp. 938–43. Reprinted by permission of Prentice-Hall, Upper Saddle River, N.J.

Pages 251–61: Burns/Peltason/Cronin/Magleby, *Government by the People*, 15th ed., © 1993, pp. 439–48. Reprinted by permission of Prentice-Hall, Upper Saddle River, N.J.

Pages 271–77: Robert V. Kail/Rita Wicks-Nelson, *Developmental Psychology*, 5th ed. © 1993, pp. 244–50. Reprinted by permission of Prentice-Hall, Upper Saddle River, N.J.

Pages 283–91: Barrett and others, *Biology* © 1986, pp. 319–29. Reprinted by permission of Prentice-Hall, Upper Saddle River, N.J.

Pages 297–307: Larry Long, *Introduction to Computers and Information Processing*, 3rd ed., © 1991, pp. 11–26, 13, 17. Reprinted by permission of Prentice-Hall, Upper Saddle River, N.J.

Pages 311–13: Barbara Zigli, "Are We Tolerating More Dishonesty?" *USA Today*, April 12, 1984, p. 30. Reprinted with permission of *USA Today*.

Pages 317–19: Adrienne Popper, "I'm Going to Buy the Brooklyn Bridge," *Woman's Day*, September 11, 1984, p. 152. Reprinted by permission of the author.

Pages 323–24: Susan Gilbert, "Wildlife on Main Street," *Science Digest*, September 1984, p. 21. Reprinted by permission of *Science Digest*, © 1984 by the Hearst Corporation.

Pages 327–30: Norman Strung, "Hard Times," *Field & Stream*, January 1984, pp. 36–37. Reprinted by permission.

Pages 335–37: "The Open Window," from *The Short Stories of Saki* (H. H. Munro). Copyright 1930, renewed copyright © 1958 by The Viking Press. Reprinted by permission of Viking Penguin Inc.

Pages 341–43: "In the Blink of an Eye," by Shawna Vogel, published in *Discover* February, 1989. © 1989 *Discover Magazine*. Reprinted with permission of *Discover Magazine*.

Pages 349–51: "The Chaser," by John Collier from *The New Yorker*. Copyright © 1940, renewed 1968 by John Collier. Reprinted by permission of Harold Matson Co., Inc.

Pages 355–61: "They Dared Cocaine—and Lost," by Henry Hurt. Reprinted with permission from the May 1988 *Reader's Digest*. Copyright © 1988 by The Reader's Digest Assn., Inc.

Pages 367–73: "The Necklace," by Guy de Maupassant, translated by Edgar V. Roberts, from *Literature: An Introduction to Reading and Writing*, 3rd ed. by Roberts/Jacobs, © 1992. Reprinted by permission of Prentice-Hall, Inc., Upper Saddle River, N.J.

Pages 379–80: "One Good Turn," by Witold Rybczynski, copyright © 1999 by the New York Times Co. Reprinted by permission.

FIFTH EDITION

Reading Skills

for

College Students

PART ONE

Context Clues

BUILDING YOUR VOCABULARY

Vocabulary plays an important role in reading. While good word recognition skills will not guarantee good comprehension, these skills are necessary in order to comprehend fully what you read. A good vocabulary helps you read with more understanding and enables you to express yourself better when you speak or write. Your friends and associates are influenced not only by your appearance and actions but also by what you say and how you say it. Successful people usually have large vocabularies and good word-recognition skills that enable them to use the right word in the right place at the right time.

There are two basic ways to communicate with others—speaking and writing. Vocabulary development is essential for both. If you fail to understand what your instructors say, one of the reasons could be the failure to understand the words that were used. For your reading, writing, and speaking skills to be up to par, you must have a good command of words.

Good vocabularies do not just happen. Instead, a good vocabulary is usually the result of a systematic, planned program designed with the individual in mind. Of all the vocabulary improvement methods available, the best one is simply *to read*. Reading widely exposes you not only to many words and their meanings but to ideas as well. These ideas then increase your interest in many areas, which in turn makes you want to read even more.

As you read for vocabulary improvement, use the following sample plan, which can be adapted to your needs and mode of learning.

1. **Take inventory of your vocabulary.** Before you can correct any deficiency, you must know the extent of the problem. You probably took a diagnostic test during the first few days of this class. If so, how well did you score on the vocabulary section? If not, are you comfortable with words, especially difficult words? Do you always know the appropriate words to express what you are thinking? Do you always understand when others speak and when you read? If you answer "no" to these questions, you should carefully follow the next four steps.

2. **Be on the alert for new words.** Look for them in everything you read, and listen for them when others are speaking. Most people tend to overlook what they do not really want to see. Therefore, you should consciously look for words you do not know.

3. **Write down the word, its definition, and its pronunciation.** Your creativity can be utilized in this step. Create your own system, such as a general vocabulary notebook, a subject notebook, or a file of note cards.

4. **Use the word.** In the notebook or on the note card, write a sentence or short paragraph using the word. Try to use the word in a way that has a special meaning for you.

5. **Review.** Use the words often and go back to them until they become a permanent part of your vocabulary.

In order to succeed with your improvement plan, or any plan to build your vocabulary, you should strive to master certain skills. Three very important skills are (1) use of context clues, (2) structural analysis, and (3) dictionary use. Occasionally these skills are used alone, but most often they are used in combination. These skills are studied in the next three chapters in this text.

USING CONTEXT CLUES

Using context clues in word recognition means figuring out the meaning of a word based on clues in the surrounding context. These clues could be found in the sentence containing the word, in the sentences before, or in the sentences following the word. Most authors realize that some readers have problems with difficult words and deliberately put in clues that will enable the reader not only to recognize the words but also to get the meaning of the words. Authors also write in such a way as to prevent misreading due to personal interpretation. A word could have a different meaning to different people with differing backgrounds of knowledge and experience. The author will include a clue in the writing to indicate to the reader the interpretation that is intended.

Context clues will be easier if you are familiar with some of the kinds of clues often found in sentences. Following are some common kinds of clues with examples and an explanation of each.

Restatement

1. *Animosity,* a feeling of strong dislike, developed among the workers when some refused to join the union.
2. *Polygamy,* the practice of having many mates, is unlawful in the United States.

A restatement is merely stating the word in another way, usually in simpler terms. A restatement is usually set off by commas. In the first example, the author defines *animosity* as a feeling of strong dislike. In the second example, the author defines *polygamy* as the practice of having many mates.

Synonyms

1. The old man was *cantankerous.* He was ill-tempered, mean, and extremely quarrelsome.
2. At first I was doubtful that I could do the job. After one successful week, however, I am much less *dubious.*

A synonym is one of two or more words that have the same or similar meaning. When an author uses a difficult word, the author often will also use a more familiar word to make it easy to understand. In the first example, the author defines *cantankerous* as ill-tempered, mean, and quarrelsome. The second example uses the word *dubious,* which means doubtful.

Antonyms

1. The sea lion is a *cumbersome* animal on land, but in the water it is one of the most graceful.
2. In contrast to their enjoyment of their country home, the Jones family found it difficult to adjust to *urban* life.

An antonym is a word of opposite meaning. In the first example just given, the "but" signals that an opposite is being used. Therefore, *cumbersome* is the opposite word of graceful and means clumsy. Example 2 uses "in contrast to" in order to indicate that *urban* is the opposite of country.

Definitions

1. A disease that can be spread from one person to another is said to be *contagious*.
2. An *incoherent* statement is a statement that is not logically connected.

It is not unusual for an author to put in a statement that clearly defines a difficult word. In these examples, *contagious* means spreading from one person to another person and *incoherent* means not logically connected.

Explanation

1. We should be *skeptical* of get-rich-quick plans because financial success usually requires long hours and hard work.
2. Marilyn is a *versatile* musician. Not only does she sing and play the piano, but she plays many other instruments as well.

As an aid to the reader, difficult words are sometimes explained to make the meaning clearer. In the first example, *skeptical* is explained in the same sentence and is signaled by the word "because." As used in the sentence, *skeptical* means doubtful or questioning. In the second sentence, *versatile* is explained by additional information in the sentence that follows. The sample sentence, then, means that Marilyn is competent in many aspects of music.

Relationships

1. The students were *jubilant* when they learned that their school had placed first in the competition.
2. Each time you drive in excess of the speed limit, especially when traffic is heavy, you *jeopardize* not only your own life but the lives of others as well.

This type of clue is less concrete and requires more thinking on the part of the reader. Here, you must identify a relationship between the difficult word and something the author has stated with little explanation and few clues. In the first example, think about how students would feel if they placed first in a competition. Some synonyms for *jubilant* would be joyful, rejoicing, or elated. Likewise, in the second example, you identify the relationship between excessive speed and a danger to your life. Thus, *jeopardize* means endanger.

EXERCISE 1: Context Clues

NAME _____ **DATE** _____

I. A. Use context clues to select the best meaning for each of the underlined words in the following sentences. Write the letter of your choice on the short line provided. In addition, determine whether the type of clue is a restatement, a synonym, an antonym, a definition, an explanation, or a relationship. Write the kind of clue on the longer line provided.

_____ 1. The prisoner was placed in <u>solitary</u> confinement. He was not allowed even one visitor.

   a. unified   b. separate   c. obsolete

_____

_____ 2. It has been a <u>tradition</u> in our family for generations to give a silver spoon to each new baby.

   a. pleasure   b. chore   c. custom

_____

_____ 3. The necklace was unusual not only in the way it was made but also in the color combination. It could certainly be described as <u>unique</u>.

   a. unusual   b. expensive   c. beautiful

_____

_____ 4. Personally, I enjoyed the <u>diverse</u> weather conditions we had during our vacation. We never knew what it would be like from one day to the next.

   a. divine   b. pleasant   c. varied

_____

_____ 5. <u>Compassion</u> is the ability to understand and appreciate another person's feelings.

   a. harmony and cooperation
   b. understanding and tenderness
   c. compulsiveness and forcefulness

_____

_____ 6. It looks as if the strike will not be settled by midnight. Labor and union officials will <u>negotiate</u> until each side is satisfied.

    a. argue   b. bargain   c. advise

_____ 7. Although I did not totally approve of the contest, I <u>sanctioned</u> it for the sake of the students in the class.

    a. disapproved   b. approved   c. defied

_____ 8. Because I could not afford to purchase the original painting, I purchased a <u>replica</u>. An inexperienced eye could not tell the difference.

    a. twin   b. copy   c. proxy

_____ 9. There has been so little <u>precipitation</u> this month that the crops are parched and dying.

    a. haste   b. labor   c. rainfall

_____ 10. <u>Idolatry</u>, the worship of idols, was practiced by many primitive people.

    a. primitive people   b. golden objects   c. worship of idols

B. Use context clues to define in your own words the underlined words in the following sentences. Write the kind of clue on the shorter line provided.

1. When you cause someone to become very angry, you <u>infuriate</u> him or her.

_____

_____

2. The <u>tranquil</u> family life in the child's foster home is a sharp contrast to the turmoil she has always known.

_A_ _____

_____

3. The small boy tries to <u>emulate</u> his father in everything he does. He even copies the way his father walks.

_____

_____

4. It was <u>inevitable</u> that the student would fail the course. Poor study habits will always result in poor grades.

Rela _____

_____

5. The driver who failed to yield the right-of-way and ignored the stop sign was charged with <u>negligence.</u>

_____

_____

6. The woman accused of the crime had always been known as a <u>rebel.</u> Even as a young woman she could not abide the rules and regulations imposed by her family.

_____

_____

7. Lately I have been assigned to every <u>tedious</u> task imaginable. On the other hand, my partner seems to get interesting, exciting tasks each day.

_____

_____

8. There are many storybooks written for children that have historical value. Photographs lend <u>authenticity,</u> or reality, to these books as well as teach the lesson in an enjoyable manner.

_____

_____

9. We were not surprised that he chose to teach kindergarten because he had always had an <u>aptitude</u> for working with young children.

_____

_____

10. <u>Geriatrics,</u> the medical treatment of the elderly, is a rapidly growing branch of medicine.

_____

_____

II. *Use context clues to select the best meaning of the underlined words in the sentences that follow. Write the letter of your choice on the line provided.*

___c___ 1. People who have stressful occupations should choose an <u>avocation</u> that allows for complete relaxation as well as enjoyment.
    a. attraction   b. business   c. hobby

___b___ 2. When the hungry ranch hands finally stopped for dinner, they ate everything on the table with <u>relish</u>.
    a. pickles   b. enjoyment   c. sauce

___c___ 3. I felt that the sentence given to the criminal was much too <u>lenient</u>. Murder should carry the maximum penalty.
    a. soothing   b. tiresome   c. merciful

___a___ 4. It took a lot of hard work and dedication for her to reach the <u>acme</u> of her career before she was thirty years of age.
    a. peak   b. consequence   c. modification

___c___ 5. After all the children had left home, the couple put their <u>commodious</u> house up for sale. It was too large for only two people.
    a. secluded   b. conspicuous   c. spacious

___c___ 6. The <u>squall</u> was so strong it blew the roof off the greenhouse and destroyed many of my prize orchids.
    a. harsh scream   b. lightning   c. violent storm

___c___ 7. Most executives consider <u>compatibility</u> to be a desirable characteristic for their employees. Internal bickering can be very disruptive.

a. ability to type rapidly
b. ability to get to work promptly
c. ability to work harmoniously

_b_ 8. The gang's <u>arrogance</u> was exceeded only by a total lack of concern for the teacher's feelings.

a. consideration   b. haughtiness   c. sensibility

_c_ 9. Children of <u>migrant</u> <u>workers</u> must adjust to a different school every few months. The harvest season for most crops is relatively short.

a. workers who work in a mine
b. workers who immigrate to another country
c. workers who move from place to place to harvest seasonal crops

_c_ 10. I was shocked by the <u>audacity</u> of Bill's request. He is usually a quiet and shy person.

a. reasoning   b. lavishness   c. boldness

_____ 11. Dogs seem to have an <u>uncanny</u> instinct for recognizing people who are not friendly.

a. mysterious   b. burdensome   c. uncouth

_____ 12. The elderly couple enjoyed <u>reminiscing</u> about all the good times the family had when the children were young.

a. thinking back   b. complaining   c. bragging

_____ 13. I was surprised when the motion was approved <u>unanimously</u> by the members of the organization. I had expected some opposition.

a. without question
b. without opposition
c. with compromise

_____ 14. My roommate gives her textbooks such a <u>cursory</u> reading, it is a wonder she ever passes a test.

a. hasty   b. thorough   c. customary

_____ 15. The carpenter did not have the exact tools needed for the job; therefore, he had to <u>improvise</u> with what he could find.

a. improve upon   b. make do   c. incorporate

_____ 16. It is a privilege to live in a free country that protects the rights of individuals. We owe the United States our <u>allegiance</u> as well as our gratitude.

    a. money   b. loyalty   c. impudence

_____ 17. Very old people are often more <u>vulnerable</u> to the misleading tactics employed by swindlers.

    a. likely to need   b. easily understood   c. open to attack

_____ 18. Record low temperatures forced the mountain climbers to give up the climb before they reached the
    a.

13 sameness, tediousness
14 disorder,

_____ 19. The _____ miner put the hea
    a.

15 cheating, unpredictable
16 changed, change
17 deadly, fatal

_____ 20. Air _____ alarming problem por _____ the animals, including clu
    a. i

18 thriftily, economicaly
19 prevention, restriction
20 delay, put off, postpone
21 perfect, flawless
22 questioning

III. Use context clues _____ ed word in the following sentences. Write the meaning on the line provided.

1. If you attend college outside the state in which you <u>reside</u>, you must pay out-of-state fees.

_____

2. It is <u>imperative</u> that a student learn to read. Success in college depends to a great extent on one's reading ability.

_____

3. The lost child was found asleep in the old abandoned house <u>clad</u> only in short pants and a T-shirt. He would have frozen by morning in the subzero weather.

_____

4. When I meet someone who has truly suffered, I feel ashamed of my own <u>petty</u> complaints.

_____

5. So many animals have been hunted to near <u>extinction</u> that the balance of nature is threatened.

   _____

6. All the paintings in the store are <u>facsimiles</u>. This would not be a good place for collectors of original art to shop.

   _____

7. Because food is so scarce in some countries, many children die of <u>malnutrition.</u>

   _____

8. Although each individual grade counts, it is the <u>cumulative</u> grade-point average that determines whether a student meets graduation requirements.

   _____

9. Rice grows well on the island because of the <u>abundance</u> of water. It rains nearly every day during the growing season.

   _____

10. The death of their only child caused the parents <u>profound</u> grief.

    _____

11. Mary received a pay raise and better benefits when she became <u>affiliated</u> with the new company.

    _____

12. The couple decided to buy the old house because their <u>meager</u> savings were short of the price of a new house.

    _____

13. After the <u>monotony</u> of the long drive and boring scenery, the children enjoyed the excitement of the county fair.

    _____

14. When the instructor returned to the room, he found utter <u>chaos.</u> It took him fifteen minutes to restore order.

    _____

15. Although we all know that honesty is the best policy, <u>fraud</u> is often used in many business deals.

    _____

16. The instructor's mood <u>fluctuated</u> to such a degree we never knew what to expect when we went to class.

_____

17. All household products should be kept out of the reach of small children. Some of these products are poisonous and would be <u>lethal</u> if swallowed.

_____

18. Even if I won a million-dollar lottery, I would continue to live <u>frugally</u>. Not having a lot of money has become a way of life.

_____

19. All traffic laws should be obeyed since they are our chief <u>deterrent</u> of reckless driving.

_____

20. Unlike my sister who pays her bills as they come in, I <u>procrastinate</u> until the very last minute.

_____

21. In contrast to his wife's untidy appearance, John is always <u>impeccably</u> dressed.

_____

22. After a brief <u>interrogation</u>, the suspect was released on bond. Questioning alone does not establish guilt.

_____

23. Cindy was from an <u>affluent</u> family; therefore, she could afford to spend a year touring Europe before attending a fashionable school in Paris.

_____*rich*_____

24. A lawyer in the suburbs will have a <u>lucrative</u> practice because of her wealthy <u>clientele</u>.

_____*profitable*_____*customer*_____

25. It was the <u>consensus</u> of the party that its candidate could easily win the election.

_____*agreement*_____*unanimous*_____

IV. *Use the context of the sentences that follow to determine the meaning of the underlined word. Write the letter of your choice on the line provided.*

_____C_____ 1. Cypress trees are <u>indigenous</u> to the state in which I live. Local residents use the wood to make shingles for roofs.

      a. incredulous   b. mysterious   c. native

_____C_____ 2. Although my friend survived his recent stroke, the <u>prognosis</u> for a complete recovery is not encouraging.

      a. proposal   b. procedure   c. prediction

_____C_____ 3. Some homemakers dislike <u>mundane</u> tasks, such as ironing and mopping, whereas others seem to enjoy these tasks.

      a. murky   b. cleaning   c. ordinary

_____a_____ 4. The salesperson used every <u>subtle</u> scheme imaginable to sell the expensive item.

      a. cunning   b. exciting   c. precocious
       clever

_____a_____ 5. Even with <u>explicit</u> directions to the coliseum, we lost our way.

      a. clearly stated   b. ambiguous   c. exorbitant

_____b_____ 6. The IRS auditor <u>meticulously</u> checked the firm's financial records during the investigation.

      a. very impassively   b. very carefully   c. very secretively

_____C_____ 7. Her remarks were infrequent as well as short and to the point. She was certainly not a <u>loquacious</u> woman.

      a. friendly   b. resentful   c. talkative

_____a_____ 8. Although the professor's lectures are clear and to the point, his test questions are <u>ambiguous</u>.

      a. vague   b. ambitious   c. difficult

_____a_____ 9. Even though the two sisters seem to care deeply for each other, they cannot be together long before they begin to <u>wrangle</u>.

      a. argue   b. talk   c. waver

_____C_____ 10. When Chad realized that his brother had betrayed him for a second time, an <u>acrimonious</u> quarrel ensued.

      a. cautious   b. sulky   c. bitter

_____a_____ 11. Some organ recipients want to know the organ donor, whereas others wish the donor to remain <u>anonymous</u>.

    a. unknown   b. answerable   c. attentive

_____c_____ 12. With <u>trepidation</u> we entered the old abandoned mine in search of the two missing children.

    a. intense pain   b. careful disguise   c. fearful uncertainty

_____b_____ 13. The widow's pension is so <u>minuscule</u>, she has difficulty paying her rent, food, and utility bills each month.

    a. unpredictable   b. small   c. inflated

_____b_____ 14. Habitual drug abuse is one of the most <u>pernicious</u> habits a person can develop.

    a. frivolous   b. destructive   c. pertinent

_____c_____ 15. Even though he was told he might never walk again, the young man worked <u>tenaciously</u> to regain full use of his legs.

    a. halfheartedly   b. temporarily   c. persistently

_____b_____ 16. The young woman was such a <u>gregarious</u> individual that she found it hard to live on the isolated island.

    a. domestic   b. sociable   c. docile

_____a_____ 17. The remarks made by the witness were <u>vindictive</u>. It was clear that the witness felt the accused deserved to be punished for the crime against his family.

    a. revengeful   b. resourceful   c. doubtful

_____c_____ 18. It was a time of haste and confusion. The police could <u>inadvertently</u> overlook a clue that would help to find the missing child.

    a. incredibly   b. deplorably   c. unintentionally

_____b_____ 19. The lawyer questioned the <u>veracity</u> of the suspects after they gave two different accounts of the events leading to their arrest.

    a. verdict   b. truthfulness   c. intention

_____a_____ 20. There was no excuse for the customer's <u>pugnacious</u> reply when told by the clerk that the item had been sold.

    a. quarrelsome   b. conscientious   c. prudent

NAME _____ **DATE** _____

Use context clues to determine the meaning of each underlined word in the following paragraphs. Write the letter of your choice on the line provided.

Criticisms of computers for children also exist. The concerns revolve in part around the possible <u>inhibiting</u> effect on social and communication skills. Children who devote too much time to computer games may not learn to interact successfully with their peers. Computer <u>advocates</u> <u>counter</u> that these games increase children's ability to use words, numbers, and pictures to express themselves. Computers are neither <u>inherently</u> good nor bad; it is our responsibility to apply them constructively.

____a____ 1. <u>inhibiting</u>

      a. restricting   b. combining   c. duplicating

____c____ 2. <u>advocates</u>

      a. illiterates   b. adults   c. supporters

____b____ 3. <u>counter</u>

      a. contradict   b. argue   c. demand

____c____ 4. <u>inherently</u>

      a. continually   b. eternally   c. basically

Advertising for tobacco products is the most <u>pervasive</u> evidence of company efforts to keep their products in the public eye. Full-page ads in magazines and on billboards portray young, healthy, successful, physically fit people enjoying tobacco products in a variety of circumstances ranging from <u>opulent</u> restaurants and apartments to rafting, boating, and wind surfing.

____b____ 5. <u>pervasive</u>

      a. pertinent   b. common   c. perfected

____c____ 6. <u>opulent</u>

      a. bizarre   b. ornate   c. expensive

In today's society, all people have the freedom to explore and develop their potentials. We each carry with us responsibility to pursue emotional well-being. During our lifetime we each will be faced with choices to grow or choices to <u>stagnate</u>. Our emotional growth depends upon our ability to take active roles in its development.

_____ 7. <u>stagnate</u>

     a. commence   b. stand still   c. endure

Addictions <u>evolve</u> gradually, often from very <u>innocuous</u> beginnings. A person who feels unhappy, overwhelmed, threatened, or bored finds a subject or behavior that produces a state of being the person desires or suppresses what the person wants to forget. Moderate use of these behaviors—for example, having an occasional drink or party with friends—does not constitute an addiction. Some people, however, reach a point where they can experience security or pleasure only when they are involved with this object or behavior. Withdrawal of the object produces anxiety and despair. At this point, the person has lost control and cannot function without the object; he or she is addicted.

_____ 8. <u>evolve</u>

     a. develop   b. shrink   c. evade

_____ 9. <u>innocuous</u>

     a. carefully planned   b. harmless   c. mysterious

As we grow, we learn that very few of our decisions are <u>irrevocable</u>. Unless the decision is life- or health-threatening, we usually can select an alternative if we want to.

_____ 10. <u>irrevocable</u>

     a. unchangeable   b. detachable   c. comprehensible

A **service** is any activity or benefit that one party can offer to another that is essentially <u>intangible</u> and does not result in the ownership of anything. Its production may or may not be tied to a physical product. Renting a hotel room, depositing money in a bank, traveling on an airplane, visiting a psychiatrist, getting a haircut, having a car repaired, watching a professional sport, seeing a movie, having clothes cleaned at a dry cleaner, getting advice from a lawyer—all involve buying a service.

_____ 11. intangible

     a. incapable of being touched or perceived

     b. inaccessible to being enjoyed

     c. intended to benefit the owner

Weather is in an almost constant state of change, sometimes in seemingly erratic fashion. Yet in the long-run view, it is possible to generalize the variations into a composite pattern, which is termed climate. Climate is the aggregate of day-to-day weather conditions over a long period of time. It encompasses not only the average characteristics but also the variations and extremes. To describe the climate of an area requires weather information over an extended period, normally several decades at least.

_____ 12. erratic

     a. flawed   b. unpredictable   c. prescribed

_____ 13. composite

     a. distinct   b. composed   c. balanced

_____ 14. aggregate

     a. understanding   b. determination   c. accumulation

The impact of the message depends not only on *what* is said, but also on *how* it is said—its message execution. The advertiser has to present the message in a way that wins the target market's attention and interest.

_____ 15. execution

     a. extinction   b. challenge   c. delivery

Understanding consumer behavior is difficult enough for companies marketing within the borders of a single country. For companies operating in many countries, however, understanding and serving the needs of consumers can be daunting. Although consumers in different countries may have some things in common, their values, attitudes, and behaviors often vary dramatically. International marketers must understand such differences and adjust their products and marketing programs accordingly.

_____ 16. daunting

     a. baffling   b. daring   c. dangerous

Complicated and challenging problems take time to acquire the information and understanding necessary for a good solution. It also takes time for an adequate preliminary evaluation. A hurried approach may give us a brief sense of accomplishment and temporary relief from pressure, but only until the solution fails. Even worse, a quick and haphazard approach may <u>exacerbate</u> the problem. For example, a quickly and poorly thought-out decision to engage the enemy in war instead of in <u>diplomatic</u> <u>dialogue</u> could grow into global warfare. On a lesser scale, imagine the consequences of making a hasty decision on our major in college, whom to marry, or how to deal with a serious relationship issue. Some problem solutions can be revoked with little or no effect; others, however, may leave <u>irretrievable marks</u>.

_____ 17. <u>exacerbate</u>

      a. overstate   b. eliminate   c. worsen

_____ 18. <u>diplomatic</u>

      a. legal   b. tactful   c. political

_____ 19. <u>dialogue</u>

      a. exchange of ideas

      b. required action

      c. definition of terms

_____ 20. <u>irretrievable marks</u>

      a. conditions that favor the individual

      b. effects that cannot be recalled

      c. targets that are untraceable

NAME _____ DATE _____

Read the following passage and select the best meaning for the underlined words as used in the passage. Write the letter of your choice on the line provided.

OCMULGEE NATIONAL MONUMENT*

A Mississippian Outpost
on the Macon Plateau

Ocmulgee is a memorial to the <u>antiquity of man</u> in this corner of the North American continent. From Ice-Age hunters to the Creeks of historic times, there is evidence here of 10,000 years of human <u>habitation</u>. One period stands out. Between A.D. 900 and 1100 a skillful farming people lived on this site. Known to us as Mississippians, they were part of a distinctive <u>culture</u> which crystallized about A.D. 750 in the middle Mississippi Valley and over the next seven centuries spread along riverways throughout much of the central and eastern United States. The Mississippians brought a more complex way of life to the region. Though far removed from such Mississippian centers as Cahokia in Illinois and Moundville in Alabama, the people here were the heirs of an <u>ascendant</u> culture and enjoyed a life as rich as any north of Mexico.

The Mississippians at Ocmulgee were <u>intruders</u> of a sort. They apparently displaced the native woodland Indians, though there is no evidence of conflict. The newcomers were a <u>sedentary</u> people who lived mainly by farming bottomlands for crops of corn, beans, squash, pumpkins, and tobacco. They built a compact town of thatched huts on the bluff overlooking the river. More than a thousand persons lived here at one time. For their public ceremonies, they leveled an area near the river and began constructing a series of earth mounds—places important in their religion and politics. They did not build the mounds to full height all at once but raised them at <u>intervals</u> over the years, perhaps as new leaders came to power or in response to cycles about which we can only speculate.

Another structure central to life here was the earthlodge. There were several at Ocmulgee. The one best preserved has been reconstructed. It is 42 feet in diameter. Opposite the entrance is a clay platform shaped like a large bird. There are three seats on the platform and 47 on the bench around the wall. In

*See page 173 for a map of Ocmulgee National Monument.

the center of the lodge is a firepit. This building may have been either a winter temple or a year-round council house. The 50 or so persons who met here were probably the group's leaders.

The mound on the town's west side was apparently a place for burials. Like the temple mounds, the Funeral Mound was flat-topped and equipped with steps leading up the side to some kind of <u>mortuary</u> building. More than 100 burials have been found here. Some had elaborate shell and copper ornaments, suggesting high status, but most had no offerings.

The Mississippians seem to have had some influence on the surrounding population (mound-building, <u>rudimentary</u> farming), but we are far from knowing the real nature of the transactions between them. Nor do we know why the town declined or what happened to the inhabitants—whether they died out, <u>migrated</u> elsewhere, or were <u>assimilated</u>. Whatever their fate, by 1100 Ocmulgee was no longer a thriving outpost of Mississippian culture.

Over the next two centuries, the native Indians, their style of life <u>irrevocably</u> altered, made occasional use of the old townsite. Then in the 1300s a new culture arose and spread widely through the Southeast. Known as the Lamar culture, it appears to have been a blending of Mississippian and Woodland elements. The Lamar people were farmers, skilled hunters, and mound-builders whose distinctive pottery <u>employed</u> designs peculiar to both their Woodland and Mississippian <u>predecessors</u>. They also made some use of the site, then fallen into ruins. One of their major centers was the Lamar site, several miles away in the swamps along the Ocmulgee River. This village contained two temple mounds and was surrounded by a stockade. It was the Lamar people that Hernando de Soto encountered in 1540 on the first European expedition into this region.

The arrival of Europeans was <u>catastrophic</u> for the natives. Disease caused <u>staggering</u> losses, and they were drawn into the white man's trading world and political disputes, with a <u>corresponding</u> collapse of their traditional way of life. The English set up a trading post at Ocmulgee sometime around 1690, and Creeks settled here in numbers. By 1715 the site was again abandoned as warfare between English and Spanish colonials <u>inflamed</u> the frontier. Within a few decades there were few <u>vestiges</u> of Mississippian life anywhere and virtually no understanding of the culture. When the pioneer naturalist William Bartram saw Ocmulgee in the 1770s, he spoke with respect mingled with <u>incomprehension</u> of "the wonderful remains of the power and grandeur of the ancients in this part of America."

_____ 1. <u>antiquity of man</u>
   a. the complexity of man
   b. how long man has lived
   c. the racial blend of man

_____ 2. habitation
a. dwelling   b. handiwork   c. customs

_____ 3. culture
a. growth   b. simplicity   c. civilization

_____ 4. ascendant
a. progressive   b. fading   c. insignificant

_____ 5. intruders
a. guests   (b.) trespassers   c. thinkers

_____ 6. sedentary
a. selective   b. wasteful   c. stationary

_____ 7. intervals
a. times of rapid growth
b. times between events
c. times of convenience

_____ 8. mortuary
a. recreational bulding   b. exhibit hall   c. funeral home

_____ 9. rudimentary
a. complex   b. basic   c. crude

_____ 10. migrated
a. communicated   b. visited   c. moved

_____ 11. assimiliated
a. incorporated   b. rejected   c. assisted

_____ 12. irrevocably
a. carefully   b. irreversibly   c. reversibly

_____ 13. employed
a. hired   b. occupied   c. used

_____ 14. predecessors
a. partners   b. ancestors   c. enemies

_____ 15. catastrophic
a. beneficial   b. characteristic   c. disastrous

_____ 16. <u>staggering</u>
a. stabilizing   b. swaying   c. astonishing

_____ 17. <u>corresponding</u>
a. vaulted   b. subsequent   c. written

_____ 18. <u>inflamed</u>
a. burned   b. agitated   c. suppressed

_____ 19. <u>vestiges</u>
a. traces   b. changes   c. growth

_____ 20. <u>incomprehension</u>
a. amazement   b. enlightenment   c. understanding

SUGGESTIONS FOR FURTHER STUDY

- Begin a vocabulary notebook and resolve to add 10 new words each day.
- Select words from your vocabulary notebook and make sentences using the words in another context.
- Find unfamiliar words in your local newspaper and use context clues to determine their meanings.
- Rely heavily on context clues to answer the vocabulary questions in Part Two and Part Three of this textbook.

2

Structural Analysis

USING ROOT WORDS

Structural analysis means analyzing a word according to what the parts of the word are and how the parts are combined. These word parts are usually in the form of prefixes, suffixes, roots, and compounds. If even one of the parts of a word is familiar, the meaning will be clearer. If in the word *microbiology* you know that *micro* means "small," *bio* means "life," and *logy* means "study of," then you know that microbiology means "the study of small life." This approach, when used in conjunction with context clues, will aid you in gaining a better understanding of words as you read. You will also be able to learn new words that will enable you to express yourself more effectively.

In order to utilize this approach effectively, you must become familiar with some common roots, prefixes, and suffixes. Do not attempt to learn the word parts in isolation only, but rather by how they combine with other parts to make words.

The root of a word expresses the primary meaning. Some common roots, their meanings, and examples are given in the list that follows. Study the list and add an example on the lines provided. Use your own dictionary if needed.

Root	Meaning	Examples
alpha	beginning	alphabet,
alt	high	altitude,
amor	love	amorous,
anthrop	man	anthropology,
aqua	water	aquarium,
arch	first, ruler	monarch,
audio	hearing	audiovisual,
bene	well	beneficial,
biblio	book	bibliography,
bio	life	biology,
cardi	heart	cardiac,
ceed, cede, cess	to go, to yield	proceed, recede, success,
cent	hundred	century,
chroma	color	chromatic,
chrono	time	chronic,
corp	body	corporation,
cosmo	universe, order	cosmos, cosmetic,
cracy, crat	govern	democracy, autocrat,
crit	judge	critical,
demo	people	democracy,
derma	skin	epidermis,
dicta	to speak, word	diction,
div	separate	divorce,

Root	Meaning	Examples (cont.)
dormi	sleep	dormant,
duc, duct	to lead	induce,
		conduct,
dyna	power	dynamite,
ego	self	egotistic,
fide	faith	confide,
fix	to place	prefix,
flex	to bend	flexible,
fract, frag	break	fraction,
		fragile,
frat	brother	fraternity,
gamos	marriage	bigamy,
gen	origin, birth	generation,
geo	earth	geography,
geri	old age	geriatric,
graph	to write	graphics,
gyn	woman	gynecology,
hemo	blood	hemoglobin,
hetero	different	heterogeneous
homo	same, man	homogeneous,
		Homo sapiens,
hydro	water	hydrate,
iatrics, iatry	medical treatment	pediatrics, psychiatry,
itis	inflammation of	tonsillitis,
logy	study, science of	biology,
loqui	to speak	eloquent,

Root	Meaning	Examples (cont.)
manu	hand	manuscript,
mater, matri	mother	maternal, matriarch,
micro	small	microfilm,
multi	many	multiply,
neuro	nerves	neurotic,
onym	name	synonym,
paleo	ancient	Paleozoic,
pater, patri	father	paternal, patriarch,
patho	disease, feeling	pathology, sympathy,
ped	child, foot	pediatrics, pedestal,
philo	loving	philosophy,
phobia	fear	pyrophobia,
phono	sound	phonetics,
prim	first	primary,
psycho	mind	psychotic,
pyro	fire	pyrometer,
scop	instrument to see	microscope,
scrib, script	write	subscribe, transcript,
spect	see, behold	spectator,
sphere	round	hemisphere,
tele	far off	television,
therma	heat	thermal,

Root	Meaning	Examples (cont.)
terra	earth	terrace,
theo	God	theology,

USING PREFIXES

A prefix is a word part added before the word to change or modify the meaning. Some prefixes have more than one meaning; therefore, you should always consider the context of the word when determining the meaning.

The list that follows contains some common prefixes you should know for good word recognition. Study the list and add an example on the lines provided.

Prefix	Meaning	Examples
a	not, up, out	atypical, arise, away,
ab	not, away	abnormal,
anti	against	antifreeze,
auto	self	automatic,
be	to make, to act	belittle,
bi	two, twice	bicuspid,
circum	around	circumstance,
co	together, joining	coed,
contra	against, opposite	contradict,
de	away, from, off	decrease,
dia	through, across	diagonal,
dis	not, separate	disability,
ex	from, beyond, former	exchange,
extra	outside, beyond	extraordinary,
fore	before (in time, in place)	forecast,
hemi	half	hemisphere,
hyper	above, excessive	hyperactive,

Prefix	Meaning	Examples (cont.)
hypo	under, less than	hypocrite,
il, ir, in	not, without	illogical,
		irregular,
		inaccurate,
inter	between, among	interchange,
intra, intro	within	intravenous,
		introvert,
mal	bad, ill	malignant,
mis	wrong, bad	misjudge,
mono	one, single	monotone,
multi	many	multicolored,
non	not	nonviolent,
peri	around	perimeter,
poly	many	polygraph,
post	after, later	postpone,
pre	before	prefix,
pro	before, forward	proclaim,
		proceed,
pseudo	false	pseudonym,
re	back, again	recall,
retro	back, behind	retroactive,
semi	half, twice in a period	semicircle
		semiannual,
sub	beneath, lesser	subhead,
sym, syn	together, with	sympathy,
tri	three	triangle,
ultra	beyond, excessive	ultramodern,

Prefix	Meaning	Examples (cont.)
un	not, opposite of	unlock,
under	beneath, lower	underneath,

USING SUFFIXES

A suffix is a word part added at the end of a word. A suffix can modify the meaning of a word and/or change the part of speech of the word. For example, one meaning of *employ* is "to engage the services of; hire" and is a verb. Adding the suffix *ee* or *er* to *employ* modifies the meaning to "someone who is employed" or "someone who employs" and results in the words *employee* and *employer*, which are nouns.

Following is a list of common suffixes, their meanings, and examples of each. Study the list and add an example on the lines provided.

Suffix	Meaning	Examples
able, ible	able, capable	durable,
		feasible,
acy	quality or state of	privacy,
age	condition, state of	marriage,
al	of, like, suitable	renewal,
ance	act, state of being	acceptance,
ant	one who is, state of being	accountant,
		militant,
ation	act, condition	demonstration,
		separation,
cide	to kill	insecticide,
ee	one who is	absentee,
er	one who is or does,	writer,
er	to compare	faster,
est	most	finest,

Suffix	Meaning	Examples
ful	full of	beautiful,
ic	of, like	alcoholic,
ion	act or condition of, result of,	action, correction,
ish	like	foolish,
ism	act or condition of, devotion to	terrorism, capitalism,
ist	one who is	artist,
ive	nature of	permissive,
less	without	breathless,
ly	in a certain manner	softly,
ment	result, act, condition	excitement, movement, employment,
meter	measure	thermometer,
ness	quality of, state of being	likeness,
or	one who is	visitor,
ous	full of	anxious,
tude	state, condition	gratitude,

EXERCISE 4: Roots, Prefixes, and Suffixes

NAME _____ DATE _____

I. Use the preceding list of roots to help you match the following words ending in **logy** with the appropriate meaning. (Note on the root-word list that **logy** means "study or science of.") Put the number of the meaning on the line provided.

Words

5   1. biology
9   2. cardiology
16   3. psychology
11   4. pathology
18   5. theology
1   6. gynecology
3   7. cosmology
20   8. paleontology
2   9. dermatology
14   10. chronology
12   11. cosmetology
7   12. audiology
8   13. microbiology
4   14. geology
19   15. archaeology
10   16. anthropology
15   17. sociology
6   18. neurology
17   19. phonology
13   20. genealogy

Meanings

1. women's illnesses and diseases
2. the skin
3. the universe
4. the earth's crust
5. living plants and animals
6. the nervous system
7. hearing
8. small living plants and animals
9. the heart
10. man, characteristics, and customs
11. the nature of disease
12. beautifying the face and hair
13. one's family descent (ancestors)
14. measuring time and dating events
15. social relations
16. the mind
17. sounds of language
18. God and religious doctrines
19. life and cultures of ancient people
20. prehistoric life through the study of fossils

II. Select from the list that follows the word that best completes the numbered sentences. You may need to refer to the list of prefixes and their meanings.

circumference   except   submit
monologue   postpone   antifreeze
synchronize   monopoly   intervene
nonconformist   hypodermic   triplets
pronoun   multimillionaire   intercollegiate
tripod   illogical   postscript
misquote   misjudge   predicts
contradict   abnormal   bifocals
symphony   preface   disregarded
disoriented   hypersensitive
ultramodern   malfunction

preface

1. After reading the ___preface___, I knew what to expect in the novel.

abnormal

2. There has been an ___abnormal___ number of absences this month. This could be due to hotter than usual temperatures.

3. The root *dict* means "to speak" or "to tell." If you speak against a person, you ___contradict___ him or her.

4. When a person states what he or she believes will happen, he or she ___predicts___, or foretells, the events.

5. If you fail to judge a person correctly, you ___misjudge___ that person.

6. The proud father could hardly believe his ears when the nurse told him that his wife had just given birth to ___tripods___. Imagine his excitement at increasing his family from two to five in one day!

triplets

7. Eyeglasses that have lenses ground with one part for close focus and one part for distance focus are called ___bifocals___.

8. A person who will not conform to a particular action is called a ___nonconformist___.

9. The student was asked to figure the distance around the earth, that is, the ___circumference___ of the earth.

10. A person who is _____hyper_____ could not deal objectively *hypersensitive* with child abuse.

11. The needle used to inject medicine under the skin is a _____ needle. *hypodermic*

12. Each winter motorists put _____ in their cars to protect against freezing. *antifreeze*

13. _____Intercollegiate_____ football between the two universities attracts large crowds at the stadium.

14. A word used in the place of a noun is called a _____pronoun_____.

15. A person with a million dollars is called a millionaire; a person with many millions is called a _____multimillionaire_____.

16. If you put off doing something until a later time, you _____postpone_____ it.

17. The accident occurred because the driver totally _____disregarded_____ all the warnings about road conditions.

18. You must _____submit_____ all your credentials by the appointed time if you wish to be considered for the job.

19. It is _____illogical_____ to expect a passing grade in the class if all your assignments have been late or incomplete.

20. When I awoke in the strange room, I was so _____ that it took several minutes for me to get my bearings. *disoriented*

21. In contrast to his brother's _____ultramodern_____ home in the suburbs, David built a rustic log cabin with no modern conveniences.

22. The root *loqui* means "to speak." A speech or skit that involves only one person is a _____monologue_____.

23. The _____malfunction_____ in the machine caused a reduction in production for the day. When the machine functions properly, the production is increased.

24. The root *chron* means "time." If we want to be sure we have exactly the same time, we should _____synchronize_____ our watches.

25. The root *phono* means "sound." A _____symphony_____ is a large orchestra that plays a harmony of sounds in different rhythms.

III. *Select a word to fill in the blanks in the sentences that follow by adding or changing the suffix of the underlined word.*

1. The couple decided to <u>separate</u> for three months. They were hopeful that the trial _separation_ would give them time to work out their problems.

2. Try not to <u>excite</u> the young child just before bedtime. Too much _excitement_ at this time can prevent the child from going to sleep promptly.

3. The five-year-old boy loves anything that requires <u>action</u>. He is a very _active_ boy.

4. Most people have a <u>tender</u> feeling toward their child; therefore, they treat the child _tenderly_.

5. Many household products have a <u>danger</u> warning on the label. These products could be _dangerous_ if swallowed.

6. My sister plays the piano <u>professionally</u>. She is a _professional_.

7. Because children are full of <u>joy</u> during the Christmas season, we see Christmas as a _enjoyable/joyful_ time.

8. The team was <u>disappointed</u> when the game was called off because of rain. The _disappointment_ of not playing can be worse than losing the game.

9. Mark is studying <u>chemistry</u> at the state university. He plans to work as a _chemist_.

10. The couple could not afford a <u>modern</u> house; therefore, they decided to _modernize_ their old house.

11. The salesperson tried to <u>demonstrate</u> how the gadget worked, but few people actually watched the _demonstration_

12. You would need a <u>guide</u> through the remote jungle. Even with expert _guidance_ you could lose your way.

EXERCISE 5: Roots, Prefixes, and Suffixes

NAME _____ **DATE** _____

I. Use the lists of roots, prefixes, and suffixes to answer all the questions in this exercise. Follow the directions for each section.

A. Use the following words to fill in the blanks.

suicide   germicide
homicide   biocide
                 matricide

1. _____matricide_____ the act of killing one's mother
2. _____germicide_____ an antiseptic used to kill germs
3. _____homicide_____ the act of one person killing another
4. _____suicide_____ the act of intentionally killing oneself
5. _____biocide_____ a chemical substance that can kill living organisms

B. Match the following words and meanings.

_b_	1. benefit	a.	an invocation of a blessing
_e_	2. benefactor	b.	to help, aid, do good
_a_	3. benediction	c.	kindness
_c_	4. benevolence	d.	anyone receiving benefits
_d_	5. beneficiary	e.	one who gives help or an endowment

C. Use the following words to fill in the blanks.

century   bicentennial
centennial   centimeter
                percentage

1. _____percentage_____ a given part in every hundred

2. _Century_ one hundred years
3. _Centennial_ one-hundredth anniversary
4. _Centemeter_ unit of measure, equal to 1/100 meter
5. _becentennial_ two-hundredth anniversary

D. Match the following words and meanings.

_d_ 1. Philadelphia   a. to engage lightly in love affairs

_a_ 2. philander   b. loving or devoted to music

_e_ 3. philanthropy   c. one who is learned in philosophy; a lover of wisdom

_b_ 4. philharmonic

_c_ 5. philosopher   d. city of brotherly love

     e. a love for and desire to help mankind

E. Use the following words to fill in the blanks.

corporation   corporal

corpse   corps

       corpulence

1. _Corporal_ of the human body, physical
2. _corpulence_ obesity, fatness
3. _Corpse_ a dead body
4. _corps_ a body of people with common goals and directions
5. _Corporation_ a group organized to operate a business as one body

F. Add a prefix to make a word that matches the meaning.

1. _bi_ cuspid—a tooth having two points
2. _sub_ title—a lesser or explanatory title
3. _pre_ historic—the period before recorded history
4. _re_ union—to come together again
5. _tri_ angle—a figure having three angles and three sides

G. *Use the following words to complete the sentences.*

monogamy   monologue
monorail   monotheism
          monarch

1. A hereditary head of state, such as a king or queen, is known as a *monarch*

2. The practice of having only one mate is known as *monogamy*

3. A long speech by one speaker is called a *monologue*

4. A single rail serving as a track for cars suspended from it or balanced on it is called a *monorail*

5. The belief in one God is known as *monotheism*

H. *Add or change the suffix of the underlined word to fill in the blanks in the following sentences.*

1. One who is <u>appointed</u> is an ___*appointer*___.
2. The act of being <u>baptized</u> is called ___*baptism*___.
3. If you are full of <u>remorse</u>, you are ___*remorseful*___.
4. If you are <u>hungrier</u> than all the others, you are the ___*hungriest*___.
5. If you are very <u>determined</u>, you have ___*determination*___

I. *Read the following sentences and underline the correct answer.*

1. If you get <u>retroactive</u> pay, you receive (back, advance) pay.

2. If you <u>contradict</u> someone, you (agree, disagree) with him or her.

3. If you have a <u>relapse</u> of an illness, you (have it again, get well).

4. If you consider yourself to be an <u>antiabortionist</u>, you are (for, against) abortion.

5. If you are <u>hyperactive</u>, you are (more, less) active than others.

6. If you cut a circle <u>diagonally</u>, you cut (across, around) the circle.

7. If you are an <u>introvert</u>, you tend to (keep your feelings within, express your feelings openly).

8. If your situation is <u>atypical</u>, it is (typical, not typical).

9. If you drive the <u>perimeter</u> of the city, you drive (across, around) the city.

10. If you sing in a <u>monotone</u>, you sing (in a single tune, in many tunes).

11. If you include a <u>postscript</u> in your letter, you (put it at the beginning, add it at the end).

12. If you use a <u>polychromatic</u> color scheme, you use (few, many) colors.

13. If you are <u>egocentric</u>, you are (self-, people) centered.

14. If you are <u>semiconscious</u>, you are (fully, not fully) conscious.

15. If you are <u>ultraconservative</u>, you are (more, less) conservative than most people.

16. If you <u>retrieve</u> an object, you (let it go, get it back).

17. If you <u>extinguish</u> the fire, you (start it, put it out).

18. If you attend a <u>polytechnic</u> school, you study (one, many) scientific and technical subjects.

19. If you <u>contrast</u> two people, you tell how they are (alike, different).

20. If you are in the <u>intermediate</u> group, you are (first, in the middle, last).

II. Match the following words and definitions. Carefully analyze the roots, prefixes, and suffixes before making your choice. Put the number of the word on the line by the definitions that follow.

1. matricide
2. posthumous
3. polysyllabic
4. micrometer
5. sympathy
6. hydrophobia
7. theocentric
8. amoral
9. primer

10. physicist
11. patriarchy
12. dehydrate
13. congenital
14. autocrat
15. criterion
16. audiovisual
17. hypersensitive

18. recede
19. egotistic
20. psychopath
21. dermatology
22. fragile
23. introspect
24. subscript
25. geriatrics

_14_ 1. a ruler with absolute power

_13_ 2. existing as such at birth

_24_ 3. written below

_15_ 4. a standard by which to judge

_1_ 5. act of killing one's mother

_17_ 6. excessively sensitive

_3_ 7. having many syllables

_19_ 8. self-centered or selfish

_20_ 9. a person suffering from a mental disorder

_8_ 10. without morals

_7_ 11. centering on God

_25_ 12. medical treatment of the elderly

_21_ 13. branch of medicine dealing with the skin

_23_ 14. to look into one's own mind

_22_ 15. easily broken

_2_ 16. happening after death

_10_ 17. a specialist in physics

_5_ 18. a feeling of compassion for another

_12_ 19. to remove water from a substance

_9_ 20. a book giving the first principles of a subject

_18_ 21. to go back

_6_ 22. abnormal fear of water

_16_ 23. involving both hearing and sight

_11_ 24. government or rule by a man

_4_ 25. an instrument that measures small distances

III. *Select from the list that follows the word that best completes each of the numbered sentences. You may need to refer to the list of roots, prefixes, and suffixes and their meanings.*

aqueduct	critique	thermometer
intercollegiate	egocentric	subzero
chronological	dehydrated	precursors
aquatic	monosyllabic	extracurricular
literacy	dermatitis	illiteracy
trilogy	matriarch	retroactive
multitude	introverted	polychromatic
primary	polygamy	bimonthly
dormant	bigamy	critical

1. Eugenia Price has written three books on the study of St. Simons Island. *Lighthouse* is the first book in this ___trilogy___.

2. After being without water for two days, the stranded motorist became ___dehydrated___.

3. An inflammation of the skin is known as ___dermatitis___.

4. If a college activity is outside the curriculum of the college, it is said to be an ___extracurricular___ activity.

5. Although our school does not play competitive sports, it does participate in ___intercollegiate___ debate among the colleges in our state.

6. A ___monosyllabic___ word is a word having only one syllable.

7. While living near the ocean, the family became interested in all kinds of ___aquatic___ sports.

8. From the three ___primary___ colors—red, yellow, and blue—all the other colors can be made.

9. There was such a ___multitude___ of people at the rally, I could not see any of the speakers.

10. No one could deny that my grandmother was the ___matriarch___ of the family. She ruled the entire household with a quiet, gentle dignity.

11. Americans are viewing the spread of ___illiteracy___ with growing alarm. Reading and writing are basic survival skills.

12. When I checked the ___thermometer___, I was shocked to realize the child's temperature was dangerously high.

13. Monogamy is the practice of having only one mate. Countries that allow a male to have many mates practice ___polygamy___.

14. A magazine that is published every two months is a ___bimonthly___ magazine.

15. One who is interested only in his or her own thoughts and feelings is said to be ___egocentric___.

16. When we put events in the order in which they happened, we put them in ___chronological___ order.

17. A high temperature and headache are often ___precursors___ of a more serious illness.

18. I love the spring when all the trees that have been ___dormant___ during the winter suddenly burst forth with new life.

19. Because of the ___subzero___ weather, all outside activities were canceled. Few people would venture out with the temperature below zero.

20. The instructor required the students to ___critique___ their classmates' oral reports but reminded them that their own report would also be judged.

IV. Define the following words by dividing each word into roots, prefixes, and suffixes, and then put the meanings together. Do not use your dictionary but refer to pages 24–30 if needed.

1. precede

   pre = before cede = giving Precede = come before

2. geologist

   geo = earth ist = one who is geologist = the person who studies the earth

3. autocrat

auto (self ?) + crat (......)

4. postscript

Postscript = Post = after   Script = Handwriting.
Postscript = A message added to a letter after the
writer's signature

5. audiovisual

audio = sound visual = sense of sight
audiovisual: Both audiable and visible

6. polychromatic

Ploy = many. Polychromatic: decorated in
many colors

7. infidelity

in = without   infidelity = lack of fidelity
or loyalty, especially to a spouse

8. loquacious

ous = full of   loquacious = very talkative

9. pseudonym

nym = name.
Pseudo = false   pseudonym = A fictitous name
assumed by an author.

10. geriatrics

geri = old age   geriatics: The branch of
medicine that deals with the diagnosis
and treatment of diseases and problems
specific to old age

SUGGESTIONS FOR FURTHER STUDY

- Add at least one additional example on pages 24–30 in this chapter.
- Add additional roots, prefixes, and suffixes as you encounter them in your reading and dictionary use.
- Combine structural analysis with context clues in order to make your word attack skills more accurate and efficient.

3

Dictionary Skills

USING THE DICTIONARY

The dictionary is one of the most valuable learning aids for a student. Although dictionaries vary in format, most of them contain the same basic information. However, dictionaries have limitations, and no one volume can answer all your questions. Indeed, it is hoped that as you use your dictionary, it will raise questions in your mind and send you in search of the answers in other dictionaries as well.

Dictionaries give not only the meanings of the word but also the pronunciation, syllabification, parts of speech, synonyms, and often illustration and examples of the word in use. Some dictionaries also give the slang meaning of the word.

To understand better the use of the dictionary, you should know some of the common terms and their meanings. As you study each term that follows, look also at the sample dictionary page on page 47, which shows the location and use of each term.

Entry Words

Entry words are the terms in the dictionary for which a definition and explanation are given. Entry words are arranged in the dictionary in alphabetical order and are usually in boldface type.

EXAMPLES: dulse, Duluth, duly

Guide Words

Guide words are usually at the top of the page to guide the user in finding a word alphabetically. The guide word on the left is the first entry word on the page, and the one on the right is the last entry word.

EXAMPLES: dulse, Dunkers

Syllabification

Syllabification is shown in the entry word, and syllables are separated in the word by a dot.

EXAMPLES: Du • luth, du • ly, dumb • wait • er

Pronunciation

The phonetic pronunciation, along with the accents, are given inside parentheses following the entry word.

Syllables to be accented are indicated within the parentheses along with the pronunciation. A primary, or strong, accent is indicated by a heavy mark (´) following the syllable. A secondary, or weak, accent is indicated by a lighter mark (').

The key to pronunciation on page 45 shows the symbols used to guide you in pronouncing unfamiliar words. (These symbols vary slightly from dictionary to dictionary.) Study the pronunciation key carefully, and use it to pronounce the words in the examples. Also note the accent marks.

EXAMPLES: Duluth (də looʹth)
duly (dooʹle)
dumbbell (dumʹbelʹ)
dungeon (dunʹjən)

An abbreviated form of this key appears at the bottom of every alternate page of the vocabulary.

Symbol	Key Words	Symbol	Key Words
a	asp, fat, parrot	b	bed, fable, dub
a	ape, date, play	d	dip, beadle, had
ä	ah, car, father	f	fall, after, off
		g	get, haggle, dog
e	elf, ten, berry	h	he, ahead, hotel
e	even, meet, money	j	joy, agile, badge
		k	kill, tackle, bake
i	is, hit, mirror	l	let, yellow, ball
ı	ice, bite, high	m	met, camel, trim
		n	not, flannel, ton
o	open, tone, go	p	put, apple, tap
ô	all, horn, law	r	red, port, dear
oo	ooze, tool, crew	s	sell, castle, pass
oo	look, pull, moor	t	top, cattle, hat
yoo	use, cute, few	v	vat, hovel, have
yoo	united, cure, globule	w	will, always, swear
oi	oil, point, toy	y	yet, onion, yard
ou	out, crowd, plow	z	zebra, dazzle, haze
u	up, cut, color	ch	chin, catcher, arch
ur	urn, fur, deter	sh	she, cushion, dash
		th	thin, nothing, truth
ə	a in ago	*th*	then, father, lathe
	e in agent	zh	azure, leisure
	i in sanity	ŋ	ring, anger, drink
	o in comply		
	u in focus		
ər	perhaps, murder		

Parts of Speech

The part of speech of the entry word is indicated immediately following the pronunciation of the word. If the entry word can be used as another part of speech in a different context or by adding a suffix, the other part of speech is also indicated.

EXAMPLES: dumb *adj.*, dumbly *adv.*, dumbness *n.*

Etymology

The history of the word's existence in another language follows the pronunciation and is usually in brackets.

> **EXAMPLES:** dungeon [ME. *dongoun* < OFr. *donjon*, prob. < Frank. *dungjo*, earth-covered cellar for storing fruits: see DUNG]

Note that the *ME.* stands for Middle English, a forerunner of Modern English. You can look up *OFr.* and *Frank.* in the list of abbreviations and symbols in the front of your dictionary.

Illustrations

Pictures of lesser-known objects, maps, and so forth, are given so that the reader gets a clear concept of the definition.

> **EXAMPLE:** DUMBBELL

Synonyms

In some cases the dictionary gives synonyms for the entry word. The synonym is indicated by *SYN* at the end of the entry explanation. Knowing a word that means the same sometimes helps you to choose the exact word that you need to convey the meaning intended.

> **EXAMPLES:** dumb—see VOICELESS
> dumbfound—see PUZZLE

Geographical and Biographical Entries

Pertinent information about persons and places is given in condensed form. Some dictionaries have a special geographical and biographical section, while others list places and names as regular entry words. The sample dictionary page lists them as regular entries.

> **EXAMPLES:** Duluth, Minnesota
> Dumas, Alexandre

dulse (duls) *n.* [Ir. & Gael. *duileasg*] any of several edible marine algae (esp. *Rhodymenia palmata*) with large, red, wedge-shaped fronds

Du·luth (də lōō′th′) [after Daniel G. *Du Lhut* (or *Du Luth* 1636?–1709?, Fr. explorer] city and port in NE Minn., on Lake Superior: pop. 101,000

du·ly (dōō′lē, dyōō′-) *adv.* in a due manner; specif., *a*) as due; rightfully *b*) when due; at the right time; on time *c*) as required; sufficiently

Du·ma (dōō′mä) *n.* [Russ. < Gmc., as in Goth. *doms*, ON, *domr*, OE. *dom*, judgment: see DOOM¹] the parliament of czarist Russia (1905–17)

Du·mas (dü mä′; *E.* dōō′mä) 1. Alexandre, 1802–70; Fr. novelist & playwright: called *Dumas père* 2. Alexandre, 1824–95; Fr. playwright & novelist: son of *prec.*: called *Dumas fils*

du Mau·ri·er (dōō môr′ē ā′, dyōō) **George** (**Louis Palmella Busson**) 1834–96; Eng. illustrator & novelist, born in France

dumb (dum) *adj.* [ME. & OE., akin to G. *dumm* (Goth. *dumbs*), mute, stupid < nasalised var. of IE. **dheubh:* see DULL] 1. lacking the power of speech; mute 2. unwilling to talk; silent; reticent 3. not accompanied by speech 4. temporarily speechless, as from fear, grief, etc. 5. producing no sound 6. lacking some normal part, characteristic, or quality ☆7. [G. *dumm*] [Colloq.] stupid; moronic; unintelligent —*SYN.* see VOICELESS —**dumb′ly** *adv.* —**dumb′ness** *n.*

Dum·bar·ton (dum bär′t'n) city in W Scotland, on the Clyde River: pop. 26,000

dumb·bell (dum′bel′) *n.* [DUMB + BELL¹: from orig. shape] 1. a device usually used in pairs, consisting of round weights joined by a short bar, by which it is lifted or swung about in the hand for muscular exercise ☆2. [cf. DUMB, sense 7] [Slang] a stupid person

DUMBBELL

dumb·found, dum·found (dum′found′) *vt.* [DUMB + (CON)FOUND] to make speechless by shocking; amaze; astonish —*SYN.* see PUZZLE

dumb show 1. formerly, a part of a play done in pantomime 2. gestures without speech

dumb·struck (dum′struk′) *adj.* so shocked as to be speechless: also **dumb′strick′en** (-strik′ən)

dumb·wait·er (-wāt′ər) *n.* 1. a small, portable stand for serving food, often with shelves ☆2. a small elevator for sending food, trash, etc. from one floor to another

☆**dum-dum** (dum′dum′) *n.* [Slang] a stupid person; dumbbell: also sp. **dumb-dumb**

dum-dum (bullet) (dum′dum′) [< *Dumdum*, arsenal near Calcutta, India < Hindi *damdama*, hill, fortification] a soft-nosed bullet that expands when it hits, inflicting a large, jagged wound

Dum·fries (dum frēs′) former county of S Scotland, on Solway Firth: now part of a region called **Dumfries and Galloway**, 2,462 sq. mi.; pop. 133,000

dum·my (dum′ē) *n., pl.* **-mies** [< DUMB + -Y²] 1. a person unable to talk; mute: now vulgar in this sense 2. a figure made in human form, as for displaying clothing, practicing tackling in football, etc. 3. an imitation or sham; substitute for the real thing, as an empty container or false drawer 4. a person secretly acting for another while apparently representing his own interests 5. [Slang] a stupid person 6. *Bridge, Whist*, etc. *a*) the declarer's partner, whose hand is exposed on the board and played by the declarer *b*) the hand thus exposed 7. *Printing* the skeleton copy, as of a magazine or book, upon which the format is planned and laid out —*adj.* 1. imitation; sham; fictitious 2. secretly acting as a front for another /a *dummy* corporation/ 3. *Bridge*, etc. played with a dummy —**dummy up, -mied, -my·ing** [Slang] to refuse to talk or tell what one knows

dump¹ (dump) *vt.* [ME. *dompen*, to plunge, throw down; prob. < ON. base akin to Dan. *dumpe*, Sw. *dompa:* for IE. base see DEEP] 1. to throw down or out roughly; empty out or unload as in a heap or mass 2. *a*) to throw away (garbage, rubbish, etc.) esp. in a place set apart for the purpose *b*) to get rid of in an abrupt, rough, or careless manner 3. to sell (a commodity) in a large quantity at a very low price, esp. abroad so as to maintain a higher domestic market price ☆4. *a*) to transfer (data in a computer memory) to another section of storage *b*) to print out (data in a computer memory) ☆5. *Football* to throw (a short pass) into the flat —*vi.* 1. to fall in a heap or mass 2. to unload rubbish 3. to dump commodities —*n.* 1. a rubbish pile ☆2. a place for dumping rubbish, etc. ☆3. *a*) a listing of data stored in a computer *b*) a printout of such data 4. *Mil.* a temporary storage center in the field, as of ammunition, food, or clothing ☆5. [Slang] a place that is unpleasant, ugly, run-down, etc. —☆**dump on** [Slang] to treat with contempt; demean —**dump′er** *n.*

dump² (dump) *n.* [prob. < Du. *domp*, haze, dullness, akin to DAMP] [Obs.] 1. a sad tune or song 2. any tune or song —(**down) in the dumps** in low spirits; depressed

dump³ (dump) *n.* [< ? DUMPY¹] [Brit.] a small, shapeless lump or chunk, as of lead

dump·ish (-ish) *adj.* [see DUMP²] [Rare] gloomy; depressed

dump·ling (dump′liŋ) *n.* [< ? DUMP² + -LING¹] 1. a small piece of dough, steamed or boiled and served with meat or soup 2. a crust of dough filled with fruit and steamed or baked 3. [Colloq.] a short, fat person or animal

☆**dump truck** a truck whose contents are unloaded by tilting the truck bed backward with the tailgate open

dump·y¹ (dum′pē) *adj.* **dump′i·er, dump′i·est** [prob. < DUMP³] 1. short and thick; squat; stumpy 2. [Slang] ugly, run-down, etc. —**dump′i·ly** *adv.* —**dump′i·ness** *n.*

dump·y² (dum′pē) *adj.* **dump′i·er, dump′i·est** [see DUMP²] melancholy; depressed

dumpy level a surveyor's level in which the mounted telescope rotates only horizontally

dun¹ (dun) *adj.* [ME. & OE., akin to OS. *dun*, chestnut-brown, ult. (? via Celt.) < IE. **dhus-no* < **dhus*, dust-colored, mist-gray, whence DUSK, DUST] dull grayish-brown —*n.* 1. a dull grayish brown 2. a dun horse 3. an artificial fishing fly of this color 4. *same as* MAY FLY —**dun′ness** *n.*

dun² (dun) *vt., vi.* **dunned, dun′ning** [? dial. var. of DIN] 1. to ask (a debtor) insistently or repeatedly for payment 2. to annoy constantly —*n.* 1. a person who duns 2. an insistent demand, esp. for payment of a debt

Du·na (dōō′nä) *Hung. name of the* DANUBE

☆**Dun and Brad·street** (dun′ ən brad′strēt′) an agency that furnishes subscribers with information as to the financial standing and credit rating of businesses

Du·nant (dü nän′), **Jean Hen·ri** (zhän än rē′) 1828–1910; Swiss philanthropist: founder of the Red Cross society

Du·nă·rea (dōō′när yä) *Romanian name of the* DANUBE

Dun·bar (dun′bär) 1. **Paul Laurence**, 1872–1906; U.S. poet 2. **William**, 1460?–1520?; Scot. poet

Dun·bar·ton (dun bär′t'n) former county of W Scotland, now in Strathclyde region

Dun·can (duŋ′kən) [Gael. *Donnchadh*, lit., brown warrior] 1. a masculine name 2. in Shakespeare's *Macbeth*, the aged king of Scotland, murdered by Macbeth 3. **Isadora**, 1878–1927; U.S. dancer

Duncan Phyfe designating or of furniture in a modified Empire and Directoire style designed by Duncan PHYFE

dunce (duns) *n.* [< John DUNS SCOTUS: his followers, called *Dunsmen, Dunses, Dunces*, were regarded as foes of Renaissance humanism] 1. a dull, ignorant person 2. a person who learns more slowly than others

dunce cap a cone-shaped hat that children slow at learning were formerly forced to wear in school

Dun·dalk (dun′dôk) suburb of Baltimore, in C Md.: pop. 85,000

Dun·dee (dun′dē) seaport in E Scotland, on the Firth of Tay: pop. 185,000

dun·der·head (dun′dər hed′) *n.* [< Du. *donder*, thunder, associated by rhyme with BLUNDER (cf. BLUNDERBUSS) + HEAD] a stupid person; dunce —**dun′der·head′ed** *adj.*

dune (dōōn, dyōōn) *n.* [Fr. < ODu. *duna:* for IE. base see DOWN¹] a rounded hill or ridge of sand heaped up by the action of the wind

☆**dune buggy** a small, light automobile generally made from a standard, compact, rear-engine chassis and a prefabricated, often fiberglass body: orig. equipped with wide, low-pressure tires for driving on sand dunes

Dun·e·din (də nē′d'n) city on the SE coast of South Island, New Zealand: pop. (with suburbs) 109,000

Dun·ferm·line (dan furm′lin) city in E Scotland, near the Firth of Forth: pop. 50,000

dung (duŋ) *n.* [ME. & OE., prob. identical with *dung*, a prison, orig., cellar covered with dung for warmth, as in OS. *dung*, OHG. *tung*, cellar where women weave < IE. base **dheng-*, to cover] 1. animal excrement; manure 2. filth —*vt.* to spread or cover with dung, as in fertilising land —**dung′y** *adj.*

dun·ga·ree (duŋ′gə rē′) *n.* [Hindi *dungrī*] 1. a coarse cotton cloth; specif., blue denim 2. [*pl.*] work trousers or overalls made of this cloth

dung beetle any of various beetles (family Scarabaeidae) that breed in dung and feed on it

dun·geon (dun′jən) *n.* [ME. *dongoun* < OFr. *donjon*, prob. < Frank. *dungjo*, earth-covered cellar for storing fruits: see DUNG] 1. *same as* DONJON 2. a dark underground cell, vault, or prison —*vt.* [Rare] to confine in a dungeon

dung·hill (duŋ′hil′) *n.* 1. a heap of dung 2. anything vile or filthy

dung·y (-ē) *adj.* **dung′i·er, dung′i·est** of, like, or soiled with dung; filthy; vile

dun·ite (dun′īt) *n.* [< Mt. *Dun*, in New Zealand + -ITE] a dense, igneous rock consisting largely of olivine

☆**dunk** (duŋk) *vt.* [G. *tunken*, to steep, dip, soak < OHG. *dunchōn:* for IE. base see TINGE] 1. to dip (bread, cake, etc.) into coffee or other liquid before eating it 2. to immerse in a liquid for a short time ☆3. *Basketball* to put (the ball) into the basket by means of a dunk shot

Dun·kerque (dön kerk′) *Fr. name of* DUNKIRK

☆**Dunk·ers** (duŋ′kərz) *n.pl.* [G. *tunker*, dipper < *tunken* (see DUNK): so named from practice of immersion] a sect of German-American Baptists opposed to military service

fat, āpe, cär; ten, ēven; is, bīte; gō, hôrn, tōōl, look; oil, out; up, fur; get; joy; yet; chin; she; thin, then; zh, leisure; ŋ, ring; ə for *a* in *ago*, *e* in *agent*, *i* in *sanity*, *o* in *comply*, *u* in *focus*; ′ as in *able* (ā′b'l); Fr. bal; ü, Fr. coeur; ö, Fr. feu; Fr. mon; b, Fr. coq; ʒ, Fr. duc; r, Fr. cri; H, G. ich; kh, G. doch. See inside front cover. ☆ Americanism; ‡foreign; °hypothetical; <derived from

47

NAME _____ **DATE** _____

I. *Use the sample dictionary page to answer the following questions.*

1. What are the guide words?

   _____

2. Give two facts about <u>George du Maurier</u>.

   _____

   _____

3. Give the location of <u>Dunedin</u>.

   _____

4. What is the population of <u>Duluth</u>?

   _____

5. Give a slang meaning of <u>dumpy</u>.

   _____

6. What is the etymology of <u>dungaree</u>?

   _____

7. Make a sentence using <u>dun</u> as a verb.

   _____

8. Make a sentence using <u>dun</u> as an adjective.

   _____

9. Make a sentence using <u>dumbbell</u>.

   _____

10. Give the meaning of <u>dumb</u> as used in the following sentences.

    a. That was a <u>dumb</u> thing to do.

    _____

    b. When the gun fired unexpectedly, the youth was struck <u>dumb</u>.

    _____

more physical

disguise (costume: sth to act on)

guise (just pretend, not wear sth)

II. A. *Use your dictionary to give the syllabification of the following words.*

1. university _____   6. scholastic ___scholastic___

2. institution _____   7. dictionary _____

3. registration _____   8. graduation _____

4. orientation _____   9. career _____

5. professor _____   10. campus ___campus___

B. *Use your dictionary to give the pronunciation of the following words. Be sure to mark the primary and secondary accented syllables.*

1. priority _____   6. plagiarize _____

2. educate _____   7. cumulative _____

3. library _____   8. occupation _____

4. schedule _____   9. concentration _____

5. hypothesis _____   10. technology _____

C. *Use the pronunciation key on page 61 to identify the following words.*

1. stud ´ e _____   6. kwes ´ chən _____

2. di fin ´ _____   7. dôr ´ mə tôr ´ e _____

3. ik splan ´ _____   8. kri tek ´ _____

4. ek ´ sər sız ´ _____   9. sek ´ rə ter ´ e _____

5. par ´ ə graf ´ _____   10. ig zam ´ ə na ´ shən _____

D. *Place the accent marks on the correct syllable in each of the following words.*

1. col lege   6. ad vise

2. flu ent   7. dis ci pline

3. dis close   8. ex pi ra tion

4. cur tail   9. syn drome

5. met a phor   10. ma nip u late

III. Use your dictionary to find the meaning of the underlined words in the following sentences. Fill in the blanks with an appropriate word or words.

1. A <u>merino</u> is one of a hardy breed of _____ (wool).

2. <u>John F. Kennedy</u> was the _____ president of the United States.

3. A <u>lapin</u> coat is made of _____ fur that has been dyed to resemble other fur.

4. A <u>periwinkle</u> could be a _____ or _____.

5. <u>Jasper</u> is an opaque variety of colored _____.

6. If the weather is <u>torrid</u>, it is extremely _____.

7. <u>Spirea</u> is a beautiful plant of the _____ family with clusters of small white flowers that bloom in the spring.

8. The <u>Inca Indians</u> lived in _____ until the Spanish conquest.

9. To call a boy an <u>urchin</u> is to say that he is _____.

10. A <u>garnet</u> gem would be _____ in color.

11. A synonym for <u>mallet</u> could be _____.

12. You would likely wear <u>mukluks</u> in places where the weather is very

_____.

13. A common name for <u>pertussis</u> is _____.

14. A <u>fallow</u> field is one that has not been _____.

15. <u>Farina</u> is usually eaten as a cooked _____.

16. <u>Psoriasis</u> is a disease of the _____.

17. An object made of <u>pewter</u> is a _____ color.

18. <u>Organdy</u> is a fabric made from the _____ plant.

19. A <u>parable</u> teaches a _____ lesson.

20. If you receive an <u>honorarium</u> for something that you did, you would get

_____.

IV. *Use your dictionary to find the meaning of the underlined words in the following sentences. Answer the questions with* **YES** *or* **NO.**

_____   1. Could you eat a <u>bonito</u>?

_____   2. Would you use a <u>carbuncle</u> on your car?

_____   3. Could you have a <u>nevus</u> on your face?

_____   4. Would you be unhappy if your friend behaved <u>atrociously</u>?

_____   5. Could you have a <u>beadle</u> for a pet?

_____   6. Would you find an <u>aquanaut</u> in your aquarium?

_____   7. Could you wear an <u>ascot</u>?

_____   8. Would you enjoy a <u>savory</u> meal?

_____   9. Could you drive through an <u>impasse</u>?

_____   10. Would you need a wheelchair if you were <u>ambulatory</u>?

_____   11. Could you use <u>cyclamen</u> as farm workers?

_____   12. Would you use a <u>fuselage</u> in your electrical box?

_____   13. Could an ocean liner sail down a <u>lagoon</u>?

_____   14. Would you <u>embroil</u> a steak to enhance the flavor?

_____   15. Could you eat a <u>papaw</u>?

_____   16. Would you <u>braise</u> your hair?

_____   17. Could you <u>mulch</u> on snacks while watching television?

_____   18. Would you like a business partner noted for his <u>rectitude</u>?

_____   19. Could you use <u>asphodels</u> to brighten your home?

_____   20. Would you put <u>brilliantine</u> on your light fixtures?

_____   21. Could you catch a train at a <u>despot</u>?

_____   22. Would you ride in a <u>hansom</u> for fun?

_____   23. Could you eat a <u>quince</u> for lunch?

_____   24. Would it be safe to pet a <u>piranha</u>?

_____   25. Could you lease your apartment to a <u>tenet</u>?

IV. *Use the pronunciation key on page 61 to rewrite the following sentences.*

1. Thə   best   mem´ər e   in shoor´əns   iz   thʉr´o   lʉr´niŋ.

_____

_____

2. Thə   nooz´pa´pər   iz   pər haps´   *thə*   most   wīd´le   red   sôrs
   uv   in´fər ma´shən   ə va´lə b'l.

_____

_____

3. Stood´´'nts   shood   re´ə lis´tik le   ig zam´ən   *ther*   golz   ənd
   pri ôr´ə tez   in   ôr´dər   too   sək´sed´   in   käl´ij.

_____

_____

_____

SUGGESTIONS FOR FURTHER STUDY

- Select an up-to-date collegiate dictionary to use for your college study.
- Form the habit of checking the dictionary for exact meanings and other information.
- Locate and familiarize yourself with the different kinds of dictionaries in your college library.

4

Main Ideas

READING WITH COMPREHENSION

Reading with comprehension means getting meaning from what you read. It is an active, thinking process that depends not only on comprehension skills but also on your own experiences and previous knowledge. Comprehension involves understanding the vocabulary, seeing relationships among words and concepts, organizing ideas, recognizing the author's purpose, evaluating the content, and making judgments.

Perhaps the one most important factor in determining the degree of comprehension is word recognition skills. Attempting to comprehend with an inadequate vocabulary is almost impossible, just as developing a good vocabulary while ignoring comprehension skills is a waste of time and effort.

Specific comprehension skills cannot be completely isolated because they are so interrelated that one skill depends to some degree on another skill. But in a broader sense, comprehension could be divided into three levels of skills: (1) literal, (2) inferential, and (3) critical.

Literal reading refers to the ideas and facts that are directly stated on the printed page. In fact, literal ideas and facts are usually so clearly stated that you could go back in the passage and underline the information if you desired. The literal level of comprehension is fundamental to all reading skills at any level because you must first understand what the author actually wrote before you can draw an inference or make an evaluation. The literal level is considered the easiest level of reading comprehension because you are not required to go beyond what the author actually wrote; therefore, less thinking is involved.

To get inferences, or implied meanings, from your reading, you must "read between the lines." Inferences are ideas that you receive when you go beneath the surface to sense relationships, put facts and ideas together to draw conclusions and make generalizations, and detect the mood and tone of the material. Making inferences requires more thinking on your part because you must depend less on the author and more on personal insight.

The third level, critical reading, requires an even higher degree of skill development and perception. Critical reading requires that you read with an inquiring mind and with active, creative participation. To read critically does not mean merely looking for false statements; rather, it means questioning, comparing, and evaluating.

In order to read with the degree of comprehension necessary to succeed in the academic environment, you must be proficient in each of the reading levels. As in most skills, each reading skill depends, to a certain degree, on another skill. For example, you cannot expect to make an inference or to evaluate what the author stated or implied unless you fully understand the facts and concepts actually presented in the material.

FINDING MAIN IDEAS

One of the most important specific comprehension skills is finding main ideas. This could be a literal skill if the idea is directly stated, or an inferential skill if it is not directly stated. The main idea is the essence of a piece of writing, or what the author is trying to get across to the reader. If you were to discard the main idea, the remaining sentences would be practically meaningless.

In order to simplify this discussion, we will concentrate on finding main ideas in paragraphs. The same procedure would be followed if you were finding the main idea, or central theme, in a passage, a chapter, or even a book.

Some paragraphs contain a topic sentence that tells you the exact main idea that the author wants you to know. This topic sentence would include who or what the paragraph is about (the topic) and what the author wants you to understand about the topic. This topic sentence would be the *stated main idea*. A stated main idea is often found in the first sentence in a paragraph, and is followed by supporting details. But this is not always the case. Some authors prefer to give the supporting details first and to end with the main idea. Others give some details, the main idea, and then more details. In some paragraphs, all the information is equally important and you must summarize the entire paragraph in order to get the main idea. On the other hand, there are paragraphs that do not directly state the main idea but that require you to infer the meaning based on the information given. Therefore, you get the *implied main idea* by "reading between the lines." Because it could be found anywhere in the paragraph and could be stated or implied, you should have a plan to facilitate finding the main idea. This could be done by asking yourself the following questions after you read a paragraph or passage.

1. **What is the topic of the paragraph?** The topic of the paragraph is who or what the paragraph is about—the subject being discussed. For example, the topic could be onions, the space shuttle, Abraham Lincoln, or drug abuse. You cannot determine the main point the author is trying to make until you know what he or she is talking about. However, merely knowing what topic the author is discussing will not give you the main idea. After you determine the topic, or subject, of the paragraph, you should then answer the next two questions about the topic.

2. **What aspect of the topic is the author discussing?** Is the author discussing the color, the nutritional value, how it is made, how it affects the air we breathe, the impact it has on world affairs, the definition of it, or the relationship to another topic? Most topics are broken down into small aspects. For example, if the subject is onions, the author might discuss how they are grown, how they are marketed, the varieties of onions, unique ways to cook them, how to chop them without crying, or even the beauty of their layered construction. When you determine the aspect of the subject that the author is discussing, you are then ready to ask the third question, which will give you the main idea, whether it is stated or implied.

3. **What main idea does the author want you to know about the topic in relation to the aspect being discussed?** After you have determined the topic and the aspect of the topic being discussed, you can determine what idea the author wants you to know. If the author's topic is *onions*, and the aspect is *chopping onions without tears*, then he or she might want you to know that *chopping a chilled onion submerged in water can prevent eye irritation—thus no tears.*

The following examples are explained in detail to help you to understand fully how to find stated and implied main ideas. Read and study each example carefully before going on to the practice exercises.

Example 1

Alcohol is a depressant and can lessen a person's normal inhibitions. Because people may feel more free to act in certain ways when drinking, they may think that the drug is a stimulant. It is not, but the excitement of feeling "free" certainly can be. During the euphoric period, a person's diminished self-control can result in social embarrassment, injury, or automobile accidents. Prolonged and excessive use of alcohol can damage the brain, liver, and other internal organs and can change the personality of the alcoholic.

1. What is the topic of the paragraph?
   alcohol

2. What aspect of alcohol is the author discussing?
   what it is and its effects on a person

3. What main idea does the author want you to know about what alcohol is and the effects it has on a person?
   Alcohol is a depressant and can lessen a person's normal inhibitions.

The main idea in this paragraph is found in the first sentence (a stated topic sentence).

Example 2

Atoms are inconceivably small particles that form the building blocks of matter, the smallest complete units of which all matter is made. To visualize the size of an atom, one can think of placing millions of them on the sharpened end of a pencil and still having room for more. Everything about us, everything we can see or touch, is made of atoms—the food we eat, the atmosphere, the water in the oceans, the smoke coming out of the chimney.

1. What is the topic of the paragraph?
   atoms

2. What aspect of atoms is the author discussing?
   the definition of atoms

3. What main idea does the author want you to know about the definition of atoms?

   Atoms are the building blocks of matter, the smallest complete units of which all matter is made.

In this paragraph the main idea is found in the first sentence (a stated topic sentence).

Example 3

No management can afford to ignore its competition. When they do, they pay a very serious price. Many problems incurred by the railroads, for instance, have been attributed to their failure to recognize who their competitors were. They believed they were in the railroad business, when, in fact, they were in the transportation business. Trucking, shipping, aviation, and bus and private automobile transportation are all competitors of railroads. Ten years ago, the three major broadcasting networks—ABC, CBS, and NBC—virtually controlled what you watched on television. If your set was on, the probability was better than 90 percent that you were watching one of the major networks. Today, with the rapid expansion of cable, VCRs, and the syndicated programs sold to local stations, less than half of the average television viewer's time is spent watching programming from the major networks. These examples illustrate that competitors—in terms of pricing, services offered, new products developed, and the like—represent an important environmental force that management must monitor and be prepared to respond to.

1. What is the topic of the paragraph?

   competition in management

2. What aspect of competition in management is the author discussing?

   how to face and meet the competition

3. What does the author want you to know about facing and meeting the competition in management?

   Management cannot ignore its competition but rather must monitor and be prepared to respond to the competition.

In this paragraph the first and last sentences are combined to create a main idea statement.

Example 4

Since the beginning of the twentieth century, the world population has more than tripled. While most of the phenomenal growth is attributed to modern medicine, better famine relief, and more sanitary living conditions, one factor is usually ignored. There has been more food because, during most of the twentieth century, and between 1935 and 1965 in particular, the farmers of the world have enjoyed a uniquely favorable warm, wet, and stable climate.

1. What is the topic of the paragraph?

   world population

2. What aspect of world population is the author discussing?

   the increase and reasons for the increase

3. What main idea does the author want you to know about the increase and reasons for the increase?

   World population has tripled in the twentieth century because of modern medicine, better famine relief, more sanitary living conditions, more available food, and especially a favorable climate.

In this example, there is no one topic sentence that gives the entire idea that the author wants you to know. Therefore, the main idea is a summary of all the sentences.

Example 5

Many of us think of ourselves as consumers only when we purchase a product or utilize a service. If we buy a suit or dress, we are part of the large mass of clothing consumers. If we sit down and eat a hamburger, we are consumers of fast foods. For most people, the concept of "consumerism" is fairly narrow. As a consequence of this limited focus, many people fail to understand that their individual decisions and actions affect other people. They become concerned about consumer issues only when they must deal directly with consumer problems. All too often, by the time they realize that they are not equipped to handle a consumer problem, it is too late. They have already become victims.

1. What is the topic of the paragraph?

   consumers

2. What aspect of consumers is the author discussing?

   the need to be concerned consumers

3. What main idea does the author want you to know about the need to be concerned consumers?

   To avoid and be ready to handle consumer problems, we should be concerned consumers in everything we purchase—even before problems arise.

There is no one topic sentence in this paragraph that states the complete main idea. Therefore, you have to use the information given to arrive at an implied main idea statement.

EXERCISE 7: Finding Main Ideas

NAME _____ **DATE** _____

Read each of the following paragraphs and answer the three questions. Keep in mind that if you correctly answer the first two questions, the third answer will be the main idea.

1. Covering just about everything on the lunar surface is a layer of fine, powderlike soil or dust. In some places it is mixed with rocks and pebbles. It varies in depth from place to place, and when it is mixed with the rocky rubble, it can be as deep as 65 feet (19.5 m). The fine soil is actually the result of billions of years of meteorites hitting the lunar surface and breaking up the rocks. It is ground up, or pulverized, rock. The astronauts were not hampered by its presence on the surface since they never sank more than a few inches into it. However, it did cling to their space suits as they moved about on the lunar surface.

1. What is the topic of the paragraph?

    Covering just about everything on the lunar

2. What aspect of the topic is the author discussing?

    lunar surface

3. What is the main idea that the author wants you to know about this aspect of the topic?

    The fine soil is actually the result

2. All of us, whatever our position, be it a student, in government, in business, too often take the easy route and say that it is the company that is doing this or that wrong or the town that is shortchanging us or the school that is not fulfilling its obligations. All too often, we do not appreciate that all of these institutions are made up of all of us as individuals. Each of us has a share in helping to change those areas that can be improved.

1. What is the topic of the paragraph?

Individual ~~to~~ muse take responsibility   take an innicrative for maley chay.

2. What aspect of the topic is the author discussing?

_____

3. What is the main idea that the author wants you to know about this aspect of the topic?

_____

_____

====================

3. Humankind has known about tides and their relationship to the phases of the moon since the time of the ancient Egyptians. Tides, the periodic rise and fall of the waters of the earth, are highest at the new-moon and full-moon phases and lowest when the moon is in its first and last quarter. People in ancient times had no explanation for this mysterious connection between the phases of the moon and the tides. It is not hard to understand how astrology came into being. After all, if a phenomenon as impressive as the tides is somehow influenced by the position of the moon, it was an easy step for people to believe that events in their everyday lives could be influenced by the positions of the stars.

1. What is the topic of the paragraph?

_____

2. What aspect of the topic is the author discussing?

_____

3. What is the main idea that the author wants you to know about this aspect of the topic?

_____

_____

====================

4. By itself, punishment simply inhibits responses. Ideally, punishment should be paired with reinforcement of the desired behavior. This is a more productive approach, since it teaches an alternative behavior to replace what is

促使

being punished. Children who mispronounce words while reading might learn faster if the teacher, besides scolding them, also praises them for pronouncing other words correctly. The praise acts as a positive reinforcement for learning to pronounce words correctly. It also makes the children less fearful about learning in general.

1. What is the topic of the paragraph?

_____ the punishment & reinforcement _____

2. What aspect of the topic is the author discussing?

_____

3. What is the main idea that the author wants you to know about this aspect of the topic?

_____

_____

5. For your own safety, as well as for the safety of your family and society, you should learn to swim. With the heavy increase in the number of aquatic facilities and equipment, both public and private, safety in and around water becomes a daily necessity. If you cannot swim, it is extremely unwise to participate in aquatic activities. The ability to swim safely and the prudence to recognize and practice safety procedures are of prime importance to you.

1. What is the topic of the paragraph?

_____

2. What aspect of the topic is the author discussing?

_____

3. What is the main idea that the author wants you to know about this aspect of the topic?

_____

_____

NAME _____ **DATE** _____

Read the following paragraphs and circle the best choice for the main idea.

1. A carefully chosen, appropriate slang expression can sometimes add interest and liveliness to writing. It can be helpful in establishing a humorous or casual tone. More significantly, in a few cases, it can suggest an attitude or a shade of meaning that a more conventional expression could not. By and large, slang is inappropriate for the comparatively formal, analytical writing that college courses demand. But when you feel sure that a slang expression can genuinely communicate something you would not otherwise be able to get across, don't be afraid to use it. Incidentally, forget about the coy little quotation marks that many writers put around slang expressions to show that they are really sophisticated people who could use better language if they wanted to. Good slang should seem natural, and if it is natural, it doesn't need quotes.

a. Slang expressions suggest an attitude or a shade of meaning that is usually distasteful.

b. Authors use quotation marks around slang to let the reader know the word or statement is slang.

c. If carefully chosen, slang expressions can add interest and liveliness to writing.

d. Most informal writing should and does contain slang expressions.

2. Throughout history, a solar eclipse has been a fearful experience, especially in the days when its cause was not understood. At such times, many thought that the end of the world was at hand. The early Chinese thought that a dragon was swallowing the sun, and they made a great commotion in an effort to induce the dragon to release the sun. Such noisemaking during eclipses was common to many early cultures, and even occurs presently among some tribes. Naturally, the drumbeating and cymbal clanging always seemed to be a complete success. The sun always returned, shining as brightly as ever.

a. No one knows the cause of a solar eclipse.

b. The Chinese thought an eclipse was caused by a dragon swallowing the sun.

c. A solar eclipse was a fearful experience before the cause was understood.

d. A solar eclipse could be a sign that the end of the world is at hand.

---

3. Song is the most natural form of music. Issuing from within the body, it is projected by means of the most personal of all instruments, the human voice. From time immemorial singing has been the most widespread way of making music. In folk music we have a treasury of song that reflects all phases of life—work songs, love songs, drinking songs, cradle songs, patriotic songs, dance songs, play songs, marching songs, songs of mourning, narrative songs. Some are centuries old, others are of recent origin; but all come out of human experience and affirm the indissoluble bond between music and life.

a. Song is the most natural form of music.

b. Song affirms the indissoluble bond between music and life.

c. Song is the most natural form of music because it comes from the human voice and human experiences.

d. All folk songs are centuries old.

---

4. While the game of volleyball is a unique sport in many ways, it is similar to most forms of athletic endeavor in one very important aspect. To win and win consistently a team must make fewer errors than its opponents. Since only the serving team may score in volleyball, an error on the serve is an error that must be avoided. Many teams playing top level tournament volleyball feel that the number of serving errors must be kept at a minimum before winning is possible. Even in the most basic beginning classes, instructor and players are aware of the futility and loss of time in a game in which there are numerous serving errors.

a. Only the serving team scores in volleyball.

b. Volleyball is a unique sport.

c. Volleyball is the most active of all sports.

d. In order to win in volleyball, serving errors must be kept at a minimum.

5. Halley's Comet is unquestionably the most famous of all the comets. Some historians believe that Halley's Comet is the Christmas star, or star of Bethlehem, depicted in nativity scenes. Almost everyone recognizes the comet's name, and many people are truly surprised to learn that Halley's Comet is just one of many comets that ride through the sky. Half a dozen or more are seen every year. Two or three of these are on well-predicted return visits. But Halley's is well-known because it is one of the few that is bright enough to be seen easily with the naked eye. Also, some people have the opportunity to see the comet twice in their lifetime.

a. Many people have never seen a comet.

b. All comets have unpredictable orbits.

c. Halley's Comet is the only comet ever seen by the naked eye.

d. Halley's Comet is the most famous and well-known because it is bright enough to be easily seen.

6. Open book exams are usually given when your teacher is interested in evaluating how well you can apply what you have learned. If you are to be given such an exam, don't waste your time memorizing facts or formulas. They are in your text or your notebook. It is much better to practice working out problems that require you to demonstrate understanding and application. Don't be misled: open book exams can be among the hardest you will take. Chances are such exams will emphasize various types of essay questions that will require you to analyze problems or situations and create an answer. Be sure you are familiar with your text and its problems. Concentrate on application, not memorization.

a. The purpose of open-book exams is to assess how well the student knows the textbook.

b. The purpose of open-book exams is to give the student an easier way to take an exam.

c. The purpose of open-book exams is to evaluate how well a student can apply what has been learned.

d. The purpose of open-book exams is to demonstrate the different types of questions that could be used to evaluate what a student has learned.

7. On January 28, 1986, the space shuttle *Challenger* exploded shortly after lift off, claiming the lives of all seven crew members. The incident captured the world spotlight, with millions of people focusing on death as a bold, dramatic, and unfortunate tragedy. Two months later, the Centers for Disease Control (CDC) in Atlanta, Georgia, revealed that nearly 11,000 AIDS patients had died since 1981 and indicated that incidence of the fatal disease was escalating. Public attention again was drawn to death, but in this case death was seen as a silent stalker threatening each of us. Then, on April 26, 1986, a failure of the cooling system at the Chernobyl nuclear power plant in the Ukraine resulted in the worst nuclear accident in history. The world was stunned, angry, and fearful in response to this tragedy. We were all again reminded of our mortality and the possibility of mass annihilation in this age of nuclear tragedy.

a. The space shuttle *Challenger* exploded on January 28, 1986, claiming the lives of all seven crew members.

b. According to the Centers for Disease Control, the incidence of AIDS is escalating.

c. The *Challenger* disaster, the rise in the number of AIDS patients, and the Chernobyl nuclear power plant accident are reminders to us of our mortality and possibility of mass annihilation.

d. The *Challenger* disaster, the rise in the number of AIDS patients, and the Chernobyl accident are the worst disasters the world has known in this century.

8. Sunlight, or white light, contains the elements of all colors in such a mixture that each color is canceled. White light can be broken into its component colors by projecting it through a prism. An object is seen as a particular color because it absorbs some elements of white light and reflects others. That is, an apple is red when it reflects those elements of light that we have named red and absorbs the others.

a. Sunlight is a white light.

b. An object is seen as a particular color because it absorbs some elements of white light and reflects others.

c. An apple is red because it absorbs all the red light.

d. White reflects the elements of all the colors.

9. The term *drama* often is used as a synonym for theatre. Such usage is not entirely accurate. As a genre, drama refers to plays that have serious intent but do not fall within the definition of tragedy. In a drama we do not necessarily have an unhappy ending, but the subject matter is treated in a serious fashion. The events tend to be of lesser magnitude than in tragedy. The heroes are of everyday stuff.

a. A drama is a play that has serious intent but is not a tragedy.

b. Drama and theatre are synonymous.

c. Dramas are the most enjoyable of all theatrical products.

d. Some dramas have unhappy endings.

10. Problem solving is affected by many other influences other than simply the problem. These include anxiety, anger, and frustration resulting from the problem-solving process itself or from other sources in your life at that time. If these emotions are present to any extent, they may interfere with your finding a smooth solution to a problem. Severe anxiety may impair your ability to answer the questions on an exam, and frustration at not being able to work a crossword puzzle may block the right word from coming to you. Sometimes, however, these factors can help you solve a problem. For example, a very competitive person, anxious to succeed, might actually become more efficient when solving a problem.

a. Anxiety and frustration may prevent you from working crossword puzzles.

b. A very competitive person is always more efficient at problem solving than a noncompetitive person.

c. In addition to the problem, problem solving is affected by anxiety, anger, and frustration caused by the problem or other sources in life.

d. Anxiety, anger, and frustration are emotions that lead to poor physical health.

11. Understanding does not mean coercing someone to your point of view. The manipulator tries to do this. He or she sees understanding as having someone else come around to *his* or *her* point of view. Then *he* or *she* is being understood. This is faulty thinking.

The understanding person communicates a sense of acceptance and understanding verbally and nonverbally, even if there is not agreement; if there happens to be agreement, that is great. But the understanding communicator does not insist on agreement. Understanding goes both ways; if you want to be understood, you need to understand the other party as well. Both communicating parties have wants and feelings that need to be expressed if two-way communication is going to occur.

a. Understanding is accepting a point of view whether or not there is agreement.

b. Understanding is changing someone's point of view to agree with your own.

c. Understanding is a demanding type of communication.

d. Understanding is faulty thinking.

12. You cannot hope to write a coherent paper until you have decided on your purpose, because that purpose will determine what you will include and what you will leave out. The purpose gives focus to your paper. If, for example, your purpose is to describe a forward pass, you will not discuss the excitement cheerleaders can generate in a crowd or the intricate formations marching bands can produce during halftime ceremonies. Your purpose is to describe a particular play, and you will do just that in the clearest manner possible. If, on the other hand, your purpose is to convince a reader that attending a football game can be exciting even to one who knows little about the sport, you might very well mention not only the gymnastic feats of cheerleaders and the skill of marching bands, but you might also describe the sandwich vendors and the colorful attire of a football crowd.

a. When writing about football games, it is important to describe the sandwich vendors and colorful attire.

b. A coherent paper is one that is clear and to the point.

c. The purpose of most papers is to describe some event.

d. A coherent paper has a clear purpose that gives focus to the paper.

13. If a problem cannot be denied or repressed completely, it may be possible to distort its nature so that it can be more easily handled. One example of this is **projection,** the attribution of one's own repressed motives, ideas, or feelings to others. We ascribe feelings that we do not want to someone else, thus locating the source of our conflict outside ourselves. A corporation executive who feels guilty about the way he rose to power may project his own ruthless ambition onto his colleagues. He is simply doing his job, he believes, while his associates are all overly ambitious and preoccupied with power. A high-school student talks his girlfriend into sneaking away with him for the weekend. It is a bad experience for both of them. Days later he insists that it was she who pushed him into it. He is not lying—he really believes that she did. Perhaps he feels guilty for insisting that they sneak away together, angry with her for not talking him out of it, disturbed by what he felt during the experience. To pull himself together, he locates the responsibility outside himself. In both cases, the stressful problem has been repressed and then translated into a form that is less stressful and easier to handle.

a. There is nothing wrong with blaming misfortunes and misdeeds on other people.

b. The best way to handle a big problem is to reduce it into many smaller, manageable problems.

c. One possible way to handle a problem is to assign the feelings or actions to someone or something outside ourselves, thus reducing the amount of stress that we feel.

d. The best problem-solvers are people who never accept responsibility for their actions and are satisfied with letting others fend for them.

---

14. As a consumer of goods and services, you will sometimes need to communicate with a manufacturer or provider concerning the quality of what you have purchased. Notes of praise take very little effort and can make a big difference to the receiver. It is especially thoughtful in the case of direct service. A waiter or waitress, gas station attendant, health care practitioner, teacher, or flight attendant—all deserve positive feedback. Sending an acknowledgment to the management of the organization that provided the service is a means of communication that consumers can use more often. These contacts can be made in writing or verbally.

a. Positive feedback is a thoughtful way of showing that you are pleased with a product or service and is welcomed by manufacturers and providers of services.

b. Thank-you notes should be sent to manufacturers on a regular basis.

c. Positive feedback is desirable and is practiced by most consumers since it requires so little time and effort.

d. Most manufacturers welcome positive feedback but discourage suggestions and complaints.

---

15. Art, like love, is easier to experience than to define. That is because, like love, it is experienced on different levels. There is art that serves as entertainment and offers a pleasant escape from the cares of life. There is art that propagates the artist's point of view, whether religious, political, or philosophical. There is art that fulfills Aristotle's precept by purging our emotions "through pity and terror." There is art that leads us to a broader understanding and compassion.

a. Art is very much like love in many ways.

b. Art is easier to experience than to define because it is experienced on different levels.

c. Art leads us to a broader understanding and compassion.

d. Art in the days of Aristotle aroused viewers' emotions.

---

16. Through a fortunate accident, Planet Earth is the right distance from the sun to make the existence of life-giving water possible. Closer to the sun the heat is so intense that water would be vaporized; farther away, water would be permanently frozen. Only Mars, of the other planets in the solar system, is in the narrow temperature band in which water can exist in its three states. But only Earth is blanketed by a living, water-built biosphere, in which the life force itself seems to issue from water's evaporation, precipitation, runoff, seepage, transpiration from plants, respiration from animals, melting, freezing, and flowing. Earth, so far as we know, is the only Water Planet.

a. Earth is the right distance from the sun to make the existence of life-giving water possible.

b. It was an accident that provided the earth with water.

c. Water is plentiful on Mars as well as on Earth.

d. Earth is nicknamed the Water Planet.

---

17. The library is an intellectual time machine. It allows you to understand the past and present so you can better enter the future. The library is a silent meeting that comes to order when you ask a question of a librarian, open a book, listen to a tape cassette, or watch a filmstrip. The library is a study place. You can meet with yourself or, through multimedia resources, with thousands of other people. Each will have his or her own knowledge allowing you the opportunity to comprehend, apply, analyze, evaluate, and synthesize. The word *college* means a group of people gathered together for a common purpose. You can find no greater gathering than that in your college library.

a. The library is a quiet place to study that allows you to study through multimedia resources.

b. The library is one of the best places to meet friends and relax.

c. The library is an intellectual time machine.

d. The word *college* means a group of people gathered together for a common purpose.

---

18. If you ask a group of people to give a one-word description of *listening,* some would say *hearing.* And that can be a problem, because the word hearing is not an adequate substitute. It doesn't describe the process of listening. Hearing is physical. If your ears are not impaired, you can hear. You make no special effort to hear sound. But you do make a special mental effort if you want to follow and understand the sound (determining whether steps are approaching or receding, the nature of a baby's cry, someone speaking). The special effort is what distinguishes listening from hearing. Hearing is simply receiving sound. Listening is following and understanding the sound. It is hearing with a purpose.

a. Listening can accurately be defined as hearing.

b. Since hearing is physical, it is different from listening.

c. Listening is following and understanding sound that has a purpose.

d. It takes an expert to distinguish between hearing and listening.

19. Just before the Civil War, about 225,000 Indians shared the plains and mountains with the buffalo, the wild horse, the jack rabbit, and the coyote. But they would soon be overwhelmed as white Americans stormed into this area at a breathtaking pace. The speed with which prospectors, ranchers, and farmers conquered the last frontier was made possible by the transcontinental railroads that criss-crossed the region, transporting settlers and supplies and providing access to outside markets. Eager to attract settlers, the railroads made land available at low prices. The federal government also played a critical role. It proved to be as liberal in giving away land to corporations and prospective farmers as it was thorough and ruthless in moving the Indians to the less desirable places. At the same time its policies undermined Indian culture and made them the wards of government bureaucrats.

a. The United States was liberal in giving land to corporations and farmers.

b. The two things that helped conquer the last frontier were the transcontinental railroads and government land grants to corporations and farmers.

c. The Indians were pushed off the plains as the white settlers stormed in.

d. Before the Civil War there were about 225,000 Indians on the plains.

20. We should be wiser, I believe, to think of the arts more as we think of people. We learn, most of us, at a very early age that an adequate adjustment to the world cannot be made from social responses that simply divide the "good people" from the "bad people." We have learned to be skeptical even of such categories as "the people I like" and "the people I don't like." If we do maintain such divisions, we find individuals constantly moving from one group to the other. Eventually we find human differences too subtle for easy classification, and the web of our relationships becomes too complex for analysis. And we try to move toward more and more sensitive discrimination, so that there are those we can learn from, those we can work with, those good for an evening of light talk, those we can depend on for a little affection, and so on—with perhaps those very few with whom we can sustain a deepening relationship for an entire lifetime. When we have learned this same sensitivity and adjustment to works of art—when we have gone beyond the easy categories of the textbooks and have learned to regard our art relationships as part of our own growth—then we shall have achieved a dimension in living that is as deep and as irreplaceable as friendship.

a. The arts are easier to place in categories than people because the arts are more stable than people.

b. We should think of the arts in the same ways that we think of people.

c. In the same way that people whom we value do not fall into predetermined groups, the arts we value should also move beyond these easy textbook categories.

d. It is hard to categorize people because each individual is constantly moving from one group to another.

EXERCISE 9: Expressing Main Ideas

NAME _____ **DATE** _____

Read each of the following paragraphs and write the main idea in your own words. Remember to think about the three-question formula studied earlier in this chapter.

1. People who do not use drugs are touched every day through the latest media story about cocaine or other massive drug arrests funded by taxpayer dollars. Those who don't use drugs are also affected by the estimated 12 percent of the entire United States work force under the influence of illicit drugs or alcohol on any given day. When our co-workers use drugs, the effectiveness of our own work is diminished. If the car we drive was assembled by a drug user at the plant, we are in danger. Our safety is jeopardized if the driver, engineer, or pilot is using drugs while transporting us.

_____
_____
_____

2. One way to fight off boredom is to alternate one subject with another when you study. There is no rule that you have to spend a four-hour block of time on one subject. Another way to reduce boredom is to take study breaks every hour or so. Try to do something different for five or ten minutes. When you are in the middle of writing a paper, a break to write a letter may not be as relaxing as a break in which you walk the dog. Taking a break is always better than staring at a book without absorbing anything. Not only does the staring stop you from resting, but it also establishes the habit of nonconcentration while studying.

_____
_____
_____

3. Educators have tried to change people's attitudes about free time to help them to get more pleasure and satisfaction from leisure activities. Teaching people how to do various activities, however—such as games and crafts— is one thing; but teaching them to enjoy them and to value doing them is something else. Perhaps leisure will only be accepted as worthwhile and honorable when people feel as positive about it as they do about work.

In order to enjoy leisure activities people must consider them worth while.

4. The two ways of marking a textbook are underlining (or highlighting) and making marginal notes. Many students underline too much: they underline whole paragraphs or sometimes a full page. Some students go to the other extreme, marking only the words in boldface or italics. Neither method serves the purpose of underlining, which is to provide a quick way of reviewing so that you don't have to reread the whole book when studying for a test. If you underline 10 percent of your book, then you've saved yourself rereading 90 percent of the material. You shouldn't underline more than 20 percent of a book or article unless the material is highly technical.

5. The mathematical system that has stood the longest test of time is undoubtedly the natural number system. The permanence of the natural numbers is due to the fact that they are the counting numbers; and man, from the earliest times, found it convenient to count objects. Just like the farmer today, the primitive shepherd kept record of his flock by counting the animals. The symbols for, and names of, the various numbers have changed, but the counting concept remains the same.

the counting number remains the

6. Listening to generate test questions is not only an excellent way to improve lecture listening skills, but is also an effective approach to test taking. With practice, some students become extremely proficient at predicting test items, using these as they study and review for examinations. As they have opportunities to compare their own items with test items actually appearing on an instructor's examinations, they learn to rephrase, sharpen, and refine their questions while at the same time becoming more aware of the kinds of questions certain teachers tend to ask.

_____

_____

_____

7. Colonial newspapers served as the most important public tie among the colonies. Their circulations were small by modern standards. Many backwoods farmers rarely saw one, even if they knew how to read. Yet the newspapers were passed from hand to hand and read aloud at crossroad stores. They served as a vital network of communication among a relatively literate people. And as time went on, that communication link became more and more vital to their interests.

_____

_____

_____

8. Some job-related distress is related to unrealistic expectations grounded in irrational beliefs. Many of us pretend to have competencies that we do not have. In so doing, we guarantee additional strain and pressures in the workplace. Realizing that progress takes time and setting reasonable goals for ourselves are the beginnings of stress management in the workplace. Time-management skills are also important if we are to meet deadlines for projects and reports.

9. The population explosion in the American colonies had several important effects. It stimulated economic growth and helped raise the standard of living, since a growing population meant more mouths to feed and a growing market for farmers. A small settlement could not afford to undertake activities other than growing food and making clothes and shelter. A larger one could support a greater variety of jobs.

_____

_____

_____

10. The sounds that we hear seldom result from pure tones. Unlike a tuning fork, which can produce a tone that is almost pure, musical instruments produce **overtones**—accompanying sound waves that are different multiples of the frequency of the basic tone. A violin string, for example, not only vibrates as a whole, it also vibrates in halves, thirds, quarters, and so on all at the same time. Because of physical differences in their construction, a violin and a piano playing the same note will be "in tune" but produce different overtones. Thus, the two instruments can play the same melody yet retain their distinctive sounds. This complex pattern of overtones determines the **timbre,** or "texture," of the sound. Music synthesizers can mimic different instruments electronically because they produce not only pure tones but also the overtones that produce the timbre of different musical instruments.

_____

_____

_____

SUGGESTIONS FOR FURTHER STUDY

- Select the main idea of each of the paragraphs in Chapter 7. Notice how finding the main idea helps you determine the organizational pattern.
- Practice writing paragraphs and essays with predetermined main ideas.
- Read articles in the local or campus newspapers and select the main idea.

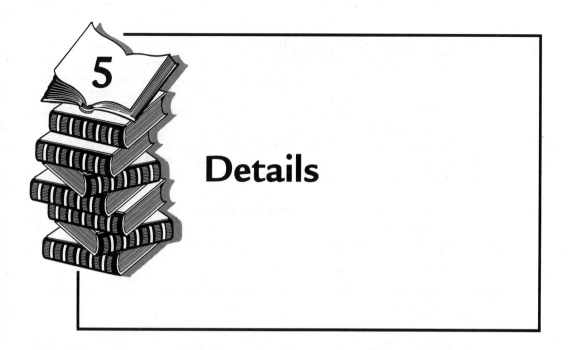

Details

MAJOR AND MINOR DETAILS

When you find the main idea in a passage you have the most important idea the author intended. But in order for you to gain a complete understanding, this main idea may need to be defined, explained, proved, or analyzed. In other words, the author uses details to fill in this important information. Some of these details directly support the main idea and are essential to understanding the idea. These are the *major details* in the passage. Authors use *minor details* to indirectly support the main idea. Although these details make the reading more interesting and they relate to the main idea, it is not essential to remember them to comprehend the passage. If a major detail were omitted, the meaning might not be clear since basic information has not been included. If a minor detail were omitted, the material might not be as readable but would be just as understandable.

In this age of information, you are presented with more reading material than you can possibly assimilate, so it becomes increasingly important to be able to distinguish major details from minor details.

The main idea and major supporting details are often all you need for a clear and complete understanding of a reading passage. However, there are times when both the major *and* the minor details would be very important. For example, if you learned that you had a certain illness, you would be more likely to want to read detailed information about it, and you would be interested in every detail—from the major details giving the cause, symptoms, progression, and treatment, to the minor details such as the effects that aspirin would have on the illness. Also, in deciding whether minor details are needed, how can you overlook the fact that minor details make your reading more interesting?

When deciding whether a detail is major or minor, you should determine your purpose and need for the information as well as the main idea that the author wants you to understand.

The passage in Example 1 is about solar energy. The main idea is that *the sun is the primary source of energy to support life on Earth*. As you read the paragraph, note that the underlined major details directly support this main idea.

Example 1

The sun is the only important source of energy for the Earth and its atmosphere. Millions of other stars radiate energy, but they are too far away to affect the Earth. Energy is also released within the Earth, primarily from the decay of radioactive minerals, and this heat flows upward to the crust; some also escapes to the atmosphere through volcanoes and geysers, but its quantity is insignificant. Tidal energy, resulting from the combination of terrestrial, lunar, and solar gravity, is also of minor importance in totality. Thus the sun supplies essentially all the energy that supports life on Earth, and it energizes most of the atmospheric processes.

The sun is a star of average size and average temperature, but its relative proximity to the Earth gives it a far greater influence on our planet than all other celestial bodies combined. The sun is a prodigal generator of energy. In a single second it produces more energy than has been used by humankind since civilization began. The sun functions as an enormous nuclear reactor, producing energy by fusion, which burns only a very small portion of the sun's mass but provides an immense and continuous flow of radiant energy that is dispersed in all directions.

The passage in Example 2 discusses how scientific information is gathered and organized. Note that most of the first paragraph is introductory, with minor details that set the stage, whereas the second paragraph contains major details that a scientist would need to remember when gathering and organizing information.

Example 2

Science is a method of gathering and organizing information that involves observation, hypothesis formation, and experimentation. Information regarding these principles is collected using whatever tools for observation are available. In some cases, the "tools" may be the observer's eyes, ears, or other unaided senses. In other cases, elaborate equipment may be used to assist the gathering of information. Often the tools used are overwhelming in complexity, which gives a somewhat erroneous and inflated impression of the actual work being done by a scientist.

Once new information has been collected, the scientist tries to fit the information into the existing framework to gain a clearer picture of the real world. It is usually more productive for a scientist to have a working hypothesis as a guide. A **hypothesis** is a logical guess about how things work. It helps to focus a person's thinking on the critical questions to be asked. If a hypothesis is used for a long period of time and is continually supported by new facts, it is often formally stated as a **theory**. Scientific theories are those unifying principles that tend to bind large areas of scientific knowledge that are not known to be true in *every* case because it would be impossible to test *every* case.

In Example 3 you will read the advantages of seeking employment with large and small corporations. First, read only the underlined major details. Note that you then have the basic information you need. Next, reread the passage, including the minor details. The minor details strengthen your understanding but do not give additional advantages.

Example 3

Corporations as a group offer a bonanza of jobs. Most large companies send recruiters to campus to interview graduating seniors with the required academic training. A large university may have more than 500 companies a year knocking on its doors. Big firms are your best bet for a job because their normal growth, employee retirements, and turnover create thousands of jobs nationwide each year.

Corporations, however, illustrate the maxim that the biggest isn't always the best. Many small firms with just a few hundred employees have positions that may coincide with your career goals, too. Such firms may not have the time, budget, or need to send recruiters around to your campus; you'll probably have to contact them yourself either directly or through an employment agency. Don't ignore these little companies. Their salaries are usually competitive and the chances for advancement and recognition even stronger than those of a big firm. You could become a big fish in a small pond, reaching a high-level position more quickly than you would if you had climbed the more competitive ladder of a corporate giant.

For example, a small company may need a bright engineering, accounting or management graduate who would report directly to the senior vice-president of engineering, the company controller, or the general manager. In larger firms it may take years to reach that level and accumulate similar in-depth experience. In addition, responsibilities may come faster in a small firm with less specialization and fewer lower-level employees to receive delegated authority.

NAME _____ **DATE** _____

Read the following passage, and then answer the questions that follow. Note that the major details have been underlined.

The Common Cold

On an everyday basis, perhaps no ailment is as bothersome as the runny nose, itchy eyes, and generally uncomfortable feeling associated with the common cold. Cold-related symptoms are responsible for more days lost from work and more uncomfortable days spent at work than any other ailment.

Caused by any number of viruses (some experts claim there may be over 100 different viruses responsible for the common cold itself), colds are *endemic* (present to some degree) among people throughout the world. Current research indicates that otherwise healthy people carry cold viruses in their noses and throats a majority of the time. These viruses are held in check until a person's resistance is lowered. Thus, in the true sense of the word, it is possible to "catch" a cold from the airborne droplets of another person's sneeze or from skin to skin or mucous membrane contact. In fact, recent studies indicate that the *hands* themselves may be the greatest avenue of cold and other viral transmission. It should be obvious that covering your mouth with a tissue or handkerchief when sneezing is better than covering it with your bare hand, particularly if you next use your hand to touch food in a restaurant, shake your friend's hand, or open the door.

Although numerous theories exist as to how to "cure" the cold, including taking megadoses of vitamin C, there is little hard evidence to support any of them. The best rule of thumb is to keep your resistance level high. Also, avoiding people with newly developed colds (colds appear to be most contagious during the first 24 hours of onset) appears to be advisable. Once you contract a cold, bed rest, plenty of fluids, and aspirin for relief of pain and discomfort are the most "tried and true" remedies. Depending on the nature of the symptoms, several over-the-counter preparations have proven to be effective on a short-term basis.

1. The common cold is caused by _any number of the viruses_

2. Three ways that colds spread are from _airbone droplets from another person's sneeze or from skin to skin_

3. The best way to prevent having a cold is _keep your resistance high level and also avoiding people with newly developed colds or mucus membrane contact_

4. What is the recommended treatment for the common cold?
bed rest, plenty of fluids, and aspirin to relief of pain and discomfort

Read the following passage, underline the major details, and then answer the questions that follow.

Walk, Don't Run

ELLEN DARION

Walking is probably the most overlooked and underpraised route to fitness. Like other exercises, it can help control weight; strengthen the heart, lungs and bones; tone muscles; ease stress; and boost energy. *Unlike* many exercises, walking is safe, convenient and simple. It's also ideal for anyone who has been leading a sedentary life or who must curtail activity due to injury or illness.

To build a strong cardiovascular system, "you have to go fast, without stopping," says Dr. Lenore R. Zohman, director of the Exercise Laboratory and Cardiac Rehabilitation Program at Montefiore Medical Center in New York. That means walking at least half an hour a day at a pace of four miles per hour, three or four times a week.

If you haven't done any conscious exercise in years, work up to the pace slowly. You'll begin to see and feel an improvement in muscle tone as early as three to five weeks after you start. (You'll also have sore muscles. Don't forget to warm up first—stretching the calf muscles is important.)

So how to get the most out of walking? If you're already walking as fast as you can, cover longer distances or rougher terrain. Try hills, walking in the snow or on sand. Don a five- or ten-pound pack or carry hand-held weights. All of these variations make you work harder, which means you burn more calories. Supplement your walks with sit-ups to condition the upper body.

Or try race-walking—"health-walking," if you remove the competitive factor. In health-walking you take longer strides and perform a vigorous pumping of arms, which firms and strengthens muscles, abdomen and back, and also lets you walk faster. (The elbow is bent at a right angle in front of the body, forearm held parallel to the ground.) The buttocks and thigh muscles are worked harder in health-walking than in running. Walkers also take more steps per minute, so they have more muscle contractions, which trim and tone their legs. "But the best thing about race-walking is that it is virtually injury-free," says former Olympic race-walking champion Howard Jacobson, founder and president of the New York Walkers Club and author of *Racewalking to Fitness*. "Walking offers a smooth transfer of weight, since you always have one foot on the ground, while a runner pounds the ground with three to four times the usual force."

Dr. John Walker, Jr., chief of the Foot and Ankle Service at New York's Lenox Hill Hospital, agrees. He describes running as a "series of jumps. The knee is the shock absorber, and it's overloaded." In walking, however, "injury is unlikely, especially with a cushioned, properly fitted shoe."

Dr. Walker recommends a running shoe with an index finger's breadth between the tip of the toe and the front of the shoe when you stand up; your foot shouldn't push the shoe out of shape. It should provide protection and support, but still be flexible.

Remember that it is possible to overdo anything, even walking. Be careful not to overexert yourself or become dehydrated, especially in hot weather. Dizziness, a pain under the sternum and an irregular heartbeat are all warning signs that you're doing too much. Slow down, and if the symptom doesn't go away, stop. If it persists, call a physician.

"The trick," says Dr. Zohman, "is to make walking a daily habit." So when you get home tonight, don't head for your favorite chair; hit the sidewalk instead.

1. Briefly compare and contrast walking with other types of exercise.

_____

_____

_____

2. How far should you try to walk at least three or four times a week?

_____

3. How long should it take you to walk this distance?

_____

4. What is the basic equipment needed for walking?

_____

5. What are the signs of overexertion?

_____

_____

The following passage is longer but easy and interesting. Read the passage carefully, and then fill in the blanks. The main idea has been stated for you.

Great Auk
(Pinguinis impennis)

The first bird to be called a "penguin" lived in the coastal waters of the North Atlantic and was known to Europeans and Native Americans long before the discovery of the Antarctic bird we today call penguin. Despite a striking resemblance, the two species are not related. The northern penguin was a great auk, largest member of the auk family. Tasty and flightless, living along well-traveled routes, it was hunted to extinction by 1844.

The great auk stood about 30 inches (76 centimeters) tall, with a stocky body, disproportionately small wings, and webbed feet. Its thick, waterproof plumage was gray-black on the back, dark brown on the head, and white on the belly. During the mating season a large white spot appeared on each cheek. The auk's black bill was as long as its face, curved at the end, and etched with deep white grooves.

Unable to fly and clumsy on land, great auks spent most of their time in the water feeding on fish and crustaceans. They were powerful divers and fast, strong swimmers, able to outlast humans pursuing them in rowboats. Well-adapted to the water, they even slept at sea for most of the year. Unfortunately, however, they had to come ashore to lay their eggs; and it was during the summer nesting seasons that hunters from Europe and America wiped out a population once numbering in the millions.

The slaughter of great auks began in prehistoric times, when their range evidently extended down the North American coast to Florida. Excavations at Indian camp-grounds in New England have uncovered heaps of fossil auk bones. Nine hundred years ago, Viking sea rovers also took their toll in the North Atlantic. And then, in the fifteenth century, European fishers sailing west in search of cod began to plunder the auks' nesting colonies.

Auk eggs were a highly prized delicacy, and the birds themselves were fat and delicious. One needed no special skill to club one of these tame, awkward waddlers on its nest and remove its egg, thus destroying two generations with one blow. During the next two centuries the killing increased as people discovered new uses for the birds. Surplus meat was good for bait. The feathers made fine featherbeds. Auk fat was an excellent fuel for lamps and stoves; and the whole dried auk, its body full of oil, could be used as a torch. To make the slaughter more efficient, the hunters built stone corrals into which they drove the birds and clubbed them en masse.

By the late eighteenth century, great auks survived only on the rocky islets around Newfoundland, Greenland, and Iceland and on the isle of St. Kilda near Scotland. The early 1800's saw a rapid decline in their numbers; for, although large hunting parties had stopped, egg hunters still raided nests. After 1821, when the last St. Kilda auk vanished, the birds withdrew, first to the Auk Rocks near the southwest tip of Iceland and then to Geirfuglasker, a remote outcropping where they were finally safe from man. But in 1830 a volcanic eruption led to violent undersea quakes, and Geirfuglasker disappeared beneath the waves. Remarkably, fifty surviving birds found their way to Eldey Island, a small steep mass of volcanic rock nearby. Suddenly naturalists and museum directors noticed that the species, once so abundant, was virtually extinct, and—what they considered most alarming—only two museums had stuffed auks in their collections.

At this point the frantic scramble began as collectors offered great sums for whole skins, skeletons, and undamaged eggs. No one gave a thought to the preservation of the species; by nineteenth-century standards, a mounted specimen was worth more than a living bird. The world's last two great auks earned one hundred crowns a piece for the Icelandic fishers who killed them for collectors.

Main idea: The great auk, a magnificent and interesting bird that resembled the bird we know as a penguin, became extinct by the year 1844.

1. The great auk closely resembled the _____ in appearance.

2. The auk became extinct by the year _____.

3. This magnificent bird became extinct because it was

   _____ and _____ .

4. Describe the great auk.

   _____

   _____

   _____

5. The auk's main food was _____ and

   _____ that were found in the

   _____ .

6. The auk spent most of the time in the water and went ashore only to

   _____ .

7. The auk can be traced back to _____ time.

8. Besides eating the auk and its eggs, what other uses did humans find for these birds? (Name three.)

   _____

   _____

   _____

9. Where in the United States have fossil remains of the auk been found?

   _____

10. How much were the Icelandic fishermen paid for the last two great auks known to exist?

    _____

The following passage is about a famous jazz musician and composer. In this passage you should note the minor details about his life as well as the major details outlining the factors that made him famous.

Read the passage, and then answer the questions that follow.

Duke Ellington

It has become increasingly common for the name of Duke Ellington to be numbered among the great American composers. His claim to that position rests on a huge body of music, including everything from simple tunes, theater songs, piano pieces, works for jazz septet and octet, to instrumental compositions for full jazz orchestra and, in a few instances, for jazz orchestra and symphony orchestra combined.

Edward Kennedy Ellington was born in Washington, D.C., on April 29, 1899, and he began his musical career in that city. By the mid-1920s he had established himself as an ensemble leader in New York. And by the early 1930s, he had begun to achieve international recognition as a composer. His nickname "Duke" was first conferred because of his sartorial elegance. It became his professional name and, as Albert Murray has observed, it was appropriate because Ellington was, personally and musically, a natural aristocrat. He died in New York City on May 24, 1974.

Ellington used the American dance band as his means of expression. "He plays piano," said his frequent collaborator Billy Strayhorn, "but his real instrument is the orchestra." Most of his best works are therefore instrumental miniatures conceived within the unpretentious conventions of twentieth-century dance music. But they are realized as works of high musical art.

In his orchestrations, and most particularly in his scoring of individual chords, Ellington proved himself to be one of the truly original musicians of our time. And through instrumental doublings by his reed players on various saxophones and clarinets, through ingenious combinations of instruments, and through the carefully crafted use of various mutes and combinations of mutes by his brass players, he achieved a rich variety of sonorities and textures from his ensemble—which in his early years numbered as few as ten musicians.

Ellington learned a great deal from his immediate predecessors and contemporaries—largely from the Fletcher Henderson orchestra—about how to transform the jazz-influenced dance band (with its reed, brass, and rhythm sections) into a true jazz orchestra. But it was when he encountered nightclub "show" work, with its call for overtures, choruses, dance accompaniments, and other demands of the miniature musical "review" which these establishments featured, that his talent began to develop. He made his dance band into a show band, and his show band a vehicle for a collaborative yet personal artistic expression.

Ellington worked with the individual talents of his musicians in the same way that dramatists of the past worked with their actors or choreographers with their dancers. Indeed, his harmonic originality was initially dictated not so much in the abstract, as by, let us say, how this particular player's A flat sounded, and how it in turn might sound when juxtaposed with that player's highly individual G in the upper register.

1. Duke Ellington was born in the year _____.

2. Why is Duke Ellington considered a great American composer?

   _____

   _____

   _____

3. Although his band was small, he was able to produce a rich variety of textures in his jazz music. How did he accomplish this?

   _____

   _____

   _____

4. Duke Ellington's jazz orchestra is best known for playing in

   _____.

*Indicate on the lines provided whether the following statements are **true** or **false**.*

_____ 5. Edward Kennedy Ellington was nicknamed "Duke" because of his aristocratic elegance.

_____ 6. Duke Ellington played the trumpet in his band.

_____ 7. He was popular and was destined to be an outstanding musician because he followed tradition without introducing new variations.

_____ 8. Duke Ellington wanted his players to double on instruments, a requirement that made it hard to find talented players.

_____ 9. Most of Duke Ellington's best works are instrumental miniatures that are still recognized as works of high musical art.

_____ 10. Much of his success is due to the fact that he considered each musician's individual talent, which he used to good advantage.

NAME _____ **DATE** _____

The following passage deals with the greenhouse effect, which could eventually affect life on earth as we know it. The passage explains the reasons for this global warming and what can be done to reverse or at least to slow the process. In the passage there are unfamiliar words that you must learn in order to fully comprehend the details.

Read the passage, and then answer the questions according to the directions that precede each section.

Global Warming and the "Greenhouse Effect"

We have noted that "greenhouse effect" is a term of questionable appropriateness that refers to an important atmospheric process. In essence the term alludes to the fact that the atmosphere inhibits the escape of long-wave terrestrial radiation, thereby increasing temperature, and that a concentration of atmospheric impurities enhances this process. In the last decade this concept has received considerable attention by the media and the general public. There is some evidence that the atmosphere is warming, and there are strong indications that an intensified greenhouse effect is at least partly responsible.

It is apparent that there has been an increase of global temperature of about 1/2% during this century—with the 1980's being the warmest decade on record—although the record goes back only about a century, which is very short range for discerning climatic trends. Although there is still no clear evidence that a long-term heating trend is in effect, even the short-term results could be serious enough to warrant considerable concern.

It should be noted that humans did not create the greenhouse effect—it has been part of the basis of life on Earth since the atmosphere first formed. Without it, our planet would be a frozen mass, more than 30% colder on average than it is now. The greenhouse effect is natural, but we seem to have turned up the heat. It is well known that climate undergoes frequent natural fluctuations, becoming warmer or colder regardless of human activities. Such events as the episodic warming of seawater in the tropical Pacific is likely to be at least partly responsible for atmospheric warming.

There is, however, an increasing body of evidence that indicates that anthropogenic (human-induced) factors are responsible for recent temperature increases. The "culprits" are popularly referred to as "greenhouse gases"—carbon dioxide, water vapor, methane, nitrous oxide, ozone, and chlorofluorocarbons—which have a low capacity for transmitting long-wave radiation, and as their concentrations in the atmosphere increase, more terrestrial radiation is retained in the lower atmosphere, thereby raising the temperature.

Human activities are clearly accountable for the increasing release of most of these gases into the air. Chlorofluorocarbons (CFCs) are synthetic chemicals that were very popular for a variety of uses until recently. Nitrous oxide comes from chemical fertilizers and automobile emissions. Methane is produced by grazing livestock, rice paddies, burning wood, and the use of natural gas, coal, and oil. All these gases have been released at an accelerating rate in recent years.

Carbon dioxide (CO) however, appears to be the principal culprit; some studies indicate that it accounts for about half the recent global warming. In the last quarter century, concentrations of carbon dioxide in the atmosphere have increased by about 25 percent. Carbon dioxide is a principal byproduct of the combustion of anything containing carbon, particularly coal and petroleum. The world consumption of fossil fuels has been increasing at a rate of 2 percent to 2.5 percent per year recently, which is only about half the rate that prevailed before the energy crisis of the mid-1970s but is more than enough to continue exacerbating the problem. Indeed, it is estimated that assuaging the warming trend would require a decrease of at least 50 percent in burning fossil fuels. Moreover, the forests of the world, particularly the tropical rainforests, are rapidly being depleted. Trees are major absorbers of carbon dioxide, and with fewer trees, more carbon dioxide floats into the atmosphere.

The long-term climatic result of the buildup of greenhouse gases is still unknown, but the predicted scenarios are serious. Certainly, temperature and precipitation patterns would change. Heat and drought would become more prevalent in much of the midlatitudes, and milder temperatures would prevail in higher latitudes. Some arid lands might receive more rainfall, ice caps would surely melt, and global sea levels would rise. Current living patterns over much of the world would be affected.

What can be done to ameliorate the situation? The bottom line is to reduce emissions, particularly from smokestacks and internal combustion engines. Coal and petroleum are major offenders; natural gas produces fewer emissions; solar, wind, and nuclear energy sources are "clean," insofar as carbon dioxide is concerned.

The United States is the world's leading producer of carbon dioxide; Russia ranks second. These two nations combined yield about 45 percent of the world total. Serious efforts to reduce emissions are now being made by industrialized nations. Most developed countries (the United States, Canada, the nations of western Europe, Japan, Australia) are now burning less oil and coal than they did a decade ago. Developing countries, on the other hand, are increasing emission output as they attempt to build their own industrial infrastructures. Addressing the obvious economic needs of developing nations while attempting to curb carbon dioxide emissions presents an especially painful dilemma. These nations argue that industrialized nations created the problem and now want the developing countries to forego the benefits of industrialization in order to protect the atmosphere.

Global warming is a very complex issue, the <u>parameters</u> of which are still unclear. Its effects on the earthly environment and the human habitat, however, are likely to be profound.

Use your dictionary and context clues to select the best meaning for each of the following terms. Write the letter of your choice on the line provided.

_____ 1. <u>alludes</u>
        a. testifies   b. points   c. contests

_____ 2. <u>terrestrial radiation</u>
        a. radiation in outer space
        b. deadly radiation
        c. radiation on the earth

_____ 3. <u>episodic</u>
        a. occasional   b. constant   c. uniform

_____ 4. <u>combustion</u>
        a. control   b. manufacture   c. burning

_____ 5. <u>fossil fuels</u>
        a. fuel derived from wood products
        b. fuel derived from water power
        c. fuel derived from organic materials

_____ 6. <u>exacerbating</u>
        a. intensifying   b. examining   c. exaggerating

_____ 7. <u>assuaging</u>
        a. equalizing   b. assuming   c. lessening

_____ 8. <u>arid</u>
      a. wet   b. cold   c. dry

_____ 9. <u>ameliorate</u>
      a. improve   b. destroy   c. justify

_____ 10. <u>parameters</u>
      a. particulars   b. limits   c. products

Read the following statements, and then fill in the blanks.

1. During the twentieth century there has been an increase in the global temperature of _____ percent.

2. The decade of the _____ had the warmest global temperature on record.

3. Records of global warming have been kept for about one _____ .

4. Is this record proof of the long-term effects of the greenhouse effect?

   _____

5. Studies indicate that carbon dioxide in the atmosphere accounts for about _____ of the recent global warming.

6. Emissions from _____ and _____ are the major producers of carbon dioxide.

7. In order to have a major impact on the greenhouse effect, we would need to decrease the burning of fossil fuels by _____ percent.

8. What country produces the largest amount of carbon dioxide?

   _____

9. Efforts to decrease the greenhouse effect are being made by _____ nations, while the _____ nations are producing more damaging gases.

Answer the following questions on the lines provided.

  1. Define "greenhouse effect."

     _____

     _____

2. When did the greenhouse effect begin?

_____

_____

3. What would happen if there was no greenhouse effect?

_____

_____

4. What conditions affect global temperature in addition to the greenhouse effect?

_____

_____

5. Name the gases that contribute greatly to the greenhouse effect. Which gas is the most damaging? How is it produced?

_____

_____

_____

_____

_____

6. Why do the gases that you named cause temperature warming?

_____

_____

_____

_____

_____

7. In addition to your answer in question 6, what is another reason why there is so much carbon dioxide in the atmosphere?

_____

_____

_____

8. What are the predicted consequences of a major increase in global warming?

_____

_____

_____

_____

_____

_____

9. What is the attitude of developing countries concerning the efforts to decrease the greenhouse effect?

_____

_____

_____

_____

10. What can be done to decrease the greenhouse effect and slow global warming?

_____

_____

_____

SUGGESTIONS FOR FURTHER STUDY

- After selecting the main ideas in Chapter 4, list the major supporting details.
- Select a passage from the lessons in Part Two of this textbook and list the major details.
- Find an article in the newspaper or library that has special meaning for you. List all the details—major and minor—that serve a purpose for you.

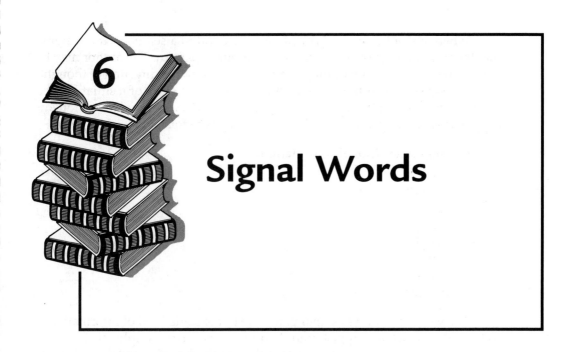

Signal Words

UNDERSTANDING SIGNAL WORDS

Signal words are like traffic lights or road signs. They help you get your bearings, warn you of abrupt changes in direction, and guide you smoothly along the path of thought set down by the author. Signal words can be a valuable aid in anticipating what is coming next; they can also help to identify the pattern the author is using to get the point across. Signal words may be found anywhere in a paragraph or may be used to provide a smooth transition from one paragraph to the next.

Some commonly used signal words are grouped and explained here.

   a. **Signals a contrast or reversal of thought:**

      although
      but
      however
      on the other hand
      nevertheless
      on the contrary
      instead
      yet
      unlike
      conversely

When one of these words or phrases is found in a sentence, it is a signal that there is a change of some kind in the thought pattern. The author may be comparing or contrasting or may simply be reversing the direction of thought. In other words, the author is presenting two or more sides of a situation. If a sentence begins, "Although the sun is shining today . . . ," you know immediately that something not so good about the day is to follow.

b. Signals additional information:

also
in addition
furthermore
and
likewise
moreover
besides
another

The words or phrases signal that more of the same kind of information is to be added to what you just read. You may read, for example, "It is the responsibility of each student to obtain the required books and materials for each course; furthermore, ..." *Furthermore* in this sentence signals that additional responsibilities are required of the student.

c. Signals reasoning and explanation:

because
the reason for
in order that

When you are reading especially difficult material, information is easier to understand and remember when the author gives reasons for the information. For example, if you read, "The new proposal on tax exemptions could have a devastating effect on the economy," you might not understand how or why and might question the fact. But if the author has added, "Because . . . " or "The reason for this is . . . ," you would find the statement easier to understand and accept. Also, the additional information helps to make difficult words easier to understand by providing an explanation.

d. Signals an example or illustration:

for example
for instance
in other words
such as

Most of us understand ideas, whether simple or complex, much better if an example or an illustration is given. You might read in your English text, "Irony is an expression in which the intended meaning of the words used is the opposite of their meaning." This idea might be difficult to grasp, but it becomes very clear when it is followed by, "An example of irony is. . . . " Therefore, when an idea or concept is difficult and you see one of these signal words, you should take note and benefit from the example relationship.

e. Signals enumeration, such as time order, sequence or listing:

one, two, three
first, second, third
next
then
finally
time of day
dates (day, month, year)

These signal words indicate that it would be helpful for you to understand the time order or sequence in which something did or should take place or that there is more than one factor to consider. Usually information that is presented in some kind of order is easier to understand. Therefore, when you see these words in reading material, it is important that you take notice of the order in which the material is arranged.

f. Signals a summary or conclusion:

therefore
consequently
thus
in summary
in conclusion
in short

Often, at the end of a paragraph, a passage, or a chapter, the author will signal the reader that a summary or conclusion will be forthcoming. You will do well to take note of this aid. After all, who could summarize or point out the most accurate conclusion better than the author?

EXERCISE 12: Identifying Signal Words

NAME _____ **DATE** _____

I. To better understand this reading skill, read the following sentences and note
the underlined signal word or words in each sentence. On the lines provided,
indicate the type of signal of each underlined word, using the following key.

    a. a contrast or reversal of thought

    b. additional information

    c. reasoning or explanation

    d. an example or illustration

    e. enumeration

    f. a summary or conclusion

___a___ 1. The plane was scheduled to depart at 8:05 P.M. but due to a bomb
threat, it was not cleared for take-off until two hours later.

___a___ 2. Ralph was a bright, highly motivated, and successful student. On
the other hand, he was unable to excel in even one sport.

___d/b___ 3. Birds are beneficial to humans in many ways. For example, wild
birds eat insects, wild seeds, and certain rodents. In addition,
many domestic birds provide food.

___f___ 4. Fruits contain important vitamins and minerals, aid in digestion,
and may be eaten in a variety of ways. Consequently, they are a
popular food in most diets.

___e___ 5. When selecting a campsite, you must consider several things.
First, select a fairly open spot, level enough to be comfortable but
sloped enough for water drainage. Next, consider whether there
are trees and a wood supply nearby. Finally, be sure to choose a
site with available water for drinking and bathing.

___a___ 6. Although the criminal had a brilliant defense lawyer, he was sen-
tenced to life in prison.

___a___ 7. Entrance test scores are one of the most important considerations
for acceptance into college. However, high school grade-point
average and accomplishments are also considered.

II. *Read the following sentences, and then underline the best signal word(s) in the parentheses.*

1. Reading is one of the privileges and joys of life. (However, In other words), in order to get the most out of your reading, you should develop a love of reading (instead of, as well as) your ability to read.

2. Some readers firmly believe every book should be read slowly and intently. (Consequently, On the contrary), there are books that deserve only a cursory glance.

3. (Nevertheless, Although) he was a wealthy man by the time he was 40 years old, he still enjoyed the simple things of life.

4. Jane does not like chemistry; (however, furthermore), she is taking the course this quarter and has a B average.

5. Most domesticated animals are gentle and tame enough for small children to pet; (therefore, however), a mother dog with young puppies can be very dangerous.

6. Many of her friends insisted that she was too old to return to school. (Thus, Nevertheless), she completed her requirements in record time and graduated with honors.

7. Bugs and beetles are alike in many ways and are often mistaken for one another. (However, Therefore), the lightning bug, the ladybug, and the June bug are not bugs at all (since, but) are beetles.

8. (For instance, Although) some animals, such as the tortoise, move very slowly, there are those who can run faster than our speed limit allows. (In summary, For example), the cheetah can run up to 65 or 70 miles per hour.

9. (Because, Although) Jim is the youngest student in the class, he has the highest grade-point average. (Also, Finally), he won honors in football and track each year while he was in high school. (For example, In addition), he has a good personality and gets along well with his teachers. His sister, (in conclusion, on the other hand), does not make good grades and has not adjusted well in school.

10. Most people are afraid of snakes and consider all of them to be harmful. (On the contrary, As a result), most snakes are helpful because they eat rats, mice, and insects. (However, In addition), some snakes are poisonous, and their bite can be fatal. Rattlesnakes, moccasins, copperheads, and king cobras (finally, for instance), are well-known poisonous snakes and have earned their bad reputation.

11. The two girls have the same parents, (but, thus) they have different personalities and natures. (In conclusion, For example), one is shy and extremely sensitive, while the other is aggressive with a selfish nature. (Then, On the other hand), because of their environment, the girls are likely to have some behavior patterns that are very much alike. Heredity gives individuals their behavioral traits, whereas environment helps to regulate how these traits are used.

12. In order to solve a problem, you must follow at least three steps. (Thus, First), you must identify the problem and accept the fact that it is a problem that needs to be solved. (Since, Next), you should explore possible solutions and analyze each one. (Finally, But), after careful consideration, you accept the solution that best fits your situation.

13. Daydreaming can be a harmless and pleasant way to relieve the pressure of daily life. (Therefore, However), daydreams can become harmful when they prevent an individual from facing reality. (In order that, In other words), daydreams become harmful when they are substituted for action in solving a problem.

14. There are basically three types of family units in today's society. The (one, first) of these types is the nuclear family, which consists of mother, father, and children. The (two, second) is the extended family, composed of the mother, father, children, and grandparents. On the increase in our society is a (three, third) type, the single-parent family, which has only one parent with one or more children.

15. What a day! (Since, First), my alarm did not go off, and I was late for work. (Then, Instead), my boss informed me I would need to work overtime (because, although) a co-worker was ill. (Finally, Thus), as if I needed something else to go wrong, my computer was down all morning. (Conversely, In short), I needed to go home and start all over again!

SUGGESTIONS FOR FURTHER STUDY

- Make sentences with the signal words given on pages 97–99.
- Organize into groups in class (or outside of class), prepare a signal words test, and then exchange with other groups.
- Make a conscious effort to use signal words in letters and essays.

Organizational Patterns

7

UNDERSTANDING ORGANIZATIONAL PATTERNS

Earlier in this text you learned that the main idea is what the author wants you to understand about the topic being discussed. The main idea is supported by details, both major and minor, that help you understand the topic. Authors use a variety of patterns to relate the supporting details to the main idea. Six of these patterns are (1) explanation, (2) examples, (3) comparison-contrast, (4) cause-effect, (5) definition, and (6) enumeration.

In some paragraphs, the author uses only one pattern that is clearly definable. In other paragraphs, the author might use two patterns, in combination, to get the main idea across more effectively.

Explanation

An explanation is given when the author feels the need to give reasons for the ideas set forth. He or she may explain how to do something or why something is the way it is, or may give an interpretation of what is said.

Read the following paragraph to understand how the author uses explanation to relate the ideas.

The colors of an artist's palette are referred to as warm or cool depending upon which end of the color spectrum they fall. Reds, oranges, and yellows are said to be warm colors. Those are the colors of the sun, and therefore call to mind our primary source of heat. So they carry strong implications of warmth. Colors falling on the opposite end of the spectrum—blues and greens—are cool colors because they imply shade, or lack of light and warmth. Here we have, as we will notice frequently, a stimulation that is mental but has a physical basis. Tonality and color contrast also affect our senses, by creating impressions of liveliness or subdued relaxation.

The main idea of this paragraph is stated in the first sentence. In order to make this statement clear, the author explains which colors are considered to be warm and gives reasons why. Then, the colors on the other end of the spectrum are described as cool, named, and reasons are given for describing them as cool colors.

Example

Main ideas and supporting details are often made clearer to the reader when examples are provided. Signal words such as "for example" and "for instance" aid in identifying this type of relationship.

Read the following paragraph and the explanation that follows to understand the example pattern.

Most of us use our hands when we talk. Words do not seem adequate sometimes; we feel that we must use our hands to describe something, to add emphasis, or to illustrate our meaning. The small gestures that a person makes convey a lot of meaning. For example, a teacher usually can tell if the class is comprehending by their facial expressions and their gestures. The pencil tapper, the clock-watcher, and the doodler convey their uncaptivated attention without a word.

The main idea of this paragraph is that *gestures carry meaning*. To make this idea clear to the reader, the author gives examples of the pencil tapper, the clock-watcher, and the doodler.

Comparison-Contrast

This pattern relates two things, one to another, by showing either how they are alike or how they are different. Within one paragraph, an author may use comparison, contrast, or a combination of both to relate one idea to another.

Read the following paragraph to see how the author compares learning to write an essay with learning to drive a car.

Learning to write a good essay is like learning to drive a car. The beginning driver feels overwhelmed by the number of operations he must perform to keep a car moving—controlling the brake and the accelerator, staying in his lane, watching the cars in front of him while keeping an eye on the rear-view mirror. In addition, he must observe all traffic laws. The tasks seem insurmountable. Yet, in time, some of the operations become almost automatic and the driver relaxes enough that he can even look at the scenery now and then. So it is with the beginning writer. At first, he wonders how he can make an outline for a paper, write clear topic sentences, develop paragraphs, provide transitions, write good instructions and conclusions, and still observe all the rules of English grammar. As with driving, part of the process eventually becomes automatic, and the writer relaxes enough to concentrate primarily on the idea he wishes to develop.

The author of this paragraph shows how both tasks, writing an essay and driving a car, require learning the operations (how the task is performed) and then how each has laws or processes that govern performance. Finally, in each task the process becomes easier with practice.

Cause-Effect

In a paragraph using this pattern, you are given a cause of something and the effects that could result.

Read the following paragraph to understand the cause-effect pattern.

Clearly, how you feel about college will affect your life there. If you believe that college is an unpleasant experience, one that will demand too much of you and make you miserable, then you may not succeed. If you think that the years before you will be full of work, success, and enjoyment, then—generally speaking—you probably will succeed. Students who begin the first semester with a negative attitude toward the college experience start with potential trouble. Even though they may have been introduced to effective study skills and habits before college, their attitude acts as a handicap.

Many times authors use a combination of organizational patterns. In the preceding paragraph, the author uses explanation in addition to cause-effect to help convey to the reader that a negative attitude (cause) can contribute to failure in college (effect) whereas a positive attitude (cause) can foster success (effect).

Definition

Authors will usually define terms and concepts when an exact meaning or interpretation is needed by the reader.

Read the following paragraph to see how the definitions help you understand the paragraph.

Maturation is an automatic unfolding of development that begins with conception. Boys and girls mature at different rates and have different body compositions. The greatest sex differences become evident at puberty, when both boys and girls go through a period of rapid growth followed by the development of the secondary sexual characteristics. *Developmental norms* are standards of growth that indicate the ages by which an average child should reach various developmental milestones. Normal development can occur within a range of ages, so these norms are only general guidelines.

In the preceding paragraph, the definitions of *maturation* and *developmental norms* help to understand better about rates and standards of development. Also, knowing what the terms mean would help you understand additional information that would follow.

Enumeration

When an author wants you to know the time order, the sequence in which something occurred, or merely that there is more than one factor to be considered, he or she will use the enumeration pattern. This pattern uses such clues as "one, two, three," "first, second, third," "first, then, finally," or the dating of events as in the following paragraph.

As the debate between the supporters and the opponents of the new constitution developed, ratification became more difficult. Delaware ratified first, and unanimously, on December 7, 1787. Five days later Pennsylvania ratified, followed six days later by New Jersey. Georgia and Connecticut ratified in early January 1788, but there were bitter struggles in Massachusetts before it agreed. Maryland and South Carolina followed, and on June 21, New Hampshire became the ninth state to ratify. That was enough to put the Constitution into effect formally. But Virginia and New York were such important states that their acceptance was essential. After desperate struggles, both ratified during the summer. North Carolina did not ratify for another 15 months, and Rhode Island became the last state to agree, on May 29, 1790.

This enumeration pattern shows a time-order relationship in the ratification of the new constitution. On December 7, 1787 . . . , Five days later . . . , in early January 1788 . . . , on June 21 . . . , for another 15 months . . . , on May 29, 1790.

NAME _____ **DATE** _____

Read the following paragraphs and decide which pattern is used in each to relate the main idea and the supporting details. Indicate your choice by underlining the correct pattern in the parentheses that follow. Then give reasons for your choice (as was done for you in the preceding examples).

---

1. The key to success in choosing a career, then, is to select one in which the interaction between your personality and the work will be harmonious—that is, a career in which you will grow and develop in the direction that will provide you with satisfaction, and in which what you bring to the career enhances the potential for success.

(explanation, cause-effect)

_____

_____

_____

_____

_____

---

2. Like the woodwinds, brass instruments produce sound by sending a vibrating column of air through pipe-shaped tubing. The significant difference, however, is where the vibrations come from. In a brass instrument the mouthpiece is shaped like either a cup or a funnel. As the player blows into the mouthpiece, the vibrations of the lips function much like those of the reed in the woodwinds.

(cause-effect, comparison-contrast, example)

_____

_____

_____

_____
_____
_____

3. Dependency on alcohol may occur in stages. People drink to unwind or to ward off anxiety—a few drinks at a party or at lunch or before dinner make them feel better. They then feel that they cannot cope without those few drinks. Sometimes this dependency is followed by a phase of drinking sprees, in which they drink themselves unconscious for days or even weeks. After drinking regularly for some time, these people find that if they do not drink heavily they feel withdrawal symptoms: depression, nausea, the shakes. Continued overuse of alcohol usually causes severe physical harm, mainly to the brain and the liver.

(explanation and enumeration, comparison-contrast)

_____
_____
_____
_____
_____

4. Jupiter and Saturn each have giant storms that show up as oval patterns. The most prominent is Jupiter's Great Red Spot. This giant storm is an anticyclone. It has survived for hundreds of years, much longer than storms on earth. One reason for this may be that it gets energy from below, deep in Jupiter's depths, while storms on earth get most of their energy from above. Also, Jupiter has no solid surface to break up the storm.

(example, explanation)

_____
_____
_____
_____
_____

5. The factors known to aid or to hinder learning can be classified into three main groups. First is the learner himself—the factors that endow him with greater or lesser ability to learn. Included in these personal factors are the amount and kind of his previous learning. Second is his methods of learning— how he goes about it. And third is the kind of material he has to learn.

As for the learner himself, individuals naturally vary in all sorts of ways, psychological and otherwise. Some of their psychological characteristics have little to do with their ability to learn; others are very important. Four big factors can be distinguished: (1) intelligence, (2) age, (3) arousal and anxiety, and (4) transfer from previous learning.

(enumeration and explanation, example and explanation)

_____

_____

_____

_____

_____

6. The term *groundwater* includes not only water above ground, washing the topsoil away visibly, but also underground water. Though we cannot see it happen, underground water is carving out caverns and undermining the top-soil from below. The water does this both by mechanical action of abrasion and sweeping of particles, and also by chemical action of dissolving minerals. The dissolved minerals are deposited later as different substances, sometimes being the glue that cements together the rock particles that came along for the ride.

(definition and explanation, enumeration and example)

_____

_____

_____

_____

_____

7. While science and technology are closely related, they are not exactly the same. Science is a process of uncovering fundamental laws and interrelationships. Technology is considered to be the application of the discoveries of science. However, engineers in the course of working on a technological application often uncover very basic knowledge. Conversely, scientists searching for basic knowledge frequently invent technology. The fact remains that science has been directly or indirectly responsible for nearly all of our present technology. Electricity is an outstanding example. It is used in a high percentage of modern appliances, instruments, and equipment. Without the work done by scientists to discover the fundamental principles of electricity it is unlikely these devices would exist.

(example and comparison-contrast, explanation and cause-effect)

_____

_____

_____

_____

_____

8. If you lift a hammer, you perform work on it, equal to the product of the hammer's weight and the height over which you raise it. Once in the air, if the hammer is dropped, it is capable of doing work itself: hitting a nail into a board, for example. In general, when work is performed on a body, that body becomes capable of doing work itself. In physics we say that the body has received energy. Energy, then, is defined as the thing enabling an object to do work.

(explanation and definition, cause-effect and definition)

_____

_____

_____

_____

_____

9. The methods that scientists use have five basic characteristics. First, the behavior must be observable. For observable behavior can be measured. Second, the methods and data must be objective. That is, the opinions of the experimenters must enter into the gathering and interpreting of data as little as possible. Third, the procedures must be repeatable. Other individuals who wish to do the same experiment or expand upon the data must be able to do so. Fourth, scientists must be able to communicate the results to others. They often do this at scientific meetings or through articles in professional journals. What good would the data be if no one but the experimenter knew about them or could understand them? Finally, experimenters must use a systematic approach. This means that they must follow an orderly arrangement of procedures. They must stick to a fixed plan that they determine before starting the experiment.

(example and cause-effect, enumeration and explanation)

_____

_____

_____

_____

_____

10. Energy from the sun is the key to the water cycle. When the sun shines on the oceans and other bodies of water, its heat changes some of the liquid water into water vapor through evaporation. The percentage of water vapor or moisture in the atmosphere is the _humidity_. Air at a given temperature can hold only so much water vapor, with warm air being able to hold more water vapor than cool air can. Air is _saturated_ when it holds all the water vapor it can at a given temperature. _Relative humidity_ indicates the percentage of saturation; when the relative humidity is 90%, the air is holding 90% of the water vapor it can hold at that temperature. If air cools enough, it becomes saturated even though the amount of water in it does not change. The temperature at which air becomes saturated is its _dew point_. Fog or dew forms if the air cools further.

(definition and cause-effect, enumeration and explanation)

_____

_____

_____

_____

_____

_____

11. The use of structural clues becomes even more important when dealing with technical vocabulary. Most scientific words, for example, are relatively recent. They were created to fit specific needs, and are often made up of old parts! For example, when scientists discovered various drugs that could be used to reduce the physiological effects associated with histamine production in allergies and colds, they simply took a widely used prefix that meant "against" and coined the word *antihistamine.* Because so many scientific words have been constructed from old Latin and Greek roots plus common affixes, the study of word structure can pay you big dividends as you learn technical vocabulary.

(example and cause-effect, example and explanation)

_____

_____

_____

_____

_____

12. We have seen two types of reasoning at work in the development of mathematics: *inductive* and *deductive.* Inductive reasoning is the process of reasoning that arrives at a general conclusion based on multiple observations or multiple occurrences. It is this type of reasoning that is used by the chemist in his laboratory when, after observing that certain chemicals behave in a particular manner during repeated experiments, he concludes that these chemicals will always behave in the same manner in the same circumstances. . . .

Deductive reasoning, on the other hand, is the process of reasoning that arrives at a conclusion based on an accepted set of premises. It is this type of reasoning that the chemist employs when he predicts the behavior of chemicals based on accepted principles. It is this type of reasoning that is employed in establishing proofs of theorems in mathematics.

(definition and comparison-contrast, cause-effect)

_____

_____

_____

_____

_____

13. When the sun and the moon pull along the same line, as they do at full or new moons, the highest tides—*spring tides*—result. At the time of the first and last quarter moon, when the sun and moon pull at different angles, smaller *neap* tides result.

(example, cause-effect)

_____

_____

_____

_____

_____

14. When the sun's energy falls on the earth, it has many large-scale effects on the hydrosphere and the atmosphere, effects that serve to store this solar energy. *Hydropower,* energy generated by water-powered turbines like the ones at dams, is the clearest example. The sun's energy is what lifts the water into the atmosphere as water vapor in the clouds. At this point, some of the solar energy has been stored as potential energy in the earth's gravitational field.

(cause-effect and example, enumeration and example)

_____

_____

_____

_____

_____

15. Fast reading is not necessarily good reading. The speed at which you should read depends on four factors. First is the difficulty of the material: even the best readers read obscure material slowly. Second is the purpose for which you are reading. Material that you must memorize for an exam should be read more slowly than material you read for relaxation. The third factor is your level of skill. If you are good at picking out main ideas, if you are familiar with college-level vocabulary, and if you have a wide background of experience so that the ideas you are reading are not completely new to you, you will read faster than someone who is less adept at reading. The fourth factor is the absence of bad reading habits that slow you down: reading one word at a time rather than phrases, moving your lips even on easy material, and looking back (regressing) at what you have already read. Even the most proficient readers do some of these things when the material is very difficult, but they should never become habits.

(enumeration and explanation, comparison-contrast)

_____

_____

_____

_____

_____

SUGGESTIONS FOR FURTHER STUDY

- Go back to Chapter 4 and determine the organizational patterns used in each paragraph.
- Look for organizational patterns as you read the newspaper and your textbooks.

Inferences

DRAWING INFERENCES

You have learned how to read what is stated on the printed page and determine the author's literal meaning. Not all meaning is clearly stated, however. Most authors expect a reader to "read between the lines," or to draw inferences, in order to get a clearer understanding of the ideas presented. Inferences are not simply pulled from the air to add zest and excitement to reading and to allow stories to end to our satisfaction. Even though not clearly stated, they are inferred from definite sources. Often you can get inferences by merely looking at something or someone. You might get an inference through conversation—how someone said something or maybe what was left unsaid. Inferences may be drawn by analyzing characters and their actions, and by determining the mood of the material. They may be based on facts and must be assembled by the reader. A fact can usually be found in the passage and underlined, but an inference is more of a feeling drawn from reasoning.

To understand better how to draw an inference, read the following examples and the explanation that follows each example.

Example 1

Oh! for a refreshing glimpse of one blade of grass—for a snuff at the fragrance of a handful of the loamy earth! Is there nothing fresh around us? Is there no green thing to be seen? Yes, the inside of our bulwarks is painted green; but what a vile and sickly hue it is, as if nothing bearing even the semblance of verdure could flourish this weary way from land. Even the bark that once clung to the wood we use for fuel has been gnawed off and devoured by the captain's pig; and so long ago, too, that the pig himself has in turn been devoured.

From this paragraph you can infer that the narrator is aboard a ship and has been at sea for so long that he is longing for land. It would make him happy to see "one blade of grass," "a handful of the loamy earth," or any "green thing."

You can further infer that food is in short supply because the captain's pig has eaten the bark from the wood for fuel and in turn has himself been eaten.

Example 2

We see the poor fellows hobbling back from the crest or unable to do so, pale and weak, lying on the ground with the mangled stump of an arm or leg, dripping their life-blood away; or with a cheek torn open, or a shoulder mashed. And many, alas! hear not the roar as they stretch upon the ground with upturned faces and open eyes, though a shell should burst at their very ears. Their ears and their bodies this instant are only mud.

If you read carefully, you can see that the passage describes what is happening during a battle because the "roar" of battle continues even though some cannot hear it. Most of the men are injured with mangled bodies or bleeding badly; and others are dead. We know this because "their ears and their bodies this instant are only mud."

EXERCISE 14: Inferences

NAME _____ **DATE** _____

Read the following passages and select the best answer for each question. Write the letter of your choice on the line provided.

_____ 1. If you have widely divergent interests, your marriage is not doomed to failure, but on the other hand do not expect marriage to suddenly present you with some interest in common. Your engagement period should provide you with a time for further developing some common interests. You should ask, "Just what do we both like to do?" If one of you is an avid skier and the other hates the sport, it is likely either that one will have to give up the sport or go alone, or that the other will have to tag along or take up the sport under protest—either of which could mean further separation in interests.

With which of the following statements would the author agree?

    a. Common interests would guarantee success in marriage.

    b. Both marriage partners should like all the things that the other likes.

    c. Common interests enhance marriage; therefore, these should be developed before and during the engagement period.

    d. If only a few common interests exist, the marriage is likely doomed.

_____ 2. Cheating is the ultimate trick a student plays on him- or herself. Aside from the primary point of making an absolute mockery of the purpose of a college education, there is also the fact that there is no way a student can avoid being found out—there is at least one person who will always know about it.

Which one of the following statements would the author support?

    a. Students should not cheat because someone will always know about it and tell.

    b. Cheating not only carries the assurance of being discovered but also harms the student.

c. Students should not cheat because cheating is merely a game of trickery.

d. A certain amount of cheating is to be expected.

_____ 3. The high birth rate also shaped early American society by making it very youthful. Today, half the people of the United States are under the age of thirty. In the seventeenth and eighteenth centuries, half the people were under the age of sixteen. This youthfulness had several important effects. Obviously, only a relatively small number of men could take part in politics and government. It also meant that the military power of the colonies was relatively small. The colonists did their best to meet the situation by setting the age for service in the colonial militias between sixteen and sixty. People often referred to the "men and boys" of the colonial armies, as did the song "Yankee Doodle" during the American Revolution.

You can infer from the passage all the following statements *except:*

a. In today's society, there are more older people than in the seventeenth and eighteenth centuries.

b. The average family in the early American society was large.

c. Because of the youthfulness of early American society, boys of sixteen and eighteen usually became prominent political figures.

d. Because of the youthfulness of early American society, the same men were important in many areas.

_____ 4. Often history books describe great ancient civilizations as though a curtain had one day risen on them, and then fallen just as suddenly hundreds of years later. But time-line charts don't account for subtle shifts in conditions that are the true catalysts of history. Ancient Rome did not fall as if from a cliff; it gradually came apart. While there are clearly social and political reasons for the decline, there are environmental reasons as well, which suggest all too bluntly our own possible course. A large part of Rome's dissolution can be traced to its indifferent natural resource management: the agricultural base of the society weakened, combining with other factors, of course, to culminate in the demise of Rome.

With which of the following statements would the author *not agree?*

a. History books are grossly inaccurate.

b. Nations change slowly but surely.

c. Environmental influences affect a civilization as surely as social and political influences.

d. Indifference to management of its natural resources greatly influenced the fall of Rome.

_____ 5. While in college, you have a part-time job as an assistant purchasing agent for a supermarket chain. You issue purchase orders, follow up with suppliers, and do assorted tasks assigned to you by your boss. One afternoon, your boss gives you the following instructions: "Here's a half-dozen orders that appear to be only partly filled. Go out to the warehouse and double-check the paperwork to see if the remainder of the orders have been received. If not, get on the phone to each vendor and find out when we can expect the rest of their shipments." Would you comply with your boss's request? What if your boss had said, "I want you to come over to my house on Sunday. The carpets need vacuuming. You'll need to mop the floors, too. After that, you can wash the outside windows and mow the lawn." Would you comply with *this* request? I would expect that you could comply with the first because you see it as within your boss's authority. The second request, however, is not likely to be accepted. Why? Asking employees to do their boss's household chores is not seen by many workers to be a legitimate right that goes with a superior's job.

You can infer from the passage which of the following statements?

a. The boss mentioned in the passage would be unreasonable in both requests.

b. There are limitations as to the types of tasks accepted by employees.

c. College students have problems deciding which requests to obey.

d. The second request is unreasonable because few people like to do housework.

_____ 6. There is something radically wrong in our Industrial system. There is a screw loose. . . . The railroads have never been so prosperous, and yet agriculture languishes. The banks have never done a better . . . business, and yet agriculture languishes.

Manufacturing enterprises never made more money, . . . and yet agriculture languishes. Towns and cities flourish and "boom," . . . and yet agriculture languishes.

With which of the following statements would the author *not agree?*

a. Railroad, banks, and manufacturing are flourishing.
b. Agriculture is not flourishing.
c. The industrial system in our country is unbalanced.
d. The problems with the system are due to loose screws.

7. The liveliest of the "lively arts" of the twenties, the movies, was also the most highly mechanized, the most highly capitalized, the one closest to big business in production and distribution methods. The movies began as a peep show in a penny arcade. The viewer put a nickel in a device called a kinetoscope (invented by Thomas A. Edison about 1896) and saw tiny figures moving against blurred backgrounds. Edison thought little of his invention, but others took it up and soon succeeded in projecting images on a screen for large audiences. By 1905, more than 5000 "nickelodeons," housed in converted stores and warehouses, were showing films for 5 cents admission.

From the passage you would know that:

a. Thomas Edison invented the kinetoscope, but it was soon outmoded. Others got the idea and improved on it until today we have projectors that produce lifelike images on large screens.
b. Thomas Edison invented the kinetoscope, which was the beginning of movie viewing. He improved it until the modern screen and projectors were introduced.

8. Two hundred years after the birth of the nation, the American Dream, though flawed and losing its luster, still persisted. Ronald Reagan had vowed to make that dream a reality in the lives of all Americans. But so had every American president in the twentieth century. Reconciling technological advances with persistent economic failures and a decline in the quality of life would be a formidable challenge for any president of the 1980s. Nor was the challenge unique to the United States. The betrayed

aspirations of masses of people were making for an increasingly turbulent and revolutionary world.

You can infer all of the following *except:*

a. Most presidents promise the people that their administration will be good for all citizens.

b. Ronald Reagan promised, as no other president before him, to fulfill the dreams of every American.

c. The dream of a good life is shared by all people in our country.

d. Many of the problems of the world are the result of unfulfilled aspirations of the people.

9. "The influence and circulation of newspapers," wrote an astonished visitor to the United States about 1830, "is great beyond anything known in Europe . . . Every village, nay, almost every hamlet, has its press." Even today, despite the recent tendency toward consolidation of American newspapers, the American press remains much more diversified than that of European countries. During the first third of the nineteenth century, the number of newspapers rose from 200 to 1200. Most were weeklies. The larger cities had many daily papers, and competition was ferocious. New York City in 1830 had 47 papers, and only one daily among them claimed as many as 4000 subscribers. Enterprising editors reduced the price of their papers to a penny and sought to lure readers by featuring "robberies, thefts, murders, awful catastrophes, and wonderful escapades."

On the lines provided, write *yes* if the statement can be inferred from the passage, and write *no* if it cannot be inferred.

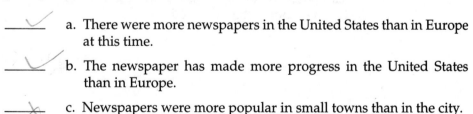

a. There were more newspapers in the United States than in Europe at this time.

b. The newspaper has made more progress in the United States than in Europe.

c. Newspapers were more popular in small towns than in the city.

d. Violence and catastrophes were reported more as a lure to attract readers than to report the news.

e. Although the United States had more newspapers than Europe in 1830, that is not true today.

_____ 10. "Conspicuous consumption" reached absurd heights in the cities during the 1890s, even while the business system was sunk in a deep depression. The follies of the rich made newspaper copy that later returned to haunt them. At one party the guests, all on horseback, rode their mounts into a luxurious hotel. At another great dinner, cigarettes rolled in hundred-dollar bills were passed out to the guests and smoked after coffee. Harry Lehr staged a dog dinner at which his friends' dogs were invited to sup on rare dainties. Perhaps the most irritating single event was the notorious Bradley Martin ball, given at a cost of $369,000 during the severe depression winter of 1896–1897. The hostess appeared as Mary Queen of Scots, displaying among her ornaments a massive ruby necklace once worn by Marie Antoinette. One of the guests, August Belmont, wore a $10,000 suit of steel armor inlaid with gold. The reaction to the ball persuaded the Bradley Martins to leave New York and take up permanent residence in England. Yet the extravagances went on. On upper Fifth Avenue in New York City, the palaces of the rich rivaled those of the titled families of Europe. High-priced architects reproduced ancient forms in limestone and marble, while their clients decorated the interiors with genuine treasures of Europe's artistic past as well as fraudulent reproductions.

The author would agree with all the following statements *except:*

a. The lavish entertainment in the late 1800s was extravagant and ridiculous.

b. The entertainment of the era was the only way in which the people could forget their workaday problems.

c. The extravagant way of living was at least indirectly responsible for the fall in economy that followed.

EXERCISE 15: Inferences

NAME _____ **DATE** _____

The passages in the preceding exercise were examples of inferences found in study materials. Most of the inferences were drawn after combining facts and reasoning. The following passages are examples of recreational materials in which you must make inferences about settings, situations, and characters.

Read the passages and then answer the questions that follow.

---

1. According to custom Tom's coffin was open, placed in the middle of the McHone cabin. Opal had covered the outside of the raw yellow poplar coffin with black calico, the inside with white muslin. With infinite care she had tried to make it fancy by fringing the edge with scissors. A little American flag and a badge reading, "God Is Our Trust and Confidence" had been pinned on one lapel of Tom's "best" suit in which he had been dressed. Opal had tucked one of her aprons in at his feet.

It was the apron that hurt me most. I looked at that faded apron, and suddenly it became a symbol of the heartbreak of women in a man's world where fighting and violence and vendettas and wars must always go on—and on—and on. For what? For a man's compulsive inner pride, driven or ordered by what he calls "honor" or "integrity," his own or his family's or his nation's, with the result that in every century and in every country women are stripped of those whom they most love. Then there is nothing left except to bow the head and to handle the grief and the emptiness as best they can. And—tuck an apron in at the feet.

1. Do you think Tom died a natural death or was killed, perhaps in a fight or duel?

   _____

2. Were these people from the wealthy class, or were they very poor?

   _____

3. What was the author questioning?

   _____

4. What do you think could have been the reason that the apron was placed in the coffin?

_____

_____

2. "When I was young I had no life of my own. . . . There was only my mother's. I was with her all the time . . . reading to her . . . talking to her . . . towards the end doing everything for her. She was very ill and suffered a lot of pain. I loved her dearly. It was hard watching her. She wanted to die but she couldn't. She just had to go on lying there suffering . . . waiting for the end. It is unbearable watching someone you love suffer, Kate. I thought constantly of how I could alleviate her pain. One night . . . I gave her an extra dose of the pain-killing medicine the doctor had given her. She died peacefully then. I didn't regret it. I knew I had done the right thing. I was happy because I had done that and saved her from the terrible nights of pain.

"Then I came to you and you were all so warm-hearted and you accepted me in Evie's place and you seemed to be so fond of me. I loved the life. It was so different from what it had been. I was fond of everyone in the village. Such nice good kind people . . . particularly the twins. I was drawn to them . . . mainly because of Faith. Poor Faith, she wasn't happy, was she? She was always afraid. I suppose we all have a certain amount of fear in us, but Faith had a double share because she had her sister's as well. I knew she was very unhappy and tried to hide it because she didn't want to spoil everything for her sister. Did you know at one time Hope almost decided not to marry because she knew it would break that close tie between herself and her twin? She was desperately worried about how Faith would get on without her. They were like one person. Well, Faith wasn't happy. Hope wasn't happy . . . but when Faith wasn't there, Hope could be. They used to confide in me, both of them . . . so I saw the picture from both sides.

"There was that spot, you remember. Rather like the one here. That dangerous drop. What was it called? Bracken's Leap? Well, I talked with Faith. We talked together and we talked and we talked . . . and there we were looking down. I didn't plan it. It just came to me that it was the right thing to do. And it was. Hope is very happy now. Those lovely children she's got, they are charming. It's such a happy family. And they visit the grandparents, and all the tragedy is forgotten now . . . because joy came out of it. Faith is forgotten now . . . as you would have forgotten the Baronne.

"Then there was your father. He pretended to come to terms with his blindness, but he never did really. I knew him so well and I knew how sad he was. Once he broke down and told me what the loss of his sight meant to him. 'I am an artist,' he said, 'and I am going into a dark, dark world. I shan't see anything ... the sky ... the trees ... the flowers and you and Kate and the boy. ... ' I knew his heart was broken. I knew that to take his eyes away from an artist was about the most cruel thing life could do. One day he said to me, 'Clare, I'd be better off dead.' Then I knew what I had to do. I remembered how easy it had been with my mother."

1. How do you think Clare, the speaker, feels about the person being addressed?

   _____

2. What happened to Clare's mother?

   _____

3. Who were Faith and Hope?

   _____

4. Contrast Faith and Hope.

   _____

   _____

   _____

5. What happened to Faith?

   _____

6. How did Clare justify what happened to Faith?

   _____

   _____

7. How did the father who was mentioned in the passage want people to think he had accepted his blindness?

   _____

8. What happened to him?

   _____

9. How did Clare feel about her role in all the things that had happened?

_____

10. How do you think the author wants you to see Clare?

_____

_____

Danny

JAY SIMPSON

The old man sat on the front porch of the unpainted, lonesome house. He had on his Sunday suit and his good hat lay beside the rocking chair where he sat. Sounds of the clanging of pots and pans and the pumping of water came through the screen door.

"Hey, Ma, somebody's comin' up the road," said the old man slowly.

"Who is it, Jed? Can you see?"

"Can't see nothin' but their dust yet. They'll be here directly."

Jed got out of his chair and watched as the dust cloud came nearer. He watched a shiny new car round the bend and stop under the huge sycamore tree in the front yard. A man in an army uniform opened the door and got out.

"How do you do, Sir. Are you Jedediah Meador?"

"'At's right, Son. Who are you?"

"Captain Harris—David Harris. I was Danny's commanding officer."

"Right proud to have you here, Capt'n Harris. Come on up and set."

Jed sat down in his rocking chair and Captain Harris took the other one beside it.

"Ma, come out here. We got company."

A gray-haired lady pushed open the screen door and walked out onto the porch. Captain Harris rose from his seat, but the older man remained seated.

"This here's Captain David Harris. He was Danny's commanding officer."

"Captain Harris," said the old lady.

"Pleased to meet you, Ma'am."

"I reckon the Captain'll be stayin' to dinner, Ma. Better set another place."

"Thank you, sir."

The old lady turned and scurried back inside, wiping her hands on her apron. Captain Harris resumed his seat.

"The woman and me been havin' tryin' times, Son. Reckon you'd know that. Danny meant more to us than anything. Losin' im that way—not seein' or knowin' how it happened . . ."

"Yes sir. I know how hard it must have been. I'd like to hear about Danny—how he was before going into the Army. That's why I came. I didn't get much of a chance to get to know him before he . . . ahh . . . died."

Jed reached into the pocket of his coat and brought out a pipe and a pouch of tobacco. He began to talk as he slowly filled the pipe.

"Well, Danny was an independent sort of boy—had his own mind about what he wanted to do. Hard to figger out sometimes."

"He was about seventeen when he came to me and said he wanted a car. I didn't hardly know what to say. Ma and me always got by without one. The young folks think they need one though. I asked him if he couldn't do without for a little while—maybe just till cotton come in and we could sell a bale. He wouldn't have none of it though. He said he was gonna leave home if he didn't get one. So one Saturday I took a little money we had saved and went into Little Rock and paid down on one. Thought I'd surprise him. He didn't come in that night, but I gave it to him the next morning. He didn't like it at first, but he drove it till he went to the Army. Ma and me was always sorry we didn't have enough to do right by the boy. 'Specially now's he's gone."

Jed fished a match from his pocket and struck it on his shoe sole. He gestured with the flaming match before he used it to light his pipe.

"'Bout two weeks after the night Danny didn't come home, Sheriff Newby came by. Wanted to talk to Danny. I called Danny out, and the sheriff wanted to know where he'd been that night. Danny didn't remember—couldn't be expected to. Sheriff seemed to think he'd swiped some hubcaps. Said the ones helped him told on him. Way I figger those boys got caught and tried to drag Danny into it. Sorry thing for one man to do to another. Anyhow, after it was all hashed out, they all got a suspended sentence. Danny didn't deserve it, 'cause he told me so. But there wa'n't nothin' we could do only take it."

The screen door opened and the old lady let it slam behind her. She wiped her hands on her apron.

"Jed, dinner's ready."

"Good. You ready to eat, Captain?"

"Yes, sir. Thank you."

Jed opened the screen door and walked in first. Captain Harris held the screen door open as Ma walked in. A platter of fried chicken was at the head of the table where Jed took his seat. He pointed to the seat on the other end of the table for the captain. Ma took the only other chair. The three bowed their heads.

"Thank you, dear Lord, for this thy bountiful blessing. Bless it to the nourishment of our bodies and forgive our sins, Amen."

Jed took a piece of chicken and passed the platter across the table to Captain Harris. One by one the other dishes were passed around.

"Ma and me get comfort from Danny's memory," said Jed as the others began to eat. "He give his life for his country. We—all of us—owe him something for that. He never had what the other boys had. Reckon he come out pretty good startin' out with so many things again' 'im. If we had any other children, I think we'd want 'em to be like Danny."

The room was silent as the three ate the meal.

When the meal was finished, the two men rose and went back toward the porch while Ma started clearing off the table. Jed held open the screen door for Captain Harris and the captain took it and kept it from slamming. They stood atop the porch steps and looked down the dusty, empty road.

"Tell me, son. Were you there when Danny was shot?"

"Yes sir. I was the one who . . . I had to . . . yes sir, I was there."

"Tell me what happened."

"I was a lieutenant then. Danny was in my platoon. Our company had taken a hill and the Chinese were counter-attacking. They came running up the slope, yelling and screaming so loud you couldn't hear anything else. There must have been thousands of them."

"We were all in the trenches. Danny was standing next to me. We were waiting till they got close to open fire. Suddenly Danny jumped up out of the trench. I turned around and he was . . . I yelled to him to stop, but he wouldn't. I had to . . . God, I didn't want to, but I had to."

"Must be hard on a man seein' another one shot down like that. Shot by some Chinese. Almost wish you hadn't told me now. Reckon that'll be hard to forget."

"No, sir. You don't understand. I . . ."

"Yes, I understand, Captain. I understand that I was blessed with a lovin' wife and a son. I understand that we was always so poor that he couldn't be like other boys and get the things he wanted. I understand how those boys got him into trouble when he hadn't done nothin'. I understand how he got a letter saying he was needed to defend his country and how he didn't want to go, but did anyway. And then he was up on some hill somewhere and ran out to fight for his home and his country and some Chinese shot him dead."

Jed took off his rimless glasses and wiped his face with his handkerchief.

"Ain't nothin' left of Danny but his memory and what he did for his country. That's about all we got now. Never did have much—but we ain't so poor with that."

Captain Harris looked down at his shiny shoes on the rough gray porch and said nothing. Jed looked at him and put his arm around his shoulders.

"It meant a lot havin' you come here, Captain. I hope you'll come back now and then."

"Yes sir. I'd like that."

The two men walked down the steps and toward the car. Captain Harris got in and started the motor.

"Thank you for the meal, Sir. I enjoyed it."

The old man stood under the sycamore tree and watched the dust cloud disappear down the road.

_____ C 1. Captain Harris says he has come to find out what Danny was like before he joined the Army. He wants to know about Danny because

    a. like any good commanding officer, he takes an interest in his men.

    b. he feels guilty and is afraid he made a tragic mistake.

    c. he wants to confirm that Danny is no good in order to justify his own action.

    d. he admires Danny's heroism and wants to find out about his upbringing.

_____ d 2. What did Jed mean when he said, "They'll be here directly"?

    a. The visitor would come directly to the house.

    b. The visitor would take the most direct route.

    c. The visitor would come without fail.

    d. The visitor would be there in a few minutes.

_____ C 3. Danny's father believes his son was a good boy, but the author implies that

    a. Danny was good only because he had the strength of character to overcome the obstacles of his upbringing.

    b. Danny's mother doesn't share Jed's view about his character.

    c. Jed was not facing reality to see that Danny was selfish, spoiled, and a thief.

    d. Danny was an all-American boy who was too mischievous to be called good.

_____ d 4. The author implies that Danny's friends were

    a. more morally responsible than Danny.

    b. numerous and fond of Danny.

    c. tattle-tales who would tell anything to get Danny in trouble.

    d. were of similar character to Danny.

_____ b 5. What Danny actually did for his country was to
  a. die heroically.
  b. attempt to desert.
  c. sell military secrets to the Chinese.
  d. become a draft dodger.

_____ a 6. How did Danny die?
  a. Captain Harris deliberately shot him.
  b. He accidentally shot himself.
  c. Captain Harris accidentally shot him.
  d. He was killed by the Chinese.

_____ d 7. Captain Harris
  a. tries to tell Jed the truth about Danny's death, but Jed will not listen.
  b. lies to Jed about Danny's death because he feels sorry for the old man.
  c. never intended to tell Danny's parents the whole truth.
  d. tells half-truths about Danny's death and covers up his own part in the whole affair.

_____ a,d 8. Which of the following statements would *not* be a reason Captain Harris left without making sure Jed understood how Danny died?
  a. He decided that it was best to leave the old man with good memories of Danny.
  b. After meeting Jed and Ma, he decided they would have problems understanding the real situation.
  c. He decided that Jed and Ma did not want to know the true circumstances of Danny's death.
  d. He was afraid the old man would take him to court.

9. Look back at the choices in question 8. Select the best reason, in your opinion, that the Captain did not make sure Jed understood how Danny died. Explain why your choice is the best.

_____

_____

_____

_____

_____

NAME _____ **DATE** _____

The following excerpts are from The Red Badge of Courage, *by Stephen Crane. Read each excerpt, and then answer the questions that follow on the lines provided.*

The setting for The Red Badge of Courage, *written in the late 1800s, is the Civil War; the story has only one main character. Henry Fielding, often referred to as "the youth," is a young, naive man who is struggling with all the rites of passage from childhood into adulthood. He fluctuates between wanting to go to war and acknowledging that his mother is right in her arguments that he should stay at home. He finally makes his decision. . . .*

eager

He had <u>burned</u> several times to enlist. Tales of great movements shook the land. They might not be distinctly Homeric, but there seemed to be much glory in them. He had read of marches, sieges, conflicts, and he had longed to see it all. His busy mind had drawn for him large pictures extravagant in color, <u>lurid</u> with breathless deeds.

But his mother had discouraged him. She had <u>affected</u> to look with some contempt upon the quality of his war ardor and patriotism. She could calmly seat herself, and with no apparent difficulty give him many hundreds of reasons why he was of vastly more importance on the farm than on the field of battle. She had had certain ways of expression that told him that her statements on the subject came from a deep conviction. Moreover, on her side, was his belief that her ethical motive in the argument was <u>impregnable</u>.

At last, however, he had made firm rebellion against this yellow light thrown upon the color of his ambitions. The newspapers, the gossip of the village, his own picturings, had aroused him to an uncheckable degree. They were in truth fighting finely down there. Almost every day the newspapers printed accounts of a decisive victory.

One night, as he lay in bed, the winds had carried to him the clangoring of the church bell as some enthusiast jerked the rope frantically to tell the twisted news of a great battle. This voice of the people rejoicing in the night had made him shiver in a prolonged ecstasy of excitement. Later, he had gone down to his mother's room and had spoken thus: "Ma, I'm going to enlist."

"Henry, don't you be a fool," his mother had replied. She had then covered her face with the quilt. There was an end to the matter for that night.

Nevertheless, the next morning he had gone to a town that was near his mother's farm and had enlisted in a company that was forming there. When he had returned home his mother was milking a brindle cow. Four others stood waiting. "Ma, I've enlisted," he had said to her <u>diffidently</u>. There was a short silence. "The Lord's will be done, Henry," she had finally replied, and had then continued to milk the brindle cow.

When he had stood in the doorway with his soldier's clothes on his back, and with the light of excitement and expectancy in his eyes almost defeating the glow of regret for the home bonds, he had seen two tears leaving their trails on his mother's scarred cheeks.

Still, she had disappointed him by saying nothing whatever about returning with his shield or on it. He had privately <u>primed</u> himself for a beautiful scene. He had prepared certain sentences which he thought could be used with touching effect. But her words destroyed his plans.

1. Give the meaning of the following words as used in the excerpt. (Use context clues and your dictionary.)

   a. <u>burned</u> _____   d. <u>impregnable</u> _____

   b. <u>lurid</u> _____   e. <u>diffidently</u> _____

   c. <u>affected</u> _____   f. <u>primed</u> _____

2. How does Henry view the battles of the war?

   _____

   _____

3. What does Henry's view of the war tell you about him?

   _____

   _____

4. In paragraph 3, what does the sentence "he had made firm rebellion against this yellow light thrown upon the color of his ambitions" mean?

   _____

   _____

   _____

5. What are Henry's feelings when he tells his mother that he has enlisted?

   _____

   _____

   _____

6. What does the excerpt tell you about Henry's mother?

_____

_____

_____

After telling his mother that he has enlisted, he then goes to tell his friends. Here the news of his enlistment is taken quite differently. . . .

From his home he had gone to the seminary to bid adieu to many school-mates. They had thronged about him with wonder and admiration. He had felt the gulf now between them and swelled with calm pride. He and some of his fellows who had donned blue were quite overwhelmed with privileges for all of one afternoon, and it had been a very delicious thing. They had strutted.

A certain light-haired girl had made vivacious fun at his martial spirit, but there was another and darker girl who he had gazed at steadfastly, and he thought she grew demure and sad at the sight of his blue and brass. As he had walked down the path between the rows of oaks, he had turned his head and detected her at a window watching his departure. As he perceived her, she had immediately begun to stare up through the high tree branches at the sky. He had seen a good deal of flurry and haste in her movement as she changed her attitude. He often thought of it.

7. Give the meaning of the following words as used in the excerpt.

   a. seminary _____ c. martial _____

   b. adieu _____ d. demure _____

8. Contrast the way in which the news of his enlistment is regarded by his friends to the way in which his mother reacted. How do you account for the difference?

_____

_____

_____

_____

9. How does the reaction of the "light-haired girl" and the "darker girl" in paragraph 2 affect Henry's moments of glory with his friends?

_____

_____

_____

Henry's regiment is treated lavishly as they went from station to station on their way to camp. After several months in camp, however, it was a different story. . . .

On the way to Washington his spirit had soared. The regiment was fed and <u>caressed</u> at station after station until the youth had believed that he must be a hero. There was a lavish expenditure of bread and cold meats, coffee, and pickles and cheese. As he basked in the smiles of the girls and was patted and complimented by the old men, he had felt growing within him the strength to do mighty deeds of arms.

After complicated journeyings with many pauses, there had come months of <u>monotonous</u> life in a camp. He had had the belief that real war was a series of death struggles with small time in between for sleep and meals; but since his regiment had come to the field the army had done little but sit still and try to keep warm.

He was brought then gradually back to his old ideas. Greek like struggles would be no more. Men were better, or more timid. <u>Secular</u> and religious education had <u>effaced</u> the throat-grappling instinct, or else firm finance held in check the passions.

He had grown to regard himself merely as a part of a vast blue demonstration. His <u>province</u> was to look out, as far as he could, for his personal comfort. For recreation he could twiddle his thumbs and speculate on the thoughts which must <u>agitate</u> the minds of the generals. Also, he was drilled and drilled and reviewed, and drilled and drilled and reviewed.

10. Give the meaning of the following words as used in the excerpt.

    a. <u>caressed</u> _____ d. <u>effaced</u> _____

    b. <u>monotonous</u> _____ e. <u>province</u> _____

    c. <u>secular</u> _____ f. <u>agitate</u> _____

11. How did the treatment of the regiment on the way to Washington affect Henry?

    _____

    _____

    _____

12. How does Henry's life in the camp compare with his fantasies about the war?

    _____

    _____

While waiting day after day to go into battle, all the men in the regiment exhibit behavior typical in stressful situations. The youth begins to wonder how he will measure up when put to the test. . . .

He went slowly to his tent and stretched himself on a blanket by the side of the snoring tall soldier. In the darkness he saw visions of a thousand-tongued fear that would babble at his back and cause him to flee, while others were going coolly about their country's business. He admitted that he would not be able to cope with this monster. He felt that every nerve in his body would be an ear to hear the voices, while other men would remain <u>stolid</u> and deaf.

13. Give the meaning of the following word as used in the excerpt.

   <u>stolid</u>

14. Study the figurative statement "he saw visions of a thousand-tongued fear that would babble at his back and cause him to flee." What is the author implying?

   _____

   _____

15. After the "visions," what decision does Henry make about himself?

   _____

Finally, the battle is upon them. The regiment is able to hold off the first wave, but after a short interval, there is another onslaught. . . .

The youth stared. Surely, he thought, this impossible thing was not about to happen. He waited as if he expected the enemy to suddenly stop, apologize, and retire bowing. It was all a mistake.

But the firing began somewhere on the regimental line and ripped along in both directions. The level sheets of flame developed great clouds of smoke that tumbled and tossed in the mild wind near the ground for a moment, and then rolled through the ranks as through a gate. The clouds were tinged an earthlike yellow in the sunrays and in the shadow were a sorry blue. The flag was sometimes eaten and lost in this mass of vapor, but more often it projected, sun-torched, <u>resplendent</u>.

To the youth it was an onslaught of redoubtable dragons. He became like the man who lost his legs at the approach of the red and green monster. He waited in a sort of a horrified, listening attitude. He seemed to shut his eyes and wait to be gobbled.

A man near him who up to this time had been working feverishly at his rifle suddenly stopped and ran with howls. A lad whose face had borne an expression of exalted courage, the majesty of he who dares give his life, was, at an instant, smitten <u>abject</u>. He <u>blanched</u> like one who has come to the edge of a cliff at midnight and is suddenly made aware. There was a <u>revelation</u>. He, too, threw down his gun and fled. There was no shame in his face. He ran like a rabbit.

16. Give the meaning of the following words as used in the excerpt.

    a. <u>resplendent</u> _____   c. <u>blanched</u> _____ face _____

    b. <u>abject</u> _____   d. <u>revelation</u> _____

17. When the battle is upon them, how does Henry see the approaching enemy, and how does he feel?

    _____

    _____

18. As the enemy draws near, what does Henry do?

    _____

Henry eventually makes his way back to camp, rejoins his regiment, and performs courageously and at times even heroically. Finally, the war is over. . . .

With this conviction came a <u>store</u> of assurance. He felt a quiet manhood, nonassertive but of sturdy and strong blood. He knew that he would no more <u>quail</u> before his guides wherever they should point. He had been to touch the great death, and found that, after all, it was but the great death (and was for others). He was a man.

19. Give the meaning of the following words as used in the excerpt.

    a. <u>store</u> _____   b. <u>quail</u> _____

20. After all the fighting is over, how does Henry see himself?

    _____

SUGGESTIONS FOR FURTHER STUDY

- Give special attention to inference questions in the Reading Selections of this textbook.
- Read a novel and look closely for inferences. Notice how much more you enjoy the book.
- Write a creative essay and incorporate as many inferences as possible.

9

Critical Reading

QUESTIONING, COMPARING, AND EVALUATING

In preceding chapters you have learned how to read in order to obtain literal comprehension of what an author actually states on the printed page. You have also learned that after you comprehend what is stated, you need to read "between the lines" to get a clearer meaning by understanding the author's implied meanings. To be a truly successful reader, you must now read beyond what is stated and implied so that you can analyze the material according to your purpose for reading. Critical reading is an active, creative skill that requires you to *question*, *compare*, and *evaluate*. Critical-reading skills are necessary in order to determine the value of reading material, to detect faulty logic and information, to separate facts from opinions, and then to determine whether you need to accept or reject the information.

If you never questioned what you read, you would accept every bit of information as fact and every author's opinions as your own. Simply because material is published does not make it relevant to your needs.

If you never compared what you read, you would have no standard by which to judge and would not be able to select the best information for your needs. Comparison is essential, especially when you read conflicting information and interpretations.

If you never evaluated, you would never know whether what you read or hear is valuable or whether it is worthless. In other words, you would not know whether the reading material was worth your valuable time needed to read it.

Critical reading could be considered a form of critical thinking. You think critically each day in everything you do. It is the means by which you make each decision, purchase any product, and decide what to say or do in any situation. Critical thinking also guides you in developing opinions of major and minor happenings in your life. For example, you use critical thinking (and reading) when you decide which brand of jeans to buy. First you *question* the cost, shrinkage, durability, and appearance. Next, you *compare* the brand you are considering with other brands you have worn, heard about from friends, or seen advertised. Finally, you *evaluate* on the basis of your own needs, budget, and personal taste. Then, and only then, are you ready to make the purchase that is best suited for you. This same process can, and indeed should, be applied to everything you read. At first the process of critical reasoning sounds long and tiresome. Instead, it actually saves you time by guiding you in selecting only the material relevant to your needs and personal taste. The process also increases your total comprehension because the analysis aids you in understanding what the author actually intended.

When you read critically, the following questions will help to guide you in questioning, comparing, and evaluating what you read.

1. **What is the purpose of the material?** The material could be intended to inform, explain, define, compare, contrast, illustrate, persuade, or simply to entertain. Determining the author's purpose will aid you in setting your own purpose for reading.

2. **When was the material written?** Whether you need the latest in print or something printed years earlier will depend on what type of information you need at the time. When you need recent developments, for example, the latest-dated material you can find would be best. In our fast-changing society, ideas that were valid years ago might no longer be in use. On the other hand, just because material is not current does not mean it is useless. Much of our best information, ideas, and recreational reading was written years ago.

3. **If the material is in a periodical (a newspaper or magazine), what is the type and reputation of the publication?** When you desire movie gossip, you go to a magazine that specializes in this type of news. On the other

hand, if you need factual information about a current event, a reputable news magazine would be best.

4. **Is the author qualified to write about the subject?** Inaccurate information could be more harmful than no information. The only way to be sure you are receiving accurate information is to select books and articles by qualified authors. Often there is information about the author in front of the book. If not, the library reference section carries several books that will give you information about authors.

5. **Does the author omit or suppress information needed about the subject?** This question is appropriate to ask whenever you need to know all sides of a situation before making a decision or forming an opinion. Whenever the material is intended to persuade you to believe or act in a certain way, it is imperative that you ask this question.

6. **Does the author use emotional words and pictures to persuade you to believe as he or she believes?** Authors choose words that convey the message that they intend the reader to receive; for example, if you were reading an article that was designed to make you want to join the armed forces, the author would use such words as *patriotism, liberty, free, oppressed, brave,* and *freedom.*

7. **Is the information fact or opinion?** A fact is something that has actually happened or is true and that can be proved. An opinion is a belief that is based on a personal evaluation. Needless to say, opinions can be true and worthy of acceptance, but you, the reader, should be able to recognize the difference between a fact and an opinion and then, through critical reading, to decide your own course of action or thinking.

8. **Does the information meet a need for you?** With the wealth of informational and recreational materials available today, this is an important question. Our fast-paced lifestyle demands that we be selective. If one piece of information or book does not meet your needs, there are many others that will.

Read the following sentences and the explanation of each to help you understand how to distinguish between fact and opinion.

1. **Susie is the most beautiful girl in the class.** This statement is an opinion because "beautiful" can mean something different to each individual. Indeed, you may agree that Susie *is,* without doubt, the most beautiful girl; however, this merely means that your opinion is the same as that of the person who made the statement. Remember, an opinion is not necessarily incorrect, but it has not been proved.

2. **Susie was elected by her classmates as the most beautiful girl in the class.** Susie now has been *voted* the most beautiful girl in the class. You can prove that according to a vote, Susie is considered the most beautiful.

Therefore, a statement is an opinion when it is a belief that is based on what seems true instead of what can be proved. A fact, on the other hand, states something that has actually happened or is true.

Read the following passage. Study the questions and answers carefully to help you better understand how to read a passage critically.

Fur Coats: Where Do They Come From?

Millions of coyote, bobcat, raccoon, muskrat, and other wild animals are caught in the steel jaw leghold trap every year. The trap shuts tight on the animal's leg, like a car door slamming on your finger. The animal may be left for hours or days in panic and pain. Some chew off their own legs to escape.

Some fur animals, like mink or fox, are bred in captivity. They are often raised in small cages that are crowded together. Controlled breeding for new pelt colors sometimes causes blindness or deformities. These animals are killed by clubbing, poisoning, electrocution—methods chosen because they do not harm the pelt.

Most seal furs are obtained by clubbing the seals into unconsciousness, then stabbing and skinning them. In some hunts, the seals are harassed and driven some distance over rocks before being clubbed.

EVERY FUR COAT HURTS—DON'T BUY FUR!

1. What is the purpose of this article?

   To convince the reader that it is wrong to buy a fur coat.

2. Does the author use emotional language to persuade the reader? Give examples.

   Yes. Words and phrases such as "caught in the steel jaw leghold trap," "animal may be left for hours or days in panic and pain," "causes blindness or deformities," "killed by clubbing," and "stabbing and skinning them."

3. This article was published by the Humane Society of the United States. What is the purpose of this organization?

   To protect and ensure the rights of animals.

4. Does this article reflect that purpose?

   Yes.

5. After evaluating the information according to the purpose, what conclusion did you draw?

   That a fur coat is made at the expense of innocent and helpless animals.

List some words and phrases that a person who manufactures or sells fur coats would use to convince you to buy a fur coat. Then use these words and phrases in a short paragraph written in favor of purchasing a fur coat.

_____

_____

_____

_____

_____

_____

_____

_____

_____

_____

_____

_____

_____

_____

_____

_____

EXERCISE 17: Fact and Opinion

NAME _____ DATE _____

*Read the following sentences, and decide which are facts and which are opinions. Indicate your choice by writing **O** or **F** on the lines provided.*

___O___ 1. The best advice to follow when choosing a career is to choose the one that promises the highest income.

___F___ 2. Books are more expensive today than they were ten years ago.

___F___ 3. The sun rises in the east and sets in the west.

___O___ 4. Most people look forward to summer because there are so many more fun activities available than during the winter.

___F___ 5. Statistics support the claim that seat belts reduce accident fatalities.

___O___ 6. Every city needs at least two modern, well-staffed hospitals.

___O___ 7. Current best-selling novels are far superior to the best-sellers of past years and cover a much wider range of interests.

___O___ 8. When juveniles commit serious crimes, they should be tried as adults.

___F___ 9. Hurricanes are one of nature's most powerful and destructive forces.

___F___ 10. Mount McKinley in Alaska, at an impressive height of over 20,000 feet, is the highest mountain in North America.

___F___ 11. Alcoholism, the uncontrollable need for alcohol, is a serious disease that affects millions of people in our country.

___F___ 12. Hans Christian Andersen, who published over 150 fairy tales, is considered one of the outstanding storytellers of all time.

___O___ 13. Every young child enjoys fairy tales, especially the ones written by Hans Christian Andersen.

___O___ 14. Your purpose for reading should determine your reading rate.

___O___ 15. Since speed is a major factor in the severity of automobile accidents, everyone understands the need for a controlled speed limit on our highways.

___O___ 16. With all its vibrant colors, pleasant weather, and fun festivals, fall is the most favored of the four seasons.

___F___ 17. Light travels faster than sound.

___O___ 18. It is easy to understand why everyone would support strict laws that would curb smoking among young people.

___O___ 19. All intelligent people recognize the need for a college education.

___F___ 20. George Washington was inaugurated as the first president of the United States on April 30, 1789.

___F___ 21. Washington, D.C., is located in a federal zone known as the District of Columbia.

___O___ 22. Although there were a token number of women in combat during the Gulf War, the practice of using women in combat will never be fully accepted in our country.

___F___ 23. The telephone was invented by Alexander Graham Bell. The first message, "Mr. Watson, come here, I want you," was transmitted on March 10, 1876.

___F___ 24. The sun is our primary source of light, heat, and energy.

___O___ 25. When the sun is high in the sky, it should never be viewed with the naked eye because light from the sun's rays can cause blindness.

___F___ 26. At 105 degrees, Tuesday was the hottest day on record for Danville.

___O___ 27. There has never been a truer statement than "a picture is worth a thousand words."

___F___ 28. Figures from the police department records show a slight decrease in violent crime in our city.

___F___ 29. Alaska is the largest state in the United States.

___F___ 30. The State Department of Education issued a report that described the condition of schools in the state and outlined plans for improvements.

___F___ 31. The polio vaccine developed by Dr. Jonas Salk has practically eradicated polio throughout the world.

___O___ 32. Establishing an independent political party would guarantee each individual an opportunity to make better decisions about issues.

___O___ 33. Reading enriches our lives and is fun!

NAME _____ DATE _____

Read the following passages, and then answer the questions that follow each passage.

Public Apathy— Highway Killer

This passage is a reprint of a leaflet published and distributed by the Public Affairs Division of the Motor Vehicle Manufacturing Association of the United States.

More than 46,000 people die on the nation's highways every year. More than 38,000 of them die in motor vehicles—nearly 25,000 in passenger cars.

And, almost 4,000,000 are injured—3,766,000 of whom are occupants of motor vehicles. Many of those injured suffer permanent disability or are scarred for life.

Yet, car occupants have available the most effective life-saving and injury-reducing device for all types of vehicle accidents—the safety belt.

The 25,000 fatalities in passenger cars is a huge decrease from the 37,000 passenger car fatalities in 1969, but this number could be reduced by one-half if all occupants wore safety belts.

The carnage of America's highways continues year after year because the majority of drivers and passengers—58 percent—do not buckle the safety belts installed in all domestic passenger cars built since 1964.

And, it continues despite conclusive evidence that the chances of death and injury are reduced by 50 percent with the use of safety belts.

Safety belt use is not the panacea that will eliminate all highway death and injury. But, when used, safety belts are effective in reducing deaths . . . and they do make a difference in the types and severity of injuries suffered.

Many drivers and passengers who don't use safety belts simply don't believe they will be involved in an accident.

Believing that motor vehicle accidents "happen to someone else" can kill, injure and destroy lives and families.

According to a study done by the University of Michigan's Transportation Research Institute, a typical American is almost certain to be involved in a traffic crash during his or her lifetime and faces a 1-in-50 chance of becoming a fatality and a 50 percent probability of suffering a disabling injury.

BEING FREE IS COSTLY

"It's a free country."

Sure it is. But that's an expression used to justify doing—or not doing—almost anything.

For many people, it's a costly expression, particularly for those not using the safety belt system installed in virtually every car on the highway.

The cost of highway accidents in dollars and human suffering is far from free.

In 1986, the latest year for which complete government fatality and injury data are available, over 46,000 persons were killed in accidents on our nation's highways. Nearly 4 million were injured, about 162,000 of them seriously.

Economic losses to society from motor vehicle accidents in 1986, the last year for available data, are estimated at $27.3 billion from property damage, $16.3 billion due to lost productivity, $4.1 billion from medical treatment and $26.3 billion from emergency services, insurance administration, legal fees, medical examiner services, administration of public assistance programs and other costs.

Dr. B. J. Campbell of the Highway Safety Research Center of the University of North Carolina finds that in a survey of 24 states plus the District of Columbia with belt use laws, traffic fatalities were reduced by nearly 7 percent—some 1,300 lives.

SAFETY BELTS RESTRAIN FOR LIFE . . .

Many non-belt users feel they can brace themselves to prevent injury in an accident. But they don't realize the forces involved until an accident happens. Some live to consider the error in their thinking. Many don't.

In a 30-mile-per-hour collision with a solid object, an unbelted driver or passenger slams into the windshield, the instrument panel or the steering wheel and column at a force more than 100 times the force of gravity.

This is the g force discussed in rocket launches. A 30-mph vehicle crash exerts g forces more than 20 times stronger than those an astronaut experiences at blastoff!

Put another way, the unbelted occupant of a 30-mph vehicle crash hits the windshield or other interior surface of the vehicle with the same impact as a fall from a three-story building. Even the impact of a slower 10-mph crash is roughly equivalent to catching a 100-pound weight dropped from about six feet.

Unbelted adults holding a child on their laps in a 30-mph crash are thrown forward with the force of one and one-half tons.

The child would be crushed to death.

Safety belts help vehicle occupants "ride down" the force of the crash (the first collision) by holding them in place and preventing contact with either the interior of the vehicle or other occupants (the so-called second collision).

Belts also keep occupants inside the vehicle. Studies reveal ejection as a major factor in fatalities and severe injuries. Being thrown out of a vehicle is 40 times more lethal. Belts can prevent you from being crushed by your own car.

According to a study covering 28,000 traffic accidents in Sweden, no fatalities involving safety belt users were found at crash speeds of under 60 mph. But speeds as low as 12 mph resulted in deaths among unbelted occupants.

The evidence is clear and dramatic . . . when used, safety belts reduce death and reduce the severity and frequency of injury in vehicle crashes. In two common accidents—head-on and rollover—belt use has a dramatic effect in reducing fatalities by body area. Safety belt users, for example, experienced 80 percent fewer deaths from head injuries—and no deaths from neck injuries.

The reduction in serious injuries by body area in both types of crashes also shows a dramatic difference between use and non-use.

1. What is the purpose of the article?

_____

_____

2. To whom is it directed?

_____

3. Note the source of the article. Would this association benefit financially from the extended use of safety belts?

_____

4. Consider your answer to the preceding question. In light of your answer, would you consider the information biased or unbiased?

_____

5. Is the information mostly facts or opinions?

_____

6. What claim does the passage make about highway deaths regarding the use of seat belts?

_____

_____

_____

7. In what ways would the source be able to support its claims and statistics?

_____

_____

8. Are the claims and statistics presented and explained in such a way that the reader can totally comprehend them?

_____

9. Is the information realistic and in accord with information on the subject that you have read from other sources?

_____

10. Is there enough clear, conclusive information on which to base a decision?

_____

11. How do you feel about using safety belts? Give reasons for your answer.

_____

_____

_____

_____

_____

_____

_____

_____

_____

Librarians

Quality of Life Is Much More Than a Job

LARRY FENNELLY

Larry Fennelly is Chairman of the Developmental Studies Department at Macon State College, a reviewer for the Macon Telegraph and News, and an enthusiastic observer of the arts in Middle Georgia. His arts column is designed to inform the public of behind-the-scenes activities and special achievements of individuals and groups.

It has often been remarked that the saddest thing about youth is that it is wasted on the young.

Reading a recent newspaper report on a survey conducted among college freshmen, I recalled the lament, "If only I knew then what I know now."

The survey disclosed what I had already suspected from informal polls of students both in Macon and at the Robins Resident Center: If it (whatever it may be) won't compute, and you can't drink it, smoke it or spend it, then "it" holds little value.

According to the survey, which was based on the responses of over 188,000 students, today's traditional-age college freshmen are "more materialistic and less altruistic" than at any time in the 17 years of the poll.

Not surprising in these hard times, the student's major objective "is to be financially well off. Less important than ever is developing a meaningful philosophy of life." It follows then that today the most popular course is not literature or history but accounting.

Interest in teaching, social service and the "altruistic" fields is at a low, along with ethnic and women's studies. On the other hand, enrollment in business programs, engineering and computer science is way up.

That's no surprise either. A friend of mine (a sales representative for a chemical company) was making twice the salary of her college instructors her first year on the job—even before she completed her two-year associate degree.

"I'll tell 'em what they can do with their (music, history, literature, etc.)" she was fond of saying. And that was four years ago; I shudder to think what she's earning now.

Frankly, I'm proud of the young lady (not her attitude but her success). But why can't we have it both ways? Can't we educate people for life as well as for a career? I believe we can.

If we're not, then that is an indictment of our educational system—elementary, secondary and higher. In a time of increasing specialization, a time when 90 percent of all the scientists who have ever lived are currently alive, more than ever we need to know what is truly important in life.

This is where age and maturity come in. Most people, somewhere between the ages of 30 and 50, finally arrive at the inevitable conclusion that they were ordained to do more than serve a corporation, a government agency, or whatever.

Most of us finally have the revelation that quality of life is not entirely determined by a balance sheet. Sure, everyone wants to be financially comfortable, but we also want to feel that we have a perspective on the world beyond the confines of our occupation; we want to be able to render service to our fellow man and to our God.

If it is a fact that these four realizations do not dawn until mid-life, is it then not incumbent upon educational institutions to prepare the way for the revelation? Most people, in their youth, resent the Social Security deductions from their paychecks, yet a seemingly few short years later find themselves standing anxiously by the mailbox.

While it's true that we all need a career, preferably a lucrative one, it is equally true that our civilization has amassed an incredible amount of knowledge in fields far removed from our own and that we are better for our understanding of these other contributions—be they scientific or artistic. It is equally true that, in studying the diverse wisdom of others, we learn how to think. More important, perhaps, education teaches us to see the connections between things, as well as to see beyond our immediate needs.

Weekly we read of unions who went on strike for higher wages, only to drive their employer out of business. No company; no job. How shortsighted in the long run.

But the most important argument for a broad eduction is that in studying the accumulated wisdom of the ages, we improve our moral sense. I saw a cartoon recently which depicts a group of businessmen looking puzzled as they sit around a conference table; one of them is talking on the intercom: "Miss Baxter," he says, "could you please send in someone who can distinguish right from wrong?"

In the long run that's what education really ought to be about. And I think it can be. My college roommate, now head of a large shipping company in New York, not surprisingly was a business major. But he also hosted a classical music show on the college's FM station and listened to Wagner as he studied his accounting.

That's the way it should be. Oscar Wilde had it right when he said that we ought to give our ability to our work but our genius to our lives.

Let's hope our educators answer the students' cries for career education, but at the same time let's ensure that the students are prepared for the day when they realize their folly. There's a lot more to life than a job.

1. What is the author's purpose?

   _____

2. How is the author qualified to write about the subject?

   _____

   _____

3. To whom is this information directed?

   _____

4. Does the author present both sides of the question?

   _____

5. Can the facts stated in the article be verified? How?

   _____

   _____

6. Are the opinions that are given realistic and in accord with what you know to be true?

   _____

7. Does the author give enough evidence for you to draw a conclusion? If so, what is your conclusion?

   _____

8. What is the author's conclusion?

   _____

   _____

   _____

   _____

9. Compare your conclusion with the conclusion of the author.

   _____

   _____

EXERCISE 19: *Questioning, Comparing, and Evaluating*

NAME _____ **DATE** _____

The following two articles are concerned with using the Scholastic Aptitude Test (SAT) as a measure of academic potential. The first article supports using the SAT, and the second opposes using the test for this purpose. Read each article carefully, and then answer the questions that follow.

SAT Is the Best Way to Test Reasoning Skill

GEORGE H. HANFORD

George H. Hanford wrote this article while serving as president of the College Board.

Since its introduction in the mid-1920s, the Scholastic Aptitude Test has become the most widely used measure of individual, developed verbal and mathematical reasoning skills.

The SAT's purpose has been to provide a uniform, objective measure of academic readiness for college-level work.

Because it is relatively independent of any curriculum, it helps to compensate for differences in grading and curriculum among the nation's more than 27,000 secondary schools.

Students and their parents often see the SAT as a barrier to be overcome in reaching the goal of higher education.

The truth is that the SAT is more often a stepping stone than an obstacle.

By helping colleges to consider all students equally, the SAT has provided more opportunity to get an education, not less. It ensures that the true abilities of any student are not masked by subjective notions about group differences.

What is the SAT *not?*

First, it is not a measure of the creativity, motivation, or special talents of students—things that may very well help them succeed in college.

Second, the SAT is not a measure of the nation's "gross educational product."

The exam is taken by only one-third of all college-bound students. The proportion of students taking it in each school, district and state varies greatly. And educational programs developed to meet the disparate needs and abilities of particular students vary widely.

This is why SAT score averages must be used with extreme care and for a limited, if valuable, purpose: most notably, to assess the academic performance and needs of individual students.

What the SAT measures best are the so-called "higher order" reasoning skills—skills that are of extreme importance if today's youngsters are to function successfully in an increasingly complex and technological society.

Reports of the National Assessment of Educational Programs and recent findings by John I. Goodlad and Theodore Sizer suggest that there is *not enough* emphasis on developing these thinking skills.

It remains a simple fact that for now the SAT provides about the best means we have of assessing the ability to think critically.

The SAT is used by hundreds of colleges around the country because it *works.*

It works because it provides useful, valid information both to them and to those youngsters applying to them.

As long as it continues to do that, the SAT—or something like it—will be an important tool in our country's educational process.

1. List four reasons stated in the article that support using the test.

    (1) _____

    (2) _____

    (3) _____

    (4) _____

2. Does the article state any negative considerations? If so, what are they?

    _____

    _____

3. Is the information presented mostly facts or opinions? List examples of each.

    _____

    _____

    _____

4. Is the author qualified to write on the subject? On the basis of his qualifications, would you expect him to support or oppose the test? (One of the functions of the College Board, an educational organization, is to sponsor tests, such as the SAT, to aid colleges in the placement and guidance of students.)

Why We Need a Test to Replace the SAT

ERNEST L. BOYER

Ernest L. Boyer is a past president of the Carnegie Foundation for the Advancement of Teaching.

Every year, about a million high school students sit for $2\frac{1}{2}$ hours with soft pencils in their hands, marking up SAT score sheets. For many, it's a dramatic and frightening rite of passage.

However, I believe that the Scholastic Aptitude Test will come to play a decreasingly important role.

The SAT score is not very helpful in predicting how a student will perform in college—though when the score is combined with high school grades, the prediction rate improves.

I am troubled by the inflated attention given the SAT at a time when the majority of the nation's colleges are not highly selective and when few use the test as the primary yardstick for admission.

The Scholastic Aptitude Test was created at a time when high school standards were extremely uneven and when racial intolerance in college admissions was a harsh reality.

The SAT sought to overcome these barriers by measuring the "intellectual aptitude" of students.

Today, it's generally agreed that measuring what's sometimes called innate ability is difficult, if not impossible, to accomplish. It's also agreed that the SAT does not adequately measure what students are learning in the classroom.

Still, many people have mistakenly come to view the SAT as a reliable report card on the nation's schools.

Most students, after all, do not take the SAT. Thus there is an urgent need to give colleges a more realistic portrait of what incoming high school students actually have learned.

There is also an urgent need to help non-collegiate students figure out what they should do. It's ironic that students who need the most advice often get the least. Those not going on to college get only snippets of information about jobs from family or friends.

It is unacceptable to focus our elaborate evaluation program on those moving on to college, while neglecting the other half who urgently need guidance.

That is why we have recommended that a new test be developed to serve all students. Its goal would be to evaluate a student's academic achievement by linking testing to the core curriculum in the school—and to help all students make academic and vocational decisions.

The aim of a standardized test should not be to screen students out of options, but to help them move on with confidence to college—and to jobs.

1. List four reasons stated in the article that oppose using the test.

   (1) _____

   (2) _____

   (3) _____

   (4) _____

2. Does the article state any support for using the test? If so, what?

   _____

   _____

   _____

3. Is the information presented mostly facts or opinions? List examples of each.

   _____

   _____

   _____

   _____

4. Is the author qualified to write on the subject? On the basis of his qualifications, would you expect him to support or oppose using the test? (One of the functions of the Carnegie Foundation for the Advancement of Teaching is to conduct and publish educational studies.)

_____

_____

Now that you have *questioned* the information in each article, you are ready to compare and then to evaluate.

Compare your answers on each article. Do you find that one author uses more facts and better logic and reasoning than the other? Is the information presented complete and objective so that you are able to draw a conclusion? Are the arguments used reasonable? Do you detect personal bias in either article? Asking yourself these kinds of questions when dealing with conflicting information will help you to detect any inconsistencies, faulty logic, and flaws in reasoning.

Evaluate by writing a short paragraph in support of or opposition to the SAT, using the information in the two articles.

_____

_____

_____

_____

_____

_____

_____

_____

_____

_____

_____

_____

_____

NAME _____ **DATE** _____

*Although women have served in the military for many years, they have not been
allowed in combat. However, their more active role in the Persian Gulf War has
raised the question of allowing women to fight alongside men. The following passages present both sides of the issue. Read the passages, answer the questions
that follow, and then cirtically analyze your own ideas concerning women in combat.*

*Should Women Be Allowed
in Combat?
Yes*

Becky Constantino

*Becky Constantino is a former chairwoman of the Defense Advisory Com-
mittee on Women in the Services. The passage is from testimony before the
Senate Arms Services Subcommittee on Manpower and Personnel, June
18, 1991.*

The performance of American servicewomen in the Persian Gulf War
calls into question existing combat restrictions for women—and highlights the
benefits of fully using the capabilities of all personnel to further enhance combat readiness and to optimize the quality of the military. The time has come to
give the chain of command the flexibility to use their best people to accomplish the tasks which our country asks of them. . . .

Physical gender differences, which could negatively impact combat
readiness, would be valid reasons for closing positions for women. But limitations based on substantiated rationales would be more acceptable than the
current limitations, which are strictly gender-related with an assumed intent
of protecting the military women's exposure to hostile fire.

Servicewomen go through the same training, make the same sacrifices
and sign the same contract as servicemen. They want an opportunity to fulfill

their commitments and serve their country to the best of their abilities. They do not expect special treatment or want standards to be reduced to assure their success. . . . They know that equal opportunity means equal responsibility, and they are willing to accept the responsibility and corresponding risks.

Sometimes those who fight in opposition to women being in the military and in combat roles forget the reason these women join. They join for the same reasons the men join—to be full-fledged defenders of our country and our military.

The spirit of the U.S. servicewoman was captured when Major Marie Rossi said: "I think if you talk to the women who are professionals in the military, we see ourselves as soldiers. We do not really see it as man versus woman."

As a nation, we now know what we will do if women become prisoners of war. We will wear yellow ribbons for them and pray for their early return. We now know what we will do if women die for their country. We will grieve for them and bury them beside their brothers in Arlington Cemetery.

The lesson of the Gulf War is that those who support a strong defense and those who want to expand opportunities for women in the military are on the same team. In spite of the inequities servicewomen face, they set aside personal frustrations and become part of a team whose objective is to protect and defend the United States.

Should Women Be Allowed in Combat?
No

General Robert H. Barrow

General Robert Barrow is a former commandant of the United States Marine Corps. The passage is from testimony before the Senate Armed Services Subcommittee on Manpower and Personnel, June 18, 1991.

The issue of women in combat is not about women's rights, equal opportunity or career assignments for enhancement purposes for selection to higher rank. It is most assuredly about combat effectiveness, combat readiness, winning the next conflict, and so we are talking about national security.

Those who advocate change have some strange arguments, one of which is that there is a de facto women-in-combat situation already, that women have been shot at, that they have heard gunfire, that they have been in areas where they could have been hit with missiles. But exposure to danger is not combat; combat is a lot more than that. It is a lot more than getting shot at or even getting killed by being shot at. Combat is finding and killing or capturing the enemy. It is killing, that is what it is.

And it is done in an environment that is often as difficult as you can possibly imagine—extremes of climate, brutality, deaths, dying. It is uncivilized, and women cannot do it. Nor should they be even thought of as doing it. And I may be old-fashioned, but I think the very nature of women disqualifies them from doing it. Women give life, sustain life, nurture life, they do not take it.

I just cannot imagine why we are engaged in this debate about even the possibility of pushing women into the combat part of our profession. The most harm that could come would probably come to what it would do to the men in that kind of situation. I know in some circles it is very popular to ridicule something called male bonding, but it is real, and one has to have experienced it to understand it. . . . It is cohesiveness. It is mutual respect and admiration. It is one for all and all for one. . . .

The other attendant problems to being in a combat situation—sexual harrassment, fraternization, favoritism, resentment, male backlash—would be insurmountable for anyone to deal with. Who would deal with it? Not some faceless political appointee over there in the Pentagon, but the corporals and sergeants and the lieutenants and the captains would have to maintain good order and discipline and also fight the war. . . .

If you want to make a combat unit ineffective, assign some women to it. It is a destructive proposition, and the thing that puzzles me about this, there is no military requirement for it. . . . We have all the men we need for those requirements. . . .

I. 1. In the first passage, what is the stated reason that women join the military?

_____

_____

2. What does Ms. Constantino state as the only valid reason for not allowing women in combat?

_____

_____

3. What is the reason currently used for not allowing women in combat?

_____

_____

4. What does Ms. Constantino state as the major benefits of allowing women in combat?

_____

_____

_____

_____

5. List three arguments stated in support of this issue.

_____

_____

_____

_____

_____

6. How does Ms. Constantino foresee the reaction of the nation when women become prisoners of war or are killed in combat?

_____

_____

_____

_____

_____

7. According to General Barrow in the second passage, the issue of women in combat is not about women's rights. What does he say it is about?

_____

_____

_____

8. Contrast *exposure to danger* and *combat* as discussed in the passage.

_____

_____

_____

9. What argument does General Barrow use in regard to the nature of a woman to support not allowing women in combat?

_____

_____

_____

10. According to the second passage, how would women in combat harm the men who serve in combat?

_____

_____

11. List three broad arguments in opposition to allowing women in combat as discussed in the second passage.

_____

_____

_____

_____

_____

12. In addition to the broad arguments you listed in question 11, what other problems does General Barrow consider insurmountable? Why does he consider these problems insurmountable?

_____

_____

_____

_____

_____

II. Now that you have *questioned* the information in each passage, you are ready to *compare* and then to *evaluate*. Compare your answers on each passage, question what you have learned about each side of the issue, and then evaluate. Write a short essay <u>in support of</u> or <u>opposition to</u> allowing women in combat. (Use this space and a sheet of your own paper—if needed—to answer.)

_____

_____

_____

_____

_____

_____

_____

_____

_____

_____

_____

_____

_____

_____

_____

_____

_____

SUGGESTIONS FOR FURTHER STUDY

- Select a current controversial topic, and read information for and against the controversy. Question each side, compare the information, and then evaluate.
- Read editorials in the local newspaper, determine whether each is in favor of or is opposed to the topic being discussed, and then write an essay taking the side not favored in the editorial.

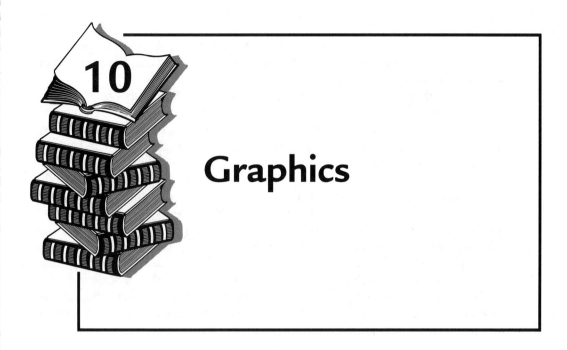

Graphics

UNDERSTANDING GRAPHICS

You have probably heard the saying "a picture is worth a thousand words." This saying aptly applies to any graphic material you may encounter when reading text. *In this context, a graphic is any form of visual information other than written material.* It could be a graph, chart, table, map, diagram, picture, or even a spreadsheet from your computer. Authors use graphics to simplify, condense, explain, and/or summarize written information. A graphic can display a wealth of information in a small space and, at a glance, give the reader information that would take much longer to read from text.

This chapter will help you learn about, interpret, and practice using graphs, charts, tables, and maps. Learning to read and interpret these will better equip you to understand any type of graphic you may encounter as you read for study or pleasure.

Graphs

A graph is used extensively in printed material because it is a simple but dramatic way to give information and to compare and show relationships between two or more items. A well-constructed graph can give a clear picture of statistical data and information and can make the most mind-boggling concepts easier to understand.

As with all graphics, you should first note the *title* of the graph, which tells you at a glance what the graph shows. In addition, the *source* of the graph should be noted so that you can critically determine the reliability of the information. (If the information was gathered and the graph constructed by the same person who wrote the text, there will not be a credit line.)

Various kinds of graphs include line graphs, bar graphs, and circle (or pie) graphs. All of these, except the circle graph, are presented in grid form with two *scales* or *axes*. The *grid* is a framework of evenly spaced vertical and horizontal lines that shows the scale by which the graph is interpreted. You should examine the scales carefully to determine what each represents. One of the scales (either the vertical or horizontal) will indicate *what* is being measured, and the other will indicate *how* it is being measured. The scale may also indicate that the quantity given on the graph represents hundreds, thousands, millions, etc. You should also note the *legend* (sometimes called a *key*) that indicates what each color, picture, or type of line represents.

Line Graphs. A *line graph* is one of the simplest of graphs and perhaps the easiest to interpret. It is useful in showing trends and changes over a period of time. A line graph is preferred for this information because it provides a quick and often dramatic picture of a trend or change.

Study the line graph in Figure 10–1. Note the title—*The Poverty Rate in the United States, 1960–1990.* The source is the U.S. Bureau of the Census, so you know that the information is reliable. At a glance you can see that approximately 22 percent of the people in the United States lived in poverty in 1960. There was a downward trend in the poverty rate until the early 1980s, when it showed a sharp increase followed by another downward trend. You can easily conclude that over the past 30 years, the poverty rate has dropped significantly. However, the line indicates the possibility of another increase in the 1990s.

Bar Graphs. A *bar graph* is used to compare quantities by using vertical or horizontal bars. Multiple comparisons can be made with the use of two or more sets of bars. As with line graphs, you determine which scale (the vertical or horizontal) indicates what is being measured and which indicates how it is measured.

For example, by noting the title of the bar graph in Figure 10–2, you see that it shows the number of men and women in the labor force. The vertical scale indicates that it is shown as a percentage, and the horizontal scale

FIGURE 10–1 The Poverty Rate in the United States, 1960–1990

Year

Source: U.S. Bureau of the Census.

FIGURE 10–2 Men and Women in the U.S. Labor Force

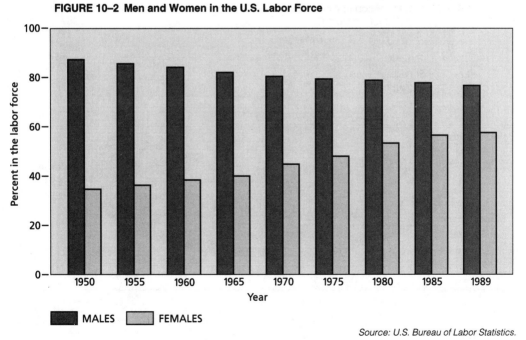

Year

MALES   FEMALES

Source: U.S. Bureau of Labor Statistics.

indicates that the percentage of males and females in the labor force is given for each year from 1950 through 1989. Note in the legend that the *dark* bar represents males and the *light* bar represents females. A quick study reveals that the percentage of males in the labor force has shown a slight decline, whereas the percentage of females has steadily increased.

Circle Graphs. The *circle graph* is sometimes called a *pie graph* or *pie chart*. It is used to show the relation of parts to a whole and is usually stated in percentages. The graph is in the form of a circle, with the entire circle representing 100 percent. The information is shown by dividing the circle into wedges like a piece of pie—thus the name pie graph or pie chart. Keep in mind that other graphics can show percentages as well as circle graphs.

The circle graph in Figure 10–3 shows the reader how the American Cancer Society allocated the funds in its 1991–1992 budget of $380,339. You can quickly see that research is the number one priority, with prevention coming in as number two, and so on. This information is valuable to contributors because it shows exactly how the money is being spent and in a format that is very easy to read and understand.

FIGURE 10–3 Allocation of American Cancer Society Funds Based on Total 1991–1992 Budget—$380,339

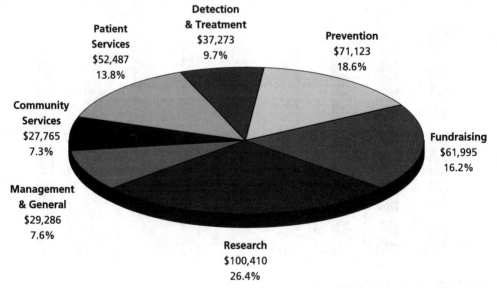

Source: Figures taken from 1991 Annual Report (in thousands).

Charts

A *chart,* which can be any graphic aid that presents information, usually appears in the form of a graph, table, or map. Charts are discussed here as a group in order to include the organization charts and flowcharts that are used so extensively in business, computer technology, and marketing.

Organization Charts.   An *organization chart* is used to show the hierarchy of any type of organization. The relationships and responsibilities of each position may also be included. Some charts also show the organization of a concept, a problem-solving process, or a decision-making process.

The organization chart in Figure 10–4 shows the organization of an information services department. You can readily trace the hierarchy all the way from the director to the operators and librarian.

FIGURE 10–4 Organization Chart—Medium-Sized and Large Information Services Departments

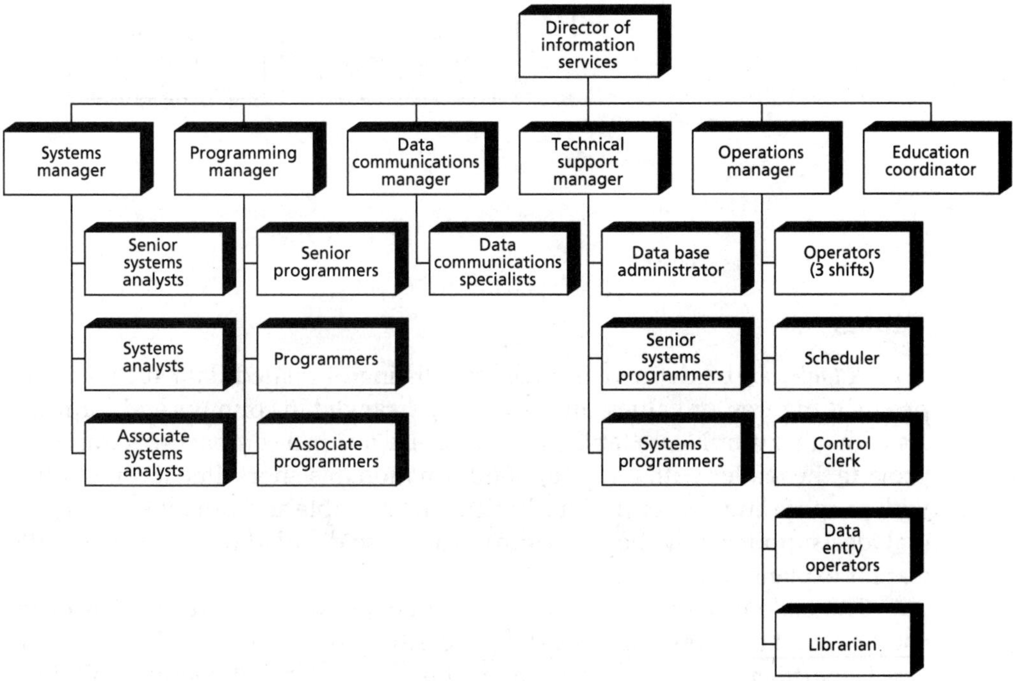

Note: No two information services departments are organized in the same way, but the example is, in general, representative.

Flowcharts. A *flowchart* is similar to the organization chart in format but serves a different purpose. It is used to show a process or procedure from beginning to completion. It may or may not give additional information. Keep in mind that organization charts and flowcharts may overlap. Your major objective is not as much to name them as to understand the message that they convey.

A flowchart can show something as simple (in concept) as the succession of objectives in managing a salesforce as shown in Figure 10–5, to illustrating how a bill becomes a law (Figure 10–11 on page 180.)

FIGURE 10–5 Major Salesforce Management Decisions

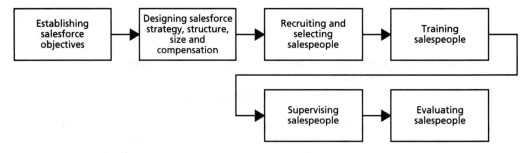

Tables

A *table* can be defined as a compact listing of related data such as facts, products, figures, or values, and is usually arranged in columns and/or rows. As with other graphics, a table can summarize text in a compact space and can provide the reader with a wealth of information in a short time if it is studied with purpose and concentration. Tables can be simple and can illustrate a general idea supported by the text, or they can be so detailed that they need little text for explanation.

The table in Figure 10–6 shows how people with different levels of income spent their money in 1984–1986 according to a survey conducted by the U.S. Department of Labor. You can quickly determine that people in all three income brackets spent the bulk of their money on transportation, housing, and food. You might be interested in comparing other categories.

FIGURE 10–6 Distribution of Consumer Spending for Different Income Levels

Expenditure	Income Level		
	$10,000– 15,000	$20,000– 30,000	Over $40,000
Food	16.1%	15.2%	12.1%
Housing	18.0	17.2	17.9
Utilities	8.8	6.7	4.8
Clothing	5.4	5.5	6.0
Transportation	19.5	20.9	19.7
Health Care	6.8	4.9	3.4
Housekeeping Supplies	1.6	1.5	1.1
Household Furnishings	3.5	3.8	5.1
Entertainment	4.0	4.6	5.1
Personal Care	1.5	1.3	1.2
Reading	.6	.6	.6
Education	1.2	.8	1.8
Tobacco	1.5	1.0	.5
Alcohol	1.2	1.2	1.1
Contributions	2.8	3.5	4.4
Insurance and Pensions	5.2	9.1	13.0
Other	2.3	2.2	2.2

Source: Consumer Expenditure Survey: Integrated Survey Data, 1984–86, U.S. Department of Labor, Bureau of Labor Statistics, Bulletin 2333, August 1989, pp. 164–66.

Maps

Maps are used to locate places, to give directions, and to give information about such things as types of terrain, climate, population, and products. In fact, a map can be used to give any information that has a relationship to location. When reading maps, it is imperative that you note all the basic characteristics of graphics discussed in this chapter—especially the legend. The legend on a map communicates to the reader the symbols that are used on the map, such as what each color, picture, or type of line (straight, broken, wavy, etc.) represents. The legend on maps such as road and street maps also indicates the scale of miles. For example, 1 inch might represent 10 miles or 100 miles.

There are many kinds of maps—*general reference, physical, political, thematic,* and *mobility.* (The name of each suggests the purpose of the map.) Because of space restrictions, this chapter will look more closely at only two of these—thematic and mobility.

Thematic Maps. A *thematic map* gives information about a selected theme, such as bushels of corn produced in each state, number of people who voted for a certain candidate, or areas with the lowest or highest population.

The map in Figure 10–7 shows the projected population growth for the United States in 1900–2000 according to the U.S. Department of Commerce, Bureau of Census. This type of map can provide valuable information to support the text and can aid people and companies in making personal and business decisions. Locate your state and determine the percent of population increase or decrease. Look up the current population of your state in an encyclopedia, and determine how many people are expected to live there in the year 2000.

FIGURE 10–7 Projected Population Growth Rates: 1990–2000

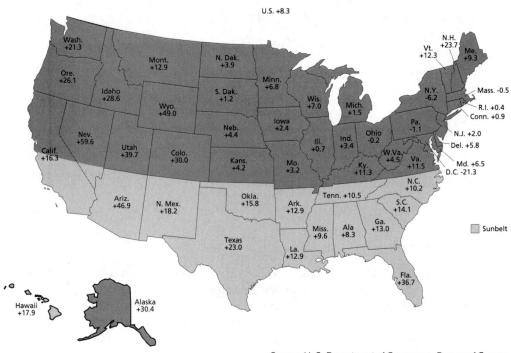

Source: U. S. Department of Commerce, Bureau of Census.

Mobility Maps. A *mobility map* is designed to locate places and provide directions. Maps of roads, streets, transit systems, and special areas are examples of mobility maps.

The map in Figure 10–8 is a map of the Ocmulgee National Monument in Macon, Georgia. Not only does this map show you the major highways to

FIGURE 10–8 Ocmulgee National Monument

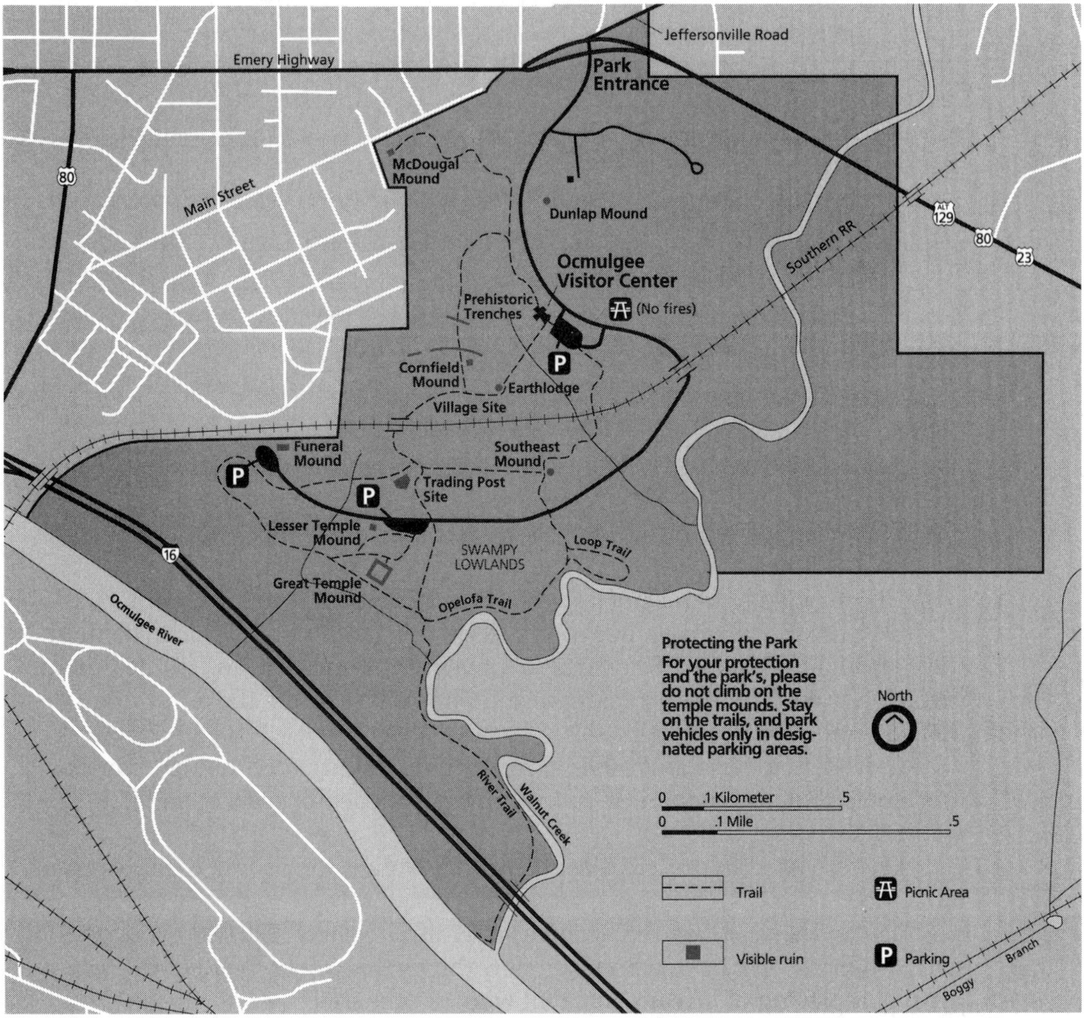

Jeffersonville Road

Emery Highway

Park Entrance

McDougal Mound

Dunlap Mound

80

Main Street

Southern RR

ALT 129

80 23

Ocmulgee Visitor Center

Prehistoric Trenches

(No fires)

P

Cornfield Mound

Earthlodge

Village Site

Funeral Mound

Southeast Mound

P

Trading Post Site

P

Lesser Temple Mound

16

SWAMPY LOWLANDS

Loop Trail

Great Temple Mound

Opelofa Trail

Ocmulgee River

River Trail

Walnut Creek

Protecting the Park
For your protection and the park's, please do not climb on the temple mounds. Stay on the trails, and park vehicles only in designated parking areas.

North

0   .1 Kilometer   .5
0   .1 Mile   .5

- - - - - Trail

■ Visible ruin

Picnic Area

P Parking

Boggy Branch

Source: National Park Service.

reach the park site, but also it gives other information. Note that the legend of the map indicates the trails, visible ruins, picnic areas, and designated parking areas. Whether you planned to see the park in a few hours or spend the day, the map and the information it contains would make your visit more enjoyable.

NAME _____ **DATE** _____

Read the following passages, study the graphics, and then answer the questions that follow.

Technology Is Blamed for Rising Health Costs

Experts: Greed, concern for profits are not to blame

Remember iron lungs? They went into storage after the polio vaccine was invented.

That cheap, simple vaccine ended the need for all that bulky, expensive equipment and care.

Unfortunately, that's not how most medical breakthroughs work.

"We are the victims of our own success as a biomedical research community," said Dr. William Schwartz, a physician-economist and professor of medicine at the University of Southern California. "Most of the new things we do add enormously to expenses."

Indeed, Schwartz and other experts agree that it is technology, not doctors' greed or drug companies' profits, that drives health costs relentlessly upwards.

Doctors used to prescribe aspirin and a walker for people with diseased hip joints.

"Now we do a hip replacement operation costing $20,000 or $25,000," said Schwartz. "We have wonderful new things that are both effective and expensive replacing old treatments that were both ineffective and cheap."

Americans will pay $912 billion for health care this year, for everything from aspirin to open heart surgery, dental work to nursing home bills. The tab is rising by $80 billion a year and consumes 14.6 percent of the gross domestic product.

When Medicare was launched back in 1965, Americans spent just $42 billion, or 5.9 percent of the gross domestic product, on health care. The soaring cost of health insurance—typically $4,000 per worker—has caused workers' real wages to stagnate.

President Clinton promises a major overhaul of the health system and warns that his economic recovery efforts are doomed if rising health costs are not slowed.

"Everywhere you look everything is conspiring to increase costs," said the Urban Institute's Marilyn Moon.

New diagnostic techniques like the magnetic resonance imaging machine—at $1,000-plus per patient—allow doctors to detect tumors or blood clots without painful exploratory surgery.

"The new technology tends to add on, not replace, the old technology," said Moon. "You do an X-ray first, then a CT scan and then an MRI. You're doing all three."

Dr. James S. Todd, executive vice president of the American Medical Association (AMA), said, "Technology in medicine is not like technology in industry. If you put a robot on an assembly line, you've saved money. If you put an MRI in a hospital, you've added 10 people to the payroll."

"We have a system with no brakes on it," said Robert Reischauer, director of the Congressional Budget Office.

A recent AMA study blamed the cost spiral in part on Americans being "overinsured" and paying only 20 percent of costs out of pocket.

Polls show many Americans believe the problem could be solved if doctors and drug companies, hospitals and insurers stopped raising fees so rapidly.

But most experts agree that prices will keep climbing as technology marches on—unless society restricts access to the latest advances.

1. Figure 10–9 shows the cost of health care in the United States from the

   years _____ to _____.

2. In the year 2000, it is projected that the cost of health care in the United

   States will be _____ dollars per year. The figure is

   an increase of _____ dollars since 1990.

3. The circle graph shows three sectors of spending—state and local, federal, and private. Of the three, the largest amount of money is spent in

   the _____ sector.

4. The federal government spent more on _____ than on any other program.

5. In the private sector, most of the money was spent on

   _____.

6. In 1993, the American people paid _____ dollars out-of-pocket for health care.

FIGURE 10–9 Rising Cost of Health Care

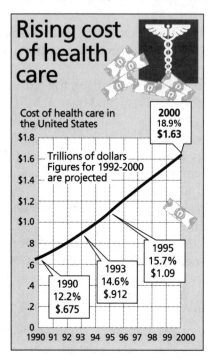

Rising cost of health care

Cost of health care in the United States

Trillions of dollars. Figures for 1992-2000 are projected

2000	18.9% $1.63
1995	15.7% $1.09
1993	14.6% $.912
1990	12.2% $.675

1990 91 92 93 94 95 96 97 98 99 2000

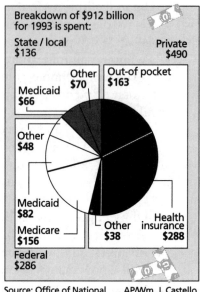

Breakdown of $912 billion for 1993 is spent:

State / local $136

Private $490

Other $70

Out-of pocket $163

Medicaid $66

Other $48

Medicaid $82

Medicare $156

Other $38

Health insurance $288

Federal $286

Source: Office of National Health Statistics   AP/Wm. J. Castello

7. According to the passage, what is the major source of blame for the increase in health care spending? Explain briefly.

_____

_____

8. What does the American Medical Association (AMA) study blame for the spiraling costs?

_____

_____

9. What do many Americans believe could curb the cost of health care in the United States?

_____

_____

_____

_____

Market Usage Rate

Markets can also be segmented into light-, medium-, and heavy-user groups. Heavy users are often a small percentage of the market but account for a high percentage of total buying. Figure 10–10 shows usage rates for some popular consumer products. Product users were divided into two groups, light users and heavy users, according to their buying rates for the specific products. Using beer as an example, the figure shows that 41 percent of the households studied buy beer. But the heavy users accounted for 87 percent of the beer consumed—almost seven times as much as the light users. Clearly, a beer company would prefer to attract one heavy user to its brand rather than several light users. Thus, most beer companies target the heavy beer drinker, using appeals such as Schaefer's "one beer to have when you're having more than one" or Miller Lite's "tastes great, less filling."

FIGURE 10–10 Heavy and Light Users of Common Consumer Products

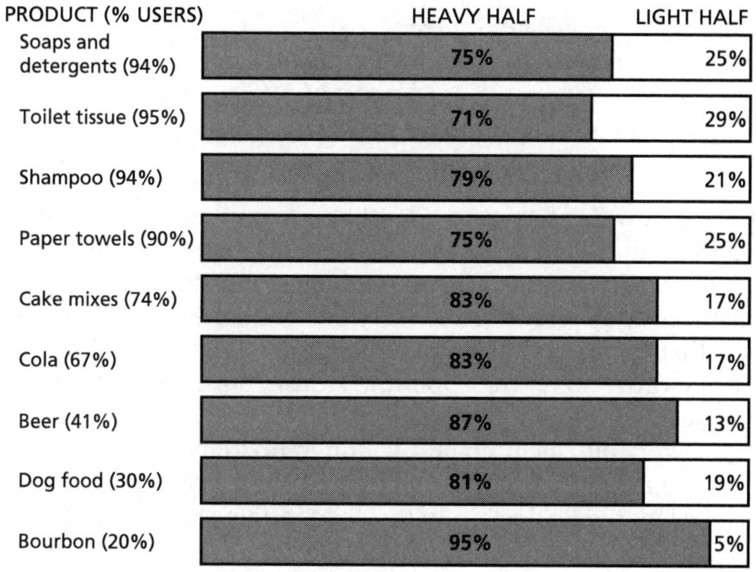

PRODUCT (% USERS)	HEAVY HALF	LIGHT HALF
Soaps and detergents (94%)	75%	25%
Toilet tissue (95%)	71%	29%
Shampoo (94%)	79%	21%
Paper towels (90%)	75%	25%
Cake mixes (74%)	83%	17%
Cola (67%)	83%	17%
Beer (41%)	87%	13%
Dog food (30%)	81%	19%
Bourbon (20%)	95%	5%

1. The title of the bar graph in Figure 10–10 is

_____.

2. The vertical scale shows
   percentage of product used.

3. Of the people studied, _____*94*_____ percent used soaps
   and detergents.

4. Of the people studied, _____*26*_____ percent did *not* use
   cake mixes.

5. If 100 people were studied, _____*30*_____ used dog food. Of
   these, _____*23*_____ were heavy users and
   _____*7*_____ were light users.

6. According to the passage, why do companies direct their advertisements
   toward heavy users of their product?
   Heavy users is in a high percentage of user market

The Legislative Obstacle Course

Congress operates under a system of multiple vetoes. The framers dispersed powers so they could not be accumulated by any would-be tyrant. In addition to the checks of bicameralism, Congress has also developed an elaborate set of customs to accompany these constitutional features that serve to distribute power. Let's follow a bill through the legislative process and we will see this *dispersion of power* (see Figure 10–11). Procedures and rules of the Senate differ somewhat from the House, but in each chamber power is fragmented and influence is decentralized.[1]

Every bill, including those drawn up in the executive branch, must be *introduced* in the House and the Senate by a member of that body. Bills are then *referred* by the leadership to the appropriate standing committee. Roughly 90

---

[1] For three well-written studies that follow legislation through the process, see Jeremy H. Birnbaum and Alan S. Murray. *Showdown at Gucci Gulch: Lobbyists and the Unlikely Triumph of Tax Reform* (Random House, 1988); Eric Redman, *The Dance of Legislation* (Simon & Schuster, 1973); Paul C. Light, *Forging Legislation* (Norton, 1992). For a more detailed study of rules and procedures, see Walter J. Oleszed, *Congressional Procedures and the Policy Process* 3rd ed. (Congressional Quarterly Press, 1989).

percent of the bills introduced every two years die in a subcommittee for lack of support. For bills that have significant backing, a committee or subcommittee holds *hearings* to receive opinions. It then meets to *mark up* (discuss and amend) and vote on the bill. If the subcommittee and then the parent committee vote in favor of the bill, it is *reported,* that is, sent to the full chamber, where it is debated and voted on. In the House the bill must go first to the Rules Committee for a *rule* that sets the time limit for debate and indicates whether floor amendments are allowed.

In the Senate, it is not uncommon for legislators to attach **riders**—provisions that may have little relationship to the bill they are riding on; for example, riders that have little to do with spending money can be attached to appropriations bills. The House of Representatives has stricter rules that require amendments to be germane to the bill, but no such rule is enforced in the Senate. Senators use riders to force the president to accept legislation attached to a bill that is otherwise popular, because the president must either accept the entire bill or veto it.

On most important topics (aside from taxes) both chambers consider their own bills, often at roughly the same time. There is no requirement that one act first. If only one chamber passes the bill, it dies. If both houses pass bills on the same subject but there are differences between the bills—and there often are—the two versions must go to a **conference committee** for reconciliation. If a bill does not make it through both chambers in identical form in the same Congress (two-year term), it must begin the entire process in the next Congress.

When a bill has passed both houses in identical form, it then goes to the president, who may sign the bill into law or veto it. If the Congress is in session and the president waits ten days (excluding Sundays), then the bill becomes law without his signature. If the Congress has adjourned and the president waits ten days without signing the bill, it is then defeated by a **pocket veto.** Except for the pocket veto, when a bill is vetoed, it is returned to the chamber of its origin by the president with a message explaining the reasons for the veto. If a bill has been vetoed and returned to Congress, Congress can vote to override the veto with a two-thirds vote in each chamber, but assembling such an extraordinary majority is often difficult.

1. What is the first step necessary in making a bill into a law?

_____

_____

2. According to the flowchart in Figure 10–11, what step is followed in the House that is not followed in the Senate?

FIGURE 10–11 How a Bill Becomes Law

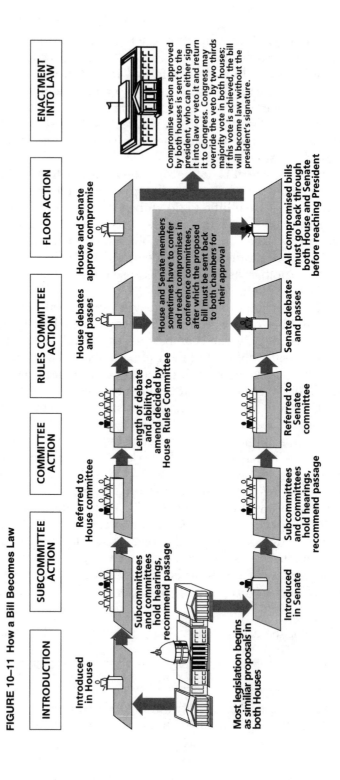

3. What is a "rider"?

4. Why is the practice of attaching riders to bills often used?

5. What happens to a bill if it passes one chamber but fails in the other?

6. According to the flowchart, the House and Senate Rules Committee sometimes reach a compromise on a bill. After a compromised version is proposed, what happens to the bill?

7. If the president vetoes a bill, how can Congress override the veto?

8. How can a bill become a law without the president's signature?

9. Referring to information in the passage and the flowchart, why do you think so many bills that are introduced never become law?

Postindustrial Sunbelt Cities

Along with the new postindustrial economy, people are not only spilling beyond the boundaries of central cities, they are also migrating from the Snowbelt to the Sunbelt. The Snowbelt—the traditional industrial heartland of the United States—includes the Northeast and Midwest, and contained almost 60 percent of the population in 1940. By 1975, however, the Sunbelt—the South and the West—passed the Snowbelt in overall population; by 1990, the Sunbelt was home of 55.6 percent of the population.

This demographic shift is shown in Figure 10–12, which compares the ten largest cities in the United States in 1950 and in 1990. In 1950, eight of the ten largest U.S. cities were industrial cities of the Snowbelt; in 1990, by contrast, six of the top ten were postindustrial cities of the Sunbelt. The box provides a snapshot of how our country's urban profile changed during the 1980s.

FIGURE 10–12 The Ten Largest Cities in the United States, 1950 and 1990

1950			1990		
Rank	City	Population	Rank	City	Population
1	New York	7,892,000	1	New York	7,323,000
2	Chicago	3,621,000	2	Los Angeles	3,485,000
3	Philadelphia	2,072,000	3	Chicago	2,784,000
4	Los Angeles	1,970,000	4	Houston	1,631,000
5	Detroit	1,850,000	5	Philadelphia	1,586,000
6	Baltimore	950,000	6	San Diego	1,111,000
7	Cleveland	915,000	7	Detroit	1,028,000
8	St. Louis	857,000	8	Dallas	1,007,000
9	Boston	801,000	9	Phoenix	983,000
10	San Francisco	775,000	10	San Antonio	936,000

Source: U.S. Bureau of the Census.

Why are Sunbelt cities faring so well? Unlike their counterparts in the Snowbelt, they are postindustrial cities that grew *after* urban decentralization began. Since suburbs take the form of a politically independent ring enclosing the Snowbelt cities, outward migration drew people out of central cities. Newer Sunbelt cities, by contrast, are not locked in by suburbs, so these cities have simply expanded outward, gaining population in the process. Chicago, for example, covers 228 square miles, whereas Houston is now over 556. Through physical expansion, Sunbelt cities have retained population even as people moved outward from the city's center, added new population as surrounding towns are enveloped, and enlarged their tax base to gain financial strength.

The great sprawl of the typical Sunbelt city does have drawbacks, however. Traveling across town is time-consuming, and automobile ownership is almost a necessity. Lacking a dense center, Sunbelt cities also generate far less of the excitement and intensity that draw people to New York or Chicago. Critics have long tagged Los Angeles, for example, as a vast cluster of suburbs in search of a center.

1. What is the source of the table in Figure 10–12? Would this information be reliable?

   _____

2. What was the second largest city in the United States in 1950? In 1990?

   _____

3. Name the city/cities that held the same rank in 1990 as in 1950.

   _____

4. Which cities were among the ten largest in 1950 and again in 1990?

   _____

5. What was the population difference between the largest and second largest city in 1950? In 1990?

   _____

   and the table in Figure 10–12, how is the

   _____

   tes is considered the Snowbelt in the passage?

   _____

   _____

   ount for the larger area of Sunbelt cities?

   _____

   _____

   annex surrounding areas to expand their city

   _____

   _____

People and the Environment: Rainforest Removal

Tropical rainforests comprise the climax vegetation over an area of nearly 3 billion acres (1.2 billion ha*), or about 8.3 percent of the Earth's total land surface. These remarkable forests are shared by some 50 countries on five continents. This vegetative association represents a biome of extraordinary diversity. Biologists believe that rainforests are the home of perhaps half the world's biotic species, about five-sixths of which have not yet been described and named.

Throughout most of history, rainforests were considered to be remote, inaccessible, unpleasant places, and as a consequence they were little affected by human activities. In the present century, however, rainforests have been exploited and devastated at an accelerating pace, and in the last decade or so, tropical deforestation has become one of the Earth's most serious environmental problems. The rate of deforestation is spectacular—51 acres (21 ha) per minute; 74,000 acres (30,000 ha) per day; 27 million acres (11 million ha) per year. More than half of the original African rainforest is now gone; about 45 percent of Asia's rainforest no longer exists; the proportion in Latin America is approaching 40 percent.

The current situation varies in the five major rainforest regions:

1. The rate of deforestation is highest in *southern* and *southeastern Asia*, primarily associated with commercial timber exploitation.

2. The current rate of deforestation is relatively low in *central Africa.*

3. Timber harvesting and agricultural expansion are responsible for a continuing high rate of forest clearing in *West Africa.* Nigeria has lost about 90 percent of its forests; Ghana, 80 percent.

4. Deforestation of the *Amazon region* as a percentage of the total area of rainforest has been moderate (about 5 percent of the total has been cleared) and it continues at an accelerating pace.

5. Very rapid deforestation persists in *Central America,* mostly due to expanded cattle ranching.

As the forest goes, so goes its animal life. In the mid-1980s it was calculated that tropical deforestation was responsible for the extermination of one species per day; by 1990 it is estimated that the rate was one species per hour.

*A hectare (ha) is a metric unit of area equal to 2.471 acres.

Moreover, loss of the forests contributes to accelerated soil erosion, drought, flooding, water quality degradation, declining agricultural productivity, and greater poverty for rural inhabitants. In addition, atmospheric carbon dioxide continues to be increased because there are fewer trees to absorb it and because burning of trees for forest clearing releases more to the air. Other broad-scale climatic alterations have been postulated, but these are still speculative.

The irony of tropical deforestation is that the anticipated economic benefits are usually illusory. Much of the forest clearing, especially in Latin America, is in response to the social pressure of overcrowding and poverty in societies where most of the people are landless. The governments throw open "new lands" for settlement in the rainforest. The settlers clear the land for crop growing or livestock raising. The result almost always is an initial "nutrient pulse" of high soil productivity, followed in only two or three years by a pronounced fertility decline as the nutrients are quickly leached and cropped out of the soil, weed species rapidly invade, and erosion becomes rampant. Sustainable agriculture generally can be expected only with continuous heavy fertilization, a costly procedure.

The forests, of course, are renewable. If left alone by humans, they can regenerate, providing there are seed trees in the vicinity and the soil has not been stripped of all its nutrients. The loss of biotic diversity, however, is much more serious. Extinction is an irreversible process. Valuable potential resources—pharmaceutical products, new food crops, natural insecticides, industrial materials—may disappear before they are even discovered. Natural genotypes that could be combined with agricultural crops or animals to impart resistance to disease, insects, parasites, and other environmental stresses may also be lost. Last, but not least, is the possibility that many small, isolated valuable groups of indigenous people may be wiped out.

Much concern has been expressed about tropical deforestation, and some concrete steps have been taken. The development of agroforestry (planting crops with trees, rather than cutting down the trees and replacing them with crops) is being fostered in many areas. In Brazil, which has by far the largest expanse of rainforest, some 46,000 square miles (119,000 km) of reserves have been set aside, and Brazilian law requires that any development in the Amazon region leave half of the land in its natural state. In 1985 a comprehensive world plan, sponsored by the World Bank, the World Resources Institute, and the United Nations Development Programme, was introduced. It proposes concrete, country-by-country strategies to combat tropical deforestation. It is an $8 billion, five-year project, dealing with everything from fuel-wood scarcity to training extension foresters. Its price tag makes its implementation unlikely.

Meanwhile, the sounds of the axe and the chainsaw and the bulldozer continue to be heard throughout the tropical forest lands.

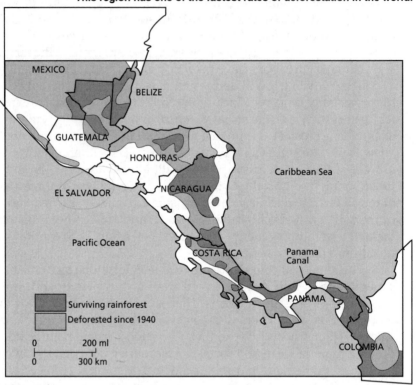

FIGURE 10–13 The shrinking Central American rainforest in the last half-century. This region has one of the fastest rates of deforestation in the world.

1. The purpose of the map in Figure 10–13 is to

   _____

   _____.

2. The map legend shows that approximately _____ equals 200 miles.

3. According to the map, _____ , a Central American country, has no rainforest.

4. According to the passage, tropical rainforests cover

   _____ acres or _____ percent of the Earth's surface.

5. According to the passage, the country of _____ has the most rainforests.

6. The rate of deforestation is _____ acres per minute.

   At this rate, _____ acres would be destroyed in a 24-hour period.

7. In addition to the loss of the forest and animal life, other problems caused by deforestation are

   _____

   _____.

8. It is evident that the destruction of the forest products in deforestation is detrimental to the future of our planet. However, the extinction of

   animals and biotic diversity is even more serious because

   _____.

9. How does the passage account for the lack of success in curbing

   deforestation?

   _____

   _____

SUGGESTIONS FOR FURTHER STUDY

- Use a road map of your city to calculate distances from your home to designated locations.
- Use a road map of your state to locate and plan a route to a recreational area in your state.
- Use a road map to plan a "dream vacation" for your family.
- Incorporate a graphic in your next research paper.

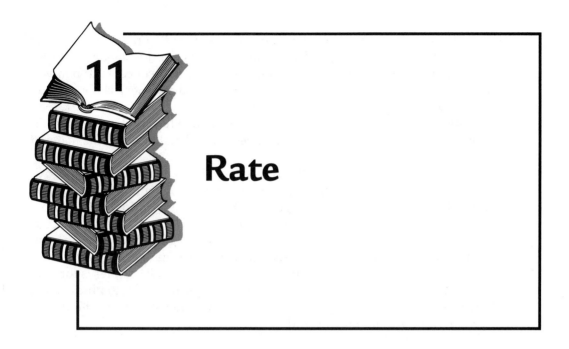

11

Rate

RATE AND COMPREHENSION

As a student in our fast-paced society, you are probably trying to manage classes, hold down a part-time job, and still leave some time for personal activities. Therefore, it is desirable to acquire the most efficient study and reading techniques possible in order to meet the increasing demands on your life. You probably have a designated amount of time each day to spend studying, but if your rate of reading is below par, you'll find yourself leaving reading assignments unfinished. Consequently, you may miss out on information vital to your success.

This chapter is concerned with rate of reading and with reading techniques that will enable you to read faster, with more enjoyment, and with better comprehension. At present you should be concerned not with rate alone but also with comprehension. If you read a book at an impressive 800 words per minute and have no idea what you have read, your reading has been useless and has been a waste of time. Your aim should be to read at the fastest possible rate to fulfill your purpose for reading. If you needed only a general idea from the material, you would read at a much faster rate than if you were reading to understand all the concepts presented by the author. In other words, your purpose for reading, along with the type and difficulty of the material, should determine how fast you read.

The more efficiently you read, the more your reading rate will vary. You can adjust your reading speed not only from passage to passage but also within a passage as you encounter difficult words and concepts. When you drive, you speed up when the road is smooth and the scenery is boring; you slow down when you want to take a closer look at something or when the road is rough. The same is true in reading. You speed up while reading easy, familiar material and slow down when you need more detail or when the material is difficult.

It has been estimated that the average reading rate for adults is approximately 200–250 words per minute. In college work, you will find that this rate is too slow to enable you to complete all the reading required. In addition, your comprehension usually suffers when you read everything slowly. Your mind, which is capable of comprehending rapidly, begins to wander when information is received as slowly as 200–250 words per minute.

If you are reading at a rate below your potential, this chapter is for you. You will learn how the reading process affects your rate, how to phrase read, how to establish a purpose for reading, and how to adjust your rate to fit your purpose and the material you read.

THE READING PROCESS

In order to reach your maximum reading rate, you need to understand the physical factors involved in the reading process and the way that these factors affect the rate at which you read.

Eye Movements

The visual symbols you see on the printed page are the means by which your mind interprets what you read. In other words, reading is a visual as well as a mental process. This section is intended to explain the visual role in the total reading process.

Fixations. In reading, a fixation is made when the eyes stop to focus on a word or a group of words. Very slow readers fixate, or focus, on each word in the sentence. Some slow readers may even fixate on each syllable. The duration of the fixation is as important as the number of fixations. The eyes usually remain on a word until the mind perceives the meaning; therefore, if the number of fixations is large and the duration long, the reading process will be exceedingly slow. The fewer and shorter the fixations, the faster the reading rate.

Recognition Span.   The number of words you recognize and perceive during one fixation is called your recognition span. Many studies have been made to determine the number of words the eyes are capable of seeing at one time. The results of these studies indicate that the eyes can actually see no more than two to three words per fixation. However, with the use of your peripheral vision you can see more words at one fixation. Generally speaking, the longer the recognition span, the better the reader.

Later in this chapter, the section "Phrasing" will explain a simple way to reduce the number of fixations and lengthen the recognition span.

Regressions.   In the reading process, you regress when you go back and reread what you have just read. Some regressions are normal, even necessary, in order to gain complete understanding of what you read. However, habit-ual regressions not only decrease your speed but also lower your level of comprehension. Often, regressions are a signal that you are not concentrating or that you feel insecure in handling the material. Ideally, if you develop good habits and concentration, improve your comprehension and vocabulary, phrase read, and adjust your reading rate to your purpose, the need to regress will lessen. All these skills are discussed in this book.

Lip Movements

As mentioned earlier, reading is both a visual and a mental process. The mind is capable of perceiving the message directly from the eye contact with the printed page. Therefore, lip movements are seldom necessary and, in fact, will interfere with your rate of reading.

Vocalizations.   If you move your lips or whisper each word as you read, you are vocalizing. This indicates that you are fixating on each word and pronouncing the word as if you were reading orally.

This practice will limit your reading rate to your speaking rate. The rate at which a person can speak varies with the individual but is seldom over 200 words per minute.

Subvocalizations.   Although you might not actually whisper or move your lips while reading, you might "say" the words to yourself. In other words, you subvocalize. Since thinking is essential to the reading process, you cannot successfully eliminate all subvocalizations. They are undesirable when you "say" each word rather than "think" each idea.

Phrasing

In order to comprehend what you read, you must read for ideas. An idea is seldom contained in a single word, but rather in a group of words. When you speak, you do not distinctly say each individual word. Instead, you speak in phrases. Everything you read is something someone has said. Therefore, when you read in phrases, you increase not only your speed but your comprehension as well.

Read the following paragraph one word at a time. Notice that the material is boring and that the meaning is unclear when you read words rather than ideas.

The / more / efficiently / you / read, / the / more / your / reading / will / vary. / You / can / adjust / your / reading / speed / not / only / from / passage / to / passage / but / also / within / a / passage / as / you / encounter / difficult / words / and / concepts. / When / you / drive, / you / speed / up / when / the / road / is / smooth / and / the / scenery / is / boring; / you / slow / down / when / you / want / to / take / a / closer / look / at / something / or / when / the / road / is / rough. / The / same / is / true / in / reading. / You / speed / up / while / reading / easy, / familiar / material / and / slow / down / when / you / need / more / detail / or / when / the / material / is / difficult.

Reread the same paragraph, using short phrases rather than reading word for word. Practice reading the paragraph and others, using short phrases. As soon as you are comfortable with your progress, you can lengthen the phrases as indicated later. As you lengthen your phrases, the material you read will be more interesting and meaningful.

The more efficiently / you read, / the more / your reading rate / will vary. / You can adjust / your reading speed / not only / from passage to passage / but also / within a passage / as you encounter / difficult words / and concepts. / When you drive, / you speed up / when the road / is smooth / and the scenery / is boring; / you slow down / when you want / to take a closer look / at something / or when the road / is rough. / The same is true / in reading. / You speed up / while reading / easy, familiar material / and slow down / when you need / more detail / or when / the material is difficult.

The more efficiently you read, / the more your reading rate will vary. / You can adjust your reading speed / not only from passage to passage / but also within a passage / as you encounter difficult words and concepts. / When you drive, / you speed up when the road is smooth / and the scenery is boring; / you slow down / when you want to take a closer look at something / or when the road is rough. / The same is true in reading. / You speed up / while reading easy, familiar material / and slow down / when you need more detail / or when the material is difficult.

Phrase reading is a necessary skill if you are to become the efficient reader that college studies demand. By reading for *ideas,* you gradually decrease the number of fixations and lengthen your recognition span. Phrase reading also eliminates unnecessary regressions and vocalizations. By reading in phrases, you "see an idea" and then automatically "think the idea," thus eliminating the need to "say the idea." With practice, reading for ideas will begin to come naturally, and undesirable habits will subside.

FLEXIBILITY IN RATE

To be a successful reader, you must learn to adjust your rate to the material you read. Flexibility in reading is definitely a mark of an efficient reader.

In order to be a flexible reader, you must establish a purpose for reading, determine the appropriate rate required to accomplish your purpose, and then use the proper techniques to maintain the desired rate.

Purpose

Reading without a purpose is like driving without a destination. Establishing a purpose for reading gives you the direction you need to accomplish the task. Your purpose will determine *how* and *how fast* you read—whether to read carefully and slowly for minute details or whether to skim for an overview of the material. For example, your history lesson that you will be tested on requires a closer reading than a magazine article that just happens to catch your eye. Before reading anything, you should decide why you are reading and what you want to learn from the material. A purpose for reading also creates a desire to learn and motivates you to read and enjoy a variety of materials.

Once you have established your purpose for reading, your next step is to decide the proper speed needed to accomplish that purpose.

The following discussions on the types of reading will give you some suggestions on how to adjust your rate to fit your purpose.

Study Reading

Study reading is the most *intensive* reading you are required to do. Study reading is usually slow reading. It is the type of reading you do when you are studying or reading anything that requires you to understand all the relationships and concepts presented. Therefore, you would use this technique when reading textbooks and reference books.

In study reading, you are reading to get the main idea and the supporting details and inferences, and also to evaluate critically what you read. Rapid reading of material that requires careful evaluation and analysis could result in incomplete information and lead you to draw false conclusions.

Recreational Reading

People who do not like to read are usually poor readers, and poor readers usually do not like to read. If this description fits your ability and attitude, you need to improve one or the other (or both!) immediately so that you can get off the "no-reading treadmill" and discover the joy of reading for pleasure.

Reading is one of the privileges and joys of life. Reading can carry you to exotic faraway places and permit you to experience the thrill of adventures that might otherwise be beyond your reach. Once you get "hooked on books" you will manage to find the time to read, regardless of the adjustments that might be necessary.

The rate of reading recreational materials varies with the individual reader as well as the material being read. Generally speaking, most recreational material is read at a moderate rate.

The types of recreational reading material are as varied as the people who read them. There is a wealth of material available for you to choose from, ranging from the current Hollywood gossip to the best-selling novel or classical masterpiece. Some common types of recreational reading materials include novels, magazines, and newspapers.

Novels.   Everyone loves a story—especially if the story is written by a master novelist who has the ability to give characters true-to- life personalities. The novelist can take an event that has happened—or could have happened—and tell it in such a way that you become so involved it is almost impossible to put the book down. In fact, interrupting the story would be almost like stopping some event in your life.

Novels come in assorted styles, with a style to fit each taste. Whether you like a sweet, romantic story, a mystery, or a deep plot that covers events over three or four generations, you will find many novels to choose from. Try not to be tempted to select only novels from the current "best-seller" list. These are good, but the best-sellers of yesteryear can be the best reading of this year.

Magazines. Magazines may be informative or entertaining or both. Trade magazines cater to people employed in a specific industry or trade. Consumer magazines cater to the general public, and range in subject matter from business news to bodybuilding. Whether you are interested in waterskiing or world affairs, Paris fashions or punk rock, you will find a magazine especially designed for you and others with similar interests. Most consumer magazines, even those that specialize in one area of interest, cover a variety of topics. This variety enables all who read the magazine to find an article of interest.

Newspapers. Newspapers are perhaps the most widely read sources of information available. Almost every city, town, and community (even your college) publishes a newspaper. The newspaper is written in a wide range of reading levels and covers a wide variety of topics because it serves a large number of people with varied backgrounds, abilities, and interests. Your local newspaper can keep you up-to-date on what is happening in your city, state, and country; it can also keep you informed about world affairs. You are not expected to read the entire newspaper. In fact, some big-city newspapers are so large that reading the entire paper would be nearly impossible. You are expected to read selectively—choosing only the articles that serve a purpose for you.

The newspaper is generally considered recreational reading and is read at a moderate rate. Even if you are reading the paper to get the news or to be informed about an issue, you are still reading because you want to; thus, it is a recreational activity. However, there are articles in each issue that you might read at a study rate because the details are important to you. On the other hand, you might skim some articles for the "gist" of the material or scan them for a specific bit of information.

Skimming and Scanning

Skimming and scanning are alike in that neither requires reading all the material. In addition, both are rapid-reading skills. Skimming and scanning are not ideal skills for the lazy student because each requires a high degree of alertness and concentration.

If you are a person who insists on reading each word, you will need to convince yourself that you can skip words, phrases, sentences, and often entire paragraphs. However, to be effective, skimming and scanning not only should be used on appropriate materials but also should be skillfully used according to your purpose for reading.

Although both skimming and scanning increase your reading speed, each skill is done differently, and each is used for a different purpose.

Skimming.   When you skim, you are looking for the "gist" of what the author is saying without a lot of the detail. In other words, you want only a preview or an overview of the material. Skimming is also used after you have already carefully studied and you need to review the major ideas and concepts.

In preview skimming, you read the introductory information, the headings and subheadings, and the summary (if one is provided). After this initial skimming, decide whether to read the material more thoroughly, and select the appropriate speed at which to read. (Chapter 1 contains a more thorough explanation on how to preview.)

Skimming to get an overview is an important skill for college students. You will find that more reading will be assigned and suggested to you than is humanly possible to read intensively. By skimming to get the "gist" of the material, you are able to cover all of it. However, *be certain you do not skim materials that require careful reading.* The same procedure used for preview skimming could be used to get an overview. Another method would be to read only key words.

To skim by reading key words, you must convince yourself that you can skip words and still be reading. By publishing condensed stories and books, some publishing companies have proven that not every word is essential to meaning. Skimming is done by omitting the unnecessary words, phrases, and sentences. With concentration and practice you can learn to select key words and phrases in order to cover the material more rapidly.

Remember that skimming is a skill that requires concentration, a superior vocabulary, and adequate comprehension skills. In addition, a certain amount of practice is necessary in order to skim and fulfill your purpose. If you master the skills covered in this book and practice the techniques in this chapter, you will find that skimming, when appropriate, will aid you in your college study.

Scanning.   When you need to locate specific information, you might not need to read carefully or even to skim. Instead, you might be able to scan to find the information you need. For instance, if you need a telephone number of a friend whose name begins with *R*, you would not need to read carefully all the names in the directory—or even all the R's—to locate the number.

Scanning is not a reading process in the true sense of the word. It is a *searching* process that requires you to float over the material until you find what you need. Then you stop and read as much as necessary in order to answer your question.

In order to scan efficiently, you should have a clear idea of what you are looking for, where you are likely to find it, and how you can recognize the information when you see it. If you are looking for a name, for example, capital letters might be your clue; if you are looking for a date, you would look for numbers; and so on. All the specific information that you need will not always be contained in one or two words. In this case, you scan until you locate the information, and then you read until you have all the information you are seeking.

SUGGESTIONS FOR FURTHER STUDY

- Practice phrase reading by marking off phrases in newspapers, magazines, and books. Begin with easy material and progress to more difficult material, practicing until you can mark off phrases with your eyes as you read.
- Read an abundance of recreational reading material.
- Scan newspaper articles for names, places, and dates.

Study Skills

MAKING ADJUSTMENTS

This book deals with the specific reading skills that are necessary for success in college. However, mastering these skills is only part of the total picture of reading for college students. You must also develop good study habits in order to utilize these skills effectively.

You will find (if you haven't already) that college classes are very different from high school classes. You will have more work and responsibilities without being prodded as much. On the other hand, you will have more freedom—freedom to choose what to study, when to study, or whether to study. You will need to exercise maximum self-discipline. This is the most difficult kind of discipline because it is self-imposed, and you are responsible only to yourself. The decisions you make concerning your study habits will be a determining factor in your success, or lack of success, in college.

In addition, you will discover that your instructors differ from the teachers you have had previously. They will expect you to take more initiative in your study habits and time management. Remember that much of your learning takes place outside the classroom. Your instructors are there to guide you, but the actual learning is your responsibility. Your instructors will give you additional help outside of class if there is evidence that you are putting maximum effort into the course.

In this chapter you will find suggestions and techniques to help you better organize your time and study habits, as well as suggestions for resources to help you maximize your college opportunities. There is no plan or technique that could be labeled as the best and be guaranteed to fit each individual. Learning is a very personal matter and cannot be totally standardized. Therefore, you should study each plan and technique available and then choose the one that seems right for you.

TIME MANAGEMENT

All work and no play might make Jack a dull boy, but all play and no work in college will certainly make Jack a college has-been. Probably the best way to have a short college career would be to "hang loose" and perform only when you are "in the mood."

Success in anything will not just happen. Regardless of your abilities and skills mastery, you will need to manage your time effectively in order to succeed in college. A schedule based on efficient use of time will enable you to include both work and play. When you get a job, you will soon discover that you do not work only when you wish and as you wish. In fact, you will have an organized plan of what to do and when to do it. Consider that being a good student is your job for as long as you remain in school (as indeed it is!), and organize your activities as if going to school is a business.

To achieve maximum success with your time management, you should set a workable schedule. It is a waste of your valuable time and energy to plan a schedule that is not compatible with your lifestyle. Therefore, before planning a schedule, you should consider the following.

Set Goals

In order to create a workable schedule, you must get clearly in mind what you want to do, what you need to do, what you are capable of doing, and most importantly, what you are willing to do. If you are washing your car, your goal might be to have it spick and span by 4:00 P.M., or it might be to rinse it off in thirty minutes. If you are beginning college, your goal might be to graduate in four years with an A grade-point average. Or you might be satisfied to take longer and be happy with a C average. Serious students will set goals as high as they are capable of achieving. Be sure your goals are within reach, but remember that most people do their best when there is a challenge.

Establish Priorities

It is not always easy to do what we should do instead of what we would like to do. When the weather is beautiful after days of rain, it is hard to remember that classes and study should come before an outing to the lake. Keep in mind that many "want to" and "should do" conflicts will arise, and you must decide which gets priority over the other. Most of these conflicts can be avoided by planning ahead and then exercising self-discipline.

Be Realistic

It is not realistic to expect to pass your courses in college and still be able to brag that you never opened a book. On the other hand, few people can find the time (or motivation) to spend eight hours each day studying. When you plan a schedule, be realistic in time allotments. For instance, don't allot two hours for a task that requires only thirty minutes. On the other hand, don't allow thirty minutes for a task that requires two hours.

You should also consider your home situation and your lifestyle. It is possible that your schedule is already fairly well determined, so you have little choice of times to study. If that is true in your situation, you will have to make the necessary adjustments. But if you are free to decide your schedule with few interferences, you should be careful in selecting appropriate times when you are most alert instead of trying to prove you can study any time. Another area that students often fail to consider is the study environment. Simply because your friend claims he can study effectively while lounging on the bed with the stereo turned up does not guarantee that you will be able to manage this next-to-impossible feat. Realistically, it has been proven that a quiet, pleasant atmosphere is much more conducive to effective study.

You should analyze your work and home responsibilities to help determine how many courses you should take each quarter. An already-full schedule does not mean that you should abandon your plans for college. If you are a very busy person who is already accomplishing many varied tasks each day, you probably are already a good planner. Therefore, you may need only to realistically examine your goals and priorities in order to succeed in college.

Make a Schedule

Use the following list to set a flexible schedule that will fit with your activities and lifestyle. At the end of this chapter you will find a sample schedule form to use as a pattern to make your planning easier.

1. Fill in the activities in your daily life that are already routine, such as eating, sleeping, dressing, and working.
2. Fill in class hours, making sure to include labs.
3. Fill in "must do" tasks, such as studying and going to the library.
4. Fill in "want to do" tasks, such as movies, dating, and visiting.
5. Try the schedule for a few days.

6. Make necessary adjustments.

7. Follow the schedule faithfully and consistently.

PSYCHOLOGICAL FACTORS

For centuries people have debated the degree of "mind over matter." If you have ever had a problem settling down to a task when your mind was on other matters, you would probably agree that the mind has a lot of control over your actions. It is important that you be mentally prepared to study. First, your attitude toward studying should be positive; second, you must learn to concentrate; and finally, you must learn ways to remember what you have learned.

Attitude

Of all the factors associated with learning, whether psychological or physical, a positive attitude is probably the most essential. A positive attitude will invariably produce positive results and at the same time make the things you do more enjoyable. Therefore, a positive attitude, which will include a genuine desire to succeed, will help you not only in your studying but also in all aspects of your life. In order to maintain a positive attitude, you should examine your goals and take a realistic inventory of where you are and where you want to be. A good attitude, combined with a mastery of basic skills, will assure you success.

Concentration

A common complaint among students is an inability to concentrate. To concentrate means to focus your total attention, thoughts, and efforts on whatever you are doing. There is no way you can concentrate on your English assignment if you are thinking about the party you are planning. Although there exists no "cure-all" formula that you can follow to assure total concentration, the following suggestions could help you increase your concentration.

1. **Solve as many of your personal problems as possible.** If doing this seems impossible, at least devise a plan to follow and make a positive beginning. Most of us feel better about a problem as soon as we begin to work on it.

2. **Be as physically alert as possible.** If you have neglected a medical problem, you should make every effort to correct it during your next break. In addition, you should eat properly and get plenty of rest. It is difficult to concentrate on your assignments when you are not feeling well.

3. **Study at appropriate times in relation to your lifestyle and personal feelings.** For example, if you study just before mealtime and are very hungry, there is little doubt that your concentration level will be near zero. Although some students enjoy arising at 6:00 in the morning and are alert enough to study, others do not come to life until much later. Only you know when you are most relaxed, alert, and free from tension.

4. **Strive to have as many as possible of your "must do" tasks completed before you try to concentrate on assignments.** If you can successfully manage your home responsibilities and keep up with your study assignments, frustrations will be lessened. Freedom from frustrations and a feeling of being on top of things will free your mind to concentrate.

5. **Use good judgment about how long to study, as well as when to study.** When you realize that you are not recalling anything you have read, it is time to take a break. Few people can give their total attention to study for more than one hour without a short break. (Just be sure that your break does not become a complete stop!)

6. **Be prepared to study.** You should have everything you will need: necessary books, pencils and pens, paper, dictionary, and any other supplies needed for what you are studying. Each time you have to get out of your chair to find supplies, you break your concentration.

Memory

The best memory insurance is thorough learning. You cannot expect to remember something you do not really understand, or at best, understand vaguely. If the information to be remembered is really important to you, your chances of remembering are good. Many students fail to remember because they have cluttered their minds with minute details instead of understanding and seeing the lesson or event as a whole. Also, there is a big difference between learning and memorizing. If you *learn* something, you completely understand it, and it becomes a part of you. On the other hand, you usually memorize something that is to be used at a specified time; when that time has passed, you usually forget it. Therefore, a thorough understanding of your subject matter is a *must* in remembering what you have learned.

STUDY ENVIRONMENT

Earlier in this chapter you learned that personal physical fitness is essential to success in college. In this section, "study environment" refers to your study surroundings and to distractions that can interfere with effective study.

Study Areas

It is as important that a college student have an appropriate place to study as it is for a golfer to have a golf course on which to practice! You should have a definite place to study that is attractive and comfortable, yet your place should not be so unusual that you spend your valuable study time admiring the unique decorations, and not so comfortable that you immediately fall asleep. Ideally, a comfortable chair, a desk (never a bed that doubles as a desk), good lighting, and a comfortable temperature are basic requirements for any study area. Needless to say, the more private the study area can be, the better. If you live with a large family, and space and privacy are at a premium, you would need to plan to study when younger family members are in school and you have the house to yourself. Or you may need to study in the library. If you live in the dormitory on campus, you will need to follow the same advice: Study when the room is vacant, if possible, or study in the library. Sometimes it is better to study in the library than to create conflicts with family or friends that could hinder concentration.

Distractions

Distractions can come in many forms. A picture of a loved one you especially want to be with or a memento of a special occasion might be just the thing to make your mind wander.

Many students contend that they study better with the radio or television playing. What they really mean is that they enjoy the study time more. To prove that it is a distraction, try reading something technical while a television program is on. After a few minutes, stop and determine which you remember more about—your reading or your program. Chances are your television program won hands down. Few people can concentrate on two things at once; therefore, loud music, television, and the radio should be reserved for other times.

If your study area faces a window, you can easily lose your concentration by watching the activities outside. Also, an open door to your room will invite distractions, such as visitors or noise from halls and surrounding rooms.

Some distractions are beyond your control, leaving you with only the library as an alternative. However, some distractions can be controlled if you plan well and exercise maximum self-discipline.

A STUDY PLAN

Many study plans are possible; in fact, a different one is proposed in each study skills book you read. Although they are all stated differently, they are basically the same—a few simple steps you should follow for effective study.

Preview

A preview of any reading material serves the same purpose as a preview of a movie. When you see a movie preview, you learn the title, the major actors, the type of movie (comedy, murder mystery, horror story, love story, and so on), and view a few scenes from the movie. This preview makes you want to return to the theater to see the movie. A book preview serves the same purpose and gives you the same kind of information.

You already do previewing, whether consciously or unconsciously. For example, when you read the newspaper, you do not read all of it. Instead, you select articles of interest to you. How do you select these articles? You preview them by reading the headline and quickly thinking about what each article contains.

Although you should preview everything you read, the thoroughness of the preview will vary according to the type of material and your purpose for reading. For instance, in previewing a newspaper article—reading the headline—takes only a few seconds. When you preview a story, read the title and the author's name, look at the visual aids, and then read the introductory paragraph. Read a few key sentences throughout the story to complete the preview. A chapter should be previewed much more thoroughly. First, read the title and whatever introductory material is provided. Second, note the subheadings to understand what topics are covered in the chapter. Third, if the author has ended the chapter with a summary, read it carefully. The summary will provide the important ideas and will prepare you for reading the material that explains these ideas. Finally, if there are questions at the end of the chapter, look over these to determine whether you should read for detailed information or overall ideas.

Read

You are now ready to read the material. As you read, you should keep in mind the information received during the preview and watch for the key ideas. Read the material in accordance with your purpose for reading, the difficulty of the material, and what you are required to do with the information. Remember to anticipate what is coming next by forming questions in your mind or by remembering the ones the author presented.

Recall

After you preview the material to raise questions in your mind and read to find answers to these questions, your next step is to determine whether you have accomplished your purpose for reading. To do this, you would do whatever is required of you in the way of answering questions, discussing issues, outlining, taking notes, or preparing for a class discussion. This step may be written as part of an assignment, or it may be a thought process to prepare you for the next class. Reread any sections of the material that are not clear or that you had trouble recalling.

Review

To review is to skim over the material you have already studied to refresh your memory. To benefit from this step, you might need to read over your notes or outline, to study the questions you answered, or to rethink the basic points you plan to use in class discussion. If you have done a thorough job of previewing, reading, and recalling, this step should merely be a wrap-up.

TEST TAKING

The mere thought or mention of the word *test* causes some students to go to pieces. These students have what is commonly called test anxiety. A certain amount of anxiety is normal, but excessive anxiety will result in poor performance.

The same thorough learning insurance that you use to strengthen your memory could be applied to test taking. In order to soothe the nerves, nothing works as well as a thorough knowledge of the material that the test covers. However, knowing a few simple test-taking techniques can benefit even the best-prepared student.

Objective Tests

Objective tests are true-false, multiple-choice, fill-in-the-blank, or matching tests. They require a definite answer that is either right or wrong.

Here are some simple tips that will help assure that you will get credit for all you have learned.

1. Look over the entire test before you begin. Be sure that you understand the directions and that you have the complete test. Note the length of the test and decide on your pace in relation to the time allowed. In other words, preview the test.

2. Begin by going through the entire test answering the questions that you are sure you know. This will ensure that you do not run out of time before you get credit for what you have learned. Be sure to leave spaces on the answer sheet for the answers you skip. Flag the questions you skip, so that you can return to them later.

3. When taking true-false tests, look for words such as *always, sometimes,* and *never.* Also watch for sentences stated in the negative.

4. On multiple-choice questions, be sure you carefully read all the choices before selecting the answer. Choice A might be a good answer, but choice D might be the best answer. Use the process of elimination if you know some choices are not correct.

5. On all objective tests, be alert for clues in the questions that will help you answer correctly.

6. When you have completed the test and there is time remaining, go back to those questions you skipped. Give these questions as much time as you can. It is also a good idea then to read over the entire test to gain an overall perspective.

7. If there is no penalty for guessing, make the most reasonable guess possible—after you have followed all the preceding suggestions. However, if you are penalized for guessing, do not guess unless you are reasonably sure you have narrowed the choices down to two.

8. Before turning in your paper or answer sheet, erase any unnecessary marks you have put on your paper. If you changed an answer, be sure you have completely erased your first choice, especially if the test will be scored by machine.

9. Make sure you have put your name and any other required information on your answer sheet.

Subjective Tests

Essay and open-book tests are two commonly used subjective tests. Although the answers are right or wrong just as in objective testing, you are allowed the freedom of expressing your ideas more openly, and you can be more creative in your presentation. Nevertheless, these tests are not opportunities to "shoot the breeze"; rather, they require that you carefully analyze what is asked, give concise facts and ideas, reason logically, and use adequate writing skills.

The following suggestions will help improve your skill in taking essay and open-book tests.

1. As part of your preparation for essay tests, you should become familiar with the words most often used in the directions. Some of these words are *define, explain, analyze, discuss, compare, outline, summarize,* and *enumerate.*

You must understand what these words mean in order to follow the directions on the test adequately.

2. Before beginning the test, read the directions carefully and be certain you understand exactly what is asked.

3. Read all the questions carefully, noting the ones that are easiest for you. Also note the questions that are worth the most points. Use this knowledge, plus the amount of time alloted for the test, to determine the questions you will answer first and how you will need to pace yourself.

4. Before you begin writing, you should make a brief outline. This step is especially important if the question requires a long, complex answer. If you are allowed extra paper, write your outline; if not, make a sketchy mental outline. Outlining will prevent you from wandering off the subject and assure you of covering the major points. Never just begin writing all you know about the subject.

5. Once you begin putting your answer on paper, be as brief as possible, but be sure to include all the necessary information. Remember that it is not *how much* you write but *what* you write that counts. Use facts and logical reasoning rather than vague ideas and personal opinions. It is important that you convey to the instructor that you have a complete understanding of the information.

6. Pace yourself so that you have time to complete the entire test if possible. If you see that you are running out of time, you should either quickly outline or list major points on the remaining questions. By doing this, you increase the possibility that your instructor will give you partial credit.

7. Never turn in a paper without proofreading. Even the most careful student makes common mistakes that could result in receiving less credit. If you need to change a word, draw one line through it (never scratch it out!) and neatly insert the correct word.

8. If it is an open-book test, the same suggestions should be considered. Students often fail to do their best when taking open-book tests because they have stereotyped this kind of test as easy and dismiss it lightly. One of the purposes of an open-book test is to see whether you are able to use the information you have learned. Therefore, what is required is not copying facts and ideas from the book, but taking these facts and ideas and applying them to specific situations.

9. Your handwriting should be neat and legible. If your instructor has problems reading your writing, your paper may receive a failing grade, or at best may receive fewer points.

In the case of an emergency, such as breaking your pencil point, quietly go to your instructor for help, instead of asking other students.

Regardless of the kind of test you are taking, be careful not to arouse suspicions of cheating. Remember that to give help is as grave an offense as to receive help. Study for the test and expect your classmates to do the same!

LEARNING RESOURCES

Although each college is unique in the learning resources available to students, most of them offer the services discussed in this lesson. The most common learning resources are counseling and testing centers, laboratories, tutors, and the library. The most successful students take full advantage of these services.

Counseling and Testing Centers

Counseling and testing centers offer a variety of services. One important service is counseling students with personal, academic, and career problems. Another is administration of the SAT/ACT, the CLEP (College Level Examination Program), and other tests required by the college.

Personal Counseling. The counselors in most college centers are not trained to cope with serious personal problems. However, they can help with minor problems that you might encounter in relation to your college life. In the case of severe problems, the center would refer you to other professional counselors.

Academic Counseling. Any student who is experiencing academic difficulties or who is on academic probation would benefit from a counseling session. Talking your problems over with a trained counselor sometimes helps you to gain a better insight into the cause of the difficulty.

The counseling center also advises students about specific problems encountered when transferring from one institution to another. The center usually has catalogs and other information that you would need before you transferred to another institution.

Career Information and Counseling. If you are in that small percentage of students who grew up knowing what you wanted to do with your life, you can bypass this service. But if you are among the many who still have doubts, you would benefit from counseling and information. Services offered could range from providing brochures on various occupations and professions to making available complicated computer systems that print out everything you ever wanted to know about a career. Regardless of how elaborate this service is, you can depend on getting some guidance.

Testing.　In this area there is also a wide range of services that vary from college to college. The tests available could range all the way from an aptitude test to a CLEP test that would exempt you from certain subjects. The counseling and testing staff also administer all tests that are required by the college. Because you will be required to find your way to this office at some time, why not take advantage of all the services available?

Laboratories

Although the kind and availability of laboratories vary, most colleges have reading, writing, math, and computer labs in addition to the labs required for science courses. Reading, writing, and math labs are relatively new on college campuses. These labs may serve as depositories for materials, as centers for remedial instruction, or as opportunities for enrichment for the more capable students. Regardless of your status and ability, you should investigate the kinds of labs available on your campus and then take full advantage of these learning resources.

Reading Labs.　The reading lab is sometimes used in conjunction with developmental reading courses. In this case, it is an integral part of the course, and if you take any reading course, you are required to use the lab. In some colleges it is operated on a voluntary basis, and students may go in at any time to receive whatever help they request. These labs are usually equipped with up-to-date materials designed to improve all your reading skills.

Writing Labs.　Writing across the curriculum is a strong movement in most colleges. You will find that you will be required to write in courses that traditionally have required little or no writing. Writing labs are usually equipped with materials all the way from "how to punctuate a sentence" to "how to write a thesis." Much of the material is self-paced, but usually a lab assistant is available to give you whatever help you need.

Math and Computer Labs.　In our highly technological society, math and computer training are becoming a necessary part of all students' curricula. These labs will vary from a collection of tapes on basic skills to up-to-date computer labs. As in the case of the reading and writing labs, these labs are often used as an integral part of the math and computer courses. They are also open to students on a voluntary basis.

Tutors

On most college campuses, a tutoring service is available to students who are experiencing difficulty in any given subject. Usually, tutors are students who have outstanding ability in the subject matter and have been highly recommended by their instructors. If you use the tutoring resources on your campus, it is your responsibility to keep your appointments and do the work suggested by the tutor. Remember that whether they are paid for their time or whether they are volunteers, the tutors are doing you a service and you should therefore give them your cooperation.

Library

This section on the library will combine a discussion of the old library system and the new automated system. You should then use the information as it applies to the college you attend.

College libraries vary in size and organization but basically offer the same services. Modern technology has made it possible for libraries to enhance and maximize all of the information resources and services that are available to you as a student. Libraries in colleges throughout the United States differ in the amount and kind of technological support they incorporate. The best plan of action you could follow regarding the use of the library at *your* college would be to visit the library, read any general information pamphlets that are available, and inquire about a library orientation. The library staff is always willing and eager to give any help needed to fully utilize the library resources.

Classification Systems. A system of classification is used in the library to enable the user to locate books and materials easily. There are two major systems for cataloging books in the library: the Dewey Decimal system and the Library of Congress system.

Both of these classification systems allow library materials to be grouped together according to academic disciplines. The difference is that Dewey breaks down the fields of knowledge into main categories using a strictly numeric system, while the Library of Congress system uses a combination letter and number system. You should make it a point to become familiar with whatever system is used in your college library.

The Circulation Desk. The core of the operation of the library is the circulation desk. This is where you will find the library staff and facilities for checking out and returning books. In addition, reserve books are usually kept in the circulation-desk area. Reserve books contain required reading material;

therefore, the instructors request that these books be kept on reserve for their classes.

The Reference Desk. Some libraries have a separate desk (separate from the circulation desk) where a professional librarian is available to assist you with your research.

The Card Catalog/OPAC. The card catalog is an alphabetical card index that lists all the books in the library. There are three kinds of cards: author, title, and subject cards. Every book in the library is listed on at least two cards—an author card and a title card—and most books can also be found in the subject file. Each card gives you the call number in the upper left-hand corner that will guide you in finding the book in the stacks (shelves).

Many college libraries no longer use a card catalog index. Instead, they use a computerized catalog called an On-Line Public Access Catalog (OPAC). Using these computers, you can search for any book in the library by author, title, or subject to find out the call number and other bibliographical information. Some OPACs are connected to other libraries, allowing you to search for books outside your library. You can either go to the other library to get the book or have it ordered through interlibrary loan.

Book Collection. The kind and number of books in each college library are determined by the needs of the institution. Purchasing books for the library is an ongoing process, and the librarians strive to maintain up-to-date and relevant books for all disciplines. In addition to books for academic disciplines, most college libraries have a wide choice of recreational reading materials.

Periodical Collection. Periodicals are materials that are published at regular intervals. Examples are magazines (which contain popular, general interest kinds of articles) and journals (whose articles are more scholarly). Current periodicals are usually on display in a special section of the library. Libraries have different ways of handling older issues of periodicals. Some have them bound in book form and place them in the stacks, while others store them on microfilm or microfiche.

Information in periodicals can be located by using indexes such as *Reader's Guide to Periodical Literature*. The *Reader's Guide* is a multivolume set of books that are updated monthly and that list periodical articles arranged by subject. The entries give you all the information needed to locate the article that you require.

In libraries using an automated system, the *Reader's Guide* is available on CD-ROM, which is an automated version of the same thing. The CD-ROM eliminates the task of searching through many volumes and therefore is more time efficient. Other CD-ROM databases would provide access to journal and newspaper articles.

Reference Books. Depending on the size of the library, reference books may be housed in a special section in the library or may be in a reference room. In very large college libraries, an entire floor may be used for reference books. The reference section includes such books as encyclopedias, dictionaries, atlases, directories, indexes, and yearbooks. These books can be located using the card catalog or an automated system. Reference books are usually not for circulation; therefore, they must be used only in the library.

Other Library Resources. Many libraries have collections of materials on microfilm or microfiche for use by students. Ask the library staff for assistance in locating these materials in the library. Microfilm and microfiche are viewed on special machines that magnify them to standard size and can be used only in the library.

In addition, most libraries have a media resources section, which would house audiovisual materials, music records, CDs, and audiocassettes, along with the equipment needed to use these items.

SUGGESTIONS FOR FURTHER STUDY

- Make a study schedule.
- Visit labs on campus and inquire about the services available.
- Attend a library orientation.
- Research a current event using as many library resources as possible.

NAME _____ **DATE** _____

STUDY AND ACTIVITY SCHEDULE

	Mon.	Tues.	Wed.	Thur.	Fri.	Sat.	Sun.	
6–7 A.M.								6–7 A.M.
7–8								7–8
8–9								8–9
9–10								9–10
10–11								10–11
11–12								11–12
12–1 P.M.								12–1 P.M.
1–2								1–2
2–3								2–3
3–4								3–4
4–5								4–5
5–6								5–6
6–7								6–7
7–8								7–8
8–9								8–9
9–10								9–10
10–11								10–11
11–12								11–12

NOTES and EXCEPTIONS

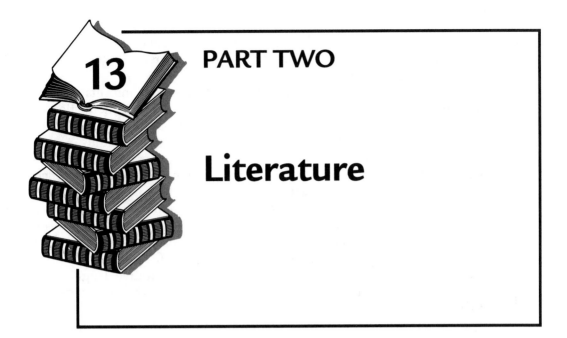

PART TWO

Literature

STUDYING LITERATURE

Regardless of what you intend as your major area of study in college, you will likely be required to take one or more courses in literature. Literature is important—not only because it meets a curriculum requirement but because it can bring so much sheer pleasure into your life. It is insurance against all forms of boredom because it can carry you to faraway places, provide an escape into fantasy, acquaint you with another culture, help you to better understand an otherwise mundane activity, or provide you with valuable information. In spite of having limited time as a student, and regardless of what your special interests and needs might be, there is some form of literature that will be right for you. But in order to truly appreciate good literature, you must explore all kinds, the old and the new, along with literature from cultures other than your own.

The study of literature is actually a study of words, in prose or verse, that express ideas of permanent interest that have been kept alive because of the style and beauty of the writing. It is a study of human expression and personal experience. A work of literature provides insight into human experiences common to all people. At the same time, literature strikes a responsive chord in each of us as we achieve a better understanding of our own experiences and emotions.

Literature takes many forms and incorporates both informative and imaginative writing. Informative writing, often referred to as nonfiction or expository writing, includes such forms of writing as essays, biographies, autobiographies, diaries, and journals. You are already adept at reading expository material since most of your textbooks contain this type of writing. Expository writing is usually concise and to the point; but as you have learned in this textbook, even this material often requires you to make inferences and always requires critical analysis. Imaginative, or fictional, writing includes novels, short stories, plays, and poetry. Imaginative writing is not necessarily "make-believe," but is often truth told with imagination. Fiction requires you to form mental images and to let the writing speak to you through your senses and your emotions. Authors use colorful, figurative language to heighten your imagination and help you to see, feel, and experience the story as they intended.

Most colleges offer a wide variety of literature courses—from the basic required courses to literature of specific historical periods and of other countries and cultures. In addition, you might be able to choose a course based on contemporary writings or even a combination of many styles. In many of these courses, you will have the opportunity to write about the literature you read or even to do some creative writing of your own. Each literature course you take will have limitations on what and how much can be covered because of time restrictions. Ideally, your first literature course will instill in you a hunger for more, and you will continue until you have experienced literature in all its many forms.

The literature lesson in this chapter is in the form of a short story. The short story is exactly what it says—a short story. It usually develops one or two characters, has only one problem, and usually contains a rather simple, straightforward plot. A short story can be an active account of an event, an insight into a character's behavior, a description of something familiar (or not so familiar), or it may merely create a particular mood through a personal experience. Whatever it is intended to do, it is usually fun to read, and if read with interest and anticipation, it can give you a meaningful insight into your life.

The story you are about to read is "Livvie," by Eudora Welty. It is the story of Livvie and Solomon. Solomon, an old man, marries Livvie when she is sixteen and carries her far from her family and friends to live in his home. First, read the story for sheer pleasure. Next, study the words in the vocabulary section of Exercise 22 and determine the meaning of each word as used in the story. Then, read the comprehension questions. Finally, read the story again for a deeper understanding before answering the questions.

Livvie

Eudora Welty

Solomon carried Livvie twenty-one miles away from her home when he married her. He carried her away up on the Old Natchez Trace into the deep country to live in his house. She was sixteen—an only girl, then. Once people said he thought nobody would ever come along there. He told her himself that it had been a long time, and a day she did not know about, since that road was a traveled road with *people* coming and going. He was good to her, but he kept her in the house. She had not thought that she could not get back. Where she came from, people said an old man did not want anybody in the world to ever find his wife, for fear they would steal her back from him. Solomon asked her before he took her, "Would she be happy?"—very dignified, for he was a colored man that owned his land and had it written down in the courthouse; and she said, "Yes, sir," since he was an old man and she was young and just listened and answered. He asked her, if she was choosing winter, would she <u>pine</u> for spring, and she said, "No indeed." Whatever she said, always, was because he was an old man . . . while nine years went by. All the time, he got old, and he got so old he gave out. At last he slept the whole day in bed, and she was young still.

It was a nice house, inside and outside both. In the first place, it had three rooms. The front room was papered in holly paper, with green palmettos from the swamp spaced at careful intervals over the walls. There was fresh newspaper cut with fancy borders on the mantel-shelf, on which were propped photographs of old or very young men printed in faint yellow—Solomon's people. Solomon had a houseful of furniture. There was a double settee, a tall scrolled rocker and an organ in the front room, all around a three-legged table with a pink marble top, on which was set a lamp with three gold feet, besides a jelly glass with pretty hen feathers in it. Behind the front room, the other room had the bright iron bed with the polished knobs like a throne, in which Solomon slept all day. There were snow-white curtains of wiry lace at the window, and a lace bed-spread belonged on the bed. But what old Solomon slept so sound under was a big feather-stitched piece-quilt in the pattern "Trip Around the World," which had twenty-one different colors, four hundred and forty pieces, and a thousand yards of thread, and that was what Solomon's mother made in her life and old age. There was a table holding the Bible, and a trunk with a key. On the wall were two calendars, and a diploma from somewhere in Solomon's family, and under that Livvie's one possession was nailed, a picture of the little white baby of the family she worked for, back in Natchez before she was married. Going through that room and on to the kitchen, there was a big wood stove and a big round table always with a wet top and with the knives and forks in one jelly glass and the spoons in another, and a cut-glass vinegar bottle between, and going out from those, many shallow dishes of pickled peaches, fig preserves, watermelon pickles and blackberry jam always sitting there. The churn sat in the sun, the doors of the safe were always both shut, and there were four baited mouse-traps in the kitchen, one in every corner.

The outside of Solomon's house looked nice. It was not painted, but across the porch was an even balance. On each side there was one easy chair with high springs, looking out, and a fern basket hanging over it from the ceiling, and a dishpan of zinnia seedlings growing at its foot on the floor. By the door was a plow-wheel, just a pretty iron circle, nailed up on one wall and a square mirror on the other, a turquoise-blue comb stuck up in the frame, with the wash stand beneath it. On the door was a wooden knob with a pearl in the end, and Solomon's black hat hung on that, if he was in the house.

Out front was a clean dirt yard with every vestige of grass patiently uprooted and the ground scarred in deep whorls from the strike of Livvie's broom. Rose bushes with tiny blood-red roses blooming every month grew in threes on either side of the steps. On one side was a peach tree, on the other a pomegranate. Then coming around up the path from the deep cut of the Natchez Trace below was a line of bare crape-myrtle trees with every branch of them ending in a colored bottle, green or blue. There was no word that fell from Solomon's lips to say what they were for, but Livvie knew that there could be a spell put in trees, and she was familiar from the time she was born with the way bottle trees kept evil spirits from coming into the house—by luring them inside the colored bottles, where they cannot get out again. Solomon had made the bottle trees with his own hands over the nine years, in labor amounting to about a tree a year, and without a sign that he had any uneasiness in his heart, for he took as much pride in his precautions against spirits coming in the house as he took in the house, and sometimes in the sun the bottle trees looked prettier than the house did.

It was a nice house. It was in a place where the days would go by and surprise anyone that they were over. The lamplight and the firelight would shine out the door after dark, over the still and breathing country, lighting the roses and the bottle trees, and all was quiet there.

But there was nobody, nobody at all, not even a white person. And if there had been anybody, Solomon would not have let Livvie look at them, just as he would not let her look at a field hand, or a field hand look at her. There was no house near, except for the cabins of the tenants that were forbidden to her, and there was no house as far as she had been, stealing away down the still, deep Trace. She felt as if she waded a river when she went, for the dead leaves on the ground reached as high as her knees, and when she was all scratched and bleeding she said it was not like a road that went anywhere. One day, climbing up the high bank, she found a graveyard without a church, with ribbon-grass growing about the foot of an angel (she had climbed up because she thought she saw angel wings), and in the sun, trees shining like burning flames through the great caterpillar nets which enclosed them. Scarey thistles stood looking like the prophets in the Bible in Solomon's house. Indian paint brushes grew over her head, and the mourning dove made the only sound in the world. Oh for a stirring of the leaves, and a breaking of the nets! But not by a ghost, prayed Livvie, jumping down the bank. After Solomon took to his bed, she never went out, except one more time.

Livvie knew she made a nice girl to wait on anybody. She fixed things to eat on a tray like a surprise. She could keep from singing when she ironed, and to sit by a bed and fan away the flies, she could be so still she could not hear herself breathe. She could clean up the house and never drop a thing, and wash the dishes without a sound, and she would step outside to churn, for churning sounded too sad to her, like sobbing, and if it made her home-sick and not Solomon, she did not think of that.

But Solomon scarcely opened his eyes to see her, and scarcely tasted his food. He was not sick or paralyzed or in any pain that he mentioned, but he was surely wearing out in the body, and no matter what nice hot thing Livvie would bring him to taste, he would only look at it now, as if he were past seeing how he could add anything more to himself. Before she could beg him, he would go fast asleep. She could not surprise him any more, if he would not taste, and she was afraid that he was never in the world going to taste another thing she brought him—and so how could he last?

But one morning it was breakfast time and she cooked his eggs and grits, carried them in on a tray, and called his name. He was sound asleep. He lay in a dignified way with his watch beside him, on his back in the middle of the bed. One hand drew the quilt up high, though it was the first day of spring. Through the white lace curtains a little puffy wind was blowing as if it came from round cheeks. All night the frogs had sung out in the swamp, like a commotion in the room, and he had not stirred, though she lay wide awake and saying "Shh, frogs!" for fear he would mind them.

He looked as if he would like to sleep a little longer, and so she put back the tray and waited a little. When she tiptoed and stayed so quiet, she surrounded herself with a little <u>reverie,</u> and sometimes it seemed to her when she was so <u>stealthy</u> that the quiet she kept was for a sleeping baby, and that she had a baby and was its mother. When she stood at Solomon's bed and looked down at him, she would be thinking, "He sleeps so well," and she would hate to wake him up. And in some other way, too, she was afraid to wake him up because even in his sleep he seemed to be such a strict man.

Of course, nailed to the wall over the bed—only she would forget who it was—there was a picture of him when he was young. Then he had a fan of hair over his forehead like a king's crown. Now his hair lay down on his head, the spring had gone out of it. Solomon had a lightish face, with eyebrows scattered but rugged, the way <u>privet</u> grows, strong eyes, with second sight, a strict mouth, and a little gold smile. This was the way he looked in his clothes, but in bed in the daytime he looked like a different and smaller man, even when he was wide awake, and holding the Bible. He looked like somebody kin to himself. And then sometimes when he lay in sleep and she stood fanning the flies away, and the light came in, his face was like new, so smooth and clear that it was like a glass of jelly held to the window, and she could almost look through his forehead and see what he thought.

She fanned him and at length he opened his eyes and spoke her name, but he would not taste the nice eggs she had kept warm under a pan.

Back in the kitchen she ate heartily, his breakfast and hers, and looked out the open door at what went on. The whole day, and the whole night before, she had felt the stir of spring close to her. It was as present in the house as a young man would be. The moon was in the last quarter and outside they were turning the sod and planting peas and beans. Up and down the red fields, over which smoke from the brush-burning hung showing like a little skirt of sky, a white horse and a white mule pulled the plow. At intervals hoarse shouts came through the air and roused her as if she dozed neglectfully in the shade, and they were telling her, "Jump up!" She could see how over each ribbon of field were moving men and girls, on foot and mounted on mules, with hats set on their heads and bright with tall hoes and forks as if they carried streamers on them and were going to some place on a journey— and how as if at a signal now and then they would all start at once shouting, hollering, <u>cajoling,</u> calling and answering back, running, being leaped on and breaking away, flinging to earth with a shout and lying motionless in the trance of twelve o'clock. The old women came out of the cabins and brought them the food they had ready for them, and then all worked together, spread evenly out. The little children came too, like a bouncing stream overflowing the fields, and set upon the men, the women, the dogs, the rushing birds, and the wave-like rows of earth, their little voices almost too high to be heard. In the middle distance like some white and gold towers were the haystacks, with black cows coming around to eat their edges. High above everything, the wheel of fields, house, and cabins, and the deep road surrounding like a moat to keep them in, was the turning sky, blue with long, far-flung white mare's tail clouds, serene and still as high flames. And sound asleep while all this went around him that was his, Solomon was like a little still spot in the middle.

Even in the house the earth was sweet to breathe. Solomon had never let Livvie go any farther than the chicken house and the well. But what if she would walk now into the heart of the fields and take a hoe and work until she fell stretched out and drenched with her efforts, like other girls, and laid her cheek against the laid-open earth, and shamed the old man with her humbleness and delight? To shame him! A cruel wish could come in uninvited and so fast while she looked out the back door. She washed the dishes and scrubbed the table. She could hear the cries of the little lambs. Her mother, that she had not seen since her wedding day, had said one time, "I rather a man be anything, than a woman be mean."

So all morning she kept tasting the chicken broth on the stove, and when it was right she poured off a nice cup-ful. She carried it in to Solomon, and there he lay having a dream. Now what did he dream about? For she saw him sigh gently as if not to disturb some whole thing he held round in his mind, like a fresh egg. So even an old man dreamed about something pretty. Did he dream of her, while his eyes were shut and sunken, and his small hand with the wedding ring curled close in sleep around the quilt? He might be dreaming of what time it was, for even through his sleep he kept track of it like a clock, and knew how much of it went by, and waked up knowing where the hands were even before he consulted the silver watch that he never let go. He would sleep with the watch in his palm, and even holding it to his cheek like a child that loves a plaything. Or he might dream of journeys and travels on a steamboat to Natchez. Yet she thought he dreamed of her; but even while she <u>scrutinized</u> him, the rods of the foot of the bed seemed to rise up like a rail fence between them, and she could see that people never could be sure of anything as long as one of them was asleep and the other awake. To look at him dreaming of her when he might be going to die frightened her a little, as if he might carry her with him that way, and she wanted to run out of the room. She took hold of the bed and held on, and Solomon opened his eyes and called her name, but he did not want anything. He would not taste the good broth.

Just a little after that, as she was taking up the ashes in the front room for the last time in the year, she heard a sound. It was somebody coming. She pulled the curtains together and looked through the slit.

Coming up the path under the bottle trees was a white lady. At first she looked young, but then she looked old. Marvelous to see, a little car stood steaming like a kettle out in the field-track—it had come without a road.

Livvie stood listening to the long, repeated knockings at the door, and after a while she opened it just a little. The lady came in through the crack, though she was more than middle-sized and wore a big hat.

"My name is Miss Baby Marie," she said.

Livvie gazed respectfully at the lady and at the little suitcase she was holding close to her by the handle until the proper moment. The lady's eyes were running over the room, from palmetto to palmetto, but she was saying, "I live at home . . . out from Natchez . . . and get out and show these pretty cosmetic things to the white people and the colored people both . . . and around . . . years and years . . . both shades of powder and rouge. . . . It's the kind of work a girl can do and not go clear 'way from home . . ." And the harder she looked, the more she talked. Suddenly she turned up her nose and said, "It is not Christian or sanitary to put feathers in a vase," and then she took a gold key out of the front of her dress and began unlocking the locks on her suitcase. Her face drew the light, the way it was covered with intense white and red, with a little patty-cake of white between the wrinkles by her upper lip. Little red tassels of hair bobbed under the rusty wires of her picture-hat, as with an air of triumph and secrecy she now drew open her little suitcase and brought out bottle after bottle and jar after jar, which she put down on the table, the mantel-piece, the settee, and the organ.

"Did you ever see so many cosmetics in your life?" cried Miss Baby Marie.

"No'm," Livvie tried to say, but the cat had her tongue.

"Have you ever applied cosmetics?" asked Miss Baby Marie next.

"No'm," Livvie tried to say.

"Then look!" she said, and pulling out the last thing of all, "Try this!" she said. And in her hand was unclenched a golden lipstick which popped open like magic. A fragrance came out of it like incense, and Livvie cried out suddenly, "Chinaberry flowers!"

Her hand took the lipstick, and in an instant she was carried away in the air through the spring, and looking down with a half-drowsy smile from a purple cloud she saw from above a chinaberry tree, dark and smooth and neatly leaved, near as a guinea hen in the dooryard, and there was her home that she had left. On one side of the tree was her mama holding up her heavy apron, and she could see it was loaded with ripe figs, and on the other side was her papa holding a fish-pole over the pond, and she could see it transparently, the little clear fishes swimming up to the brim.

"Oh, no, not chinaberry flowers—secret ingredients," said Miss Baby Marie. "My cosmetics have secret ingredients—not chinaberry flowers."

"It's purple," Livvie breathed, and Miss Baby Marie said, "Use it freely. Rub it on."

Livvie tiptoed out to the wash stand on the front porch and before the mirror put the paint on her mouth. In the wavery surface her face danced before her like a flame. Miss Baby Marie followed her out, took a look at what she had done, and said, "That's it."

Livvie tried to say "Thank you" without moving her parted lips where the paint lay so new.

By now Miss Baby Marie stood behind Livvie and looked in the mirror over her shoulder, twisting up the tassels of her hair. "The lipstick I can let you have for only two dollars," she said, close to her neck.

"Lady, but I don't have no money, never did have," said Livvie.

"Oh, but you don't pay the first time. I make another trip, that's the way I do. I come back again—later."

"Oh," said Livvie, pretending she understood everything so as to please the lady.

"But if you don't take it now, this may be the last time I'll call at your house," said Miss Baby Marie sharply. "It's far away from anywhere, I'll tell you that. You don't live close to anywhere."

"Yes'm. My husband, he keep the *money*," said Livvie trembling. "He is strict as he can be. He don't know *you* walk in here—Miss Baby Marie!"

"Where is he?"

"Right now, he in yonder sound asleep, an old man. I wouldn't ever ask him for anything."

Miss Baby Marie took back the lipstick and packed it up. She gathered up the jars for both black and white and got them all inside the suitcase, with the same little fuss of triumph with which she had brought them out. She started away.

"Goodbye," she said, making herself look grand from the back, but at the last minute she turned around in the door. Her old hat wobbled as she whispered, "Let me see your husband."

Livvie obediently went on tiptoe and opened the door to the other room. Miss Baby Marie came behind her and rose on her toes and looked in.

"My, what a little tiny old, old man!" she whispered, clasping her hands and shaking her head over them. "What a beautiful quilt! What a tiny old, old man!"

"He can sleep like that all day," whispered Livvie proudly.

They looked at him awhile so fast asleep, and then all at once they looked at each other. Somehow that was as if they had a secret, for he had never stirred. Livvie then politely, but all at once, closed the door.

"Well! I'd certainly like to leave you with a lipstick!" said Miss Baby Marie <u>vivaciously.</u> She smiled in the door.

"Lady, but I told you I don't have no money, and never did have."

"And never will?" In the air and all around, like a bright halo around the white lady's nodding head, it was a true spring day.

"Would you take eggs, lady?" asked Livvie softly.

"No, I have plenty of eggs—plenty," said Miss Baby Marie.

"I still don't have no money," said Livvie, and Miss Baby Marie took her suitcase and went on somewhere else.

Livvie stood watching her go, and all the time she felt her heart beating in her left side. She touched the place with her hand. It seemed as if her heart beat and her whole face flamed from the pulsing color of her lips. She went to sit by Solomon and when he opened his eyes he could not see a change in her.

"He's fixin' to die," she said inside. That was the secret. That was when she went out of the house for a little breath of air.

She went down the path and down the Natchez Trace a way, and she did not know how far she had gone, but it was not far, when she saw a sight. It was a man, looking like a vision—she standing on one side of the Old Natchez Trace and he standing on the other.

As soon as this man caught sight of her, he began to look himself over. Starting at the bottom with his pointed shoes, he began to look up, lifting his peg-top pants the higher to see fully his bright socks. His coat long and wide and leaf-green he opened like doors to see his high-up tawny pants and his pants he smoothed downward from the points of his collar, and he wore a <u>lu-minous</u> baby-pink satin shirt. At the end, he reached gently above his wide platter-shaped round hat, the color of a plum, and one finger touched at the feather, emerald green, blowing in the spring winds.

No matter how she looked, she could never look so fine as he did, and she was not sorry for that, she was pleased.

He took three jumps, one down and two up, and was by her side.

"My name is Cash," he said.

He had a guinea pig in his pocket. They began to walk along. She stared on and on at him, as if he were doing some daring spectacular thing, instead of just walking beside her. It was not simply the city way he was dressed that made her look at him and see hope in its <u>insolence</u> looking back. It was not only the way he moved along kicking the flowers as if he could break through everything in the way and destroy anything in the world, that made her eyes grow bright. It might be, if he had not appeared the way he did appear that day she would never have looked so closely at him, but the time people come makes a difference.

They walked through the still leaves of the Natchez Trace, the light and the shade falling through trees about them, the white irises shining like candles on the banks and the new ferns shining like green stars up in the oak branches. They came out at Solomon's house, bottle trees and all. Livvie stopped and hung her head.

Cash began whistling a little tune. She did not know what it was, but she had heard it before from a distance, and she had a <u>revelation.</u> Cash was a field hand. He was a transformed field hand. Cash belonged to Solomon. But he had stepped out of his overalls into this. There in front of Solomon's house he laughed. He had a round head, a round face, all of him was young, and he flung his head up, rolled it against the mare's-tail sky in his round hat, and he could laugh just to see Solomon's house sitting there. Livvie looked at it, and there was Solomon's black hat hanging on the peg on the front door, the blackest thing in the world.

"I been to Natchez," Cash said, wagging his head around against the sky. "*I taken a trip, I ready for Easter!*"

How was it possible to look so fine before the harvest? Cash must have stolen the money, stolen it from Solomon. He stood in the path and lifted his spread hand high and brought it down again and again in his laughter. He kicked up his heels. A little chill went through her. It was as if Cash was bringing that strong hand down to beat a drum or to rain blows upon a man, such an <u>abandon</u> and <u>menace</u> were in his laugh. Frowning, she went closer to him and his swinging arm drew her in at once and the fright was crushed from her body, as a little match-flame might be smothered out by what it lighted. She gathered the folds of his coat behind him and fastened her red lips to his mouth, and she was dazzled by herself then, the way he had been dazzled at himself to begin with.

In that instant she felt something that could not be told—that Solomon's death was at hand, that he was the same to her as if he were dead now. She cried out, and uttering little cries turned and ran for the house.

At once Cash was coming, following after, he was running behind her. He came close, and halfway up the path he laughed and passed her. He even picked up a stone and sailed it into the bottle trees. She put her hands over her head, and sounds clattered through the bottle trees like cries of outrage. Cash stamped and plunged zigzag up the front steps and in at the door.

When she got there, he had stuck his hands in his pockets and was turning slowly about in the front room. The little guinea pig peeped out. Around Cash, the pinned-up palmettos looked as if a lazy green monkey had walked up and down and around the walls leaving green prints of his hands and feet.

She got through the room and his hands were still in his pockets, and she fell upon the closed door to the other room and pushed it open. She ran to Solomon's bed, calling "Solomon! Solomon!" The little shape of the old man never moved at all, wrapped under the quilt as if it were winter still.

"Solomon!" She pulled the quilt away, but there was another one under that, and she fell on her knees beside him. He made no sound except a sigh, and then she could hear in the silence the light springy steps of Cash walking and walking in the front room, and the ticking of Solomon's silver watch, which came from the bed. Old Solomon was far away in his sleep, his face looked small, relentless, and devout, as if he were walking somewhere where she could imagine the snow falling.

Then there was a noise like a hoof pawing the floor, and the door gave a creak, and Cash appeared beside her. When she looked up, Cash's face was so black it was bright, and so bright and bare of pity that it looked sweet to her. She stood up and held up her head. Cash was so powerful that his presence gave her strength even when she did not need any.

Under their eyes Solomon slept. People's faces tell of things and places not known to the one who looks at them while they sleep, and while Solomon slept under the eyes of Livvie and Cash his face told them like a mythical story that all his life he had built, little scrap by little scrap, respect. A beetle could not have been more laborious or more <u>ingenious</u> in the task of its destiny. When Solomon was young, as he was in his picture overhead, it was the <u>infinite</u> thing with him, and he could see no end to the respect he would <u>contrive</u> and keep in a house. He had built a lonely house, the way he would make a cage, but it grew to be the same with him as a great monumental pyramid and sometimes in his absorption of getting it erected he was like the builder-slaves of Egypt who forgot or never knew the origin and meaning of the thing to which they gave all the strength of their bodies and used up all their days. Livvie and Cash could see that as a man might rest from a life-labor he lay in his bed, and they could hear how, wrapped in his quilt, he sighed to himself comfortably in sleep, while in his dreams he might have been an ant, a beetle, a bird, an Egyptian, assembling and carrying on his back and building with his hands, or he might have been an old man of India or a swaddled baby, about to smile and brush all away.

Then without warning old Solomon's eyes flew wide open under the hedge-like brows. He was wide awake.

And instantly Cash raised his quick arm. A radiant sweat stood on his temples. But he did not bring his arm down—it stayed in the air, as if something might have taken hold.

It was not Livvie—she did not move. As if something said "Wait," she stood waiting. Even while her eyes burned under motionless lids, her lips parted in a stiff grimace, and with her arms stiff at her sides she stood above the <u>prone</u> old man and the panting young one, erect and apart.

Movement when it came came in Solomon's face. It was an old and strict face, a frail face, but behind it, like a covered light, came an <u>animation</u> that could play hide and seek, that would dart and escape, had always escaped. The mystery flickered in him, and invited from his eyes. It was that very mystery that Cash with his quick arm would have to strike, and that Livvie could not weep for. But Cash only stood holding his arm in the air, when the gentlest flick of his great strength, almost a puff of his breath, would have been enough, if he had known how to give it, to send the old man over the <u>obstruction</u> that kept him away from death.

If it could not be that the tiny illumination in the fragile and ancient face caused a crisis, a mystery in the room that would not permit a blow to fall, at least it was certain that Cash, throbbing in his Easter clothes, felt a pang of shame that the vigor of a man would come to such an end that he could not be struck without warning. He took down his hand and stepped back behind Livvie, like a round-eyed schoolboy on whose unsuspecting head the dunce cap has been set.

"Young ones can't wait," said Solomon.

Livvie shuddered violently, and then in a gush of tears she stooped for a glass of water and handed it to him, but he did not see her.

"So here come the young man Livvie wait for. Was no prevention. No prevention. Now I lay eyes on young man and it come to be somebody I know all the time, and been knowing since he were born in a cotton patch, and watched grow up year to year, Cash McCord, growed to size, growed up to come in my house in the end—ragged and barefoot."

Solomon gave a cough of distaste. Then he shut his eyes vigorously, and his lips began to move like a chanter's.

"When Livvie married, her husband were already somebody. He had paid great cost for his land. He spread sycamore leaves over the ground from wagon to door, day he brought her home, so her foot would not have to touch ground. He carried her through his door. Then he growed old and could not lift her, and she were still young."

Livvie's sobs followed his words like a soft melody repeating each thing as he stated it. His lips moved for a little without sound, or she cried too <u>fervently,</u> and unheard he might have been telling his whole life, and then he said, "God forgive Solomon for sins great and small. God forgive Solomon for carrying away too young girl for wife and keeping her away from her people and from all the young people would clamor for her back."

Then he lifted up his right hand toward Livvie where she stood by the bed and offered her his silver watch. He dangled it before her eyes, and she hushed crying; her tears stopped. For a moment the watch could be heard ticking as it always did, precisely in his proud hand. She lifted it away. Then he took hold of the quilt; then he was dead.

Livvie left Solomon dead and went out of the room. Stealthily, nearly without noise, Cash went beside her. He was like a shadow, but his shiny shoes moved over the floor in <u>spangles,</u> and the green downy feather shone like a light in his hat. As they reached the front room, he seized her <u>deftly</u> as a long black cat and dragged her hanging by the waist round and round him, while he turned in a circle, his face bent down to hers. The first moment, she kept one arm and its hand stiff and still, the one that held Solomon's watch. Then the fingers softly let go, all of her was limp, and the watch fell somewhere on the floor. It ticked away in the still room, and all at once there began outside the full song of a bird.

They moved around and around the room and into the brightness of the open door, then he stopped and shook her once. She rested in silence in his trembling arms, unprotesting as a bird on a nest. Outside the redbirds were flying and crisscrossing, the sun was in all the bottles on the prisoned trees, and the young peach was shining in the middle of them with the bursting light of spring.

NAME _____ **DATE** _____

VOCABULARY

I. Use all the vocabulary skills you learned in Chapters 1, 2, and 3 to determine the best meaning of the following words as they are used in the story. Write your answer on the line provided.

____*b*____ 1. <u>pine</u>

a. languish   b. yearn   c. plug

____*c*____ 2. <u>safe</u>

a. vault for storing valuables
b. security device
c. cabinet for storing cooked food

____*a*____ 3. <u>vestige</u>

a. trace   b. attire   c. regalia

____*c*____ 4. <u>whorls</u>

a. holes   b. dirt   c. spirals

____*c*____ 5. <u>luring</u>

a. deterring   b. combining   c. trapping

____*a*____ 6. <u>reverie</u>

a. dreamy spell   b. backward glance   c. relevant noise

____*b*____ 7. <u>stealthy</u>

a. afraid of being punished
b. careful not to be seen or heard
c. determined to steal

____*a*____ 8. <u>privet</u>

a. a shrub   b. a patch of grass   c. an orchard

____*c*____ 9. <u>cajoling</u>

a. forcing   b. calculating   c. coaxing

____*a*____ 10. <u>scrutinized</u>

a. studied   b. searched   c. criticized

_____ b _____ 11. <u>vivaciously</u>
           a. somberly   b. cheerfully   c. vindictively

_____ c _____ 12. <u>luminous</u>
           a. expensive   b. luscious   c. shiny

_____ c _____ 13. <u>insolence</u>
           a. modesty   b. tastefulness   c. impertinence

_____ a _____ 14. <u>revelation</u>
           a. vision   b. concealment   c. reverence

_____ c _____ 15. <u>abandon</u>
           a. desertion   b. remoteness   c. recklessness

_____ a _____ 16. <u>menace</u>
           a. endangerment   b. protection   c. consolation

_____ b _____ 17. <u>ingenious</u>
           a. essential   b. clever   c. inherent

_____ a _____ 18. <u>infinite</u>
           a. constant   b. restricted   c. infallible

_____ c _____ 19. <u>contrive</u>
           a. restrain   b. convene   c. create

_____ a _____ 20. <u>prone</u>
           a. propped   b. profane   c. flat

_____ b _____ 21. <u>animation</u>
           a. lifelessness   b. liveliness   c. bitterness

_____ b _____ 22. <u>obstruction</u>
           a. clearing   b. obstacle   c. support

_____ a _____ 23. <u>fervently</u>
           a. passionately   b. impassively   c. festively

_____ b _____ 24. <u>spangles</u>
           a. disturbing loudness
           b. glittering movements
           c. menacing silence

_____ c _____ 25. <u>deftly</u>
           a. daintily   b. dejectedly   c. skillfully

COMPREHENSION

II. Answer the following questions on the lines provided.

1. What does Livvie gain by marrying Solomon? What does she lose?

   _____

   _____

   _____

   _____

   _____

2. In the first paragraph Solomon asks Livvie "if she was choosing winter, would she pine for spring." What does he mean?

   _____

   _____

3. What are the bottle trees? In what way might they relate to Solomon's character and his relationship with Livvie?

   _____

   _____

   _____

   _____

   _____

   _____

4. Although Livvie seems to accept passively Solomon's control over her, the reader senses that her inner feelings are in conflict with this acceptance. What evidence in the story reveals her sadness and longing to be free?

   _____

   _____

   _____

   _____

_____

_____

5. In what season of the year is the story set? Give at least two facts that support your answer. How does the author's choice of seasons relate to the plot of the story?

_____

_____

_____

_____

_____

_____

_____

_____

_____

6. The unexpected visitor, Miss Baby Marie, sells cosmetics. Why do you think the author chose a cosmetic saleswoman? What might have happened if she had come before Solomon was confined to his bed?

_____

_____

_____

_____

_____

_____

7. In what ways is Cash different from Solomon?

_____

_____

_____

8. What doubts does Livvie have about Cash?

_____

_____

_____

9. How does Solomon react when confronted by the sight of Livvie and Cash together? What is the significance of Solomon's giving his watch to Livvie? If we think of the watch as a symbol of time, why does Solomon clutch the watch so closely to his chest? Why does Livvie let it drop to the floor?

_____

_____

_____

_____

_____

_____

_____

_____

_____

SUGGESTIONS FOR FURTHER STUDY

- Write an essay on what you think will happen in Livvie and Cash's relationship.
- Contrast Livvie and Solomon's marriage to what you believe a marriage should be.
- Write a brief biography of Eudora Welty.
- Locate and read other stories by Eudora Welty.

14

History

STUDYING HISTORY

Why study history? Simply stated, analyzing and understanding the past helps you understand the present and anticipate the future. In other words, if you do not know what happened yesterday, you cannot successfully cope with today; and if you do not understand today, there is no way to plan for tomorrow.

If you are a student who regards history as a dull, boring study of facts and dates, then you probably regard everything that is happening around you as dull and boring. History is being made every minute of every day. Everything you are exposed to—newspapers, magazines, television, radio, and even activities in your own home—are manifestations of history in the making. When you study history, you are studying things that happened to people who lived years ago, just as you and those around you live today and make history to be read by others years in the future.

However, the study of history includes more than accounts of day-to-day living of ordinary citizens like you and me. One definition of history is that it is an account of the significant events that have affected a group of people such as that of a nation. It is an account of the true-life drama of humankind. Indeed, it is about people, their struggles and triumphs, their bad times and good times, their conflicts and accords, their wars and peacetimes, their defeats and victories, and their endless struggle to make their surroundings the best possible place.

People have always had a desire to learn about their past. Before history was recorded, stories of historical events were passed down from generation to generation by word of mouth and through the art and music of the people. However, with advancements in printing and research technology, modern historians now provide us with accurate information in carefully written and beautifully illustrated books that are a pleasure to read and study. A modern historian not only meticulously checks all facts and documents for accuracy but also uses other branches of science to aid in the interpretation and assimilation of historical information.

Although facts are fundamental to the study of history, a deeper analysis of events is essential. Indeed, you must know *what* happened before you can understand *how* and *why* it happened. But a history student cannot afford to be content with facts alone. It is not enough to know when World War II was fought, how many people were killed, and who won the war. You must also know why it was fought and how the issues that it settled, or left unsettled, affected nations then and now and how the ramifications of the war will continue to influence the history of the nations involved.

In order to understand history, you should (1) put events in proper perspective in relation to time and place, (2) understand the social customs of the people involved, and (3) see the events or period you are studying as a whole, rather than as a series of isolated facts.

The lesson you are asked to read in this chapter is called "The Gulf War." This lesson was chosen because of its relevance to you, since you lived through this major event in United States history. Before you read, recall all you know about the Gulf War. Perhaps you were watching television at the precise moment when it was announced that war was declared. Perhaps you had a loved one who served in some capacity in the war, and consequently you followed the war closely. Or perhaps you were one of the many who were called to serve in the war. This account of the war relates the events leading up to the war, chronicles the actual events of the war, and then discusses the aftermath and unresolved conflicts. First, read the passage for general information. Next, work through the vocabulary section in Exercise 23 to determine the meaning of the underlined words in the passage. Then, read the passage again for a deeper understanding. Look for comparisons with other wars, the sequence of events and the effects each had on the war, the roles individual people had in the war, and the eventual outcome. Finally, recall and interpret the significant information as you work through the comprehension questions.

The Gulf War

And then, in the summer of 1991, the United States was confronted with an international crisis that abruptly deflated the underline euphoria over the end of the Cold War. Suddenly it became clear that the world was still an uncertain and dangerous place and that Americans could not afford to put their heads in the sand.

Iraq Invades Kuwait. During the marathon Iraq-Iran War (1980–1988) the United States had tilted toward Iraq. Although it was the aggressor in the war and although its leader, Saddam Hussein, was a brutal tyrant who used terror and poison gas against his own people, Iraq seemed preferable to an Iran controlled by the Shiite fundamentalists who had taken American hostages a decade before. American support had helped prevent Iraqi defeat and by 1988 the two countries had arranged a cease-fire. Yet Saddam had not disarmed. Instead, with the help of the Soviet Union and enormous arms purchases from France, Germany, and even the United States, he had constructed the most formidable military machine in the Mideast.

What the American government had not taken into account was that the same fierce urge to control the oil-rich Persian Gulf region that had led to the attack on Iran had not ceased. In fact, there was a new reason for Iraqi aggression against its Gulf neighbors: its need to pay the billions in debts incurred by its ill-starred war with Iran. For months Saddam had been denouncing the rulers of the small neighboring sheikdom of Kuwait for producing too much oil, thereby keeping the price low, while simultaneously demanding border adjustments in Iraq's favor. Yet it came as a complete surprise when, on August 2, Iraqi troops and tanks plunged across the border into Kuwait and brutally seized control of the country. Soon after, Saddam announced that Kuwait would be incorporated into Iraq as its nineteenth province.

Aside from the total lawlessness of the attack, Iraq would now control a substantial portion of the world's petroleum resources and, if unchecked, would be in a position to intimidate the other major Gulf oil producers into doing his economic bidding as well.

The Iraqi invasion shocked much of world opinion. Could the international community permit naked aggression to stand unchallenged? Could it tolerate an adventurer like Saddam having a choke hold on much of the world's petroleum supply? In short order the United Nations Security Council, with powerful American support, passed a series of resolutions condemning the unprovoked aggression against Kuwait and demanding that the Iraqis withdraw from their small neighbor. To back the resolution, the UN voted to impose an <u>embargo</u> on all goods and supplies to Iraq and to block export of Iraqi oil to markets abroad.

The Iraqi invasion forced some difficult choices on President Bush. The UN by itself could not enforce the <u>sanctions;</u> it lacked military power. Clearly the United States, the world's most powerful nation, must bear the primary burden of stopping Saddam, lest his appetite grow with the eating and his example inspire other aggressors. Unpunished naked aggression would frustrate all possibility for Bush's "new world order" in the wake of the Cold War. And there was a more immediate danger. Saddam's troops in Kuwait were just over the border from Saudi Arabia, the largest petroleum producer in the world. After gobbling up Kuwait, what would stop him from conquering the fabulously rich but militarily weak Saudi kingdom, a friend of the United States in the Arab world?

Finally, there was the hazard of nuclear arms. Iraq had long sought to acquire nuclear weapons, and although Saddam's drive to make Iraq a nuclear power had been set back for years by an Israeli air attack on his nuclear facilities in 1981, he had clearly resumed the quest. Now that Saddam had revealed his aggressive policies, the nuclear issue became urgent. If he succeeded in constructing a nuclear arsenal the entire Mideast would be destabilized in ways too frightening to contemplate.

Yet U.S. intervention entailed serious risks at home and abroad. Ever since Vietnam, Americans had been wary of overseas military commitments beyond the defense of Europe through NATO. Would intervening in the Gulf produce another drawn-out, bloody war? As <u>pessimists</u> noted during the Gulf crisis: "Wait till the body bags start to arrive!" And if the war should prove costly, would the American people stay the course or would they demand withdrawal? Withdrawal without victory would, in turn, reinforce the post-Vietnam self-doubt that still burdened the nation and further undermine its capacity for world leadership. And what about the domestic political consequences of another inconclusive Vietnam-type war? Wouldn't the voters hold the administration responsible for such a <u>debacle?</u>

And there were other <u>imponderables</u> as well. What would be the reactions of the Arab peoples to an American intervention in the Gulf? During the crisis various Western "experts" on the Mideast and Islam solemnly proclaimed that Saddam would incite a holy war against the American infidels. The United States would be depicted as a latter day crusader nation moved by hatred of Islam and by a desire to protect its client, the Zionist enemy, Israel. Many skeptics also warned that any attempt to stop Saddam would ignite widespread terrorism by pro-Iraq Islamic groups. And their fears were widely shared. For the six months following the August invasion air travel, domestic and overseas, <u>plummeted</u> as tourists and business people shied away from exposure to terrorist attacks. Finally, there was the Soviet Union. It was still a great power and had been the major patron of the Iraqi military, helping to train the Iraqi army and supplying much of Iraq's planes and arms. Would it accept the _rout_ of its Mideast client?

Though beset by doubts, after consulting our NATO allies and pro-American nations in the Mideast, Bush dispatched a force of 125,000 troops to Saudi Arabia to deter any move by Saddam against that Arab kingdom. Meanwhile, on the diplomatic front, secretary of state James Baker and defense secretary Richard Cheney set off on whirlwind trans-Atlantic trips to line up military, diplomatic, and financial support for the American move. They succeeded in winning the endorsement and promise of troops and financial help from Egypt, Syria, and other Arab nations, as well as from Britain, France, Italy, and several other NATO allies. Even the Soviet Union endorsed the sanctions against Iraq, though the Soviet government remained uneasy about the massive intrusion of the United States into the sensitive Mideast, and refused to send either military help or provide financial support to what Bush soon labeled Operation Desert Shield.

During the fall and early winter of 1990 thousands of troops of the anti-Iraq _coalition_, mostly Americans, and millions of tons of munitions, planes and supplies were ferried to Saudi Arabia to confront the Iraqis and keep them _at bay._ The American troops in the Gulf reflected the new post-Vietnam army. It was all-volunteer; it included many blacks and Hispanics; and, for the first time for any American military force, it possessed a substantial proportion of women, though not in combat positions.

Meanwhile the UN embargo and the oil sanctions failed to induce the Iraqis to pull out. Instead, Saddam's army defiantly dug in along the Kuwait-Saudi border prepared to fight the kind of defensive war that had served so effectively against the Iranians. Playing to fears among the American public, Saddam thundered that his forces would turn any coalition attack into a bloodbath and might use poison gas and germ warfare. He also threatened to use the thousands of foreigners from coalition countries caught in Iraq or Kuwait when the crisis began as human shields. They would be dispersed to strategic locations where they would be injured or killed by coalition forces' bombs if Iraq were attacked. While outraging the Western nations, Saddam sought to win over the disaffected Arab masses by depicting himself as a Robin Hood who would share Gulf oil wealth with the poor and proclaiming himself a champion of the Palestinian people in their struggle against Israel. On several occasions he announced that if the coalition nations agreed to hold a Mideast conference to settle the Arab-Israeli problem, he would consider making concessions on Kuwait. The coalition considered the move little more than _propaganda_ and, reluctant to reward Saddam's aggression by accepting "linkage" of the Kuwait and Palestinian issues, it rejected these terms.

At first Americans were sharply divided over the Gulf crisis. At one end of the opinion range was a small group who believed that intervention in the region represented a shameful instance of American imperialism and war-mongering. A much larger bloc of Americans, while deploring Iraqi aggression, favored waiting longer to see if sanctions would work. Finally, even at the outset, a substantial minority of Americans were convinced that nothing except actual force would evict Saddam from Kuwait and even if he left, if unpunished, he would remain a major threat to peace to the strategically critical region.

The administration itself initially hoped that Saddam might back down if confronted by a convincing threat. To bolster UN credibility, two days after the November Congressional elections, Bush announced that he was doubling the number of American troops in Saudi Arabia. The reinforcements would include crack military units from Germany and the army's best armored equipment. The coalition forces now could not only stop any invasion of Saudi Arabia; they could also evict Saddam's forces from Kuwait if he refused to withdraw them.

The November escalation angered the antiwar forces and Americans who favored waiting for sanctions to work. In Congress prominent Democrats, including normally hawkish Senator Sam Nunn of Georgia, head of the Armed Services Committee, protested loudly. Nunn held Senate hearings in which a parade of military and foreign policy experts warned about the dangers and uncertainties, military and diplomatic, of a ground war in the Mideast. Around the country various peace groups, inspired by the Vietnam experience, began to hold rallies and demonstrations demanding the United States disengage from the Gulf.

During the Thanksgiving holiday Bush went to Saudi Arabia to visit the troops and there concluded, apparently, that Saddam would not be intimidated; that force would actually have to be used. Soon after the president returned home, the administration prevailed on the UN Security Council to go beyond the earlier resolutions and approve the actual use of force against Saddam if his forces did not leave Kuwait by January 15.

The use-of-force resolutions gave many Americans the jitters. To calm a nervous public Bush invited the Iraqi foreign minister to Washington to discuss the crisis while promising to send secretary Baker to Baghdad for similar discussions. At this point Saddam decided to release the foreign hostages. But, as a stalling tactic, he refused to see Baker until the very eve of the January 15 UN deadline.

On January 2 Bush concluded that the use of force could not be avoided. But before ordering an attack, he decided, he would send Baker to Geneva to meet with the Iraqi foreign minister for last-ditch negotiations. He also gave Baker a personal letter to deliver to Saddam reiterating the American position. Nothing was achieved at Geneva. Tariq Aziz, the Iraqi foreign minister, refused to budge and contemptuously declined to transmit the president's letter to his chief. This dismissive act played into Bush's hands. Until now, wary of a divisive debate, the administration had avoided asking Congress for authorization to use force, arguing that as commander-in-chief the president by himself had the power to order an attack. Many Americans considered this a risky abuse of executive power and the administration finally yielded to pressure. The insulting Iraqi gesture at Geneva helped the administration's cause. The debate over the authorization, especially in the Senate, was passionate. A majority of Democrats in both houses urged sticking longer with the economic sanctions; a few questioned the administration's motives. But enough Democrats joined Bush to give him the authority to use force in the Gulf. The issue of peace or war was now up to Saddam Hussein.

War and Victory. Actual shooting war, called Desert Storm, began on January 16 in the early evening, eastern standard time, when, on signal from General Norman Schwartzkopf, the commander of the Gulf forces, the United States and its coalition partners launched a massive air offensive against Iraq. The targets of the initial attacks—conducted by radar-invisible stealth fighters, navy F-15s, low flying cruise missiles, and other high-tech weapons—were Iraqi command headquarters, communications centers, electric power stations, scud missile launchers, chemical weapons factories, and H-bomb development facilities. The results were spectacular. During the next few days the American public saw pictures of incredible pin-point hits on vital Iraqi facilities achieved with few if any coalition losses. A wave of euphoria and relief swept over the nation; the war, it seemed, might be won with air power alone without the need to use ground forces. Coalition troops would not have to face the "elite" Republican Guard who, it was said, had proved deadly against the Iranians during the recent Iraq-Iran War.

Once the fighting started most public doubts fell away. A wave of patriotism swept the nation and Americans took to wearing red, white, and blue bunting and tying yellow ribbons around curbside trees to indicate support for the troops. In the Mideast, day after day coalition bombers, fighters, and missiles raced across the desert to drop their explosives on Iraqi troops, tanks, artillery, bridges, and communications facilities. Much of Iraq's water supply, sewage facilities, and electric generation plants were quickly destroyed. The coalition forces sought to avoid hitting homes, shops, and offices, but inevitably mistakes occurred and Iraqi civilians died.

The Iraqis <u>retaliated</u> by releasing millions of gallons of oil into the Persian Gulf to deter <u>amphibious</u> landings on the Kuwaiti beaches and to <u>foul desalination</u> plants in Saudi Arabia. The Iraqi airforce showed little fight, however, and before long a large proportion of its best planes escaped to Iran where they were interned for the duration of the war. The only offensive weapons the

Iraqis could wield were scud missiles, weapons of terror without military worth.

The targets of the scuds were Riyadh, the Saudi capital, and Tel Aviv, Haifa, and other Israeli cities. Israel was not a coalition nation, but Saddam believed that if he could goad the Israelis into retaliation, their response would so offend the Arab world that the hastily forged Gulf coalition would fall apart. Fortunately, powerful pressure from the United States and the loan of American-manned anti-scud Patriot missiles deterred the Israelis from counterattack. Yet the scuds were an annoyance. One disastrous scud attack killed 28 American service troops in Riyadh. The need to take them out tied up coalition planes and troops.

As the winter days passed Americans remained glued to their radios and TVs for the Gulf news. The media complained that the government did not allow reporters the free movement to roam battlefield areas as in Vietnam but, rather, insisted on filtering the news and doling it out through information pools. But most Americans were impressed with the official spokespersons who briefed the reporters and the public daily. Most effective were Colin Powell, head of the Joint Chiefs of Staff, a vigorous black general who grew up in New York City, and Norman Schwartzkopf, commander-in-chief of all the Gulf forces, a cultivated West Pointer who had lived in the Mideast and fought in Vietnam. Both officers were articulate and compassionate men who did not fit the military troglodyte image associated with the commanders in Vietnam. Schwartzkopf, especially, soon became a folk hero.

As his military "assets" eroded under the around-the-clock air and missile bombardment, Saddam sought to save himself by appealing to Gorbachev for diplomatic help. Though they had favored the UN sanctions, the Soviets were worried about the growing influence of the U.S. in the Mideast and were not averse to currying favor among the radical Arab leaders and masses who saw Saddam as a savior rather than villain. In mid-February, with a ground attack clearly imminent, the Soviets got the Iraqis to agree to leave Kuwait, but only with conditions that violated the UN resolutions. By this time the coalition leaders, convinced that, despite Soviet diplomatic efforts, Saddam would not give in to the coalition's demands, had chosen a date for launching a ground attack; and they were in no mood to make concessions that would enable Saddam to save his military forces and claim victory in confrontation with the United States. President Bush rejected the terms of the Soviet proposal and gave Iraq 24 hours to surrender. Saddam responded by launching another scud missile at Israel.

On February 23 at 8 p.m. eastern standard time, the coalition launched the long-awaited ground assault. General Schwartzkopf had deceived the Iraqis into believing that the coalition would attack amphibiously across the beaches from the Gulf and head-on from the south across the Saudi-Kuwaiti border. Instead the main armored units—U.S., British, and French—were sent far to the west to swing north and then east around the main Iraqi defenses cutting the entrenched Republican Guards and the bulk of Iraqi armor off from retreat north to Baghdad. Meanwhile, Saudi, Egyptian, and Kuwaiti troops bolstered by U.S. marines, crossed into occupied Kuwait.

For a few hours the public held its breath. No one knew for sure whether the air campaign against the dug-in Iraqi forces had been successful in eroding their fighting ability. Some observers believed that the Republican Guards, at least, would fight to the death and inflict horrendous casualties on coalition forces. And once cornered, it seemed likely that the Iraqis would use poison gas against the coalition.

The fears were misplaced. Thousands of Iraqis, waving coalition surrender leaflets, gave up without firing a shot. Where the better troops resisted they were quickly subdued. In sharp fighting south of Kuwait City, the marines defeated the main Iraqi army and forced it into headlong retreat northward. The defeated Iraqis fled on foot or in surviving tanks, military trucks, and confiscated civilian cars and buses. As they retreated they were mercilessly pounded from the air by coalition planes. The planes often had to fly through clouds of black smoke from hundreds of burning oil wells that the Iraqis had ignited before they fled Kuwait.

But the fleeing Iraqis had nowhere to go in any case. The armored sweep around the left end had smashed the Republican Guard in one brief, one-sided armor battle. In a day or two the vaunted Guard, as well as those Iraqis fleeing from the south, were cut off and forced into a pocket around Basra. In a hundred hours the Iraqi army had ceased to exist as a fighting unit and president Bush ordered a cease-fire.

Only 125 American soldiers had died in the fighting in the Gulf in the seven weeks of active air and ground conflict. The Iraqis, however, had suffered thousands of casualties and had lost most of their equipment. Saddam Hussein's military power had been largely destroyed. The victory was one of the most complete and total in the history of modern warfare.

In the Wake of Victory. The Gulf victory brought jubilation at home. Americans felt a surge of pride for their fighting men and women. They also regained much of their confidence in their technical and military prowess so badly eroded by Japanese industrial success and the catastrophic Vietnam War. Soon after the cease-fire, Bush declared that the victory had finally exorcised the ghost of Vietnam.

It also created a new sense of confidence in American leaders. President Bush's approval rating soared to over ninety percent, the highest ever recorded for a president. Americans also had two new heroes in generals Schwartzkopf and Powell. Rumors were soon circulating that both men might enter national politics. There were political losers as well, however. Republican leaders accused the Democrats of poor judgment, if not worse, for opposing the use-of-force resolution and seeking to appease Saddam. The charges were no doubt unfair, but they put the Democrats on the defensive. Observers considered it significant that as late as the spring of 1991, months later than in past years, no Democratic candidate was actively campaigning for his party's presidential nomination.

Yet Democrats clearly had no intention of giving up without a fight. The president's weak suit was domestic policy, they said. While Bush was overseeing the Gulf crisis, problems at home continued to multiply. American education remained mediocre; crime on the streets continued; U.S. industrial competitiveness was still inferior; the economy was falling into a slump; American financial institutions were in crisis; racism seemed on the rise. Winning the war was all very well, but now that it was over, Democrats said, we would have to come back to reality. And it was here, in domestic affairs, that they had better answers than the Republicans.

And not all the country's international problems were settled. With the war over what would be the new shape of international affairs? Would Saddam Hussein survive in the Mideast? Would the Palestinian problem ever be solved? Would the United States have to keep a military presence in the Gulf region indefinitely? In the wake of the victory, moreover, turmoil in Iraq propelled thousands of Shiite and Kurdish refugees from their homes requiring a major international rescue effort to keep them from starving.

And there were problems elsewhere as well. As the Gulf War ended, the Soviet Union seemed on the brink of dissolution with its economy in shambles and millions of Soviet citizens in near revolt against Communism and—among the non-Russian people—against the dominance of the central government in Moscow. Meanwhile, Gorbachev, author of Soviet reform, was himself under siege by critics to his right who wanted to return to the Brezhnev era of Communist party supremacy and a command economy, and critics to his left who wanted a democratic, multi-party system and a market economy. In the spring of 1991 no one could tell where the stresses in the Soviet Union would lead and what dangers they would pose for America and for world peace.

NAME _____ DATE _____

VOCABULARY

I. Use all the vocabulary skills you studied in Chapters 1, 2, and 3 to select the best meaning for the following words as they are used in the passage. Write your answer on the line provided.

_____ 1. euphoria
   a. concern   b. acknowledgment   c. high spirits

_____ 2. formidable
   a. dreadful   b. piteous   c. hesitate

_____ 3. ill-starred
   a. favored to win   b. made to order   c. doomed to fail

_____ 4. intimidate
   a. to drive away   b. to cause fear   c. to make shy

_____ 5. naked
   a. without clothing   b. without permission
   c. without disguise

_____ 6. embargo
   a. a restriction   b. an investment   c. an embarkation

_____ 7. sanctions
   a. coercive measures   b. collective bargaining
   c. destructive practices

_____ 8. pessimists
   a. those who expect the best   b. those who expect the worst
   c. those who make predictions

_____ 9. debacle
   a. exasperating delay   b. exhausting task
   c. overwhelming failure

_____ 10. imponderables
   a. immeasurables   b. improbables   c. implorables

_____ 11. <u>plummeted</u>
    a. plunged   b. plundered   c. increased

_____ 12. <u>rout</u>
    a. concessions   b. defeat   c. road

_____ 13. <u>coalition</u>
    a. population   b. collection   c. alliance

_____ 14. <u>at bay</u>
    a. on the shore   b. immersed in water   c. held off

_____ 15. <u>propaganda</u>
    a. proposition   b. deception   c. proposal

_____ 16. <u>escalation</u>
    a. rapid increase   b. definite course   c. accepted code

_____ 17. <u>reiterating</u>
    a. recommending   b. repeating   c. recognizing

_____ 18. <u>retaliated</u>
    a. repaid   b. retreated   c. questioned

_____ 19. <u>amphibious</u>
    a. day to night   b. air to land   c. water to land

_____ 20. <u>foul</u>
    a. fortify   b. dishonor   c. pollute

_____ 21. <u>desalination</u>
    a. food processing   b. food storage   c. salt removal

_____ 22. <u>troglodyte</u>
    a. reclusive   b. superior   c. inferior

_____ 23. <u>averse to currying</u>
    a. opposed to seeking   b. in favor of receiving
    c. subject to demanding

_____ 24. <u>vaunted</u>
    a. lifted over   b. boasted about   c. closed in

_____ 25. <u>exorcised</u>
    a. excluded   b. depleted   c. banished

COMPREHENSION

II. Answer the following questions on the lines provided.

1. What did Iraq stand to gain by conquering Kuwait?

   _____

   _____

   _____

   _____

   _____

2. What questions most concerned the nations of the world after Iraq's invasion of Kuwait?

   _____

   _____

   _____

   _____

   _____

3. Briefly define the terms *Operation Desert Shield* and *Desert Storm.*

   _____

   _____

   _____

   _____

   _____

4. What were some of the differences between American troops sent to the Gulf War and American forces of past wars?

   _____

   _____

   _____

   _____

   _____

5. What did Iraq hope to accomplish by releasing millions of gallons of oil into the Persian Gulf?

_____

_____

_____

_____

6. Who were the Republican Guard?

_____

_____

_____

7. What happened to the Republican Guard during the ground assault?

_____

8. List five major details you consider to be significant in determining the outcome of the war.

_____

_____

_____

_____

_____

_____

_____

_____

9. What was the outcome of the war? What happened to Saddam Hussein?

_____

_____

_____

_____

10. What were some of the questions left unanswered at the end of the war?

_____

_____

_____

_____

_____

_____

_____

III. *The following events happened just before and during the Gulf War. Arrange them in sequential order by placing the appropriate number on the line before each event.*

_____ Iraq released millions of gallons of oil into the Persian Gulf.

_____ The ground assault was launched on February 23, 1991.

_____ Iraq invaded and seized control of Kuwait.

_____ Troops, munitions, planes, and supplies were dispatched from the United States to Saudi Arabia and were soon joined by troops from other NATO allies.

_____ Iraq was given an ultimatum to leave Kuwait by January 15, 1991.

_____ The UN imposed an embargo on all goods and supplies to Iraq and blocked export of Iraqi oil abroad.

_____ The ground assault lasted one hundred hours and ended the war with a total defeat of the Iraqi army.

_____ The allied coalition dropped explosives with deadly accuracy on Iraqi troops, tanks, artillery, bridges, and communications facilities.

_____ When Saddam Hussein refused to pull out of Kuwait, war actually began on January 16, 1991.

_____ Iraq, under the leadership of Saddam Hussein, treated the people of Kuwait with aggressive brutality and threatened to conquer the entire Arab world.

IV. *Match each of the following persons with the position each held during the Gulf War.*

_____	1. Colin Powell	a. United States Secretary of Defense
_____	2. Norman Schwartzkopf	b. President of the United States
_____	3. George Bush	c. United States Secretary of State
_____	4. Saddam Hussein	d. head of the Joint Chiefs of Staff
_____	5. James Baker	e. commander of all Gulf forces
_____	6. Richard Cheney	f. President of Iraq

SUGGESTIONS FOR FURTHER STUDY

- Write an essay on one or more of the following topics:
  —Saddam Hussein since the Gulf War
  —Problems the UN has encountered enforcing the terms of the peace treaty
  —Effects of the Gulf War on the environment
  —Women in combat
- Interview a person who served in any capacity in the Gulf War and have that person relate to you his or her most memorable experience.

15

Political Science

STUDYING POLITICAL SCIENCE

Political science is the study of the politics and government of a state or nation. It involves the study of laws, organizations of government, and the individual's relationship to these laws and organizations.

The politics of a nation speaks in a resounding way about the people of that nation. Our government is based on democratic principles, which means that you as an individual have a say in how you are governed. This right is one of the many privileges enjoyed by all Americans. However, along with the privileges also come responsibilities. It is your responsibility to understand not only *how* the system works but *why* it works in a particular way. It is your responsibility to keep pace with current issues by watching television; reading newspapers, magazines and books; monitoring political organizations; and discussing issues and current events with family and friends. Keep in mind that it is not enough to have the right to voice your opinion or cast your vote. You should also understand why you believe as you do and how your actions will affect you and others today and in the future.

The study of political science includes more than how laws are introduced, passed, and then enforced. It includes knowledge about the people—the president and the cabinet, Congress, the courts, and all the organizations that work together to form the political structure of our country. It is also the study of ordinary people, such as you and me, who react to these issues, speak out when necessary, and exercise our right to vote. It is not enough to be concerned with general basic problems; you and I must address concrete problems one by one, search for solutions, and then persevere until each problem is resolved.

As in the study of history, facts are fundamental to learning political science. However, knowledge of the political system involves understanding why the system works the way it does and how it affects all citizens. The political system of the nation is so interwoven into your daily life that it is your responsibility to become as informed as possible, to strive to make rational decisions, and to commit yourself to becoming actively involved in the politics of your city, state, and national government.

Most colleges require all students to take at least one political science course. That it is a requirement reveals how essential it is that every individual have an understanding of how the government works and how each citizen plays an important role. However, because of time restrictions it would be possible to learn only a minimum of what you need to know about a subject as complicated and diverse as political science. Therefore, it is highly recommended that you take additional courses.

The lesson in this chapter is about presidential responsibilities and powers. As expected, there are two extremes of opinions. There are some who think the president has too much responsibility and power and tries to do too much; and there are those who think the president has too little responsibility and does not do the necessary things. As you study political science, you will build a foundation on which to form your own opinions on issues such as this one. It is only through the efforts of citizens with strong, informed opinions that our political system will remain vital and grow even more effective.

In this lesson, "The Presidency," you will learn some of the responsibilities and powers of the president. As you study this lesson, keep in mind that the passage is an excerpt from a much longer chapter. Therefore, not all the responsibilities and powers are discussed, making it difficult for you to form an opinion on whether the president does too much or too little. You might be interested in noting that although presidential responsibilities and powers have changed over the years, the desirable qualifications in the president have remained constant. First, read the passage for an overall understanding. Then, after completing the vocabulary section in Exercise 24, go back and reread the passage. After the second reading, test your understanding by answering the comprehension questions.

The Presidency

As he traveled slowly up the east coast from Mount Vernon to New York (the temporary seat of government) in 1789, newly elected President George Washington was showered with parades and fireworks. His whole trip was one long <u>ovation</u>, a celebration of the people's yearning for a strong individual who could provide continuity and leadership for the nation.

Yet Washington and his compatriots were of two minds about the power of the presidency. The framers both admired and feared leadership. They realized the country needed a more effective, centralized government, yet they were suspicious of the potential abuses of power, especially the power <u>vested in</u> a single individual. Given what they had lived through in the preceding decades, they had every right to these fears. Moreover, they hardly wanted to jeopardize the rights and liberties they had fought so hard to win in the recent revolution.

Washington knew the people needed to have confidence in their <u>fledgling</u> government, a sense of continuity with the past, a time of calmness and stability, free of emergencies and crises. He knew, too, that the new nation faced many foreign dangers.

Today, more than 200 years later, Americans still have not resolved their <u>ambivalence</u> toward the presidency. Should it be "above politics" and merely wait for a consensus to emerge from the people and Congress? Or should the institution be clearly political, *leading* the people and *leading* Congress? Should its powers be narrowly defined, or should it be granted broad authority to respond to national and international emergencies? Is an office created in an <u>agrarian</u> society adequate for the post–cold war era in which the United States is challenged to play a leading role in global trade, development, and diplomacy? Can any person meet our high expectations of the presidency? And does the greatly enlarged role of the presidency under these circumstances alter and perhaps undermine some of the fundamental checks and balances in our constitutional democracy? We'll try to answer these questions as we take a closer look at the central role of the American presidency.

WHAT DO WE LOOK FOR IN PRESIDENTS?

The framers perceived the president in the image of George Washington, the man they expected would first occupy the office. Like Washington, the American executive was to be a wise, moderate, dignified, <u>nonpartisan</u> leader of all the people. Washington had served his country in a variety of ways, most notably as commander in chief of the Continental Army for eight years and as an instigator of, and later presiding officer at, the Constitutional Convention of 1787. No one commanded the trust and respect that Washington did—as illustrated by his being unanimously elected as the first president of the new republic in 1789.

James Wilson and Gouverneur Morris, two of the delegates from Pennsylvania to the Constitutional Convention, wrote most of the constitutional provisions for Article II, which outlined the nature and scope of presidential power. They responded to Washington's calls of the prior decade for more vigorous executive leadership. Their proposed presidency was a modified version of the office of governor in New York and Massachusetts, and it even incorporated some aspects of the powers of the English Crown. The framers of the new presidency were plainly trying to remedy the inadequate provisions for leadership under the Articles of Confederation. Shaping all of these decisions, and very much influencing the delegates, was their confidence in George Washington, the man they all hoped and expected would become the first president.

Washington's misgivings about his qualifications and about the scope of presidential power faded as he set precedents and fulfilled the hopes of the people.[1] He was sensitive to the fine line between providing stronger leadership and infringing on the individual rights and liberties of the people. He knew then, as every president after him has either known or learned, that Americans have a strong streak of anti-government and even anti-authority sentiment. We want strong presidential leadership when the times demand it or when it serves our favorite causes, yet we insist that no elected official or governmental agency dare infringe on our rights.

We are not at all clear about how much power we want to vest in the president. When presidents take charge and try to run the country, they are likely to be criticized for trying to impose their will on the nation. More likely, however, they are going to be criticized because they do nothing and, even more likely, to be blamed for whatever happens to the country—for our not having a proper health policy, for a recession, for the Los Angeles riots, for inflation, for the homeless, or for the Japanese selling too many cars to Americans. People who like what the president is doing are often champions of presidential leadership, but when they are skeptical, they point to the dangers of dictatorship.

What kind of person does it take to perform this delicate balancing act? Our Constitution establishes only three qualifications for the office: a president must be at least 35 years of age, have lived in the United States for 14 years, and be a natural-born citizen. Our "unwritten presidential job description"—the one we carry around in our heads—says that a president has to be many things to many people. Every four years Americans search the national landscape for a new superstar who is blessed with the judgment of a Washington, the mind of a Jefferson, the steadfastness of a Lincoln, the calm of an Eisenhower, and the grace of a John F. Kennedy.

Americans want leadership, but what kind of leadership? We want someone who can provide a sense of purpose, someone who can remind us of our shared aspirations as a constitutional democracy and a pragmatic, hardworking, generous nation. Yet we also want someone who can pay close attention to our immediate needs—jobs, peace, prosperity.

Voters sometimes place more emphasis on a presidential candidate's character and integrity than they do on a candidate's stands on social and economic issues. This emphasis is not misguided. Presidents have enormous power, especially in times of crisis, like the Persian Gulf War. They also select the people who run the executive departments and serve on our courts, and thus they have much to do with the standards of governmental performance and ethics. Hence it is important to weigh their character.

We also pick our candidates in terms of their personalities. Can they get along with members of Congress, the press, fellow party leaders, and leaders of other nations? We also ask whether the would-be president displays vision, judgment, a grasp of history, a sense of proportion, and a sense of humor. To be sure, people prefer candidates whose views of issues accord with their own; if they like a person's personality, they trust that individual's policy ideas to be acceptable. A candidate's character and policy preferences sometimes get blurred—if not reversed—in the voter's mind.

In addition, the public wants a president to be tough, decisive, and competent. Voters recognize the need for strong leadership, even in a democracy. They yearn for a leader with foresight and personal strength. Moreover, people want someone who will simplify politics, symbolize the protective role of the state, and yet be concerned with *them*. We want *effectiveness* but also *fairness*. Do we ask too much? The novelist John Steinbeck thought so: "We give the President more work than a man can do, more responsibility than a man should take, more pressure than a man can bear. We abuse him often and rarely praise him. We wear him out, use him up, eat him up. . . . He is ours and we exercise the right to destroy him."[2]

Americans applaud presidents when things go well and blame them when things go wrong. Disasters as well as triumphs are credited to president—Wilson's League of Nations, Hoover's Depression, Roosevelt's New Deal, Johnson's Vietnam War, Nixon's Watergate, Carter's Iranian crisis, Reagan's debt. An exaggerated sense of presidential wisdom and power sometimes causes us to forget there are limits to what presidents can accomplish. Although the tragedies of American involvement in Vietnam and of presiden-

FIGURE 15–1

Who Were the Best Presidents?

A. Past surveys of *historians* have consistently obtained these results:

1. Lincoln
2. Washington
3. F. D. Roosevelt
4. Jackson
   Jefferson
   Theodore Roosevelt
   Wilson

B. But surveys of the *public* turn out differently.
A Gallop Poll asked the American people, "What three presidents do you regard as the greatest?"

1. Kennedy 52%
2. Lincoln 49%
3. F. D. Roosevelt 45%
4. Truman 37%
5. Washington 25%
6. Eisenhower 24%

---

tial involvement in the **Watergate scandal** deglamorized the presidency, the vitality of our constitutional democracy still depends in large measure on creative presidential leadership.

THE JOB OF THE PRESIDENT

The Original Intent

The framers of the Constitution created a presidency of limited powers. They wanted a presidential office that would stay clear of parties and factions, enforce the laws passed by Congress, deal with foreign governments, and help states put down disorders. They wanted a presidency strong enough to match Congress but not so strong that it would overpower Congress. They seemed to have in mind that the president should be an elected king, with substantial personal authority, who serves the common good and minimizes the negative influence of the worst factions. The framers rejected a *plural* or *collegial* executive. They also combined the ceremonial head of government with the actual head of government. The term of office would be four years, and presidents would be indefinitely eligible to succeed themselves.

Although independent from the legislature, presidents would still share considerable power with Congress. The essence of the arrangement would be in *intermingling* powers with Congress. To achieve change, the separate branches would have to cooperate and consult with one another. A president's major appointments would have to be approved by the Senate; Congress could **override** the chief executive's veto by a two-thirds vote of each chamber; and the president could make treaties only with the advice and consent of two-thirds of the senators. All appropriations (the power of the purse), of course, would be legislated by Congress, not the president.

But even a presidency with such limited powers, hemmed in by the system of checks and balances, worried some Americans in 1787. The framers deliberately outlined the powers of the president broadly. The president, they thought, should have <u>discretionary power,</u> so that this official could act when other governmental branches failed to meet their responsibilities or to respond to the urgencies of the day. They were reassured by the fact that George Washington was to be the first chief executive. Still, they recognized that Congress was truly the first branch in making laws and budgets.

A relatively unified Congress could make life pretty miserable for a president. It could, for example, refuse to confirm a president's vital nominations, reduce funds for key programs, and refuse to approve treaties. It could also override the chief executive's vetoes. But the historical record suggests most presidents have enjoyed far greater cooperation from Congress than this implies, and modern-day presidents are more powerful than those of the last century, even though their constitutional powers have not changed.

The Extension of Executive Power

Two centuries later our presidential "track record" is good. Perhaps in no other nation have leaders with so much power at their command so carefully followed the restraints imposed on them by a written Constitution. But to describe presidential power is inadequate. The exact dimensions of executive

FIGURE 15–2

Constitutional Responsibilities of a President

- Act as commander in chief
- Negotiate treaties
- Receive foreign ambassadors
- Nominate top federal officials, including federal judges
- Veto bills
- Faithfully administer federal laws
- Pardon persons convicted of federal offenses
- Address Congress and the nation

---

power at any given moment are partly the consequence of the <u>incumbent's</u> character and energy, combined with the needs of the time, the values of the citizenry, and the challenges to our nation's survival.[3] By and large, the history of presidential power is one of steady, if uneven, growth. Of the 41 individuals who have filled the office, about one-third have enlarged its powers. Andrew Jackson, Abraham Lincoln, and both Roosevelts, for example, strengthened both the institution and its powers by the way they responded to crises and set priorities.

In this extension of the executive power, Congress and the courts have often been willing partners. In emergencies Congress often rushes to delegate discretion to the executive branch; and the legislature sometimes seems incapable of dealing with matters that are highly technical or that require immediate response and constant management. Some people think what Congress lacks most is the will to use the powers it already has. But this is hardly a satisfactory explanation, as the weakness of Congress is not unique among legislative bodies. During the last two centuries in all democracies, and at all levels, power has drifted from legislators to executives. The English prime minister, the French president, the governors of our states, and the mayors of our cities all play more dominant roles than they did, generally speaking, one hundred years ago.

Several factors have strengthened the presidency. The danger of war plainly increases a president's influence on the nation's affairs. The cold war, with its enormous standing army, nuclear weapons, and widespread intelligence and alliance operations, invited presidential dominance in national security matters. Television also contributes to the growth of presidential influence. With access to prime time, presidents take their cases directly to the people. This invitation to bypass and sometimes to ignore Congress, the Washington press, and even party leaders weakens the checks once imposed on the presidency.

Growth of the federal role in domestic and economic matters has also increased presidential responsibility and contributed to an enlarged presidential establishment. Problems not easily delegated to any one department often get pulled into the White House. When new programs concern several federal agencies, someone near the president is often asked to set a consistent policy and <u>reconcile</u> conflicts. White House aides, with some justification, claim the presidency is the only place in government where it is possible to establish and coordinate national priorities. And presidents constantly set up central review and coordination units that help formulate new policies, settle <u>jurisdictional disputes</u> among departments, and provide access for the well-organized interest groups who want their views to be given weight in decision making.

The growth of the presidency is also encouraged by public expectations. Although we may dislike or condemn individual presidents, popular attitudes toward the institution of the presidency remain positive. We want very much to believe in our presidents. Perhaps this is because we have no royal family, no established religion, and no common ceremonial leadership. Sometimes, in an effort to live up to exaggerated expectations, presidents overextend themselves. Wanting to maintain presidential popularity encourages them to make frequent appeals to the general public. These public appeals become bargaining chips that may help presidents temporarily improve their public images and even win occasional fights in Congress. If used too often, though, these appeals can undermine a president's relations with Congress and render the parties less important in supplying policy ideas and in keeping presidents and other elected officials accountable.[4]

Today a president is asked to play countless roles that are not carefully spelled out in the Constitution. We want the chief executive to be an international peacemaker as well as a national morale builder, a politician in chief as well as a commander in chief, and a unifying representative of all the people. We want the president to be the architect of "a new world order" and to negotiate favorable trade pacts with major trading partners. We want every new president to be virtually everything all our great presidents have been, and then some. Rightly or wrongly, we believe our greatest presidents were models of talent, tenacity, and optimism—people who could clarify the vital issues of the day and mobilize the nation for action. We like to think of our great presidents as leaders who could not only symbolize the best in the nation and move the enterprise forward but who could summon the highest kinds of moral commitment from the American people. Such storybook images of our legendary presidents often make it tough for modern presidents to do their job.

In addition to the obvious leadership responsibilities a president has in foreign policy, economics, and domestic policy, seven broad functional kinds of leadership are expected of a president. These policy areas and functions, when examined together, permit us to develop a job profile of an American president.

Presidents as Crisis Managers

"The President shall be Commander in Chief of the Army and the Navy of the United States," reads Section 2 of Article II of the Constitution. Even though this is the first of the president's powers listed on the Constitution, the framers intended the military role to be a limited one—far less than a king's. Congress would declare war and call up the army and navy. And Congress would control the power of the purse and hence the funding of wars. Yet it was very important, the framers insisted, that the people's elected representative—the president—be in charge of the military. This principle of *civilian* control over the military is an absolutely central element in our constitutional democracy.

This principle has meant that in the United States today we do not worry, as do people in many nations around the world, whether the military establishment will accept the outcome of elections. General Douglas MacArthur tested this principle of American constitutionalism late in the Korean War when he challenged President Harry Truman. Truman, an unpopular president at the time, had to tell the popular general to leave his command—and the general went. Many people consider this civilian supremacy over the military one of our most significant contributions to the survival of constitutional democracy. We put the president, a civilian, on top.

When crises and national emergencies occur, Americans instinctively turn to the chief executive, who is expected to provide not only executive and political leadership but also the appearance of a confident, "take-charge" leader who has a steady hand at the helm. Public necessity forces presidents to do what Lincoln and Franklin Roosevelt did during the national emergencies of their day: provide the stability and continuity needed to protect the union and safeguard vital American interests.

Two centuries of national expansion and recurrent crises have increased the powers of the president beyond those specified by the Constitution. The complexity of Congress's decision-making procedures, its unwieldy numbers, and its constitutional tasks make it a more public, deliberative, and divided organization than the presidency. When major crises occur, Congress traditionally holds debates, and almost as predictably, delegates authority to a president, charging that official to take whatever actions are necessary. This is essentially what Congress did when Bush asked for its support to force Saddam Hussein out of Kuwait. And, to a lesser extent, this is what happened in 1992 after the Los Angeles riots.

The primary factor underlying this transformation in the president's function as commander in chief has been the changed role of the United States in the world, especially since World War II. In the postwar years every president from Truman to the present argued for and won widespread support for the position that military strength, especially military superiority over the now <u>defunct</u> Soviet Union, was the primary route to national security. Nations willingly grew dependent on our assistance, which rapidly became translated into a multitude of treaties, pacts, and diplomatic agreements. From then on, nearly every threat to the political stability of our far-flung network of allies became a test of whether we would honor our commitments in good faith. These commitments, plus the fear of nuclear war and the importance of deterrence, prompted Congress to give presidents great flexibility in this area.

Presidents are expected to be crisis managers in the domestic sphere as well. Whenever things go wrong, we demand presidential-level planning and problem solving. When New York City and the Chrysler Corporation were on the verge of collapse in the 1970's, and more recently many of the nation's banks, people turned to the White House for help. When terrorists attack U.S. citizens, people assume their president will retaliate. When a disastrous oil spill occurs, as it did off the Alaskan coast a few years ago, people expect the head of state to step in and assist. When riots break out in our cities, we ask what the president is going to do about it. In many crises, however, presidents are little more than victims of fast-breaking events and forces outside of their control. They are sometimes surprised, overtaken by developments, and placed on the defensive. President Bush, for example, appeared notably less effective in dealing with the 1992 recession than he had been in his commander-in-chief role during the 1991 Gulf war.

Presidents as Morale Builders

Presidents are the nation's number-one celebrities; almost anything they do is news. Merely by going to church or to a sports event, presidents command attention. By their actions they can arouse a sense of hope or despair, honor or dishonor.

The framers of the Constitution did not fully anticipate the symbolic and morale-building functions a president must perform. Certain magisterial functions, such as receiving ambassadors and granting pardons, were conferred. But over time the presidency has acquired enormous *symbolic* significance. No matter how enlightened or rational we consider ourselves, all of us respond in some way to symbols and rituals. The president's actions often affect our images of authority, legitimacy, and confidence in our political system.

Although Americans like to view themselves as hardheaded pragmatists, they—like people everywhere—cannot stand too much reality. Humans do not live by reason alone; myths and dreams are an age-old form of escape. And people turn to national leaders just as tribespeople turn to shamans—for meaning, healing, empowerment, assurance, and a sense of propose. Many people find comfort in an oversimplified image of the president as a warrior-captain at the helm of the great ship of state—liberator, prophet, defender of liberty and democracy, and spokesperson for the American Dream.

George Washington and his advisers recognized from the beginning that the job of the presidency demanded symbolic leadership. They knew that to be effective, it must epitomize the best in the community, the best in our traditions, values, and purposes. Effective leadership infuses vision and a sense of meaning into the enterprise of a nation.

The Popular Need for Leadership. A president's personal conduct affects how millions of Americans view their political loyalties and civic responsibilities. Of course, the symbolic influence of presidents is not always evoked in favor of worthy causes, and sometimes they do not live up to our expectations of moral leadership. "The Presidency is the focus for the most intense and persistent emotions," writes the political scientist James David Barber. "The President is . . . the one figure who draws together the people's hopes and fears for the political future. On top of all his routine duties, he has to carry that off—or fail."[5] Children see our political system as president-centered and tend to personalize and idealize the position.

It would be much easier for everyone, some say, if our president were only a prime minister, called on merely to manage the affairs of government in as efficient and practical a way as possible, and not also our chief of state. But this is not the case. Americans are not about to invent a head-of-state position separate from the presidency. Moreover, to do so would weaken an already fragile institution.

Presidential head-of-state duties often seem trivial and unimportant. For example, throwing out the ceremonial first baseball of the season, promoting Easter seals, pressing buttons that start big power projects, and consoling the survivors of American victims of terrorist attacks do not require executive talents. Yet our president is continuously asked to champion our common heritage, to help unify the nation, and also to create an improved climate within which the diverse interests of the nation can work together.

A Presidential Dilemma. Some expectations for presidents are fundamentally inconsistent with one another. On the one hand, the president is a party leader, spokesperson and representative of a segment of the population loosely identified with a particular party. As such the president not only directs the national party organization but—as chief legislator—also takes specific positions on issues for or against some groups. On the other hand, as ceremonial leader and chief of state, the president attempts to act for *all* the people. A chief executive must faithfully administer the laws, whether passed by Democratic or Republican majorities in Congress. Yet in making appointments and in applying the law, presidents often understandably think first of the interests of those who elected them.

The relationship between these presidential roles is uneasy. For example, usually the chief executive is granted free time on radio and television. But if an election is approaching, the opposition often charges the president is really acting as party chief and that the party should pay for the radio or television time. The same question comes up in connection with a president's inspection trips, especially when they are used as occasions for political talks and general politicking.

Most of the time combining the two roles of chief of state and party leader in one office creates no special problems. We have come to expect a president to play both roles and move from one to the other as conditions demand. The ceremonial role takes a lot of presidential time, and some worry that it keeps presidents from performing their other demanding duties. But it doubtless makes the job more enjoyable and helps them sustain the exacting burdens of their office.

The morale-building job of the president involves much more than just ceremonial, cheerleading, or quasi-chaplain duties. Presidential leadership, at its finest, radiates confidence and empowers people to give their best, to unleash the vast energies for good that exist in the nation. Our best leaders have been able to provide this special and often <u>intangible</u> element. Although it may defy easy definition, we judge a president's success and popularity by it. Still, we know all too well that it is not something that the Constitution <u>confers</u> or something conveniently stored in the White House for the use of each new occupant.

NOTES

1. Glenn A. Phelps, "George Washington: Precedent Setter," in *Inventing the American Presidency*, ed. Thomas E. Cronin (University Press of Kansas, 1989), chap. 10.

2. John Steinbeck, *America and Americans* (Bonanza Books, 1966), p. 46.

3. For a different point of view, see Benjamin I. Page and Mark P. Petracca, *The American Presidency* (McGraw-Hill, 1983), chap. 1.

4. Theodore J. Lowi, *The Personal President* (Cornell University Press, 1985).

5. James David Barber, *The Presidential Character*, 4th ed. (Prentice Hall, 1992). See also George Edwards, *The Public Presidency* (St. Martin's Press, 1983).

EXERCISE 24: The Presidency

NAME _____ DATE _____

VOCABULARY

I. *Use all the vocabulary skills you learned in Chapters 1, 2, and 3 to select the best meaning for the following words as they are used in the passage. Write your answer on the line provided.*

_____ 1. <u>ovation</u>

      a. taunt   b. overlook   c. tribute

_____ 2. <u>vested in</u>

    a. exposed to   b. given to   c. vetoed by

_____ 3. <u>fledgling</u>

    a. failing   b. flexible   c. new

_____ 4. <u>ambivalence</u>

    a. uncertainty   b. indifference   c. hostility

_____ 5. <u>agrarian</u>

    a. industrial   b. military   c. agricultural

_____ 6. <u>nonpartisan</u>

    a. nonpolitical   b. nonplussed   c. nonchalant

_____ 7. <u>recession</u>

    a. intermission between sessions of Congress
    b. suspension of business
    c. slowing of economic activity

_____ 8. <u>pragmatic</u>

    a. philosophical   b. practical   c. predominant

_____ 9. <u>factions</u>

    a. spontaneous groups   b. rioting groups
    c. dissenting groups

_____ 10. <u>intermingling</u>

    a. mixing together   b. exchanging   c. discontinuing

_____ 11. <u>discretionary power</u>

    a. the right to serve consecutively
    b. the power to dispense with any regulation deemed necessary
    c. the authority to make decisions and to act when necessary

_____ 12. <u>incumbent</u>

    a. person running for office
    b. person currently in office
    c. person most in control of opposing party

_____ 13. <u>reconcile</u>

    a. recognize   b. settle   c. construct

_____ 14. <u>jurisdictional disputes</u>
   a. employment issues
   b. harassment allegations
   c. questions of authority

_____ 15. <u>defunct</u>
   a. no longer harmonious
   b. no longer existent
   c. no longer expanding

_____ 16. <u>magisterial</u>
   a. charitable   b. majestic   c. authoritative

_____ 17. <u>shamans</u>
   a. medicine men   b. idols   c. nature

_____ 18. <u>epitomize</u>
   a. define   b. equate   c. represent

_____ 19. <u>intangible</u>
   a. patriotic   b. indefinable   c. integral

_____ 20. <u>confers</u>
   a. bestows   b. confines   c. condones

COMPREHENSION

II. *Read the following statements and decide which are facts and which are opinions. Indicate your choice by writing **F** or **O** on the line provided.*

_____ 1. George Washington was the first president of the United States.

_____ 2. Of all the United States presidents, George Washington was the most moderate and dignified.

_____ 3. James Wilson and Gouverneur Morris, two delegates from Pennsylvania to the Constitutional Convention, wrote most of Article II, which outlined presidential power.

_____ 4. The United States Constitution established only three qualifications for the office of president.

_____ 5. The president nominates the people who run the executive departments of the government and who serve on the federal courts.

_____ 6. All voters recognize the need for a president with a pleasing personality.

_____ 7. Americans ask too much of their president.

_____ 8. The framers of the United States Constitution established a system of checks and balances to assure that no one individual or group of individuals could attain too much power.

_____ 9. Congress is truly the first branch in making laws and budgets.

_____ 10. The media are solely responsible for the president's popularity (or lack of popularity).

_____ 11. The president is commander-in-chief of the armed forces of the United States.

_____ 12. With his command of international affairs, the president is the most qualified person to decide whether to declare war on another nation.

_____ 13. In the event of a national crisis, a citizen's best defense is to trust the judgment of the president.

_____ 14. Everything a president does, from going to church to signing a declaration, is of utmost interest to every American.

_____ 15. According to the Constitution, the president must faithfully administer the laws, whether proposed by the president's own political party or the opposition party.

III. *Answer the following questions on the lines provided.*

1. Did the majority of the American people approve of George Washington as the first president? Give three major details to support your answer.

_____

_____

_____

_____

_____

2. What is a major contradiction to the way Americans think regarding the scope of power the president should be given?

_____

_____

_____

_____

3. What are the qualifications for the office of president as outlined in the Constitution?

_____

_____

4. In addition to the stated qualifications, we want our president to have other qualifications. Identify some of the qualifications mentioned in the passage.

_____

_____

_____

_____

5. In paragraph 1 on page 254 under *The Job of the President,* find the sentence "The framers rejected a *plural* or *collegial* executive." Look up "plural" and "collegial" in the dictionary. Then after rereading the paragraph, explain what the sentence means.

_____

_____

_____

6. In what ways could a unified Congress (especially if the majority of the members are from the opposition party) make the president's job difficult?

_____

_____

_____

7. Have the powers of the president increased or decreased over the years? What factors often influence the extent of power?

_____

_____

_____

_____

_____

8. According to Figure 15–1 on page 254, who has been the favorite president among historians? Who was the favorite of the people? How do you account for the difference?

_____

_____

_____

_____

_____

9. What is the chief advantage of having a civilian as commander-in-chief of the armed forces?

_____

_____

_____

10. Study Figure 15–2 on page 255. According to the passage, what are some of the responsibilities we expect of the president that are not stated in the Constitution?

_____

_____

_____

_____

IV. *Think of some action taken by a president in recent years in which you felt that the president needed to take more or less action. Explain in detail on the lines provided.*

_____

_____

_____

_____

_____

_____

_____

_____

_____

_____

_____

SUGGESTIONS FOR FURTHER STUDY

- Write a research paper on one of the following:
  —President [*your choice*]'s Major Accomplishments
  —The Presidential Election of 2000
- Write a comparison/contrast essay on the presidencies of George Washington and Bill Clinton.
- Arrange a debate among class members discussing whether the president has too much or too little power.

16

Psychology

STUDYING PSYCHOLOGY

Psychology is usually referred to as the science of human and animal behavior. Psychologists are concerned with what individuals do and what makes them do it. In a broader sense, psychology covers such areas as behavior, personality, intelligence, heredity, environment, language development, and social interaction. Not only is psychology a broad field of study, but it also involves intensive research and clinical study in its efforts to understand instinctive behavior of humans and animals, ranging from simple aspects of biological behavior to the more complex behavior attributed to personality.

Before the late nineteenth century, psychology was a branch of a more abstract study of the nature of learning known as philosophy. However, by the late 1800s, outstanding philosophers had shown that the study of the behavior of humans and animals could be studied by careful observation and experimentation. Modern psychologists now study behavior as scientifically as medical scientists study the human body.

Psychology is closely related to all the other social sciences because all social interactions that foster the beliefs and attitudes of individuals affect behavior. The study is also closely related to the natural sciences, especially biology, because psychologists are interested in the workings of the nervous system and the brain that directly affect behavior.

Psychologists are not interested solely in *why* a person acts as he or she acts, but also in finding ways to help individuals understand and control their behavior and to channel it into constructive pursuits that would assure maximum use of each individual's potential resources.

For most college students, at least one psychology course is required, especially if the student is entering a career that deals directly with people. In a basic psychology course you will study the theories and teachings of well-known philosophers and psychologists such as John Locke, Jean Jacques Rousseau, Wilhelm Wundt, John B. Watson, and Sigmund Freud, just to name a few. Through the years these philosophers and psychologists have developed theories, conducted research, and accumulated information that has contributed greatly to our understanding of human behavior. It is important that you study the work of these outstanding people to see how the different theories were proved, modified, or discarded by careful research, experimentation, and observation. This study will help you to better understand the meticulous work done by modern psychologists as they strive to understand the complex behavior of the human race.

In a basic or advanced psychology course, it is essential that you make a concentrated study of the vocabulary used in the textbook and in your supplemental reading. Many psychology textbooks provide a glossary at the end of the book to enable the reader to learn the words with ease and efficiency. However, if the psychology text you use does not contain a glossary, you should use all the vocabulary skills you have learned in this textbook to learn the words.

The lesson for this chapter is "Measuring Intelligence." Intelligence level is one of the things a psychologist is interested in when studying the behavior of a person (or animal). Most modern intelligence testing is done by using standardized intelligence tests. These standardized tests may be individual tests or group tests. The lesson explains how intelligence testing began and discusses some of the earlier tests and the tests we use today. You will find it interesting to learn how an IQ is calculated from the results of such a test. Most of the vocabulary words that are essential for understanding are set **boldface** in the passage, making them easy to locate. First, read the passage, making sure that you understand the meaning of each boldfaced word. Next, test your understanding of the words by working through the vocabulary section in Exercise 25. Then, reread the passage for a deeper analysis. Finally, test your understanding by working through the comprehension questions.

Measuring Intelligence

For much of the twentieth century, intelligence tests have been used in schools. These tests are designed to determine the intellectual tasks individuals can perform. With this information, educators have tried to match instruction with ability. Poor test performance, sometimes combined with other information, has often been used as a reason for placing a child in a special class. Intelligence tests have also been used in the armed services to evaluate the success of educational programs and institutions and to select employees. To understand and evaluate this mental-testing movement, we must first know how the tests are constructed.

TEST CONSTRUCTION PRINCIPLES

Initial Selection of Items. The first step in constructing any kind of psychological test is to select appropriate items—that is, the test questions. The choice depends on the purpose of the test and the theoretical approach of the people constructing it. However, the general principle is that the items should be a representative sample of the behaviors or skills of interest.

Norms and Standardization. Next, the test items must be administered to a representative group of individuals in order to establish normative performance. This group, the standardization sample, must be chosen carefully because its scores will be used as a standard against which later scores will be compared. For example, if the test is being designed for children of varying ages and socioeconomic backgrounds, the standardization group should include appropriate proportions of individuals reflecting these backgrounds.

Still another part of standardization procedures concerns the context within which the test is administered. When classroom tests are given in school—for example, spelling or arithmetic tests—individual teachers may differ widely in their selection of content, their allotment of time for taking the test, their policy on using notes, and so forth. Such tests do not permit direct comparisons from one classroom to another. A child who correctly answered 80 percent of the questions on Mr. Jones's arithmetic test might very well have learned less—or more—than one who earned the same score on Ms. Smith's test. If we are to compare many children from different parts of the country successfully, this problem must be overcome. Standardization of test procedures is used for this purpose. A **standardized test** is one in which the apparatus, procedure, and scoring have been fixed so that exactly the same test is given at different times and places.

Some people feel that one of the weaknesses of psychological tests is the standardization, which does not allow the examiner to provide the best conditions for any one individual. But if we want to use the test for comparison with others, it must be conducted in a standardized way for all who take it.

Reliability. After a test has been standardized, efforts must be made to check its reliability. **Reliability** is a measure of how closely sets of scores are related or how consistent the scores are over various time intervals. One common method of determining reliability is to administer a test to the same individuals on two different occasions. Another consists of administering equivalent forms of the test of items from the same test form on separate occasions. In either case, the two sets of scores are then correlated. The higher the correlation coefficient, the higher the reliability.

Validity. According to many psychologists, questions of validity are the most important that can be asked about any psychological test. Simply, the **validity** of a test is the degree to which it actually measures what it purports to measure.

How does one determine validity? Usually, one or more independent criterion measures are obtained and correlated with scores from the test in question. Criterion measures are chosen on the basis of what the test is designed to measure. Anxiety exhibited in a public-speaking situation, for example, might be a criterion measure for a test to evaluate self-consciousness. If individuals who are visibly nervous when they speak publically have higher test scores than people who are relaxed while speaking, then evidence exists that the test enjoys some validity.

The validity of intelligence tests is usually determined by using as criterion tasks measures of academic achievement, such as school grades, teacher ratings, or scores on achievement tests. The reported correlations for the more widely used intelligence tests and these criterion tasks are reasonably high, typically falling between 0.4 and 0.8. Furthermore, children who have been accelerated or "skipped" one or more grades do considerably better on intelligence tests than do those who have shown normal progress. Youngsters who were held back one or more grades exhibit considerably lower than average scores (McNemar, 1942). Low scores on intelligence tests also predict poor performance in school, and this is true regardless of race or socioeconomic background (Cleary, Humphreys, Kendrick, and Wesman, 1975).

Thus, most tests of intelligence are reasonably valid, at least insofar as intelligence is reflected in school performance, and most are relatively successful in predicting school achievement. This *predictive validity* is the major reason for the wide use of tests of intelligence. You should keep in mind, however, the limits associated with the use of school achievement as the criterion measure. The evidence that we have described demonstrated that modern tests provide valid assessments of intelligence as it is required for school achievement; tests do *not* necessarily accurately measure aspects of intelligence that are necessary for success in activities in other contexts.

INDIVIDUAL TESTS FOR CHILDREN AND ADULTS

All the widely used tests discussed in this section are administered to individuals rather than to groups. Group tests have the advantage of providing information about many individuals quickly and inexpensively, often without the need of highly trained psychologists. However, individual testing optimizes the motivation and attention of the examinee and provides an opportunity for a sensitive examiner to assess factors that may influence test performance. The examiner may notice that the examinee is relaxed and that therefore test performance is a reasonable sample of the individual's talents. Or the examiner may observe that intense anxiety is interfering with performance. Such clinical judgments are not possible with group tests.

The Binet Scales. In 1905 Alfred Binet and Theophile Simon, commissioned by the minister of public education in Paris, devised the first successful test of intellectual ability. It was called the Metrical Scale of Intelligence and was made up of 30 problems ordered according to difficulty. The goal was to identify children who were likely to fail in school so that they could be transferred to special classes. Revisions of the test, in 1908 and 1911, were based on the classroom observations of students that teachers called "bright" and "dull," as well as on trial-and-error adjustments. Test scores agreed strongly with teacher ratings of intellectual ability.

Beginning with the 1908 revision, the Binet-Simon test was categorized according to age levels. For example, the investigators placed into separate groups all tests that normal 3-year-olds could pass at the three-year level, all tests that normal 4-year-olds could pass at the four-year level, and so on up to age 13. This arrangement gave rise to the concept of **mental age, MA.** A child's mental age is equivalent to the **chronological age, CA,** of children whose performance he or she equals. A 6-year-old child who passed tests that the average 7-year-old passed would be said to have an MA of 7. This simple procedure did much to popularize the mental-testing movement generally.

The Stanford-Binet Tests. The Binet-Simon tests attracted much interest, and translations soon appeared in many languages. In the United States,

Lewis Terman at Stanford University revised the test into the first Stanford-Binet test in 1916. The Stanford-Binet was a new test in many ways. Items had been changed, and it had been standardized on a relatively large American population, including about 1,000 children and 400 adults. Furthermore, Terman and his associates used the notion of the **intelligence quotient** or **IQ**—the ratio of an individual's mental age to his or her chronological age, multiplied by 100 to avoid the use of decimals. Thus:

$$IQ = MA/CA \times 100$$

This quotient was a really clever idea at the time. If a child's mental age and chronological age were equivalent, the child's IQ, regardless of actual chronological age, would be 100—reflecting average performance. The procedure also made it possible to compare the intellectual development of children of different chronological ages. If a 4-year-old boy has a mental age of 3, his IQ will be 75 ($^3/_4 \times 100$), as will that of an equally retarded 12-year-old with a mental age of 9 ($^9/_{12} \times 100 = 75$).

The Stanford-Binet test was revised in 1937, 1960, 1972, and 1986. Since the 1960 revision, an individual's IQ is calculated by comparing test results with the average score earned by those of the same age in the standardization group. Statistical procedures allow the average score for each age group to be set at 100, with approximately the same number of scores below 100 as above it. An IQ score thus reflects how near or how far, and in what direction, the individual is from the average score of his or her age group. Moreover, it is possible to calculate the percentage of individuals who will perform higher or lower than any particular IQ score. This kind of comparison is now used in many intelligence tests.

Like the earlier versions, the Stanford-Binet today consists of many cognitive and motor tasks, ranging from the extremely easy to the extremely difficult. The test may be administered to individuals ranging in age from approximately 2 years to adulthood, but not every individual is given every question. For example, young children (or older retarded children) may be asked to recognize pictures of familiar objects, string beads, answer questions about everyday relations, or fold paper into shapes. Older individuals may be asked to define vocabulary words, find the solution to an abstract problem, or decipher an unfamiliar code. The examiner determines, according to specific guidelines, the appropriate starting place on the test and administers progressively more difficult questions until the child or adult fails all the questions at a particular level. An IQ score is assigned on the basis of how many questions the individual passed compared with the average number passed by people of the same age.

The Wechsler Scales. A second set of intelligence scales widely used in assessment and research with children is based on the work of David Wechsler. The original Wechsler scale, the Wechsler-Bellevue, was published in 1939 and was geared specifically to measure adult intelligence for clinical use. Later revisions resulted in instruments for adults (Wechsler Adult Intelligence Scale, or WAIS), for schoolchildren (Wechsler Intelligence Scale for Children-III; of WISC-III), and for children 4 to 6 years of age (Wechsler Preschool and Primary Scale of Intelligence Revised, or WPPSI-R). All these tests follow a similar format.

The WISC-III was published in 1991 and is the third edition of the WISC, which was first published in 1949. Unlike the Stanford-Binet, the WISC-III includes subtests that are categorized into verbal or performance subscales; the latter taps nonverbal symbolic skills. Children are thus assessed on verbal IQ, performance IQ, and a combination of the two, the full-scale IQ. A second major difference between the WISC-III and the Stanford-Binet is that each child receives the same subtests, with some adjustment for either age level or competence or both. The subtests include puzzles, tests for vocabulary, knowledge of the social environment, and memory tasks.

The Kaufman Assessment Battery for Children. Alan Kaufman directed the 1974 revision of the WISC, and WISC-R, and he wrote a well-known book on the proper use of the WISC-R (Kaufman, 1979). From these experiences with the WISC-R, he and Nadeen Kaufman developed a new test of intelligence, the Kaufman Assessment Battery for Children, or K-ABC, for short (Kaufman and Kaufman, 1983a, b). The starting point for the K-ABC was the distinction, derived from cognitive psychology and neuropsychology, between **simultaneous** and **sequential processing.** Simultaneous processing requires that a child integrate different information simultaneously. Typifying this sort of mental synthesis would be understanding pictures, in which many elements must be integrated to form a cohesive whole. In contrast, sequential processing requires that information be integrated in sequence. An example would be language comprehension, where meaning hinges upon the particular order of words.

The K-ABC consists of three scales—sequential processing, simultaneous processing, and achievement—that can be administered to 2- through 12-year-olds. Scores on these scales can be compared with norms to determine a child's level of performance relative to other children of the same age. Measures of children's ability derived from the K-ABC in this fashion are highly correlated with IQ scores derived from the Stanford-Binet and the WISC-R (for example, Knight, Baker, and Minder, 1990).

The different subscales of the K-ABC are particularly useful in diagnosing children's academic difficulties. To see how this can be done, let's consider a typical case in which the K-ABC might be administered to a youngster who is struggling in school. If the child had higher scores on the simultaneous scale than on the sequential scale, one recommendation might be that the child is more likely to learn from instruction that emphasizes synthesis of information rather than step-by-step analysis (for example, learning to read whole words rather than parts of words phonetically). Suppose, instead, that the child had above average scores on both the simultaneous and successive scales, but below-average scores on the achievement scales. Here the interpretation might be that the child has the general intellectual skills to succeed in school; the child's failure to achieve, therefore, may be traced to motivation or attitudes toward school.

The K-ABC illustrates that more precise assessment of a child's strengths and weaknesses is possible when (a) scales are derived from a theory of mental processing and (b) achievement is distinguished from processing. In the future, these features may well be standard fare in all intelligence tests (Pellegrino, Hunt, and Yee, 1989).

Constancy of IQ Scores. One reason that intelligence tests were devised was to predict the outcome of each individual's development. The hope was that a test administered early in a child's life could be used to predict that child's intelligence as an adult (McCall, 1989). What happens when test scores obtained by children are correlated with later performance? Studies clearly show that although the relation increases progressively as time of testing approaches maturity, even tests obtained during childhood predict later performance when data for groups of people are examined.

These results at first appear to support the idea that intelligence is relatively fixed. However, when individual performance over time is examined, we see that constancy is not a hard-and-fast rule. For example, in one study in which children were tested several times between 6 and 18 years of age, almost 60 percent of the children changed by 15 or more IQ points (Honzik, MacFarland, and Allen, 1948).

In another study that involved repeated assessment of subjects' IQ scores, nearly half the children had approximately the same IQ scores at each assessment. For the remaining children, some had IQs that increased during childhood but decreased in adolescence; others declined steadily throughout childhood and adolescence; still others declined during childhood but increased in adolescence (McCall, Appelbaum, and Hogarty, 1973).

Thus, although IQ is often relatively stable throughout childhood and adolescence, this is definitely not the only pattern. For many children, IQ will change—both up and down—as they develop. As we shall see later in this chapter, heredity and environment are both implicated in these patterns.

REFERENCES

CLEARY, T. A., HUMPHREYS, L. G., KENDRICK, S. A., and WESMAN, A. (1975). Educational uses of tests with disadvantaged students. *American Psychologist, 30,* 15–41.

HONZIK, M. P., MACFARLAND, J. W., and ALLEN, L. (1948). The stability of mental test performance between 2 and 18 years. *Journal of Experimental Education, 17,* 309–324.

KAUFMAN, A. S. (1979). *Intelligence testing with the WISC-R.* New York: Wiley.

KAUFMAN, A. S. and KAUFMAN, N. L. (1983a). *K-ABC administration and scoring manual* Circle Pines, Minn.: American Guidance Service.

KAUFMAN, A. S. and KAUFMAN, N. L. (1983b). *K-ABC interpretive manual.* Circle Pines, Minn.: American Guidance Service.

KNIGHT, B. C., BAKER, E. H. and MINDER, C. C. (1990). Concurrent validity of the Stanford-Binet: Fourth Edition and Kaufman Assessment Battery for children with learning disabled students. *Psychology in the Schools, 27,* 116–125.

MCCALL, R. B. (1989). Commentary. *Human Development, 32,* 177–186.

MCCALL, R. B., APPLEBAUM, M. I., and HOGARTY, P. S. (1973). Developmental changes in mental performance. *Monographs of the Society for Research in Child Development, 38* (Whole No. 150).

MCNEMAR, Q. (1942). *The revision of the Stanford-Binet Scale: An analysis of the standardization data.* Boston: Houghton Mifflin.

PELLEGRINO, J. W., HUNT, E. B., and YEE, P. (1989). Assessment and modeling of information coordinatin abilities. In R. Kanfer, P. L. Acherman, and R. Cudeck (Eds.), *Abilities, motivation and methodology: The Minnesota symposium on learning and individual differences.* Hillsdale, N.J.: Lawrence Erlbaum.

EXERCISE 25: Measuring Intelligence

NAME _____ **DATE** _____

VOCABULARY

I. *Read the sentences, and then fill in the blanks with one of the terms listed below.*

intelligence test   mental age
achievement test   reliability
standardized test   validity
intelligence quotient (IQ)   simultaneous processing
chronological age   sequential processing

1. A _____ is one in which the apparatus, procedure, and scoring have been fixed so that exactly the same test is given at different times and places.

2. A person's _____ is the number of months or years since birth.

3. _____ is a type of mental activity that requires a person to integrate more than one kind of information at the same time.

4. A test designed to determine the intellectual tasks that individuals can perform is known as an _____.

5. The formula for determining a person's _____ is MA/CA × 100.

6. The _____ of a test is the degree to which it actually measures what it is supposed to measure.

7. A child's _____ is equivalent to the chronological age of children whose performance he or she equals on an intelligence test.

8. A test that uses _____ requires that information be integrated in sequence.

9. A test that gives consistent scores over various time intervals is said to have a high degree of _____.

10. An _____ measures levels of actual performance.

COMPREHENSION

II. Fill in the blanks and/or complete the following sentences.

1. The first intelligence test was devised in _____ by _____ and was called the _____.

2. The purpose of this first intelligence test was to

_____

3. The test was revised in _____ and called the _____ test.

4. The test you named in sentence 3 was revised again in _____. Then in _____ , it was again revised by _____ and was called the _____ , the name it is known by today.

5. This test (just mentioned) determines a person's intelligence quotient, or IQ, on the basis of the formula _____.

6. If a 10-year-old boy has a mental age of 8, his IQ will be

   _____.

7. Another set of intelligence scales, first called the Wechsler-Bellevue, was published in 1939. This test had been revised into the following:

   WAIS or _____ , WISC-III or

   _____ , and WPPSI-R or

   _____.

8. Alan and Nadeen Kaufman developed the Kaufman Assessment Battery for Children, or K-ABC, that consists of three scales:

   _____

   _____ .

9. Whereas the Stanford-Binet test is primarily designed to measure

   _____ , the Kaufman Assessment Battery is designed

   to measure _____.

10. The conclusion drawn in the last paragraph in the selection supports the

   theory that IQ is determined by both _____ and

   _____.

III. *Answer the following questions on the lines provided.*

1. How is the reliability of a test determined?

   _____

   _____

   _____

   _____

2. How is the validity of a test determined?

   _____

   _____

_____

_____

3. What is the major reason intelligence tests are widely used?

_____

_____

4. What is the major limitation of intelligence tests?

_____

_____

5. What are the major advantages of an individual test versus a group test?

_____

_____

_____

_____

SUGGESTIONS FOR FURTHER STUDY

- Write an essay on the advantages and/or disadvantages of using intelligence tests in the workplace.
- From the moment they enter school, children are subjected to a variety of intelligence and achievement tests. Some psychologists and educators view such testing as harmful. Using the _Reader's Guide to Periodical Literature_ and similar resources in your library, find and summarize some of the arguments against these tests. Follow your instructor's directions for documenting your sources.
- Most people have at least one personal success story or horror story to tell about a test-taking experience. Write a short essay describing your most memorable testing experience.

Biology

STUDYING BIOLOGY

Biology is the study of living things—from the giant sequoia tree to a thin blade of grass, from the majestic blue whale to the luminescent firefly, from complex humans to a tiny atom. The study of biology explores how these living things develop, grow, function, and reproduce. Biology is such a broad field that most biologists specialize, thus creating many branches and specialized areas of study. Each of these deals with a specific form of life. A few examples are bacteriology, which deals with the study of bacteria; marine biology, which deals with ocean life; and microbiology, which deals with microscopic organisms. In other words, one biologist might be devoting his or her time to studying a rare animal on the verge of extinction, while another is searching for a cure for cancer.

Biological knowledge dates back to prehistoric times when people learned to grow plants and raise animals for food. Each of the early efforts paved the way for further study and accumulation of information until it was realized that it is possible for people to discover and understand the natural laws that govern living plants and animals.

Biology, in any of its many specialized areas, is a truly scientific study in that all its information is based on facts gathered through careful observation, controlled experimentation, and critical evaluation. Biological study and research affect our lives in numerous ways. It has made our lives better by helping us understand the human body with all of its complexities, by discovering new drugs and cures for diseases, by developing improved seeds and plants to foster better agricultural productivity, and by introducing new methods of conservation to aid in protecting our wildlife.

To study biology will require your best, most intensive reading and study skills, because it is so detailed and deals with so many complex relationships and processes. For many students, the vocabulary will require an extra amount of concentration. As you read biology texts, watch for definitions of key words in the context of the writing. This practice is especially important in introductory biology courses because you will need an exact definition in order to understand the material and to build a vocabulary for future biology courses. Many biology books contain a glossary in the back of the book to further aid you in learning the vocabulary. If a glossary is not provided, use your dictionary.

A laboratory is usually an integral part of a biology course. Just as experimentation is a vital part of biological research, it is vital to you as a biology student. In the lab you are provided the opportunity to conduct experiments and engage in activities that will reinforce the information that you learn in class and from your biology textbook.

In most areas of college study, at least one or two courses in biology are required as part of the core curriculum. Many require specialized biology courses such as microbiology, anatomy, and physiology. In some colleges you are limited to only a few choices, while in some large colleges and universities you can choose from many specialized courses. In either case, you will have the opportunity to choose a course that is of special interest to you.

The lesson chosen for this chapter deals with immunity. The human immune system has been highlighted in the news for the past few years because of the spread of a disease known as Acquired Immune Deficiency Syndrome (AIDS). Read the passage for general information, paying close attention to the definition of vocabulary terms. Then, reinforce this learning by working through the vocabulary section in Exercise 26. You will need to refer back to the passage to be sure you know the exact meaning of each word or term as it is used in the context. Next, reread for more detailed information. Note how much easier it is to understand the passage when you know the vocabulary. Finally, check your in-depth knowledge by answering the comprehension questions.

Immunity

WHAT IS IMMUNITY?

The word *immune* was originally used to refer to people who were exempt from military service or the payment of taxes (from the Latin *immunis,* "free of taxes or burden"). The term was later applied to individuals who did not suffer further attacks of smallpox or plague once they had the disease and survived. In the broader sense, **immunity** refers to the resistance of a host organism to invasion by foreign organisms or to the effects of their products. There are two main types of immunity: nonspecific immunity, also called natural resistance, and specific immunity (Fig. 17–1).

FIGURE 17–1 Types of Immunity

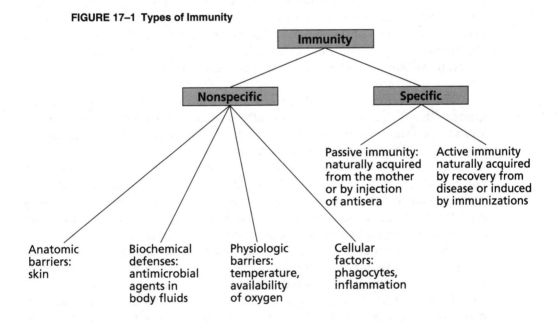

NONSPECIFIC IMMUNITY

Nonspecific immunity refers to the capacity of normal organisms to remain relatively unharmed by, or immune to, a variety of harmful agents present in the environment. This resistance to infections by microorganisms (bacteria, viruses, fungi, and protozoa) is due to anatomic, biochemical, and physiologic features of a species that represent primary and secondary lines of defense.

Human Skin

Because it covers the whole body, the skin is probably the body's most effective defense system against infection. The skin is an organ, the body's largest and one of its most important. Like all organ systems, it consists of various kinds of tissues. It is a complex organ consisting of several layers. Human skin is composed of two main layers, the **dermis** (from the Greek *derma*, "skin") and the overlying **epidermis.**

The Dermis. The dermis is a connective tissue layer well supplied with blood vessels, nerves, and sensory receptors. Glands and hair follicles are located deep in the dermis, although both have dermal and epidermal components. Hair follicles are supplied with smooth muscle fibers capable of making hair "stand on end" and producing "goose flesh." Underlying the dermis is a subcutaneous layer (from the Latin *sub*, "below," and *cutis*, "skin") of loose connective tissue containing many adipocytes (fat cells).

The Epidermis. The epidermis is composed of several layers that intergrade with each other. All of them are the products of the innermost layer, the **stratum germinativum.** The cuboidal cells of lowermost portion have central nuclei, and their organelles exhibit no specializations. The layer just above them, the **stratum spinosum,** is also composed of cuboidal cells. The cytoplasm of these cells contains bundles of fibers that converge on specific areas of the plasma membrane to form desmosomes. These intercellular connections are believed to be responsible for the cohesion among cells in the epidermis and to protect against loss of epidermal cells by abrasion.

The cells of the third layer, the **stratum granulosum,** are flattened and polygonal, also with centrally placed nuclei. They contain a well-developed Golgi complex and endoplasmic reticulum and produce a special sulfur-containing protein, **keratin.** This tough, water-repellent material is the primary constituent not only of the outer covering of the skin but of hair, nails, claws, and other secretory products of the epidermis. The stratum granulosum also synthesizes other complex molecules. But, unlike keratin, they are stored in membrane-bound granules.

The two outer layers of the skin, the **stratum lucidum** and the **stratum corneum,** are composed of flat, dead cells. They are continually worn away and replaced from below. This is what happens in the case of dandruff, a normal phenomenon. Dandruff is nothing but the dead cells that flake off. These outer layers are rich in keratin, mucopolysaccharides, and phospholipids which render them resistant to abrasion and relatively impermeable to water. Thus, they form a protective layer over the vulnerable living cells beneath them.

The Skin as a Physical Barrier

The scaly skin of lizards and snakes, the feathery skin of birds, and the hairy skin of mammals have a common evolutionary origin and serve many of the same functions. The skin has the following remarkable qualities and important functions:

1. It protects against invasion by microorganisms, parasites, fungi, and other disease organisms. Its tough second major layer, the dermis, also protects against cuts and blows. The dermis of animal skins can be tanned and used as leather.
2. When cut or otherwise injured, the skin regenerates.
3. The skin helps regulate body temperature. A layer of fat cells is located in the loose connective tissue just below the skin. This layer is especially prominent in some animals where it acts as an insulator. In animals with sweat glands, the body is cooled by the evaporation of sweat from the skin's surface. The blood vessels in the skin dilate in warm weather, bringing blood to the body surface and allowing body heat to be radiated into the environment. They constrict in cold weather, conserving body heat. The skin is thus an important homeostatic organ for the control of body temperature.
4. The skin blood vessels also contribute significantly to the control of blood pressure.
5. In mammals, epidermal cells produce cells that are modified to form hair, spines, nails, claws, hooves, horns, and scales. In birds, such specializations include scales, feathers, beak, and claws.
6. Some regions of the skin have special functions. For example, the friction ridges that form fingerprints and palm prints permit tight gripping of objects, especially valuable to an animal that swings by its hands from branches. Calluses form in response to irritation and thereby protect the hands and feet against excessive wear and injury.
7. Sebaceous glands at the base of hairs produce a fatty substance called sebum which keeps the skin and hair supple and prevents damage caused by drying.
8. The skin can be stretched. For example, it is stretched during pregnancy but comes back to its original form after delivery.

9. Human skin is pigmented. Pigment-bearing cells called **melanocytes** are located deep in the epithelium. The melanocytes expand and inject granules of the pigment melanin into epidermal cells in response to exposure to sunlight, shielding the deeper layers against ultraviolet rays. Pigmentation varies among human beings according to the amount of pigment synthesized by their melanocytes, not the number of melanocytes they possess. Pigmentation in human populations is directly related to the annual amount and intensity of sunlight and is the result of evolution. Dark skin is an advantageous trait in tropical regions. An albino, an individual unable to synthesize any pigment, born in the tropics is strongly selected against; only extreme care to avoid the sun can save an albino's life in such an environment.

10. The skin is richly supplied with sensory nerve endings, receptors that obtain information about the outside world and convey it to the nervous system.

11. Human skin has two types of sweat glands. The most numerous are the exocrine glands (those which secrete their products into ducts), which secrete water containing some dissolved material. The less numerous apocrine glands (those which secrete their products directly into tissue fluid or blood) exude a milky, odorous secretion, usually in response to stress or sexual excitement, and are found only in the armpits, navel, anogenital area, nipples, and ears. They are far more numerous in women than in men. Mammary glands, from which mammals derive their name, are believed to be modified sweat glands.

The primary defense system of the skin is enhanced by various kinds of microorganisms that live on the skin. These microorganisms provide what is known as **bacterial antagonism,** the inhibition of growth and proliferation of certain other microorganisms that might be harmful. Bacterial antagonism is based on chemical by-products of cellular metabolism, including several kinds of acids. Sweat, another kind of substance found on the skin of mammals, also has microbicidal properties (i.e., the ability to destroy very minute organisms, or microbes).

Moist mucous membranes found in various parts of the body, especially those lining the respiratory tract, act to trap invading microbes. Mucus also contains microbicidal substances. As a result of a ciliary action of the linings of the respiratory tract which brings the trapped material up into the mouth and the sucking action of the mouth, the mucus is normally carried back into the throat, where it is swallowed.

The gastrointestinal tract provides an internal barrier against microbes, supplemented by microbicidal substances in saliva and other digestive secretions. Furthermore, the high acidity of gastric juice kills most organisms that enter the stomach.

Biochemical Defenses

If an organism is able to penetrate the skin, it encounters a series of secondary defense mechanisms, including a variety of biochemical defenses. The body contains a number of substances that kill microbes. They comprise a second line of defense. One of these substances is **lysozyme,** an enzyme that is found in tissues and is highly effective in breaking down a particular kind of chemical in the cell walls of many bacteria. Another defensive substance is **beta lysin,** which is active against aerobic bacilli that form reproductive bodies called spores. Beta lysin is usually present in low levels in human blood, but its concentration greatly increases during the acute phase of an infectious disease. A third defense molecule, which has received considerable attention in recent years, is **interferon.**

Physiologic Barriers

In many animals their normal body temperature is effective in combating infection in inhibiting the growth of organisms that would otherwise flourish in their tissues. In some cases, however, temperature changes favor infection. For example, the chicken, which is normally resistant to the disease anthrax, has a normal body temperature of 40 degrees centigrade (105 degrees Fahrenheit). However, it becomes susceptible to the bacterium that causes anthrax if its body temperature is lowered to 37 degrees Centigrade (98.6 degrees Fahrenheit), the body temperature of mammals. Lizards, which have a lower body temperature than mammals and are usually resistant to anthrax, become susceptible if their body temperature is raised to that of mammals.

In some cases, the absence of certain essential nutrient molecules prevents growth and reproduction of infectious organisms. For example, most bacteria are unable to grow in the absence of iron or calcium ions. The availability of oxygen is another important factor influencing bacterial infection because, if the amount of oxygen is low, aerobic microorganisms will not multiply. Conversely, for anaerobic microorganisms, such as *Clostridium tetani,* the agent of the disease tetanus, lowered oxygen levels are favorable to multiplication. For such microorganisms, high oxygen levels are usually inhibitory.

Phagocytosis and the Inflammatory Process

Another secondary line of defense against microorganisms is a group of cells, called **phagocytes,** that engulf and digest foreign substances, including microbes. Phagocytic cells are primarily of two kinds: the circulating phago-cytic cells of the blood, which are the polymorphonuclear leukocytes, (PMNs) and monocytes; and the fixed tissue phagocytes, such as the Kupffer cells of the liver, the microglial cells of the brain, alveolar macrophages of the lung, and the macrophages of the lymphatic tissue, such as the spleen and lymph nodes. The PMNs represent a major internal defense in the destruction of mi-crobes. During the early stages of tissue injury, chemical factors, or **chemotax-ins** are released from the injured tissues, attracting circulating PMNs to the site of injury. As a result, large numbers of PMNs are produced by the bone marrow and released into the circulation during systemic infection or signifi-cant tissue damage.

Inflammation at the site of a wound is another secondary defense system. The term *inflammation* is suggested by the reddening of the affected areas. His-tamine, a molecule secreted by certain white blood cells that causes contrac-tion of smooth muscles and dilation of blood vessels, is released, blood vessels dilate, and phagocytic cells and plasma move into the affected tissues. At the same time, fibrin causes the blood to clot, closing the wound to further micro-bial penetration with a scab. Microbicidal factors in the plasma also inhibit mi-crobial growth and reproduction and thereby mediate the repair of damaged tissues.

SPECIFIC IMMUNITY

Although immunobiology is a relatively recent scientific discipline, the concept of immunity as a means of resistance to infection is an ancient one. Since the time of the Greeks it has been recognized that those who recover from plague, smallpox, yellow fever, and various other infectious diseases rarely contract the same disease again.

The first scientific attempts at artificial immunization were made in the late eighteenth century by the English physician Edward Jenner. Jenner inves-tigated the basis for the widespread belief of peasants in the rural areas in Eng-land that anyone who had had vaccinia, or cowpox (from the Latin *vacca* "cow"), a disease that affected both dairy cattle and humans, never contracted smallpox. Smallpox was not only often fatal—10 to 40 percent of those who contracted it died, and children were especially susceptible—but those that re-covered usually had disfiguring pockmarks. Yet most British milkmaids, who were readily infected with cowpox, had clear skins because cowpox was a rel-atively mild infection that left no scars.

After some 20 years of close observation, including several deliberate at-tempts to give smallpox to people who had contracted cowpox, Jenner began to immunize people by deliberately infecting them with cowpox. His first subject was a healthy, eight-year-old boy known never to have had either of these two related diseases. As Jenner had expected, immunization with the cowpox virus caused only mild symptoms in the boy. When Jenner subsequently inoculated him with smallpox virus, the boy showed no symptoms of the disease.

Jenner subsequently inoculated patients in large numbers with cowpox pus, as did other physicians in England and on the European continent. By 1800, the practice, known as **vaccination,** had begun in America, and by 1805, Napoleon commanded all French soldiers to be vaccinated.

Further work on immunization was carried out by Louis Pasteur (1822–1895), the French physician who established the scientific basis for the germ theory of disease (the fact that microorganisms are responsible for disease) and developed techniques for the maintenance and growth of bacteria in test tubes. Pasteur discovered that neglected, old cultures of chicken cholera bacilli, which had not been placed in a fresh culture medium on a regular basis, produced only a mild attack of this disease in chickens inoculated with it. He then discovered that fresh cultures of the bacteria failed to produce the disease in any chickens that had been previously inoculated with such old cultures. The organisms in the old cultures had somehow become less pathogenic, or **attenuated.** They had lost their ability to cause damage to cells and tissues, a change that Pasteur later found he could regularly produce in cultures of other kinds of aerobic bacteria by growing them for long periods of time under anaerobic conditions. To honor Jenner, Pasteur gave the name **vaccine** to any preparations of a weakened pathogen, or infective microbes, that was used as was Jenner's "vaccine virus," to immunize against infectious disease.

Pasteur used vaccination to protect animals against anthrax and people against rabies. Following Pasteur's discovery, other investigations showed that not only weakened, living microorganisms but also microorganisms killed by treatment with formalin, merthiolate, phenol, or heat could induce immunity.

Acquired Immunity

The immunity acquired following the penetration of the body by foreign substances depends on the body's ability to recognize the substances as foreign and to produce an immune response to them. Such substances are called **antigens.** This ability to distinguish self from nonself is one of the hallmarks of immunity. Such immunity may develop as a result of contracting a disease and recovering from it. This will usually result in a long-lasting immunity to another attack of the same disease, that is, the immunity is specific to the particular agent that engendered the immune response. Specificity is another hallmark of immunity.

Acquired immunity can also be artificially induced in individuals as a means of developing protection against the possibilities of future infections by specific microorganisms. This is accomplished by the injection of attenuated or killed microorganisms, or some of their metabolic products that are known to cause disease. These "shots," as they are commonly called, have been effective in developing resistance to microorganisms that cause cholera, diphtheria, measles, mumps, whooping cough, rabies, smallpox, tetanus, typhoid, yellow fever, and poliomyelitis. Because of a massive and concerted worldwide campaign of immunization against smallpox, the World Health Organization declared this once dreaded disease eradicated from the world in 1980.

Boosting the Immune Response. You may recall from your own experience that when you received a polio vaccine you had to have more than one shot. The second, or booster, shot is designed to increase immunity to a higher level than that which can be obtained with only one shot, called a primary immunization. This occurs because the immune system can recognize when it has previously encountered a given foreign substance and responds to a second immunization by producing a much larger immune response in a shorter period of time (Fig. 17–2). This secondary response is referred to as the **anamnestic response** (from the Latin *anamnesis,* "to recall") and is the third major characteristic of immunity: immunologic memory. Immunity developed by this procedure is long-lasting and may even last for the life of the individual. This accounts for the fact that many of the shots we received—such as inoculations against diphtheria, pertussis (whooping cough), tetanus

FIGURE 17–2

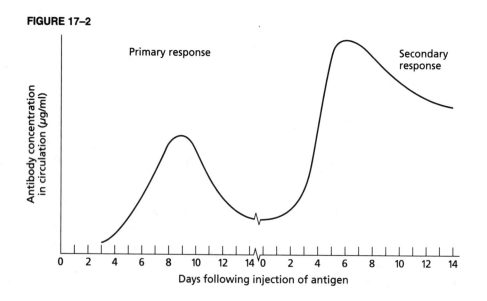

(DPT), and polio—were given to us only when we were young and have not been repeated.

Passive Immunity

Passive immunity is achieved by infecting individuals with **antibodies,** the specific protein molecules involved in immunity, that have been produced by another individual in response to a foreign substance. The protection afforded by this type of immunity usually lasts only a short time, since the antibodies are rapidly broken down and soon disappear from the circulation. Some diseases are treated by infection of a serum (the clear yellow fluid obtained from blood that has clotted) containing antibodies, called an **antiserum,** from animals that have been immunized or from humans that have experienced a disease and recovered. Passive immunization is used against such diseases as poliomyelitis and infectious hepatitis for exposed persons who have not been actively immunized to the microorganisms that cause these diseases. Tetanus antitoxin (antibody against toxic molecules, called toxins, produced by the bacterium *Clostridium tetani*) is used for people who risk infection by tetanus bacilli introduced into a dirty wound and who have not recently been actively immunized to tetanus toxoid (the pathogenic toxin produced by tetanus bacilli and treated so that it can no longer cause pathogenesis but can still induce an immune response).

Passive immunity is also naturally acquired by the transfer of antibodies from mother to child across the placenta during pregnancy. The antibodies are also absorbed through the child's intestine from the first milk of the mother, called **colostrum.** This passively acquired immunity protects newborns in the first few months of life, when their own immune system is not yet fully developed.

EXERCISE 26: Immunity

NAME _____ **DATE** _____

VOCABULARY

I. Read the following sentences, and then fill in the blanks with words from the passage.

1. A condition of being able to resist a particular disease by preventing the invasion by foreign organisms is known as ___immunity___.

2. Such things as the human skin, antimicrobial agents in the body fluids, temperature, and oxygen protect the body against harmful bacteria and viruses. This is called _nonspecific immunity_.

3. One of our most effective defenses against infection is the skin. The skin has two main layers, the _Dermis_ and the _Epidermis_, which in turn have layers.

4. The outer layer of the skin contains a substance called _Keratin_, a tough, water-repellent material that protects the living cells underneath.

5. Human skin has pigment-bearing cells called _____. These cells expand and inject granules of a dark brown or black pigment into the epidermal cells in response to sunlight.

6. The skin's defense system is enhanced by microorganisms that provide _bacterial_ _antagonism_, which restricts the growth of other microorganisms that might be harmful.

7. If a harmful organism penetrates the skin, a second line of defense goes into action. Found in body tissues are substances called

_____, which are effective in destroying bacteria. Another is called _beta_ _lyson_, which is active against bacilli that form spores. This substance fights

infectious disease. A third is known as _Interferon_, a low-molecular-weight protein that combats viral infections.

8. _Phagocytes_ are cells that engulf and digest foreign substances, including microbes. After an injury, chemicals called _Chemotaxins_ are released from the injured tissues, which attract these cells so that they in turn can prevent infection.

9. A _Vaccine_ is a weakened disease virus that is used to immunize against an infectious disease.

10. Acquired immunity can be produced after a person has a disease and the body produces substances called _antigens_, which fight the disease and produce a long-lasting immunity.

11. To achieve passive immunity, _____, the protein molecules that are involved in immunity, are injected into an individual.

Some diseases are treated with an injection of serum from an animal that has been immunized or from a person who has had the disease. This serum iscalled an ___antiserum___.

12. Another example of a substance that can be passed from one individual to another to provide passive immunity is ___Colostrum___, the first milk of a mother to an infant.

COMPREHENSION

II. *Select the best answer for the following questions. Indicate your choice on the line provided.*

__C__ 1. The purpose of the first paragraph in the passage is to explain
   a. the original meaning of the word immune.
   b. how individuals become immune to smallpox.
   c. the broad concept of immunity.

__b__ 2. The language used in the passage is
   a. informal. b. scholarly. c. argumentative.

__C__ 3. The body's most effective defense against infection is
   a. vaccination. b. mediation. c. the skin.

__C__ 4. Interferon, mentioned in the passage, has in recent years been linked to the treatment of
   a. hepatitis. b. AIDS. c. cancer.

__b__ 5. Edward Jenner developed a method of artificial immunization against
   a. smallpox. b. cowpox. c. polio.

__C__ 6. Louis Pasteur developed vaccines to protect
   a. cows against cowpox and people against smallpox.
   b. people against typhoid and polio.
   c. animals against anthrax and people against rabies.

__b__ 7. The discovery that microorganisms are responsible for disease was made by
   a. Napoleon. b. Louis Pasteur. c. Edward Jenner.

_b_   8. According to the passage and Figure 17–2, which is the most effective—a primary or secondary immunization?

        a. primary   b. secondary

_a_   9. The immune system is not fully developed at birth.

        a. true   b. false

_b_   10. One of the most outstanding hallmarks (characteristics) of immunity is

        a. that "shots" are effective in preventing infectious disease.
        b. the ability to distinguish self from nonself.
        c. that smallpox has been virtually eradicated throughout the world.

III. *Answer the following question on the lines provided.*

1. Study Figure 17–1. Select one of the ways that the body develops immunity against disease, and list at least three major details from the passage to support the effectiveness of this type of immunity.

     _____

     _____

     _____

     _____

     _____

     _____

     _____

SUGGESTIONS FOR FURTHER STUDY

- Write a research paper on the development of the polio vaccine.
- Write a research paper on the advancements of immunizing people in underdeveloped countries.
- Conduct a classroom debate concerning mandatory immunization for children before entering school.

18

Computer Science and Data Processing

STUDYING COMPUTER SCIENCE AND DATA PROCESSING

In this age of information, computer science and data processing play an increasingly important role in our society, making it imperative that all individuals possess at least a minimal knowledge of the operation and function of computers.

Early computers were used mostly for scientific calculations. In fact, until the early 1970s, most were massive central computers owned by large corporations and operated only by computer professionals. Today, in addition to these large mainframe computers, personal computers are found in large and small businesses, in most offices, and in many homes. It is doubtful that a single profession or occupation exists that does not utilize a computer system in some way. In other words, computers are used whenever and wherever data needs to be processed. Businesses ranging from the local supermarket to the largest automobile manufacturer depend on computers to maintain their accounts and inventories, calculate employees' wages, operate machinery, analyze the market, and keep track of the latest consumer demands and trends.

In addition to their use in business operations, computers are used extensively in schools. Most schools and colleges use some type of computer-assisted instruction all the way from pre-kindergarten to graduate studies. Lessons ranging from reading passages with vocabulary and comprehension questions to complex algebraic calculations are programmed into computers. Many classes use computers for composition courses, making proofreading and rewriting easier and more efficient. Computer-assisted education is especially advantageous for the disabled student who might otherwise have difficulty writing assignments. This type of instruction also allows students to progress at their own pace and helps in retention of information, since he or she is actively involved in the learning process. Well-staffed computer labs are common on college campuses and are accessible to you even if computers are not a required part of your course work. In addition to being used in the classroom, the administrative offices in your college depend on computers to keep records of grades and to handle your registration as well as to conduct the business of running the institution.

In the home, computers can take care of mundane tasks, such as turning the lights on and off, controlling the temperature, keeping inventories, preparing income tax returns, and preparing a household budget. In addition, on-line services are available that enable consumers to shop and bank at home and to get news, stock quotations, and bulletin board services. Computers can also be used for entertainment. Games on software are available for your home computer, ranging from a card game to a game of golf.

Anyone interested in becoming computer-competent would have little trouble finding a computer training class. Computer skills are included as part of most school curricula. In college you have a range of choices, from basic computer courses to specialized courses leading to a computer-oriented career. In fact, many colleges encourage computer training regardless of your major. Your career plans will determine whether you need basic computer literacy or in-depth study. Whether you plan to be a politician or a farmer, a movie star or an accountant, the president of a bank or an artist, you would benefit by becoming a competent computer user.

The lesson chosen for this chapter is designed to acquaint you with the components of a computer system, the function of each component, pertinent information about computer hardware and software, ways in which computers are used, and to give you a brief insight into future applications of computer technology. First, read the passage for general information, paying close attention to the boldfaced words and terms. In the vocabulary section in Exercise 27 you are asked to demonstrate your understanding of the vocabulary that is listed. (Your instructor may give you a specific activity for the words.) Each of the words is defined and explained in the passage. Next, reread the passage, and then answer the comprehension questions.

Using Computers

HOW OFTEN DO YOU USE THE COMPUTER?

How would you respond to the question "How often do you use computers?" Many people who are just beginning to learn about computers might say, "I don't use them at all," and most of these people would be wrong. The computer and its applications have become so much a part of our everyday routine that we tend to take them for granted. Just about everyone uses and even programs computers, even people who have never sat in front of a personal computer or video display terminal.

- Have you set up your VCR to tape a couple of movies while you sleep? If you have, then you have programmed a computer. VCRs have one or more small computers that activate internal motors based on programmed commands. If you do not have a VCR, then you probably have a programmable microwave oven or answering machine.

- Have you ever called a mail-order merchandiser and been greeted by a recorded message like this: "Thank you for calling Zimco Enterprises Customer Service. If you wish to place an order press one. If you wish to inquire about the status of an order, press two. To speak to a particular person, enter that person's four-digit extension, or hold and an operator will process your call momentarily." More and more companies are installing computer-controlled telephone systems to expedite calls. These systems permit customers to interact directly with a computer.

- Have you paid your latest electric bill? Sometimes we use the computer indirectly. Did you return a preprinted stub with your check? If you did, you were providing input into a computer system. The information on the stub, which is computer-readable, is entered directly into the computer system.

- Have you driven or ridden in a late-model automobile recently? Most of the newer cars have several on-board computer systems. A computerized warning device checks various systems and "tells" you which ones are not ready: "Please fasten your seat belt," or "A door is open." A computerized fuel-control system feeds the exact mixture of fuel and air to the engine. Another on-board computer provides travel information such as miles per gallon, average miles per hour, and so on.

- How's the temperature at home? Many homes are equipped with computer-controlled environmental systems. These systems permit you to program daily and weekly temperature settings to fit your lifestyle and your pocketbook.
- Did traffic flow smoothly this morning? If it did, then it probably was due to an automated traffic-control system. Sensors in the street feed data on your position, speed, and direction into a central computer. The system uses these data to synchronize traffic signals to optimize the flow of traffic.
- Have you ever been hungry and short of cash? It's lunchtime and you have only 47 cents in your pocket? No problem. Just stop at an automatic teller machine and ask for some lunch money.

So, as you see, computers are quietly playing an increasingly significant role in our lives. Each day technological innovations that will ultimately make life a little more convenient for all of us are being explored. For example, you may be doing your grocery shopping from the comfort of your kitchen counter (via a personal computer) within this very decade!

UNCOVERING THE "MYSTERY" OF COMPUTERS

The Computer System

Technically speaking, the computer is any counting device. But in the context of modern technology, we will define the **computer** as *an electronic device capable of interpreting and executing programmed commands for input, output, computation, and logic operations.*

Computers may be technically complex, but they are conceptually simple. The computer, also called a **processor,** is the "intelligence" of a **computer system.** A computer system has only four fundamental components: *input, processing, output,* and *storage.* Note that a computer system (not a computer) is made up of the four components. The actual computer is the processing component; when combined with the other three components, it forms a *computer system.*

The relationship of data to a computer system is best explained by showing an analogy to gasoline and an automobile. Data are to a computer system as gas is to a car. Data provide the fuel for a computer system. A computer system without data is like a car with an empty gas tank: No gas, no go; no data, no information.

How a Computer System Works

A computer system also can be likened to the biological system of the human body. Your brain is the processing component. Your eyes and ears are input components that send signals to the brain. If you see someone approaching, your brain matches the visual image of this person with others in your memory (storage component). If the visual image matches that of a friend, your brain sends signals to your vocal cords and right arm (output components) to greet your friend with a hello and a handshake. Computer system components interact in a similar way.

The payroll system in Figure 18–1 illustrates how data are entered and how the four computer system components interact to produce information (a year-to-date overtime report) and payroll checks. The hours-worked data are *input* to the system and are *stored* on the personnel **master file.** The master file is made up of **records,** each of which contains data about a particular employee (for example: name, hours worked).

The payroll checks are produced when the *processing* component, or the computer, executes a program. In this example, the employee records are recalled from storage, and the pay amounts are calculated. The *output* is the printed payroll checks. Other programs extract data from the personnel master file to produce a year-to-date overtime report and any other information that might help in the management decision-making process.

FIGURE 18–1 Payroll System

This microcomputer-based payroll system illustrates input, storage, processing, and output.

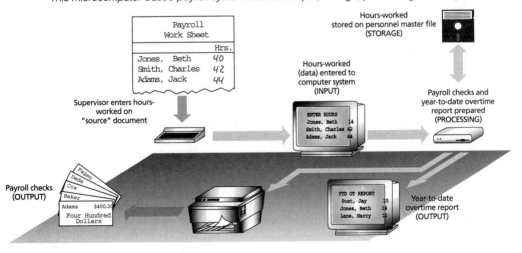

The Hardware

In the payroll example, data are entered (input) on a **video display terminal**. A **video display terminal**, or simply **terminal**, has a typewriterlike **keyboard** for input and a televisionlike (video) screen, called a **monitor**, for output such as the year-to-date overtime report. The payroll checks are output on a device called a **printer**. Data are stored for later recall on **magnetic disk**. There are a wide variety of **input/output (I/O)** and storage devices.

The principles discussed here apply equally to microcomputers and **mainframe computers**. Each has the four components and each uses data to produce information in a similar manner. The difference is that microcomputers, also called **personal computers**, are more limited in their capabilities and are designed primarily for use by *one person at a time*. Mainframe computers can service *many users*, perhaps every manager in the company, all at once.

What Can a Computer Do?

Remember from our previous discussion that the *input/output* and *data storage* hardware components are *configured* with the *processing* component (the computer) to make a computer system. Let's discuss the operational capabilities of a computer system just a bit further.

Input/Output Operations. The computer *reads* from input storage devices. The computer *writes* to output and storage devices. Before data can be processed, they must be "read" from an input device or data storage device. Input data are usually entered by an operator on a video display terminal or retrieved from a data storage device such as a magnetic disk drive. Once data have been processed, they are "written" to an output device, such as a printer, or to a data storage device.

Input/output (I/O) operations are illustrated in the payroll system example in Figure 18–1. Hours-worked data are entered, or "read," into the computer system. These data are "written" to magnetic disk storage for a recall at a later date.

Processing Operations. The computer is totally objective. That is, any two computers instructed to perform the same operation will arrive at the same result. This is because the computer can perform only *computation* and *logic operations.*

The computational capabilities of the computer include adding, subtracting, multiplying, and dividing. Logic capability permits the computer to make comparisons between numbers and between words then, based on the result of the comparison, perform appropriate functions. In the payroll-system example of Figure 18–1, the computer calculates the gross pay in a computation operation (for example, 40 hours at $15/hour = $600). In a logic operation, the computer compares the number of hours worked to 40 to determine the number of overtime hours that an employee has worked during a given week. If the hours-worked figure is greater than or equal to 40 (42, for example), the difference (2 hours) is credited as overtime and paid at time and a half.

Computer System Capabilities

In a nutshell, computers are fast, accurate, and reliable; they don't forget anything; and they don't complain. Now for the details.

Speed. The smallest unit of time in the human experience is, realistically, the second. Computer operations (such as the execution of an instruction, such as adding two numbers) are measured in **milliseconds, microseconds, nanoseconds,** and **picoseconds** (one thousandth, one millionth, one billionth, and one trillionth of a second, respectively). A beam of light travels down the length of this page in about one nanosecond!

Accuracy. Errors do occur in computer-based information systems, but precious few can be directly attributed to the computer system itself. The vast majority can be traced to a program logic error, a procedural error, or erroneous data. These are *human errors.*

Reliability. Computer systems are particularly adept at repetitive tasks. They don't take sick days and coffee breaks, and they seldom complain. Anything below 99.9% *uptime* is usually unacceptable. For some companies, any *downtime* is unacceptable. These companies provide *backup* computers that take over if the main computers fail.

Memory Capability. Computer systems have total and instant recall of data and an almost unlimited capacity to store these data. A typical mainframe computer system will have many billions of characters stored and available for instant recall. To give you a benchmark for comparison, this book contains approximately a million characters.

HOW DO WE USE COMPUTERS?

For the purpose of this discussion, we will classify the uses of computers into six general categories: *information systems/data processing, personal computing, science and research, process control, education,* and *artificial intelligence.* Figure 18–2 shows how the sum total of existing computer capacity is apportioned to each of these general categories. In the years ahead, look for personal computing, process control, education, and artificial intelligence to grow rapidly and become larger shares of the computer "pie."

FIGURE 18–2 The Way We Use Computers

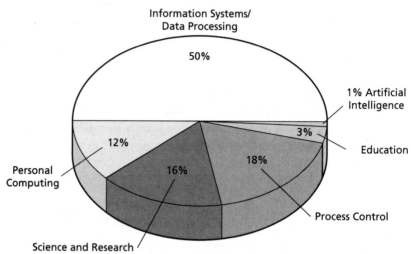

Information Systems/Data Processing

The bulk of existing computer power is dedicated to *information systems* and *data processing*. This category includes all uses of computers that support the administrative aspects of an organization. Example applications include payroll systems, airline reservation systems, student registration systems, hospital-patient billing systems, and countless others.

We combine *hardware, software, people, procedures,* and *data* to create an information system. A computer-based information system provides a manager's department with *data processing* capabilities and managers with the *information* they need to make better, more informed decisions.

To get a feeling for the widespread influence of computers, let's take a look at how the computer services the data processing and information needs of Zimco Enterprises (a fictional manufacturer of handy consumer products).

- In the *accounting* division, all financial/accounting systems are computerized.
- Zimco's *production* division uses information systems for such applications as inventory control and production scheduling.

- As competition becomes keener, the *marketing* division has turned to the information services division for assistance in fine-tuning the marketing effort.

- The *human resources development* division has automated the basic personnel functions of employment history and career planning.

- The *purchasing* division has replaced cumbersome manual systems with computer-based systems that extend its buying power through selective, time-phased purchasing.

- The *research and development* division relies on the information services division to support a variety of technical programs that include simulation and computer-aided design.

- Zimco's *headquarters staff* and top management routinely make "what if" inquiries such as: "What if the advertising budget were increased by 20%? How might sales be affected?"

The influence of computer information systems is just as pervasive in hospitals, government agencies, and colleges. A wide variety of information systems for virtually every industry is described and discussed throughout the remainder of the book.

Personal Computing

Individuals and companies are purchasing small, inexpensive microcomputers, also called personal computers, or **PCs,** for a variety of business and domestic applications. A microcomputer system, or **micro** for short, easily sits on a desktop and can be controlled by one person. The growth of this general area, called **personal computing,** has surpassed even the most adventurous forecasts of a decade ago. Some companies actually have more personal computers than telephones. Personal computers far outnumber mainframe computers. But, of course, a single mainframe computer may have the processing capacity of 1000 personal computers.

Domestic Applications for Personal Computing. A variety of domestic and business applications form the foundation of personal computing. Domestic applications include some of the following: maintaining an up-to-date inventory of household items; storing names and addresses for a personal mailing list; maintaining records for, preparing, and sending income tax returns; creating and monitoring a household budget; keeping an appointment and social calendar; handling household finances (for example, checkbook balancing, paying bills, coupon refunding); writing letters; education; and, of course, entertainment. You can purchase software for all these applications, and you can probably obtain software for your special interest, whether it be astrology, charting biorhythms, composing music, or dieting.

Business Applications for Personal Computing. Of course, virtually any business application (for example, payroll and sales analysis) discussed in this book is supported on a personal computer, but the most popular business use of personal computers is with *productivity software.* Microcomputer-based productivity software is a series of commercially available programs that can help people in the business community save time and get information they need to make more informed decisions. *Productivity software* is the foundation of personal computing in the business world. These productivity tools include the following:

- *Word processing.* **Word processing** software permits users to enter, store, manipulate, and print text.
- *Desktop publishing.* **Desktop publishing** software allows users to produce near-typeset-quality copy for newsletters, advertisements, and many other printing needs, all from the confines of a desktop.
- *Electronic spreadsheet.* **Electronic spreadsheet** software permits users to work with the rows and columns of a matrix (or spreadsheet) of data.
- *Database.* **Database** software permits users to create and maintain a database and to extract information from the database.
- *Presentation graphics.* **Presentation graphics** software permits users to create charts and line drawings that graphically portray the data in an electronic spreadsheet or database.

Information Services. Personal computers, or **PCs,** are normally used as stand-alone computer systems, but as we have seen from earlier discussions, they can also double as remote terminals. This dual-function capability provides you with the flexibility to work with the PC as a stand-alone system or to link it with a larger computer and take advantage of its increased capacity. With a PC, you have a world of information at your fingertips. The personal computer can be used in conjunction with the telephone system to transmit data to and receive data from an **information network.**

A growing trend among personal computer enthusiasts is to subscribe to the services of an information network. These information networks have one or several large computer systems that offer a variety of information services. These services include hotel reservations, home banking, shopping at home, daily horoscopes, financial information, games, up-to-the-minute news, and much more.

The services provided by information networks, coupled with the capabilities of microcomputer productivity software, eventually should make personal computers a "must-have" item in every home and business.

Science and Research

Engineers and scientists routinely use the computer as a tool in experimentation and design. Aerospace engineers use computers to simulate the effects of a wind tunnel to analyze the aerodynamics of an airplane prototype. Political scientists collect and analyze demographic data, such as median income and housing starts, to predict voting trends. Chemists use computer graphics to create three-dimensional views of an experimental molecule. There are at least as many science and research applications for the computer as there are scientists and engineers.

Process Control

Computers used for **process control** accept data in a continuous *feedback loop*. In a feedback loop, the process itself generates data that become input to the computer. As the data are received and interpreted by the computer, the computer initiates action to control the ongoing process. For example, process-control computers monitor and control the environment (temperature, humidity, lighting, security) inside skyscrapers. These computer-controlled skyscrapers are often referred to as "smart" buildings.

Tiny "computers on a chip" are being embedded in artificial hearts and other organs. Once the organs are implanted in the body, the computer monitors critical inputs, such as blood pressure and flow, then takes corrective action to ensure stability of operation in a continuous feedback loop.

Education

Computers can interact with students to enhance the learning process. Relatively inexpensive hardware capable of multidimensional communication (sound, print, graphics, and color) has resulted in a phenomenal growth of the computer as an educational tool in the home, in the classroom, and in business. Computer-based education will not replace teachers and books, but educators are in agreement that *computer-based training* (CBT) is having a profound impact on traditional modes of education.

Computers have been used for drill and practice for over a decade. Only recently has sophisticated CBT been economically feasible. Now powerful personal computers have added a dimension that is not possible with books and the traditional classroom lectures. The student controls the pace of learning and can interact directly with the computer system. Through interactive computer graphics, a CBT system can demonstrate certain concepts more effectively than can books or even teachers. The teacher-book-CBT approach has spawned a new era in education.

Artificial Intelligence

Human Beings Are Born, Not Manufactured. Today's computers can simulate many human capabilities such as reaching, grasping, calculating, speaking, remembering, comparing numbers, and drawing. Researchers are working to expand these capabilities and, therefore, the power of computers by developing hardware and software that can imitate intelligent human behavior. For example, researchers are working on systems that have the ability to reason, to learn or accumulate knowledge, to strive for self-improvement, and to simulate human sensory and mechanical capabilities. This general area of research is known as **artificial intelligence (AI).**

Artificial intelligence? To some, the mere mention of artificial intelligence creates visions of electromechanical automatons replacing human beings. But as anyone involved in the area of artificial intelligence will tell you, there is a distinct difference between human beings and machines. Computers will never be capable of simulating the distinctly human qualities of creativity, humor, and emotions! However, computers can drive machines that mimic human movements (such as picking up objects and placing them at a prescribed location) and provide the "brains" for systems that simulate the human thought process within the domain of a particular area of expertise (tax preparation, medical diagnosis, and so on).

Categories of Artificial Intelligence. Research in the field of artificial intelligence can be divided into categories: knowledge-based and expert systems, natural languages, simulation of human sensory capabilities, and robotics.

Knowledge-based and expert systems. A **knowledged-based system** relies on a **knowledge base** that is filled with "rules of thumb" (intuition, judgment, and inferences) about a specific application area, such as computer repair. Humans can use the knowledge-based system and the IF-THEN rules in the knowledge base to help them solve a particular problem. **Expert systems** are the most sophisticated implementation of a knowledge-based system. Once the knowledge of one or more human experts has been entered to an expert system's knowledge base, users can tap this knowledge by interacting with the system in much the same way they would interact with a human expert in that field. Both the user and the computer-based expert system ask and respond to one another's questions until a problem is resolved.

Natural languages. **Natural languages** refer to software that enables computer systems to accept, interpret, and execute instructions in the native, or "natural," language of the end user, typically English. For example, the end user uses a natural language when he or she enters brief English commands such as "Show me a pie chart for regional sales" to a computer system. There are, of course, limitations on the complexity of the commands that can be interpreted. The state of the art of natural languages is still somewhat primitive. Most commercial natural languages are designed to provide end users with a means of communicating with a corporate database or an expert system.

Simulation of human sensory capabilities. One area of AI research involves computer simulation of human capabilities. This area focuses on equipping computer systems with the capabilities of seeing, hearing, speaking, and feeling (touching). These artificial intelligence capabilities are possible with current technology, to varying degrees.

Robotics. **Robotics** is the integration of computers and **industrial robots.** Industrial robots, which are usually equipped with an arm and a hand, can be "taught" to perform almost any repetitive manipulative task, such as painting a car, screwing on a bolt, moving material, and even such complex tasks as inspecting a manufactured part for defects.

Computers and Opportunity

Computers provide many opportunities for us to improve the quality of both our private and professional lives. Our challenge is to take advantage of the opportunities afforded by the computer revolution and our emergence as an information society. People like you who are willing to put forth the effort and accept the challenge will be the ones who benefit the most.

EXERCISE 27: Using Computers

NAME _____ **DATE** _____

VOCABULARY

   I. In this lesson, the vocabulary words and terms you should know are in boldface or italics and are defined in the passage. Be sure you understand the meaning of each of these words and terms. If you are already adept in "computerese," you may need only to review. If you are not, you should do a complete study of the words and terms listed on page 308. Your instructor may have a special plan for you to follow as well as additional words and terms.

computer	printer
computer system	master file
microcomputer	input
mainframe computer	output
video display terminal	productivity software
keyboard	artificial intelligence
monitor	natural languages

COMPREHENSION

*II. Indicate on the line provided whether the following statements are **true** or **false**.*

_____ 1. The computer (or processor) is the intelligence of a computer system.

_____ 2. A computer can perform only objective operations.

_____ 3. The smallest unit of time realistically used by humans is the nanosecond.

_____ 4. If it takes 60 seconds to drive one mile, the time would be equal to 60,000 microseconds.

_____ 5. Most mistakes attributed to a computer system are human errors.

_____ 6. Computer systems are adept at most operations unless they are repetitive tasks.

_____ 7. Personal computers are used only for entertainment.

_____ 8. When we pay our bills each month, we provide input into a computer system.

_____ 9. Computers are practically indispensable in business and management operations but are of little use to students and educators.

_____ 10. If computer technology continues to expand as predicted, all of us not only will benefit but also will be challenged beyond our present imagination.

III. Answer the following questions on the lines provided.

1. What is the purpose of the passage?

_____

_____

2. What are the four fundamental components of a computer system?

_____

_____

3. Study Figure 18–1. What is the major advantage of using a computer system over the old ledger system for this type of business operation?

_____

_____

_____

_____

4. What is the author's purpose in the first paragraph under the heading "Input/Output Operations" on page 300?

_____

_____

5. According to the author, what are the positive characteristics of a computer?

_____

_____

_____

6. Name the six general uses of the computer listed in the passage.

_____

_____

_____

_____

7. Study Figure 18–2. What is currently the most widely used application of computers? The least widely used?

_____

_____

_____

8. Study the list of productivity software and their uses on page 302. Which of these would be the most valuable to you in writing a term paper that contains mostly text?

_____

9. Define artificial intelligence as it applies to computer use.

_____

_____

_____

_____

SUGGESTIONS FOR FURTHER STUDY

- Think of "new and innovative" ideas for future uses of the computer.
- List ideas you would present to your employer if you were asked to think of a unique way to use computers on your job. (If you do not work, use a job you would like to do.)
- Discuss advantages and disadvantages of further development of artificial intelligence.
- Discuss whether or not you think there is a computer career in your future.

PART THREE

Reading Selections

Selection One

Are We Tolerating More Dishonesty?

BARBARA ZIGLI

The government withheld taxes from the young New York waitress's wages, but not her tips. So she didn't <u>declare</u> them on this year's income tax.

"It was not a substantial amount of money, since I only worked there 11 weeks," she says in her defense. "It was just easier than figuring out how much tips I made."

The manager of a Los Angeles theater told an employee to resell some used tickets collected from <u>patrons</u> and give him the extra money. The <u>ploy</u> kept the second sales from showing up on theater records.

Convinced the funds were going into the manager's pocket, and not the theater's, the employee began to keep half.

"If he's going to force me to do this, I'm going to get a piece of it for myself," he says. "But basically, I'm a nice person."

Cheating: The income-tax deadline approaches and some taxpayers'

311

thoughts turn to it. Test time approaches and some students' thoughts turn to it. Temptation appears and some spouses consider it.

"You want something you can't get by behaving within the rules, and you want it badly enough you'll do it regardless of any guilt or remorse, and you're willing to run the risk of being caught." That's how Ladd Wheeler, psychology professor at the University of Rochester in New York, defines cheating.

Cheating represents the triumph of the "Brazen Rule" over the "Golden Rule," says Terry Pinkard, philosophy professor at Georgetown University in Washington, D.C.

"The Golden Rule says, 'Do unto others as you would have them do unto you.' The Brazen Rule says, 'Do unto others as they would do unto you if they were in your place.'"

Many experts believe cheating is on the rise. "We're suffering an <u>ethical</u> breakdown," Pinkard says. "We're seeing more of the kind of person who regards the world as a series of things to be <u>manipulated.</u> Whether to cheat depends on whether it's in the person's interest." He does, however, see less cheating among the youngest students.

Richard Dienstbier, psychology professor at the University of Nebraska in Lincoln, believes that society's attitudes account for much of the <u>upsurge</u> in cheating.

"Twenty years ago, if a person cheated in college, society said: 'That is extremely serious, you will be dropped for a semester if not kicked out permanently,'" he says.

"Nowadays, at the University of Nebraska, for example, it is the stated policy of the College of Arts and Sciences that if a student cheats on an exam, the student must receive an "F" on what he cheated on. That's nothing. If you're going to flunk anyway, why not cheat?"

Cheating is unethical, Pinkard says, whether it's massive <u>fraud</u> or failure to tell a store cashier you were undercharged.

"You're treating other people merely as a means for your own ends. You're using people in ways they would not consent to. The cheater says, 'Let everybody else bear the burden, and I'll reap the benefits.'"

Cheaters usually try to justify their actions, says Robert Hogan, chairman of the psychology department at the University of Tulsa in Oklahoma. "They never think it's their fault."

Cheaters make justifications because they want to feel good about themselves, adds Wheeler. "They don't want to label themselves as a cheater. Also, they may be anticipating the possibility of getting caught, so they work on their excuse ahead of time."

The most common justifications, psychologists say, include:

"I had to do it."

"The test was unfair."

"Everybody does it, and I have to cheat to get what's rightfully mine."

"The government wastes the money anyway."

"My wife (or husband) doesn't understand me, and we've grown apart."

Cheating is most likely in situations where the <u>stakes</u> are high and the chances of getting caught are low, says social psychologist Lynn Kahle of the University of Oregon in Eugene.

In his study, a group of freshmen were allowed to grade their own tests, while secret, pressure-sensitive paper indicated who changed answers. To raise the pressure, students were given an extremely high score as the "average" for the test and told that those who flunked would go before an inquiring board of psychologists.

About 46 percent of the male students changed answers; among the females, about 30 percent cheated.

Everybody cheats a little, some psychologists say, while others insist that most people are basically honest and some wouldn't cheat under any circumstances.

Despite the general rise in cheating, Pinkard sees some cause for hope: "I do find among younger students a much less tolerant attitude toward cheating."

Perhaps, he says, the upcoming generation is less <u>pampered</u> than the "baby boom" students who preceded them—and therefore less self-centered. "There seems to be a <u>swing</u> back in the culture."

EXERCISE 28: Are We Tolerating More Dishonesty?

NAME _____ DATE _____

VOCABULARY

I. *Select the best meaning for the following words as used in the selection. Indicate your choice on the line provided.*

_____ 1. <u>declare</u>

      a. account for   b. speak to   c. brag about

_____ 2. <u>patrons</u>

      a. patterns   b. customers   c. sponsors

_b_   3. <u>ploy</u>
        a. plea   b. scheme   c. performance

_c_   4. <u>ethical</u>
        a. ethnic   b. indecent   c. moral

_c_   5. <u>manipulated</u>
        a. worked   b. falsified   c. controlled

_b_   6. <u>upsurge</u>
        a. outcome   b. increase   c. decrease

_a_   7. <u>fraud</u>
        a. deceit   b. formulation   c. disgust

_b_   8. <u>stakes</u>
        a. posts   b. rewards   c. risks

_a_   9. <u>pampered</u>
        a. spoiled   b. dominated   c. intimidated

_c_   10. <u>swing</u>
        a. dangle   b. rhythm   c. shift

COMPREHENSION

II. *Select the best answer for each of the following. Indicate your choice on the line provided.*

_b_   1. The purpose of this selection is to
        a. convince the reader that cheating is immoral.
        b. discuss the varieties of and reasons for cheating.
        c. describe how cheaters cheat.
        d. suggest how to curtail cheating.

_c_   2. According to the passage, which of the following is true?
        a. It is ethical to cheat unless money is involved.
        b. Failure to tell a store cashier you were undercharged is not considered cheating.
        c. There has been a general rise in cheating.
        d. Most cheaters are college students.

_____d_____ 3. According to the passage, with which of the following would the author probably *not* agree?

    a. Cheating is often the result of intense pressure.

    b. Cheating is cheating, whether on a test or on income tax forms.

    c. Cheating is widespread and society is too tolerant.

    d. The Brazen Rule is a better rule than the Golden Rule.

_____c_____ 4. Regarding the future of cheating, the author seems to be

    a. depressed.

    b. optimistic.

    c. amused.

    d. bewildered.

III. *Decide whether the following sentences are facts or opinions. Write **F** or **O** on the line provided.*

_____O_____ 1. The possibility of getting caught should be the only factor in determining whether or not to cheat.

_____ 2. According to the passage, people are more likely to cheat when the rewards are high.

_____O_____ 3. Because so much money is wasted by the government, it is ethical to cheat on your income tax.

_____F_____ 4. At least one psychologist in the passage believes that cheating is unethical, whether it is massive fraud or accepting too much change from a cashier.

_____F_____ 5. Cheaters tend to justify their cheating by blaming someone else or some situation.

_____F_____ 6. Psychologists believe that cheaters do not want to be labeled as cheaters.

_____O_____ 7. If a student is likely to receive an F in a course, he or she has nothing to lose by cheating.

_____O_____ 8. More people live by the Golden Rule than by the Brazen Rule.

_____C_____ 9. According to the passage, there is a less tolerant attitude toward cheating among younger students.

_____F_____ 10. Psychologists quoted in the passage seem to agree that cheaters cheat because of society's attitudes as well as temptations and pressures.

IV. *Pretend you know someone who is on the verge of cheating on an exam and has asked for your advice. Write your advice on the following lines. Be sure to include such considerations as the risks, rewards (or lack of), as well as the moral issues involved.*

_____

_____

_____

_____

_____

_____

_____

_____

_____

_____

_____

_____

_____

_____

_____

for Monday

Selection Two

I'm Going to Buy
the Brooklyn Bridge

ADRIENNE POPPER

Not long ago I received an alumni bulletin from my college. It included a brief item about a former classmate: "Kate L. teaches part-time at the University of Oklahoma and is assistant principal at County High School. In her spare time she is finishing her doctoral dissertation and the final drafts of two books, and she still has time for tennis and horseback riding with her daughters." Four words in that description undid me: *in her spare time.* A friend who is a psychotherapist said that if I believed everything in the report, she had a bridge in Brooklyn she'd like to sell me.

My friend's joke hit home. What a <u>gullible</u> idiot I'd been! I resolved to stop pondering Kate's incredible accomplishments and to be suitably skeptical of such stories in the future.

But like a dieter who <u>devours</u> a whole box of cookies in a moment of weakness, I found my resolve slipping occasionally. In weak moments I'd comb the pages of newspapers and magazines and consume success stories by the pound. My favorite superwomen included a politician's daughter who cared for her two-year-old and a newborn while finishing law school and managing a food cooperative; a practicing pediatrician with ten children of her own; and a television anchorwoman, mother of two preschoolers, who was studying for a master's degree.

One day, however, I actually met a superwoman face to face. Just before Christmas last year, my work took me to the office of a woman executive of a national corporation. Like her supersisters, she has a husband, two small children and, according to reports, an <u>immaculate</u> apartment. Her life runs as precisely as a Swiss watch. Since my own schedule succeeds about as often as Soviet five-year grain plans, her accomplishments fill me with equal amounts of awe and guilt.

On a shelf behind her desk that day were at least a hundred jars of strawberry preserves, gaily tied with red-checked ribbons. The executive and her children had made the preserves and decorated the jars, which she planned to distribute to her staff and visiting clients.

When, I wondered aloud, had she found the time to complete such an ambitious holiday project? I should have known better than to ask. The answer had a familiar ring: *in her spare time.*

On the train ride home I sat with a jar of strawberry preserves in my lap. It reproached me the entire trip. Other women, it seemed to say, are movers and shakers—not only during office hours, but in their spare time as well. What, it prodded, do you accomplish in *your* spare time?

I would like to report that I am using my extra moments to complete postdoctoral studies in astrophysics, to develop new theories of tonal harmony for piano and bassoon, and to bake brownies and play baseball with my sons. The truth of the matter is, however, that I am congenitally unable to get my act together. No matter how carefully I plan my time, the plan always goes <u>awry.</u>

If I create schedules of military precision in which several afternoon hours are allotted to the writing of the Great American Novel, the school nurse is sure to phone at exactly the moment I put pencil to paper. One of my children will have developed a strange <u>malady</u> that requires him to spend the remainder of the day in bed, calling me at frequent intervals to bring soup, juice, tea and pheasant under glass.

Other days, every item on my schedule will take three times the number of minutes set aside. The cleaner will misplace my clothes. My order won't be ready at the butcher shop as promised. The woman ahead of me in the supermarket line will pay for her groceries with a check drawn on a Martian bank, and only the manager (who has just left for lunch) can OK the transaction. "They also serve who only stand and wait," wrote the poet John Milton, but he forgot to add that they don't get to be superwomen that way.

Racing the clock every day is such an exhausting, losing endeavor that when I actually have a few free moments, I tend to collapse. Mostly I sink into a chair and stare into space while I imagine how lovely life would be if only I possessed the organizational skills and the <u>stamina</u> of my superheroines. In fact, I waste a good deal of my spare time just worrying about what other women are accomplishing in theirs. Sometimes I think that these modern fairy tales create as many problems for women as the old stories that had us biding our time for the day our prince would come.

Yet superwomen tales continue to enchant me. Despite my friend's warning against gullibility, despite everything I've learned, I find that I'm not only willing, but positively eager to buy that bridge she mentioned. Why? I suppose it has something to do with the eternal appeal of <u>optimism</u>—and the fact that extraordinary feats have been accomplished by <u>tenacious</u> individuals who refused to believe that "you can't" was the final word on their dreams.

Men have generally been assured that achieving their heart's desires would be a piece of cake. Women, of course, have always believed that we can't have our cake and eat it too—the old low-dream diet. Perhaps becoming a superwoman *is* an impossible dream for me, but life without that kind of fantasy is as <u>unpalatable</u> as a diet with no goodies.

I know the idea of admiring a heroine is considered <u>corny</u> today; we working women are too sophisticated for that. Yet the superwomen I read about are my heroines. When my faith in myself falters, it is they who urge me on, whispering, "Go for it, lady!" It's the antidote to "Forget it, girl."

One of these days I plan to phone my former classmate Kate and shout "Bravo!" into the receiver. I hope she won't be modest about her achievements. Perhaps she will have completed her dissertation and her two books and moved on to some new work that's exciting or dangerous or both. I'd like to hear all about it. Then I'm going to phone my friend, the psychotherapist, to tell her a story: the tale of a woman who bought her own version of that bridge in Brooklyn and found that it was a wise investment after all.

EXERCISE 29: I'm Going to Buy the Brooklyn Bridge

NAME _____ DATE _____

VOCABULARY

I. *Select the best definition for each of the following words. Indicate your choice on the line provided.*

_____ 1. <u>gullible</u>
   a. swallowed hastily   b. easily misled   c. talking rapidly

_____ 2. <u>devours</u>
   a. greedily eats   b. lustfully watches   c. speedily reacts

_____ 3. <u>immaculate</u>
   a. poorly lighted   b. tastefully decorated   c. very clean

_____ 4. <u>awry</u>
   a. as planned   b. smoothly   c. wrong

_____ 5. <u>malady</u>
   a. story   b. excuse   c. illness

_____ 6. <u>stamina</u>
   a. resistance to fatigue
   b. desire to work
   c. opportunity to serve

_____a_____   7. optimism

     a. positive outlook
     b. negative attitude
     c. dangerous situation

_____c_____   8. tenacious

     a. tense   b. frivolous   c. persistent

_____a_____   9. unpalatable

     a. unacceptable
     b. uncanny
     c. unnutritious

_____c_____   10. corny

     a. fashionable   b. faddish   c. silly

COMPREHENSION

II. Select the best answer for each of the following. Indicate your choice on the line provided.

_____c_____   1. If someone says to you, "If you believe that, I have a bridge in Brooklyn I'd like to sell you," that person is implying that

     a. real estate in Brooklyn is a poor investment.
     b. the Brooklyn Bridge is not for sale.
     c. you will fall for anything.
     d. you cannot handle money responsibly.

_____c_____   2. The phrase that seemed so incredible to the author is

     a. "one of these days."
     b. "go for it."
     c. "in her spare time."
     d. "completed her dissertation."

_____a_____   3. The tone of the selection is

     a. humorous.
     b. satirical.
     c. ironic.
     d. serious.

_____d_____   4. The author gets her point across by

     a. narration.
     b. numeration.

c. analysis.

d. personal experiences.

_____ c 5. The author probably is

    a. very lazy and has no desire to be a superwoman.

    b. a gullible person who falls for every outrageous story she hears.

    c. a capable person who has a good sense of humor and is probably well-organized.

    d. a depressed person with a low self-image.

_____ d 6. Which of the following statements could you *not* infer from the selection?

    a. You can always expect something to go wrong when you are the busiest.

    b. A superperson is usually well-organized.

    c. Everyone cannot be a superperson, no matter how hard he or she tries.

    d. If you are not a superperson, your children will not respect you.

_____ b 7. The author would probably agree that if you wanted something done, the best person to ask would be

    a. someone who evidently has nothing to do.

    b. someone who is organized and very busy.

    c. someone who does not have children.

    d. someone with a college education.

_____ a 8. You could conclude from the selection that fewer people have heroes and heroines today than in the past because

    a. we consider ourselves too independent and sophisticated.

    b. there are too few people to admire.

    c. we have too much to do to be concerned with what others do.

    d. it simply is not the thing to do.

_____ b 9. You could further conclude from the selection that

    a. to admire superpersons is childish and immature.

    b. admiration for superpersons can urge you on to greater accomplishments.

    c. there are few superpersons around today.

    d. if you are considered a superperson, you need to see a psychotherapist.

_____ *d* 10. The emotion that best expresses the author's feelings toward her gift of a jar of strawberry preserves is
   a. love.
   b. hate.
   c. disgrace.
   d. envy.

III. *Pretend you are a superperson. What would you do?*

_____

_____

_____

_____

_____

_____

_____

_____

_____

_____

_____

_____

_____

_____

Selection Three

Wildlife on Main Street

SUSAN GILBERT

One thing the tour books don't tell you about London is that 2,000 of its residents are foxes. As native as the royal family, they fled the city about two centuries ago after developers and pollution moved in. But now that the environment is cleaner, the foxes have come home, only one of the many wild animals that have moved into urban areas around the world.

"The number and variety of wild animals in urban areas is increasing," says Gomer Jones, president of the National Institute for Urban Wildlife in Columbia, Maryland. A survey of the wildlife in New York's Central Park last year tallied 14 species of mammals, including muskrats, shrews and flying squirrels. A similar survey conducted in the 1890s counted only five species. One of the country's largest populations of raccoons now lives in Washington, D.C., and moose are regularly seen wandering into Maine towns. Peregrine falcons dive from the window ledges of buildings in the largest U.S. cities to prey on pigeons.

Several changes have brought wild animals to the asphalt jungles—and vice versa. Foremost is that air and water quality in many cities have improved as a result of the 1970s' pollution-control efforts. Meanwhile, rural areas have been built up, leaving many animals on the edges of suburbia. In addition, conservationists have created urban wildlife refuges.

The Greater London Council last year spent $750,000 to buy land and build 10 permanent wildlife refuges in the city. Over 1,000 volunteers have donated money and cleared rubble from derelict lots. As a result, pheasants now strut in the East End, and badgers scuttle across lawns near the center of town. A colony of rare house martins nests on a window ledge beside Harrods, and one evening last year a fox was seen on Westminister Bridge looking up at Big Ben.

For peregrine falcons, cities are actually safer than rural cliff dwellings. By 1970 the birds were extinct east of the Mississippi because the DDT had made their eggs too thin to support life. That year, ornithologist Tom Cade of Cornell University began raising the birds for release in cities, for cities afforded abundant food in the form of pigeons and contained none of the peregrine's natural predators.

"Before they were exterminated, some migrated to cities on their own because they had run out of cliff space," Cade says. "To peregrines, buildings are just like cliffs." He has released about 30 birds since 1975 in New York,

Baltimore, Philadelphia and Norfolk, and of the 20 pairs now living in the East, half are urbanites. "A few of the young ones have gotten into trouble by falling down chimneys and crashing into window glass, but overall their adjustment has been successful."

Moose Stumble into Stores. Some animals wind up in a city because development has sprawled virtually to their doorsteps. Raccoons outside Washington, D.C., follow the sewers downtown. Polar bears wander into the small Canadian city of Churchill, built right on their summer migration path. Moose, <u>disoriented</u> by hunger, stumble in from the Maine woods and, stunned by the <u>commotion</u> around them, have walked right through plate-glass storefronts.

Los Angeles has spread into the canyons, and the coyotes living there have seen no reason to leave, since they find plenty of food in the garbage cans. Recent droughts have reduced the coyotes' normal food supply, and as a result, the animals have become <u>menaces.</u> Wandering into backyards, they have bitten people and preyed on cats and small dogs. Public alarm reached its peak last year when a coyote killed a child, and Los Angeles County has resorted to shooting the animals. Similarly, in Washington, D.C., an epidemic of rabies among the raccoons has caused a health hazard, and city police have orders to shoot them on sight.

Cities can attract wild animals without turning them into pests. The trick is to create <u>habitats</u> where they can be self-sufficient but still be seen and appreciated. Such habitats can even be functional. In San Francisco, the municipal government and the National Institute for Urban Wildlife are testing different kinds of rainwater-control basins to see not only which ones retain the cleanest water but which will attract the most birds.

EXERCISE 30: Wildlife on Main Street

NAME _____ **DATE** _____

VOCABULARY

I. *The words in column A are used in the selection. Match the definition in column B to the appropriate word in column A.*

A

B

_____ 1. tallied   a. abandoned

_____ 2. prey   b. moved

_____c____ 3. derelict   c. causes for alarm

_____i____ 4. predator   d. counted

_____ 5. exterminated   e. disturbance

_____b____ 6. migrated   f. dwelling places

_____ 7. disoriented   g. feed

_____ 8. commotion   h. wiped out

_____ 9. menaces   i. enemies

_____f____ 10. habitats   j. confused

COMPREHENSION

II. *Select the best answer for each of the following. Indicate your choice on the line provided.*

_____d____ 1. The selection is primarily concerned with

a. foxes returning to London.

b. falcons in New York, Baltimore, Philadelphia, and Norfolk.

c. moose stumbling into plate-glass storefronts.

d. wildlife of all kinds returning to large cities to live.

_____c____ 2. The selection suggests that Londoners

a. have welcomed the wild birds, but find the foxes and martins a nuisance.

b. now hold foxhunts in the heart of the city.

c. have spent a great deal of money and time to make the city habitable for wildlife.

d. are taking steps to move wild animals back to the country.

_____a____ 3. An <u>ornithologist</u> is a person who

a. studies birds.

b. loves all wildlife.

c. plans ways to control pollution.

d. exterminates wildlife.

_____d____ 4. A <u>conservationist</u> is a person who

a. works to solve environmental problems.

b. protects humans from the health hazards of wildlife.

c. believes that wildlife is the least essential natural resource.

d. cares for and preserves all natural resources.

_____ 5. According to the selection, which of the following statements is *not* a reason wildlife is returning to the cities?

    a. Air and water quality have improved in the cities.

    b. Wildlife likes the noise and commotion in the cities.

    c. Food is plentiful in the cities.

    d. Wildlife refuges have been built in the cities.

_____ 6. According to the selection, the number of species of wildlife in New York's Central Park

    a. has more than doubled in the last century.

    b. is slowly decreasing in number.

    c. competes favorably with other large cities.

    d. is fast becoming a nuisance.

_____ 7. Select the most accurate characteristics that make cities good homes for peregrine falcons.

    a. bountiful nesting areas, abundant food, and rainwater control basins

    b. abundant food, buildings that resemble cliffs, and no natural predators

    c. large buildings with chimneys, other wild animals, and well-lighted nesting areas

    d. abundant food, chimneys, rubble, and windowsills

_____ 8. The most negative result of wildlife in cities mentioned by the author is

    a. attacks on humans and pets and creating a health hazard, especially rabies.

    b. the inability to provide enough food for the wildlife.

    c. educating the people to accept sharing the city with wildlife.

    d. maintaining the pollution-control efforts with animals in the cities.

_____ 9. The author seems to feel that

    a. wild animals and birds do not belong in cities.

    b. for the benefit of humans and animals, humans need to consider the needs of animals when building cities.

    c. if the migration of animals to cities continues, humans will gradually be forced into the wilderness.

    d. special wilderness preserves should be built for wildlife.

Selection Four

Hard Times

Norman Strung

1   The hard times. We don't care to remember them; we concentrate instead upon the golden days when birds were as thick as autumn leaves and fish jumped in the boat. Yet when you dig deeply enough, it is the hard times that mold us as outdoorsmen and friends.

2   Having had my share of mean experiences, I find they fall into two categories: disasters of our own making, and those that are the consequences of bad luck. I could cite many illustrations of the first state of graceless ignorance, but the one that comes most quickly to mind happened over two decades ago.

3   It was the first deer season of my life; the first year I could legally hunt big game. Without a <u>mentor</u> or personal transportation, but charged with enthusiasm at the chance of taking a deer, I made sketchy plans with two equally green friends to hitch to upstate New York for opening weekend.

4   We had no idea where we were going, and our equipment was so scant as to be skeletal: guns, knives, shells, cheap kapok sleeping bags, a Sterno stove, a pot, a pan, paper plates and cups, instant coffee, and lots of canned spaghetti.

5   Miraculously, we were picked up by two deer hunters who called themselves Jay and Tee and who dropped us off at a campground they knew of, in the middle of public hunting lands. But after that, everything went wrong. It started to rain about 3 in the morning, and by 6 our bags were soaked and soggy. We arose wet, shivering, and lusting for a hot drink, but it was so cold and damp that the Sterno didn't generate enough heat to dissolve the coffee crystals. After an hour of this had assured us that, indeed, watched pots never boil, it was breaking light and there was no time to heat the spaghetti. We ate it cold.

6   It rained all that morning. By blind chance and the custom of the day, we wore checkered-wool jackets. So long as we kept moving, we at least kept warm. As might be expected, we saw no deer.

7   The rain changed to snow that afternoon. We ate <u>tepid</u> spaghetti under the boughs of a dripping fir. Somehow deer hunting had lost most of its glamour. We started a fire by borrowing coals from a neighboring camper and tried to dry out our bags against the coming night.

8   To their credit and our gratitude, Jay and Tee stopped by to check on us just as night was falling. They had killed their deer and were headed home.

9   It took us all of 5 seconds to weigh the glory of another day afield against

their offer of a round trip. We cased our guns, crammed our meager belongings into a duffel bag, and thanked them profusely when they dropped us off near our homes.

10   There's more to this story, however, than testimony to our bright-eyed stupidity. In the shared misery of those sodden mountains, each of us received an education that would have been denied us under more <u>benign</u> circumstances: the worth of wool, the wisdom of careful planning, to name a few. We also learned to expect the unexpected and, in my case at least, to develop a distaste for canned spaghetti.

11   Although classes taught in the school of hard knocks seldom need repeating, disasters of your own making aren't limited to the untutored and tenderfooted. I now consider myself an accomplished outdoorsman, yet errors in judgment still visit me with their ruler-on-the-knuckles lessons.

12   I count whitewater rafting among my outdoor passions, as much for the superb fishing that usually comes attached to inaccessible canyons as for the thrills. Knowing that your life depends upon the quality and condition of your equipment, I always keep mine in perfect shape. But on one trip that very perfection cost me and my companions dearly.

13   Sam Curtis, Brett Friedah, and I were floating the Middle Fork of Montana's Flathead River during the bull trout run. The raft I was using was old, but it had been cared for immaculately—blown dry and powdered after each use, stored in a cool cellar, and preserved without so much as a patch to blemish its smooth skin.

14   But the invisible deterioration of age had taken its toll, and that factor, compounded by unusually abrasive rocks, shallow water, and a 2-foot misjudgment on a narrow passage, found us slamming into a sharp rock shelf that ripped the bottom of a tube wide open. The raft became a bathtub in an instant, and we were scoured into the water at the head of a particularly <u>vile</u> rapid. We lost the raft, but not our lives. Thanks to a previous education, we all knew to stay upstream of the raft; to point our legs downstream and use them as shock absorbers should we collide with a rock; and to angle toward shore with the current rather than against it. Since that trip I reserve older rafts for more leisurely floats and use only new equipment when there's danger to life or limb.

15   That Flathead trip also revealed another of the disguised gifts that accompany hard times. It was a five-star foulup in ways other than the dunking. What was forecast to be sunny July weather turned into four downhill days that went from cool and showery to a persistent downpour, ending with snow on the mountains. The only time we were dry and warm was in our bags at night. We could not even take comfort in good fishing. The bull trout had lockjaw.

16   It was a ripe environment for gripes, fault-finding, and games of pin-the-blame-on-the-next guy, but there was none of that. Rather, there was a will-

ingness to shoulder the burden and share our mutual disappointment. This smoothed out what could have been a human conflict even stormier than the weather. We pulled together, made the best of a bad situation, and made it together. To this day, I'd be willing to pitch a camp on the rimrocks of Hell if I knew Sam and Brett would be my partners.

17   Mettle of that caliber doesn't require great drama to be revealed, however. Bad luck will bring it out in smaller ways. For example, there was the week I once spent in a backpack tent, on the shores of one of the best trout lakes in the Rockies, during unexpected mountain monsoons. There were four of us, and the fishing was fair between the raindrops, but the gloomy weather, the close confines, and the incessant accommodations to the weather could easily have driven our spirits down. Instead, each of us seized every opportunity to lighten a heavy situation. We hatched an elaborate plot to lynch the weatherman. We read to each other from the labels of soup cans. We made a deck of cards from a notepad, and played poker, using the seeds of pine cones for chips. Looking back upon that week I remember a lot of laughs; despite everything, it had actually been enjoyable. That's another thing about hard times—they teach you to pick your hunting and fishing partners carefully.

18   I once went broadbill hunting with a fellow I'd known for several years. We'd fished together a few times, and walked the uplands for grouse, and he seemed a likable sort. We'd rigged thirty blocks on a deepwater point with a small pram and paddles. Around midday, a front came through, and the wind freshened from the northwest. The shooting improved as the wind grew in intensity. By 3 it was blowing a gale, and the decoys started dragging their anchors.

19   We agreed that we'd had enough for the day, and paddled out to pick up the stool, but as we reached the farthest block and turned around, it was apparent that the wind and waves were a force to be reckoned with. We paddled till our arms ached, and seemed to make no progress. Five miles of icy, open water licked at our backs.

20   "We're not gonna make it . . . I can't fight it any more," he wailed, shipping his paddle.

21   Half in shock, I yelled that if he didn't keep paddling, I'd throw him overboard to lighten the load. (I never would have. One person with one paddle in that high-profile pram was a certified dead man.) But it worked. Fear of certain drowning overcame his acceptance of probable drowning. He found a new reserve of strength and we made it inside the lee of the point, and finally to shore. But I never fished nor hunted with the man again.

22   Hard times can also forge partnerships as strong as the links in a log chain. My closest companion afield was only an acquaintance at the time, and a tough situation brought us a little closer together. We were hunting black ducks on the marshes of Long Island on a Christmas morning, and had driven

a Jeep down the beach to a place recommended to us by a friend. It was bitter cold that day, and the soft sand and marsh mud were frozen so hard that we didn't even have to engage the front hubs. With such firm footing, we drove our <u>decoys</u> right to the blind over salt meadows that would never support the vehicle in warmer weather. Although we had enough sense to return the Jeep to solid ground in case of a thaw, the hard freeze belied its location. Later that morning the weather clouded and warmed, and when I tried to move the vehicle, the wheels dug in up to the frame.

23   It was noon, and we were due at a family Christmas dinner at 2. We shored and we jacked and we levered in that accursed jelly for an hour. The Jeep fell off the jack, and slid off the slick boards we'd placed under the wheels. It started sleeting, then it poured rain. We built a corduroy road of sticks and cattails and driftwood, and we worked so hard that my partner vomited from overexertion.

24   We made it to the dinner 15 minutes late, and we were on the same marsh the next day, for the gunning had been good, and we agreed it was worth the price.

25   We were almost constant companions on trout streams the next spring, and bass ponds that summer. We endured a few other hard times during that period, but for the most part, good times prevailed. And then early that fall, before the obligations of establishing a more formal partnership could intrude upon the impending hunting season, we were married.

EXERCISE 31: Hard Times

NAME _____ **DATE** _____

VOCABULARY

I. Select the best definitions for the following words as they are used in the selection. Indicate your choice on the line provided.

_____   1. <u>mentor</u>
            a. plan   b. guide   c. partner

_____   2. <u>tepid</u>
            a. lukewarm   b. hot   c. frozen

_____   3. <u>benign</u>
            a. favorable   b. unbelievable   c. deplorable

_____   4. <u>vile</u>
            a. furious   b. beauteous   c. treacherous

_____b_____ 5. <u>mettle</u>
     a. outrage   b. courage   c. misfortune

_____c_____ 6. <u>monsoons</u>
     a. poor roads   b. steep mountains   c. seasonable rains

_____ 7. <u>incessant</u>
     a. unpleasant   b. constant   c. lack of

_____b_____ 8. <u>lee</u>
     a. hole   b. shelter   c. bottom

_____c_____ 9. <u>forge</u>
     a. force   b. hammer   c. form

_____ 10. <u>decoys</u>
     a. hooks   b. lures   c. game

COMPREHENSION

II. *Select the best answer for each of the following. Indicate your choice on the line provided.*

_____b_____ 1. The author of the selection could best be described as
     a. an inexperienced deer hunter.
     b. an experienced outdoorsman.
     c. a professional bounty hunter.
     d. a professional sports writer.

_____c_____ 2. The expression "mean experiences" most nearly means
     a. meaningful experiences.
     b. experiences in which someone is unkind.
     c. times when things go wrong.
     d. average, everyday experiences.

_____e_____ 3. According to the author, there are two kinds of mean experiences. These are
     a. disasters of our own making.
     b. pranks partners play.
     c. consequences of bad luck.
     d. the sheer roughness of the outdoors.
     e. a and c
     f. b and d

_____d_____ 4. The author remembers his first deer-hunting trip primarily because
   a. it was also his last.
   b. everything went perfectly.
   c. he shot his first deer.
   d. he received an education about the outdoors.

_____d_____ 5. According to the author, the perfect companion for an outdoorsman is one who
   a. has plenty of expensive equipment.
   b. is willing to stay at the Holiday Inn if it rains.
   c. knows everything there is to know about hunting, fishing, and whitewater rafting.
   d. is willing to pull together in bad times as well as in good.

_____a_____ 6. The author's one-time broadbill hunting partner was a poor companion because he
   a. gave up when things got rough.
   b. was older than the author.
   c. was afraid of the water.
   d. was a "sissy."

_____c_____ 7. Which of the following statements is *not* a positive result of the hard times mentioned in the selection?
   a. You learn to expect the unexpected.
   b. It is wise to plan carefully for an outdoor excursion.
   c. You learn to enjoy cold beans and stale sandwiches.
   d. Friendships and partnerships are strengthened.

_____b_____ 8. The author gets his message across by using
   a. narration.
   b. examples.
   c. comparisons.
   d. explanation.

_____c_____ 9. The author's "closest companion afield" is now
   a. Sam Curtis.
   b. Brett Freidah.
   c. his wife.
   d. a and b only.

_____d_____ 10. You could conclude from the selection that lasting friendships are formed by

    a. chance meetings and good times.

    b. physical attractions and admiration.

    c. similar ages and career goals.

    d. sharing experiences and companionship.

III. *Locate the following expressions in the indicated paragraphs, and then explain what the author meant by each.*

1. "the golden days when birds were as thick as autumn leaves and fish jumped in the boat" (1)

_____

_____

2. "state of graceless ignorance" (2)

_____

_____

3. "two equally green friends" (3)

_____

_____

4. "testimony to our bright-eyed stupidity" (10)

_____

_____

5. "classes taught in the school of hard knocks" (11)

_____

_____

6. "ruler-on-the-knuckles lessons" (11)

_____

_____

7. "a five-star foulup" (15)

_____

_____

8. "The bull trout had lockjaw." (15)

_____

_____

9. "a ripe environment for gripes, fault-finding, and games of pin-the-blame-on-the-next guy" (16)

_____everyone complains and blames_____

_____each other_____

10. "I'd be willing to pitch a camp on the rimrocks of Hell if I knew Sam and Brett would be my partners." (16)

_____

_____

IV. Write a paragraph about a "hard times" experience you have had that has strengthened a relationship.

_____

_____

_____

_____

_____

_____

_____

_____

_____

_____

_____

Selection Five

The Open Window

Saki (H. H. Munro)

"My aunt will be down presently, Mr. Nuttel," said a very self-possessed young lady of fifteen; "in the meantime you must try and put up with me."

Framton Nuttel <u>endeavoured</u> to say the correct something which should duly flatter the niece of the moment without unduly discounting the aunt that was to come. Privately he doubted more than ever whether these formal visits on a succession of total strangers would do much towards helping the nerve cure which he has supposed to be undergoing.

"I know how it will be," his sister had said when he was preparing to migrate to this rural retreat; "you will bury yourself down there and not speak to a living soul, and your nerves will be worse than ever from moping. I shall just give you letters of introduction to all the people I know there. Some of them, as far as I can remember, were quite nice."

Framton wondered whether Mrs. Sappleton, the lady to whom he was presenting one of the letters of introduction, came into the nice division.

"Do you know many of the people round here?" asked the niece, when she judged that they had had sufficient silent <u>communion.</u>

"Hardly a soul," said Framton. "My sister was staying here, at the rectory, you know, some four years ago, and she gave me letters of introduction to some of the people here."

He made the last statement in a tone of distinct regret.

"Then you know practically nothing about my aunt?" pursued the self-possessed young lady.

"Only her name and address," admitted the caller. He was wondering whether Mrs. Sappleton was in the married or widowed <u>state.</u> An undefinable something about the room seemed to suggest masculine habitation.

"Her great tragedy happened just three years ago," said the child; "that would be since your sister's time."

"Her tragedy?" asked Framton; somehow in this restful country spot tragedies seemed out of place.

"You may wonder why we keep that window wide open on an October afternoon," said the niece, indicating a large French window that opened on to a lawn.

"It is quite warm for the time of the year," said Framton; "but has that window got anything to do with the tragedy?"

"Out through that window, three years ago to a day, her husband and her two young brothers went off for their day's shooting. They never came back. In crossing the <u>moor</u> to their favourite snipeshooting ground they were all three engulfed in a treacherous piece of <u>bog.</u> It had been that dreadful wet summer, you know, and places that were safe in other years gave way suddenly without warning. The bodies were never recovered. That was the dreadful part of it." Here the child's voice lost its self-possessed note and became falteringly human. "Poor aunt always thinks that they will come back some day, they and the little brown spaniel that was lost with them, and walk in at that window just as they used to do. That is why the window is kept open every evening till it is quite dusk. Poor dear aunt, she has often told me how they went out, her husband with his white waterproof coat over his arm, and Ronnie, her youngest brother, singing, 'Bertie, why do you bound?' as he always did to tease her, because she said it got on her nerves. Do you know, sometimes on still, quiet evenings like this, I almost get a creepy feeling that they will all walk in through that window—"

She broke off with a little shudder. It was a relief to Framton when the aunt bustled into the room with a whirl of apologies for being late in making her appearance.

"I hope Vera has been amusing you?" she said.

"She has been very interesting," said Framton.

"I hope you don't mind the open window," said Mrs. Sappleton briskly; "my husband and brothers will be home directly from shooting, and they always come in this way. They've been out for snipe in the marshes today, so they'll make a fine mess over my poor carpets. So like you men-folk, isn't it?"

She rattled on cheerfully about the shooting and the scarcity of birds, and the prospects for duck in the winter. To Framton it was all purely horrible. He made a desperate but only partially successful effort to turn the talk on to a less <u>ghastly</u> topic; he was conscious that his hostess was giving him only a fragment of her attention, and her eyes were constantly straying past him to the open window and the lawn beyond. It was certainly an unfortunate coincidence that he should have paid his visit on this tragic anniversary.

"The doctors agree in ordering me complete rest, an absence of mental excitement, and avoidance of anything in the nature of violent physical exercise," announced Framton, who <u>laboured under</u> the tolerably wide-spread <u>delusion</u> that total strangers and chance acquaintances are hungry for the least detail of one's ailments and infirmities, their cause and cure. "On the matter of diet they are not so much in agreement," he continued.

"No?" said Mrs. Sappleton, in a voice which only replaced a yawn at the last moment. Then she suddenly brightened into alert attention—but not to what Framton was saying.

"Here they are at last!" she cried. "Just in time for tea, and don't they look as if they were muddy up to the eyes!"

Framton shivered slightly and turned towards the niece with a look intended to convey sympathetic comprehension. The child was staring out through the open window with dazed horror in her eyes. In a chill shock of nameless fear Framton swung round in his seat and looked in the same direction.

In the deepening twilight three figures were walking across the lawn towards the window; they all carried guns under their arms, and one of them was additionally burdened with a white coat hung over his shoulders. A tired brown spaniel kept close at their heels. Noiselessly they neared the house, and then a hoarse young voice chanted out of the dusk: "I said, Bertie, why do you bound?"

Framton grabbed wildly at his stick and hat; the hall-door, the gravel-drive, and the front gate were dimly noted stages in his headlong retreat. A cyclist coming along the road had to run into the hedge to avoid <u>imminent</u> collision.

"Here we are, my dear," said the bearer of the white mackintosh, coming in through the window; "fairly muddy, but most of it's dry. Who was that who bolted out as we came up?"

"A most extraordinary man, a Mr. Nuttel," said Mrs. Sappleton, "could only talk about his illnesses, and dashed off without a word of good-bye or apology when you arrived. One would think he had seen a ghost."

"I expect it was the spaniel," said the niece calmly; "he told me he had a horror of dogs. He was once hunted into a cemetery somewhere on the banks of the Ganges by a pack of <u>pariah</u> dogs, and had to spend the night in a newly dug grave with the creatures snarling and grinning and foaming just above him. Enough to make any one lose their nerve."

Romance at short notice was her speciality.

EXERCISE 32: The Open Window

NAME _____ **DATE** _____

VOCABULARY

I. Select the best definition for each of the following words as used in the selection. Indicate your choice on the line provided.

b _____ 1. <u>endeavored</u>
   a. continued   b. attempted   c. neglected

_____ C _____ 2. <u>communion</u>
   a. discord   b. alienation   c. accord

_____ b _____ 3. <u>state</u>
   a. declaration   b. condition   c. territory

_____ a _____ 4. <u>moor</u>
   a. marsh   b. road   c. farmland

_____ c _____ 5. <u>bog</u>
   a. mountainous terrain   b. dry, firm ground
   c. wet, spongy ground

_____ a _____ 6. <u>ghastly</u>
   a. horrible   b. enticing   c. robust

_____ c _____ 7. <u>labored under</u>
   a. worked with   b. eased into   c. was affected by

_____ a _____ 8. <u>delusion</u>
   a. misconception   b. delight   c. hindrance

_____ c _____ 9. <u>imminent</u>
   a. future   b. stupendous   c. impending

_____ b _____ 10. <u>pariah</u>
   a. gentle, domestic   b. wild, outcast   c. old, diseased

COMPREHENSION

II. Select the best answer for each of the following. Indicate your choice on the line provided.

_____ 1. The window referred to in the short story is

   a. a large picture window only eighteen inches from the floor.
   b. a small, narrow window placed horizontally in the wall.
   c. a stained-glass window with a mosaic design in the center.
   d. a French window hinged at the sides to open in the middle in the same way as a French door.

_____ 2. You would know your answer to the first question is correct because

   a. The Sappletons were able to get a panoramic view of the lawn.

    b. the house had modern lighting and air conditioning and did not need light from the outside.

    c. the Sappleton's lived in the rectory and wanted the windows to match the ones in the church.

    ✓d. the window must have served as a door, since the men walked through it leaving and entering the house.

_____ 3. The story takes place

    a. on an isolated hunting reserve.

    b. at the home of a wealthy family during an organized fox hunt.

    ✓c. at a restful country home where the men of the family enjoyed hunting.

    d. at the boarding house where Framton's sister had once lived.

_____ 4. Framton Nuttel had come to the area to

    a. engage in some hunting.

    b. recover from a nervous breakdown.

    c. sell real estate.

    d. check out where his sister had lived.

_____ 5. The story takes place in the

    a. spring.

    b. summer.   *uncomfortable*

    ✓c. fall.

    d. winter.

_____ 6. Framton tried to talk of his illness because

    a. he wanted to make it clear that he had overcome his problems.

    b. he was ill at ease and had the mistaken idea that they would be interested.

    c. he was attracted to Vera and wanted to impress her.

    d. he was a bore and told everyone he met about his personal life.

_____ 7. How did Vera relate the open window to the tale that she told Framton?

    a. Her uncles, along with their small dog, had gone through the window to go hunting and were drowned in the bog. Her aunt still expected them to return through the open window.

    b. Her uncles had gone hunting and had not returned. She and her aunt were watching for them through the window, expecting them to return at any time. They kept the window open so they could see them at a distance.

_____ 8. What made the story that Vera told so believable?

    a. Framton was gullible and was so impressed with Vera, he would believe anything she said, especially since she seemed so concerned about the men.

    b. Because Vera had seen the men leave, she was able to describe them perfectly. In addition, when Mrs. Sappleton came in, she said she was expecting the men to walk through the window at any minute.

_____ 9. The climax of the story occurred when

    a. Framton finally managed to tell the story of his illness to Vera and Mrs. Sappleton.

    b. the hunters were glimpsed in the distance.

    c. the hunters and the small dog actually walked through the window exactly as Vera had said they would.

    d. Framton met the hunters and heard their tales of the hunt.

_____ 10. When Framton saw the hunters and the dog approaching as Vera had said, he

    a. asked Vera how she knew exactly what would happen.

    b. wondered why they came through the window.

    c. congratulated them on their kill.

    d. immediately arose and ran from the house as fast as he could go.

III. *Answer the following question on the lines provided.*

1. Do you think Vera is playing a practical joke on Framton, or do you think she has a streak of evil? Give reasons for your answer.

_____

_____

_____

_____

_____

_____

Selection Six

In the Blink of an Eye

SHAWNA VOGEL

Someone should have told Richard Nixon that his eyelids were giving him away. On August 22, 1973, during his first nationally televised press conference since the Senate's Watergate investigation began six months earlier, the president maintained a calm, controlled tone of voice. But in answering such pointed questions as, "Is there any limitation on the president, short of impeachment, to compel the production of evidence?" Nixon's eyes became a blur. In an average minute he blinked 30 to 40 times. Unimpeachable adults blink only about 10 to 20 times a minute, and even that may be excessive; studies on infants show that the physical need to blink comes just once every two minutes.

All these extra blinks represent more than just watery wipes for dry corneas. Some are dust induced; others are reflex blinks, protective responses to a tap on the forehead or the pop of a balloon. What's left over is the thousands of blinks a day that seem to occur without cause and at random. But in fact these blinks are precisely timed, and they're directly linked to what's on our mind.

Excitement, fatigue, and anxiety can all be detected from someone's blinks, according to psychologist John Stern of Washington University in St. Louis. Stern has been interested in blinks ever since he watched Nixon parry press questions, and he specialized in the study on these tiny twitches, using them as sensitive probes of how the brain works.

"I use blinks as a psychological measure to make inferences about thinking because I have very little faith in what you tell me about what you're thinking," he says. "If I ask you the question, 'What does the phrase *a rolling stone gathers no moss* mean?' you can't tell me when you've started looking for the answer. But I can, by watching your eyes."

Blinks also tell Stern when you have understood his question—often long before he's finished asking it—and when you've found an answer or part of one. "We blink at times that are psychologically important," he says. "You have listened to a question, you understand it, now you can take time out for a blink. Blinks are punctuation marks. Their timing is tied to what is going on in your head."

Understandably, new acquaintances tend to squirm when Stern tells them what he does for a living. "They think I've been watching them blink," he says, "which is not the case. They'll say, 'You mean you can tell how I'm thinking by my blinks?' Then I tell them I can't listen to them and watch them blink at the same time."

But few things do more to stir the urge to blink—and thus contaminate blink research—than the thought that someone is watching your eyes. "If I tell someone I'm watching them blink," says Stern, "that immediately makes them uncomfortable. Eventually they'll stop thinking about their blinks, but until they do, they blink at an abnormal rate."

This <u>paradoxical</u> effect forced pioneers in the field to carry out their experiments <u>surreptitiously.</u> In the 1920s the first blink researchers, two Scottish scientists from the University of Edinburgh, conducted their early studies in the backs of courtrooms, secretly watching the eyes of witnesses and trying to determine how their blinks reflected their testimony. The research was limited to counting blinks and comparing the rates for different situations. Crude as these studies were, they showed indisputably that anxiety-ridden situations, such as a cross-examination, do indeed tend to <u>foster</u> more blinks.

Today's researchers have upgraded their techniques considerably, and their interests have shifted from blink rates to blink placement and <u>duration.</u> In Stern's lab, subjects are <u>wired</u> with tiny electrodes above and below their eyes to measure the difference in the electric potential of the eye when it is open and closed. The volunteers are told that the apparatus is only for measuring how the eyeball moves; in fact it times to the millisecond how long each component of a blink lasts and when the blink occurs in response to a given stimulus.

Stern has found that subjects <u>suppress</u> blinks when they are absorbing or anticipating information but not when they're reciting it. People blink later, for example, if they have to memorize six numbers instead of two. "You don't blink," he says, "until you have committed the information to some short-term memory store." And if subjects are <u>cued</u> that the set of numbers is coming in, say, five seconds, they'll curb their blinks until the task is over.

Similarly, the more important the information that people are taking in, the more likely they are to put their blinks on hold for it. Pilots blink less when they're responsible for flying a plane than when they're in the copilot's seat. Drivers routinely blink when they shift their eyes from the road to the rearview mirror. But if they see the flashing lights of a state trooper behind them, their eyes will dart unmoistened to the speedometer and back to the mirror.

This tendency to put blinks on the back burner whenever alertness is key has lured one of the nation's leading students of alertness, the Air Force, into the blink business. It is working to observe not only the frequency but also the length of blinks (which increases with fatigue) to gauge whether fliers are paying attention. "Blinks are relatively easy to monitor," says James Miller, a research physiologist at Edwards Air Force Base in California. "For very little trouble, they give us a great deal of information about what's going on in the brain."

Miller anticipates that in five or six years a blink-watching <u>apparatus</u> could be incorporated into the gear that pilots already wear. They wouldn't necessarily have to <u>don</u> electrodes; rather, an invisible infrared light shining on their eyeball could reflect back to a detector and signal whether the eye was open or closed. "If the monitor showed something unusual," says Miller, "we could then beep the pilot and perhaps pull him off the job."

Stern wishes such alertness monitors would be required for drivers as well. "What I would like to see," he says, "is every car with a big red light on top that flashes when the driver has stopped paying attention. Then if I see that light flashing, I can get out of the way."

Such dreams, however, take a backseat to Stern's latest interest: <u>tackling</u> the broader question of how people use their eyes to gather information. He's widened his focus to include the interactions of blinks with two other elements of visual activity: movements of the eyes and head. During a blink, eyes tend to move to whatever will be their next position, and Stern finds that this happens, in particular, whenever the task being performed is a complex one. It seems that under certain conditions the brain links blinks with eye movements to reduce the time the eye spends out of service.

Head movements also vary with the rigor of a task. Stern can usually identify when a reading child shifts from one line to the next because he'll move his head—not just his eyes—to scan the line. "Adults will do the same thing when they're reading difficult material," Stern says, "but not when the reading is easy."

Stern's continuing curiosity about blinks has been shared by few others over the years. But gradually the ranks of blink buffs are growing. "There are pockets of interest developing abroad," he says. "A group in Japan sent someone to work in our lab last year and a group in Germany hopes to send someone soon. People are finally discovering how much the eyes can tell us about the brain." In time, Prime Minister Takeshita and Chancellor Kohl, like President Nixon before them, may have to watch what their eyes reveal.

NAME _____ **DATE** _____

VOCABULARY

I. *Select the best definition for the following words as they are used in the selection. Indicate your choice on the line provided.*

_____b_____ 1. <u>random</u>

      a. with good intentions   b. without purpose or design
      c. with purpose

_____c_____ 2. <u>parry</u>

      a. oppose   b. perceive   c. evade

_____c_____ 3. <u>paradoxical</u>

      a. seemingly comparative   b. seemingly abnormal
      c. seemingly contradictory

_____a_____ 4. <u>surreptitiously</u>

      a. secretly   b. recklessly   c. uncertainly

_____b_____ 5. <u>foster</u>

      a. discourage   b. promote   c. forecast

_____ 6. <u>duration</u>

      a. length of time   b. method of movement
      c. ease of blink

_____c_____ 7. <u>cued</u>

      a. given   b. prompted   c. urged

_____a_____ 8. <u>apparatus</u>

      a. machine   b. electrode   c. signal

_____c_____ 9. <u>don</u>

      a. blink   b. tolerate   c. put on

_____b_____ 10. <u>tackling</u>

      a. charging   b. undertaking   c. teaching

COMPREHENSION

II. *Select the best answer for each of the following. Indicate your choice on the line provided.*

_____ 1. The author's primary purpose was to

   a. warn the reader to watch out when talking to research teams.
   b. explain how investigators judged whether Richard Nixon was telling the truth.
   c. show the relationship between the frequency and duration of eye blinks to the functions of the brain.
   d. explain about blink research with airplane pilots and automobile drivers.

__b___ 2. Blinking is to _____ as punctuation is to writing.

   a. breathing
   b. thinking
   c. reading
   d. speaking

__b___ 3. Adults who are calm and relatively free of stress blink about _____ times a minute.

   a. 0–10
   b. 10–20
   c. 20–30
   d. 30–40

__a___ 4. The first known research on blinking was conducted in

   a. 1920.
   b. 1934.
   c. 1973.
   d. 1980.

_____ 5. When a person is listening intently, the eyes tend to

   a. blink more rapidly.
   b. blink more slowly.
   c. not blink at all.
   d. blink and become watery.

d   _____ 6. On the basis of information in the passage, who do you think would benefit *least* by eye blink research?

    a. drivers
    b. pilots
    c. lawyers
    d. actors

c   _____ 7. As described by the author, the machine that measures the frequency and duration of blinks would most resemble the familiar

    a. tape player.
    b. headphone set.
    c. polygraph.
    d. siren.

d   _____ 8. Stern found that blinks were closely associated with all *but* which of the following?

    a. head movements
    b. lies and feelings of guilt
    c. excitement, fatigue, and anxiety
    d. mealtime and relaxation

b   _____ 9. Which of the following could *not* be fact?

    a. More people are beginning to see the value of studying eye blinks.
    b. The study of eye blinks should be of interest to everyone.
    c. Blink research could make airplane travel more safe in the future.
    d. Apparatus for studying eye blinks will be more sophisticated in the near future.

d   _____ 10. The author foresees a future blink-watching apparatus that uses

    _____ to monitor eye blinks.

    a. electric voltage
    b. special eyeglasses
    c. tiny electrodes
    d. invisible infrared light

III. *Indicate on the line provided whether the following statements are* **true** *or* **false.**

_____ 1. Eye blinks seem to be timed according to what is going on in the brain.

_____ 2. Blinks tend to occur more rapidly while you are listening intently.

3. Whenever you listen intently and your brain signals understanding, it is natural to blink.

4. When you know someone is watching you, you tend to blink at an abnormally slow rate.

5. You tend to blink less while absorbing information.

6. When you are warned that something important is about to be said or done, you tend to blink rapidly.

7. The more important information is, the more likely we are to hold our blink until we understand.

8. When a pilot is responsible for flying a plane, he or she blinks more often than the copilot.

9. There is a tendency to blink less when total concentration and alertness is demanded than when we are less absorbed.

10. Fatigue makes our blinks of longer duration, just as fear makes them shorter.

11. The United States Air Force at Edwards Air Force Base in California is currently using data on the duration of blinks to determine whether their fliers are paying attention.

12. According to the passage, blink research is too complicated and expensive for the amount of information received.

13. The same information gathered from blinks that would help alert pilots to fatigue could also benefit drivers.

14. When the eye blinks, it is temporarily out of service—not really seeing.

15. When reading a line, the eye usually does not blink but will blink as it moves to begin a new line.

16. Stern found that head movement along the line is most likely if the reading is easy and fun to read.

17. It is easier to control our voice when we are anxious than it is to control our eye blinks.

18. It would not be abnormal for a calm, untroubled infant to blink only once every two minutes.

_____ 19. At least two other countries have become interested in learning more about the relationship between eye blinks and the brain.

_____ 20. In the United States, there are hundreds of research studies being conducted on the eye blinks of normal adults.

IV. *Observe someone while the person is reading or listening intently to an explanation or to directions to see how your subject blinks his or her eyes. Write your observations on the lines provided.*

_____

_____

_____

_____

_____

_____

_____

_____

Selection Seven

The Chaser

JOHN COLLIER

Alan Austen, as nervous as a kitten, went up certain dark and creaky stairs in the neighborhood of Pell Street, and peered about for a long time on the dim landing before he found the name he wanted written <u>obscurely</u> on one of the doors.

He pushed open this door, as he had been told to do, and found himself in a tiny room, which contained no furniture but a plain kitchen table, a rocking chair, and an ordinary chair. On one of the dirty buff-colored walls were a couple of shelves, containing in all perhaps a dozen bottles and jars.

An old man sat in the rocking chair, reading a newspaper. Alan, without a word, handed him the card he had been given. "Sit down, Mr. Austen," said the old man very politely. "I am glad to make your acquaintance."

"Is it true," asked Alan, "that you have a certain mixture that has—er—quite extraordinary effects?"

"My dear sir," replied the old man, "my <u>stock in trade</u> is not very large—I don't deal in laxatives and teething mixtures—but, such as it is, it is varied. I think nothing I sell has effects which could be precisely described as ordinary."

"Well, the fact is—" began Alan.

"Here, for example," interrupted the old man, reaching for a bottle from the shelf. "Here is a liquid as colorless as water, almost tasteless, quite <u>imperceptible</u> in coffee, milk, wine, or any other beverage. It is also quite imperceptible to any known method of <u>autopsy</u>."

"Do you mean it is a poison?" cried Alan, very much horrified.

"Call it cleaning fluid if you like," said the old man indifferently. "Lives need cleaning. Call it a spot-remover. 'Out, damned spot!' Eh? 'Out, brief candle!'"

"I want nothing of that sort," said Alan.

"Probably it is just as well," said the old man. "Do you know the price of this? For one teaspoonful, which is sufficient, I ask five thousand dollars. Never less. Not a penny less."

"I hope all your mixtures are not as expensive," said Alan <u>apprehensively</u>.

"Oh, dear no," said the old man. "It would be no good charging that sort of price for a love-potion, for example. Young people who need a love-potion very seldom have five thousand dollars. If they had they would not need a love-potion."

"I'm glad to hear you say so," said Alan.

"I look at it like this," said the old man. "Please a customer with one article, and he will come back when he needs another. Even if it is more costly. He will save up for it, if necessary."

"So," said Alan, "you really do sell love-potions?"

"If I did not sell love-potions," said the old man, reaching for another bottle, "I should not have mentioned the other matter to you. It is only when one is in a position to oblige that one can afford to be so confidential."

"And these potions," said Alan. "They are not just—just—er—"

"Oh, no," said the old man. "Their effects are permanent and extend far beyond the mere <u>carnal</u> impulse. But they include it. Oh, yes, they include it. Bountifully. Insistently. Everlastingly."

"Dear me!" said Alan, attempting a look of scientific detachment. "How very interesting!"

"But consider the spiritual <u>side</u>," said the old man.

"I do, indeed," said Alan.

"For indifference," said the old man, "they substitute devotion. For scorn, adoration. Give one tiny measure of this to the young lady—its flavor is imperceptible in orange juice, soup, or cocktails—and however gay and giddy she is, she will change altogether. She'll want nothing but solitude, and you."

"I can hardly believe it," said Alan. "She is so fond of parties."

"She will not like them anymore," said the old man. "She'll be afraid of the pretty girls you may meet."

"She'll actually be jealous?" cried Alan in a <u>rapture</u>. "Of me?"

"Yes, she will want to be everything to you."

"She is, already. Only she doesn't care about it."

"She will, when she has taken this. She will care intensely. You'll be her <u>sole</u> interest in life."

"Wonderful!" cried Alan.

"She'll want to know all you do," said the old man. "All that has happened to you during the day. Every word of it. She'll want to know what you are thinking about, why you smile suddenly, why you are looking sad."

"That is love!" cried Alan.

"Yes," said the old man. "How carefully she'll look after you! She'll never allow you to be tired, to sit in a draft, to neglect your food. If you are an hour late, she'll be terrified. She'll think you are killed, or that some <u>siren</u> has caught you."

"I can hardly imagine Diana like that!" cried Alan, overwhelmed with joy.

"You will not have to use your imagination," said the old man. "And by the way, since there are always sirens, if by any chance you *should*, later on, slip a little, you need not worry. She will forgive you, in the end. She'll be terribly hurt, of course, but she'll forgive you—in the end."

"That will not happen," said Alan fervently.

"Of course not," said the old man. "But, if it does, you need not worry. She'll never divorce you. Oh, no! And, of course, she herself will never give you the least, the very least, grounds for—not divorce, of course—but even uneasiness."

"And how much," said Alan, "how much is this wonderful mixture?"

"It is not so dear," said the old man, "as the spot-remover, as I think we agreed to call it. No. That is five thousand dollars; never a penny less. One has to be older than you are to indulge in that sort of thing. One has to save up for it."

"But the love-potion?" said Alan.

"Oh, that," said the old man, opening the drawer in the kitchen table and taking out a tiny, rather dirty-looking <u>phial</u>. "That is just a dollar."

"I can't tell you how grateful I am," said Alan, watching him fill it.

"I like to oblige," said the old man. "Then customers come back, later in life, when they are better-off, and want more expensive things. Here you are. You will find it very effective."

"Thank you again," said Alan. "Good-bye."

"*Au revoir,*" said the old man.

EXERCISE 34: The Chaser

NAME _____ DATE _____

VOCABULARY

I. Select the best meaning for the following words as used in the selection. Indicate your choice on the line provided.

_____ 1. <u>obscurely</u>
      a. conspicuous   b. almost illegible   c. with conformity

_____ 2. <u>stock in trade</u>
      a. inventory   b. estimation   c. activity

_____ 3. <u>imperceptible</u>
   a. undetectable   b. indissoluble   c. improbable

_____ 4. <u>autopsy</u>
   a. record keeping by a medical facility
   b. preparation of food
   c. examination after death to determine cause of death

_____ 5. <u>apprehensively</u>
   a. gallantly   b. anxiously   c. flippantly

_____ 6. <u>carnal</u>
   a. sensual   b. hasty   c. indiscreet

_____ 7. <u>rapture</u>
   a. rampage   b. ecstasy   c. flight

_____ 8. <u>sole</u>
   a. sacred   b. serious   c. singular

_____ 9. <u>siren</u>
   a. warning device   b. seductive woman   c. sea nymph

_____ 10. <u>phial</u>
   a. purse   b. package   c. bottle

COMPREHENSION

II. *Answer the following questions on the lines provided.*

1. Why does Alan go to the shop on Pell Street?

   _____

2. Describe the shop and location.

   _____

   _____

3. When you form a mental picture of Alan, what do you see?

   _____

   _____

4. Consider your answer to question 3. Why, then, is Alan willing to go to the shop on Pell Street?

   _____

   _____

5. When you form a mental picture of Diana, what do you see?

   _____

   _____

6. How does Diana feel toward Alan?

   _____

7. How much does the love-potion cost? How much does the expensive potion cost? What do you think the latter is intended to do?

   _____

8. Why do you think that the old man acts so mysteriously about the expensive potion rather than just stating what it is intended to do?

   _____

   _____

   _____

9. Define love as described through the effects of the love-potion.

   _____

   _____

   _____

   _____

10. Why do you think that the old man bade Alan *au revoir* instead of good-bye at the end of the story? (In English dictionaries the meaning of *au revoir* is "good-bye," but the literal meaning in French is "to see you again.")

    _____

    _____

    _____

III. *Contrast love as defined through the effects of the love potion to what you consider true love.*

Selection Eight

They Dared Cocaine— and Lost

HENRY HURT

No one is immune to this savage infection—not the strong, not the wealthy, not the gifted. Even when cocaine does not kill the body, it devours the spirit, sucking every morsel of dignity and self-respect, often bringing an agony much worse than death.

Among professionals, cocaine addiction is notoriously widespread. It has destroyed corporate executives, lawyers, doctors, performers of every variety. Despite their initial insulation from the horrors of addiction, these professionals in the end wallow as helplessly in their misery as the most tortured back-alley junkie.

Five million Americans are regular users of cocaine. Each day 5000 more tempt self-destruction by trying the drug for the first time. Here are the stories of three people whose lives were ravaged by cocaine.

A DREAM DESTROYED

1   Stan Belin was born in the 1930s to an urban family locked in the grip of the Great Depression.* His was a fractured family—one in which his parents fought constantly. "I lived with a feeling of impending doom," he says. This fear drove him to be a model child.

2   Stan has a vivid memory of once leaning against a bridge railing as a boy and gazing at a handsome party boat passing below. He could see people on deck enjoying their outing. It was a scene of comfort and luxury he could hardly have imagined. That mental picture influenced the boy's idea of success. His goals became money, power, and prestige.

3   Stan did well in school. He found his greatest academic success in his science courses. But he lacked the confidence to pursue a medical career and turned to dentistry as a quicker route to his life's goals.

*The names of Stan and Jane Belin and Mary Shea have been changed.

Reprinted with permission from the May 1988 Reader's Digest. Copyright © 1988 by The Reader's Digest Assn., Inc.

4   He married a young woman he had known since high school, and for over 20 years Stan and Jane lived a life that many people would envy. His reputation spread, the money started rolling in and he was appointed to a prestigious position by his state government. Two healthy children were born. The family had a magnificent house, expensive automobiles and took exotic vacations.

5   The crowning touch for Stan came when he bought a luxury yacht and sailed to the bridge where, as a child, he had first glimpsed what he hoped would be his future. "I told Jane the story," he says. "As I spoke, I realized that something was all wrong. I possessed everything I had ever dreamed of, but I felt very sad and hopeless. What was worse, I knew it would never change."

6   Then in the early 1980s, a doctor friend invited Stan to dinner. The friend said he had been using cocaine as an anti-depressant. He described it as a marvelous nonaddictive drug. Stan decided the drug might be just right for his own depression.

7   "From the instant I snorted the first line of cocaine, I was addicted," says Stan. "It gave me poise, confidence, happiness—things I had believed money should buy. It made me seem a better person, a better talker, a better dentist."

8   At first Stan did not believe that he was doing anything wrong: "I thought I had finally found an anti-depressant drug that raised me from my misery. It angered me that such a wonderful drug would continue to be outlawed."

9   Two years after Stan's introduction to cocaine, his insulation from the world of street addiction was knocked asunder when his physician friend was murdered. A week later, Stan walked out of his dental office and never returned. "At the time, I believed I could not deal with the pressures of my practice, but that wasn't it. I just needed more time for my addiction."

10   He spent his days aimlessly—going shopping with his wife, and wandering from doctor to doctor to find help for his depression—all the while snorting cocaine. He took menial jobs. He frequently considered suicide.

11   By the third year of Stan's addiction, the effects of cocaine were increasingly fleeting. The high would last for only seconds before he would crash back to the depths of his depression.

12   "Finally, it reached the point where I just stood around crying," Stan says. Jane knew her husband's condition was desperate, and she persuaded him to enter an addiction center. Stan checked into a prominent institution, but he had one-half ounce of cocaine concealed in his clothes. "I was cooperative for a few days, until I had snorted up my cocaine," Stan says. Then he split—as he did other times when Jane convinced him to seek help.

13   Once when Stan believed he had finally beaten his addiction, he was washing his car and saw a small vial of cocaine, a leftover from his past, roll from beneath the carpet. "Just the sight of it made me high," he recalls. "I put

it in my pocket. I thought it would make me stronger to keep it and resist the temptation. But my mind never left that vial."

14   Like a serpent coiled in Stan's pocket, the little vial of cocaine lay quietly. A war raged in Stan's mind. Then the serpent struck with a ferocity known only to those who are powerless against their addiction.

15   Today Stan has completed an extensive rehabilitation program for his addiction and works as a counselor in a drug program. His salary is one-seventh what he earned as a dentist; his house and boat are gone.

16   Only time will reveal if he finally has beaten his addiction. Now, as he tries to build his new life, Stan is determined not to let the serpent get so close.

"TAILORED FOR ME"

17   Mary Shea was the American dream come true. Her blue eyes shining with confidence, she believed the future stretched in front of her with the same beckoning that had coaxed her from the humblest of origins. At 26, she had just received her pharmacist's license and landed a good job. She had traveled a hard road to reach this juncture.

18   Mary was one of five children in a lower-middle-class Boston family. She had worked from age nine to save money for college—a goal no one in her family had reached. Despite her accomplishments in academics, music and athletics, Mary always felt that her parents were disappointed in her—a belief that gnawed at her constantly.

19   "I looked at my mother and how she struggled to take care of five children with so little money, and I knew that wasn't for me," Mary says in her gentle voice. "I wanted to *live*, and I was determined I wasn't going to miss anything."

20   Like demons in the long night of the 1960s, drugs came at Mary from all directions. She started taking amphetamines when she was 13. These drugs literally sped up everything in her system. She could get by on four hours' sleep a night and still maintain her frenzied pace.

21   Always independent, Mary used her earnings from baby-sitting and clerking in a pharmacy to pay for drugs—but never more than she could afford. She never got into trouble, and there was never any sign of addiction. At age 21, launching a college career, Mary tossed aside the drugs. "I didn't need them anymore," she says. "I was grown and free and ready for life."

22   For the next six years, she did not use drugs. After she completed college and received her license, she got a job as a pharmacist. She and her fiancé bought a small farm. Life was crammed with hard work, running, skiing and farming.

23   It was during that first year, 1979, that the demon crept into Mary's life.

Some friends told her about their sensational experiences with cocaine. "I had walked away from drugs before with no problem. And I believed the myth that cocaine is nonaddictive," she says. "So why not try it? I loved the incredible burst of energy. Cocaine was perfectly tailored for me."

24   Over the next year or so, Mary snorted cocaine about once a month. Then one day she discovered a supply in the drugstore. No one would miss it, for it was stored among outdated drugs and not in inventory. Mary helped herself to a small amount, took it home and used it. A pattern developed, and Mary became increasingly obsessed with when and where she would snort her next line.

25   Gradually Mary's fiancé discovered what she was doing and finally confronted her. "He claimed all my values had changed," Mary says. "I guess he was right." Mary moved out, rejecting him in favor of cocaine.

26   The drug had taken control of her life and wrecked the most precious part of her future. Unable to face the daily routine of work, she quit her job and began cleaning houses. For the first time in her life, Mary lived aimlessly from day to day. Her only purpose was to find cocaine. "It was so degrading," she recalls. "I had spent my entire life trying to improve myself, and suddenly I was at the bottom—cleaning toilet bowls for other people."

27   Then, a regular cocaine user Mary knew was shot to death in a drug-related murder. "I knew I had to get out of there," she says.

28   Fear and terror of the murder jolted Mary back to her senses. She left Boston and settled into a small town in the South. She straightened herself up—still able to look bright and friendly—and quickly landed a job as a pharmacist. "She was excellent with customers and especially gentle and patient with older people," recalls the pharmacy owner who hired her.

29   "I had a wonderful opportunity to start over," Mary says. But, convinced she could use cocaine in moderation, she rationed her use to once a week. For a while this worked, and Mary was promoted to manager of the pharmacy.

30   But once more Mary lost control and began to steal cocaine from the drugstore. She even filched it from prescriptions she filled, substituting an anesthetic in its place. Cocaine offered the only relief she could find from the overwhelming depression of knowing she had thrown away her promising life.

31   Mary's body was tortured by cocaine. Her heart beat so hard that she took drugs to slow it down. She took pills in desperate attempts to sleep, to escape the real world. Determined that she could overcome any problem alone, she never even thought of asking for help.

32   In a final attempt to regain her self-respect, Mary stopped using cocaine, cold turkey. She resumed her running and began taking care of herself. Part of her strategy was to make no friends, but rather to concentrate entirely on being drug-free. "It was like I was addicted to staying *off* cocaine," she says. "I was terribly lonely."

33   Seven months later, in November 1984, Mary ran a marathon and came in seventh out of 200 women. Her self-respect surged. In her euphoria, she went out to celebrate with some acquaintances. Like a venomous serpent hidden in the grass, cocaine struck with terrifying precision.

34   Now Mary fell in with a group of heavy users, including dangerous dealers. She became their source of Valium. She would fake prescriptions, then pay for the Valium and swap it for cocaine. Soon Mary began selling cocaine herself.

35   Slowly Mary descended into levels of hell she had never imagined. She lived in constant fear of arrest. Around the end of 1984, she quit her job again. By this time, no matter how much cocaine she consumed, the effect was fleeting. Mary tried injecting it into her veins. She tried smoking it. She took crack.

36   It is clear now that Mary's greatest strengths—those of self-reliance and powerful determination—were her greatest enemy. Finally, when suicide seemed the only escape, Mary sought help.

37   Today Mary Shea's blue eyes are sad. She has successfully completed an addiction-treatment program. Theoretically she could face heavy penalties for countless violations of the federal narcotics laws, but the terms of punishment for Mary are uncertain.

38   "I'm so glad the nightmare is over," says Mary, now 35. She expects to participate in support groups like Cocaine Anonymous for the rest of her life. "It was hopeless for me to try to fight this alone. I always thought I could solve my own problems—but that was before I met cocaine."

DANCE OF DEATH

39   At the age of 21, Patrick Bissell burst upon New York as principal dancer of the American Ballet Theatre. Rarely had a man so young dazzled so many in the supercharged, intensely competitive world of ballet. He was praised, in the words of Mikhail Baryshnikov, as "one of the brightest lights in the entire ballet world."

40   Patrick Bissell also helped bury the American myth that ballet is for sissies. At six feet, two inches tall, Patrick was a tough, hard-drinking kid from Texas with a passion for motorcycles, cowboy boots and women. He was a muscle man who could twirl ballerinas into the air and make them look as graceful as butterflies.

41   Seven months after his birth in 1957, baby Bissell was not walking, according to his mother; he was actually running. When Patrick was ten, his sister bribed him with her allowance to come to her dance class, because she needed a partner. His natural gifts of coordination and stamina were stunning, and from that point on, his destiny was dance.

42   The ballet world is notoriously brutal in its physical and emotional demands. The primary goal is absolute perfection. Unlike a professional athlete, which many believe Bissell could have become, a ballet star never has the satisfaction of knowing a final score, or of beating the competition. He competes only against himself—and for a perfectionist this may be the harshest competition of all.

43   When young Bissell set off for life, his mother believes he carried with him seeds that would lead to his destruction. Patrick was one of five children born in six years to Patricia and Donald Bissell, an ambitious young couple who moved six times by the time Patrick was 12.

44   Patricia Bissell, herself terribly frustrated during those years, is convinced that her son's self-esteem was so battered by her emotional and physical beatings when he was a child that he carried with him a deep-seated hatred of himself. True or not, Patrick Bissell's life seems tormented from the time he was a very young man.

45   Every indication is that, even early in his career, Bissell was addicted to cocaine, alcohol and other drugs. But his strength and skill were so tremendous that he was able to perform the most demanding work without his managers' knowing the truth.

46   In her autobiography, *Dancing on My Grave,* ballerina Gelsey Kirkland claims that Bissell introduced her to cocaine soon after his success in New York City, thus setting their private stage for a long affair of sex and drugs. She watched Bissell's paranoia grow to the point that, when he slept, he kept a hatchet under the bed and a knife under his pillow. He would stand by the apartment door for hours with a can of Mace to fend off imagined intruders.

47   In June 1981, only three years into his career, Bissell slashed his wrist. When the paramedics reached him, Bissell smashed a bottle to use for a weapon and fought them off. Next day, he was bandaged and back onstage.

48   By this time, he and Kirkland were clearly out of control—spending weeks on cocaine binges. Increasingly they were absent from rehearsals and late for performances. Both were fired from their jobs, rehired and fired again. In the end, Gelsey Kirkland sought help.

49   Patrick Bissell did not.

50   In the fall of 1987, the ballet company sent Bissell away for treatment—to the Betty Ford Center in California. He told friends that he was ready to clean up his life. He wanted a fresh start.

51   He was released a week early and returned to New York. During December, Amy Rose, a ballerina he had become engaged to, was on tour in California and would return to New York after the holidays. Alone, Bissell got a Christmas tree and decorated it for their apartment.

52   On December 23, he had a long telephone conversation with his parents. His mother begged him to join them at home. He declined, explaining that

being alone during Christmas was a chance for him to show that he was strong enough to live without cocaine.

53   Four days after Christmas, Amy Rose let herself into the apartment. She discovered Patrick's body on the living-room couch. Patrick Bissell was dead of an overdose of cocaine and other drugs. He had just turned 30.

54   Patricia Bissell's voice breaks as she speaks of a death notice for her son in the *New York Times*. Beneath the name Bissell, it simply states: "Good night, sweet prince."

55   It is impossible to say what, if anything, could have saved Patrick Bissell once he had begun his long dance of death. His mother, realizing that her assessment runs counter to some expert wisdom, offers a powerful insight:

56   "We are quick to blame such tragedies on others—on peer pressure, stressful occupations, drug dealers, everyone except ourselves. But most of these problems begin at home, when children are being brought up. It is hard for me to admit this, but I failed to nurture in Patrick the self-esteem he needed to deal with life. No matter how well he did, he felt that he had failed. He used drugs because they allowed him to escape that feeling. When we come to understand and accept this aspect of addiction, maybe we can do something about it."

EXERCISE 35: They Dared Cocaine—and Lost

NAME _____ **DATE** _____

VOCABULARY

I. Select a word or phrase in the indicated paragraph that means

_____ 1. about to happen (1)

_____ 2. near perfect (1)

_____ 3. important (4)

_____ 4. finale (5)

_____ 5. protection (9)

_____ 6. askew (9)

_____ 7. fury (14)

_____	8. position in life (17)
_____sped up_____	9. hurried (20)
_____	10. false belief (23)
_____steal_____	11. stole (30)
_____	12. plan of action (32)
_____	13. feeling of well-being (33)
_____	14. poisonous (33)
_____	15. fate (41)
_____	16. beaten down (44)
_____	17. delusions (46)
_____	18. sprees (48)
_____	19. in opposition (55)
_____	20. promote development (56)

COMPREHENSION

II. *Select the best answer for each of the following. Indicate your choice on the line provided.*

___b___ 1. The purpose of the selection is to

  a. inform the reader that using cocaine is expensive.
  b. convince the reader that using cocaine could be deadly.
  c. inform the reader that using cocaine is not socially acceptable.

___a___ 2. The most likely audience for this article is

  a. adults who might feel it is harmless to try cocaine socially.
  b. teenagers whose friends are pressuring them into drug use.
  c. hard-core addicts.

___b___ 3. The purpose of the italicized introduction is

  a. to synopsize the article so the hurried reader won't have to
   read it all.

b. to provide an overview that serves to unite the three narra-
       tives.
   c. to tell the reader the author's purpose in writing the article.

___ 4. Stan and Mary were propelled into abusing cocaine by
   a. the realization that all their peers were using the drug.
   b. a drug dealer who coerced them into using the drug.
   c. the dream that it would help them achieve a better life.

___ 5. After becoming addicted to cocaine, both Stan and Mary realized
        that they
   a. were on their own to conquer the addiction.
   b. could help each other to conquer the addiction.
   c. needed professional help to conquer the addiction.

___ 6. You can conclude that Stan and Mary are now
   a. struggling to remain free of their addiction.
   b. likely to return to their addiction within a few years.
   c. totally free of their addiction.

___ 7. All three people in the story—Stan, Mary, and Patrick—started
        using drugs when they were teenagers.
   a. true
   b. false

___ 8. Patrick Bissell helped to dispel the theory that
   a. drugs are dangerous.
   b. it takes tough, strong men to succeed.
   c. ballet is for sissies.

___ 9. You can infer from the selection that Patrick's mother
   a. partially blames herself for his insecurities.
   b. blames his drug use on his career choice.
   c. believes he would still be alive if he and his girlfriend had
       married.

___ 10. You can conclude from the selection that
   a. Patrick Bissell's success as a ballet dance depended on drug
       use.
   b. Patrick Bissell's addiction made him very unpopular with
       other professional dancers.
   c. Patrick Bissell was a talented ballet dancer and could have
       been successful without the use of drugs.

_____ 11. The author makes his case against cocaine through
  a. comparison and contrast.
  b. example.
  c. statistical analysis.

_____ 12. The style of writing in the selection could best be described as
  a. formal and scholarly.
  b. informal and personal.
  c. objective and analytical.

III. *Indicate whether the following statements are **true** or **false** according to the passage.*

_____ 1. Although many professionals abuse cocaine and other drugs, they handle the latter stages with more dignity than nonprofessionals.

_____ 2. Some people are so influenced by what they see as the "good life" that they will go to great lengths to obtain a similar life style.

_____ 3. Most of the people in the passage used drugs to help them reach certain goals and then settled back to enjoy their accomplishments.

_____ 4. Users often try to "sell" cocaine on the premise that it is an antidepressant and is nonaddictive.

_____ 5. People who begin by taking drugs only occasionally will often increase their intake during trying times in their lives.

_____ 6. As with most addictions, a cocaine user will soon need more of the drug more often to receive the desired effect.

_____ 7. According to the first story, the user did not succeed in breaking the habit in the beginning because he would not follow through with the treatment.

_____ 8. Actually, when a person is addicted, there is little that can be done.

_____ 9. In the passage, Mary wanted a better life than her mother had but wanted a shortcut to obtain this better life.

_____ 10. The fact that Mary quit drugs, but started back several times, proves that there is no return once you use drugs.

_____ 11. Even after Mary quit using drugs and her life was filled with hard work and a satisfying personal life, she backslid and started cocaine.

_____ 12. In Mary's case, when one drug caused a reaction, she took another drug to combat the reaction; then when that one caused a reaction, she took still another. . . .

_____ 13. Since Mary's cocaine abuse went to such extremes, she will likely fight the battle for the remainder of her life.

_____ 14. Patrick Bissell was a ballet dancer who, according to the passage, could have made it big on his own merits.

_____ 15. Since Patrick Bissell's major competition was himself, his life was virtually free of stress.

_____ 16. Patrick Bissell introduced a ballerina to cocaine, and she became his partner on many of his binges.

_____ 17. He became so addicted and affected by cocaine that he could not sleep and eventually could not work.

_____ 18. Bissell's employer was totally unsympathetic and did nothing to help him.

_____ 19. Although Patrick Bissell was treated at the Betty Ford Center and released, a few weeks later he died from an overdose of cocaine and other drugs.

_____ 20. The purpose of the passage is to convey to the reader that if you dare cocaine—you lose.

IV. _Plan in detail one of the following, explaining or demonstrating the effects of drug abuse: (1) a poster, (2) a skit with two or three characters, (3) a full-page newspaper ad, or (4) a one-minute television commercial._

_____

_____

_____

_____

_____

_____

Selection Nine

The Necklace

GUY DE MAUPASSANT
Translated by Edgar V. Roberts

She was one of those pretty and charming women, born, as if by an error of destiny, into a family of clerks and copyists. She had no <u>dowry</u>, no prospects, no way of getting known, courted, loved, married to a rich and distinguished man. She finally settled for a marriage with a minor clerk in the Ministry of Education.

She was a simple person, without the money to dress well, but she was as unhappy as if she had gone through bankruptcy, for women have neither rank nor race. In place of high birth or important family connections, they can rely only on their beauty, their grace, and their charm. Their inborn <u>finesse</u>, their elegant taste, their engaging personalities, which are their only power, make working-class women the equals of the grandest duchesses.

She suffered constantly, feeling herself destined for all delicacies and luxuries. She suffered because of her grim apartment with its drab walls, threadbare furniture, ugly curtains. All such things, which most other women in her situation would not even have noticed, tortured her and filled her with despair. The sight of the young country girl who did her simple housework awakened in her only a sense of desolation and lost hopes. She daydreamed of large, silent <u>anterooms</u>, decorated with oriental tapestries and lighted by high bronze floor lamps, with two elegant <u>valets</u> in short culottes dozing in large armchairs under the effects of forced-air heaters. She visualized large drawing rooms draped in the most expensive silks, with fine end tables on which were placed knicknacks of inestimable value. She dreamed of the perfume of dainty private rooms, which were designed only for intimate tête-à-têtes with the closest friends, who because of their achievements and fame would make her the envy of all other women.

When she sat down to dinner at her round little table covered with a cloth that had not been washed for three days, in front of her husband who opened the kettle while declaring ecstatically, "Oh boy, beef stew, my favorite," she dreamed of expensive banquets with shining placesettings, and wall hangings depicting ancient heroes and exotic birds in an enchanted forest. She imagined a <u>gourmet-prepared</u> main course carried on the most exquisite trays and served on the most beautiful dishes, with whispered gallantries which she would hear with a <u>sphinxlike</u> smile as she dined on the pink meat of a trout or the delicate wing of a quail.

She had no decent dresses, no jewels, nothing. And she loved nothing but these; she believed herself born only for these. She burned with the desire to please, to be envied, to be attractive and sought after.

She had a rich friend, a comrade from convent days, whom she did not want to see anymore because she suffered so much when she returned home. She would weep for the entire day afterward with sorrow, regret, despair, and misery.

Well, one evening, her husband came home glowing; and carrying a large envelope.

"Here," he said, "this is something for you."

She quickly tore open the envelope and took out a card engraved with these words:

> The Chancellor of Education and Mrs. George Ramponneau request that Mr. and Mrs. Loisel do them the honor of coming to dinner at the Ministry of Education on the evening of January 8.

Instead of being delighted, as her husband had hoped, she threw the invitation spitefully on the table while muttering:

"What do you expect me to do with this?"

"But Honey, I thought you'd be glad. You never get to go out, and this is a special occasion! I had a lot of trouble getting the invitation. Everyone wants one; the demand is high and not many clerks get invited. Everyone important will be there."

She looked at him angrily and stated impatiently:

"What do you want me to wear to go there?"

He had not thought of that. He stammered:

"But your theatre dress. That seems nice to me . . ."

He stopped, amazed and bewildered, as his wife began to cry. Large tears fell slowly from the corner of her eyes to her mouth. He said falteringly:

"What's wrong? What's wrong?"

But with a strong effort she had recovered, and she answered calmly as she wiped her damp cheeks:

"Nothing, except that I have nothing to wear and therefore can't go to the party. Give your invitation to someone else at the office whose wife will have nicer clothes than mine."

Distressed, he responded:

"Well, okay, Mathilde. How much would a new dress cost, something you could use at other times, but not anything fancy?"

She thought for a few moments, adding things up and thinking also of an amount that she could ask without getting an immediate refusal and a frightened outcry from the frugal clerk.

Finally she responded tentatively:

"I don't know exactly, but it seems to me that I could get by on four hundred francs."

He <u>blanched</u> slightly at this, because he had set aside just that amount to buy a shotgun and go with a few friends to Nanterre on Sundays the next summer to shoot larks.

However, he said:

"Okay, you've got four hundred francs, but make it a pretty dress."

As the day of the party drew near, Mrs. Loisel seemed sad, uneasy, anxious, even though her dress was all ready. One evening her husband said to her:

"What's up? You've been acting strangely for several days."

She answered:

"It's awful, but I don't have any jewels, not a single stone. Nothing for matching jewelry. I'm going to look <u>impoverished</u>. I'd almost rather not go to the party."

He responded:

"You can wear a corsage of cut flowers. This year that's really the in thing. For no more than ten francs you can get two or three gorgeous roses."

She was not convinced.

"No . . . there's nothing more humiliating than to look ragged in the middle of rich women."

But her husband exclaimed:

"God, but you're silly! Go to your friend Mrs. Forrestier, and ask her to lend you some jewelry. You know her well enough to do that."

She uttered a cry of joy:

"That's right. I hadn't thought of that."

The next day she went to her friend's house and described her problem.

Mrs. Forrestier went to her glass-plated wardrobe, took out a large jewel box, opened it, and said to Mrs. Loisel:

"Choose, my dear."

She saw bracelets, then a pearl necklace, then a Venetian cross of finely worked gold and gems. She tried on the jewelry in front of a mirror, and hesitated, unable to make up her mind about which ones to give back. She kept asking:

"Do you have anything else?"

"Certainly. Look to your heart's content. I don't know what will please you most."

Suddenly she found, in a black satin box, a superb diamond necklace, and her heart throbbed with desire for it. Her hands shook as she took it up. She fastened it around her neck, watched it gleam at her throat, and looked at herself ecstatically.

Then she asked, haltingly and anxiously:

"Could you lend me this, nothing but this?"

"Why yes, certainly."

She jumped up, hugged her friend joyfully, then hurried away with her treasure.

The day of the party came. Mrs. Loisel was a success. She was prettier than anyone else, stylish, graceful, smiling, and wild with joy. All the men saw her, asked her name, and sought to be introduced. All the important administrators stood in line to waltz with her. The Chancellor himself eyed her.

She danced joyfully, passionately, intoxicated with pleasure, thinking of nothing but the moment, in the triumph of her beauty, in the glory of her success, in a cloud-nine of happiness made up of all the admiration, of all the aroused desire, of this victory so complete and so sweet to the heart of any woman.

She did not leave until four o'clock in the morning. Her husband, since midnight, had been sleeping in a little empty room with three other men whose wives had also been enjoying themselves.

He threw over her shoulders the shawl that he had brought for the trip home, modest clothing from everyday life, the poverty of which contrasted sharply with the elegance of the party dress. She felt it and hurried away to avoid being noticed by the other women who luxuriated in rich furs.

Loisel tried to hold her back:

"Wait a while. You'll catch cold outdoors. I'll call a cab."

But she paid no attention and hurried down the stairs. When they reached the street they found no carriages. They began to look for one, shouting at cabmen passing by at a distance.

They walked toward the Seine, desperate, shivering. Finally, on a quay, they found one of those old night-going buggies that are seen in Paris only after dark, as if they were ashamed of their wretched appearance in daylight.

It took them to their door, on the Street of Martyrs, and they sadly climbed the stairs to their flat. For her, it was finished. As for him, he could think only that he had to begin work at the Ministry of Education at ten o'clock.

She took the shawl off her shoulders, in front of the mirror, to see herself once more in her glory. But suddenly she cried out. The necklace was no longer around her neck!

Her husband, already half undressed, asked:

"What's wrong with you?"

She turned toward him frantically:

"I . . . I . . . I no longer have Mrs. Forrestier's necklace."

He stood up, bewildered:

"What! . . . How! . . . It's not possible!"

And they looked in the folds of the dress, in the creases of the shawl, in the pockets, everywhere. They found nothing.

He asked:

"You're sure you still had it when you left the party?"

"Yes. I checked it in the <u>vestibule</u> of the Ministry."

"But if you had lost it in the street, we would have heard it fall. It must be in the cab."

"Yes, probably. Did you notice the number?"

"No. Did you see it?"

"No."

Overwhelmed, they looked at each other. Finally, Loisel got dressed again.

"I'm going out to retrace all our steps," he said, "to see if I can find the necklace that way."

And he went out. She stayed in her evening dress, without the energy to get ready for bed, <u>prostrated</u> in a chair, drained of strength and thought.

Her husband came back at about seven o'clock. He had found nothing.

He went to Police Headquarters and to the newspapers to announce a reward. He went to the small cab companies, and finally he followed up even the slightest hopeful lead.

She waited the entire day, in the same <u>enervated</u> state, in the face of this frightful disaster.

Loisel came back in the evening, his face pale and haggard. He had found nothing.

"You'll have to write to your friend," he said, "that you broke a fastening on her necklace and that you will have it fixed. That will give us time to look around."

She wrote as he <u>dictated</u>.

At the end of a week they had lost all hope.

And Loisel, seemingly five years older, declared:

"We'll have to see about replacing the jewels."

The next day, they took the case which had contained the necklace and went to the jeweler whose name was inside. He looked at his books:

"I wasn't the one, Madam, who sold the necklace. I only made the case."

Then they went from jeweler to jeweler, searching for a necklace like the other one, <u>racking</u> their memories, both of them sick with worry and anguish.

In a shop in the Palais-Royal, they found a <u>string</u> of diamonds that seemed to them exactly like the one they were seeking. It was priced at forty thousand francs. They could buy it for thirty-six thousand.

They got the jeweler to promise not to sell it for three days. And they made an agreement that he would buy it back for thirty-four thousand francs if the original was recovered before the end of February.

Loisel had saved eighteen thousand francs that his father had left him. He would have to borrow the rest.

He borrowed, asking a thousand francs from one, five hundred from another, five louis here, three louis there. He made <u>promissory</u> notes, under- took ruinous obligations, did business with <u>loan sharks</u> and the whole tribe of finance companies. He compromised himself for the remainder of his days, risked his signature without knowing whether he would be able to honor it, and terrified by anguish over the future, by the black misery that was about to descend on him, by the prospect of all kinds of physical deprivations and moral tortures, he went to get the new necklace, and put down thirty-six thou- sand francs on the jeweler's counter.

Mrs. Loisel took the necklace back to Mrs. Forrestier, who said with an of- fended tone:

"You should have brought it back sooner, because I might have needed it."

She did not open the case, as her friend feared she might. If she had no- ticed the substitution, what would she have thought? What would she have said? Would she not have taken her for a thief?

Mrs. Loisel soon discovered the horrible life of the needy. She did her share, however, completely, heroically. That horrifying debt had to be paid. She would pay. They dismissed the maid; they changed their address; they rented an attic flat.

She learned to do heavy house work, dirty kitchen jobs. She washed the dishes, wearing away her manicured fingernails on greasy pots and encrusted baking dishes. She handwashed dirty linen, shirts, and dish towels that she hung out on the line to dry. Each morning, she took the garbage down to the street, and she carried up water, stopping at each floor to catch her breath. And, dressed in cheap house dresses, she went to the fruit dealer, the grocer, the butchers, with her basket under her arms, haggling, insulting, defending her <u>measly</u> cash penny by penny.

They had to make installment payments every month, and, to buy more time, to refinance loans.

The husband worked evenings to make fair copies of tradesmen's ac- counts, and late into the night he made copies at five cents a page.

And this life lasted ten years.

At the end of ten years, they had paid back everything—everything—in- cluding the extra charges imposed by loan sharks and the accumulation of compound interest.

Mrs. Loisel seemed old now. She had become the strong, hard, and rude woman of poor households. Her hair unkempt, with uneven skirts and rough, red hands, she spoke loudly, washed floors with large buckets of water. But sometimes, when her husband was at work, she sat down near the window, and she dreamed of that evening so long ago, of that party, where she had been so beautiful and so admired.

What would life have been like if she had not lost that necklace? Who knows? Who knows? Life is so peculiar, so uncertain. How little a thing it takes to destroy you or to save you!

Well, one Sunday, as she had gone on a stroll along the Champs-Elysées to relax from the cares of the week, she suddenly noticed a woman walking with a child. It was Mrs. Forrestier, always youthful, always beautiful, always attractive.

Mrs. Loisel felt <u>moved</u>. Would she speak to her? Yes, certainly. And now that she had paid, she could tell all. Why not?

She walked closer.

"Hello, Jeanne."

The other did not recognize her at all, being astonished to be addressed so intimately by this working woman. She stammered:

"But . . . Madam! . . . I don't know . . . You must have made a mistake."

"No. I'm Mathilde Loisel."

Her friend cried out:

"Oh! . . . My poor Mathilde, you've changed so much."

"Yes. I've had some hard times since I saw you last; in fact, miseries . . . and all this because of you! . . ."

"Of me . . . how so?"

"You remember the diamond necklace that you lent me to go to the party at the Ministry of Education?"

"Yes. What then?"

"Well, I lost it."

"How, since you gave it back to me?"

"I brought back another exactly like it. And for ten years we've been paying for it. You understand that this wasn't easy for us, who have nothing. . . . Finally it's over, and I'm mighty damned glad."

Mrs. Forrestier stopped her.

"You say that you bought a diamond necklace to replace mine?"

"Yes. You didn't notice it, eh? They were exactly like yours."

And she smiled with proud and childish joy.

Mrs. Forrestier, deeply <u>moved</u>, took both her hands.

"Oh, my poor Mathilde! But mine was false. At the most, it was worth five hundred francs! . . ."

NAME _____ **DATE** _____

VOCABULARY

I. Use context clues, structural analysis, and/or your dictionary to find the best meaning for the underlined words and phrases as used in the selection. Indicate your choice on the line provided.

_____C_____ 1. <u>dowry</u>

    a. money a woman receives from friends as wedding gifts

    b. money a woman is given by her husband on their wedding day

    c. money given to the husband by the bride's family

_____a_____ 2. <u>finesse</u>

    a. ability to handle delicate situations skillfully

    b. ability to use wealth to gain control of others

    c. ability to transform the working-class to a higher status

_____b_____ 3. <u>anterooms</u>

    a. a room larger than all other rooms in the house

    b. a small room leading into another room

    c. a room used primarily for entertaining

_____c_____ 4. <u>valet</u>

    a. a rack for hanging clothing

    b. an employee who parks cars at a hotel

    c. a manservant who takes care of another man's personal needs

_____c_____ 5. <u>gourmet-prepared</u>

    a. prepared by a chef in a top-rated hotel

    b. prepared by a chef certified by a famous French cooking school

    c. prepared by a skilled cook who has excellent taste in food

_a_   6. <u>sphinxlike</u>
    a. mysterious—as if keeping a secret
    b. sad—as if feeling rejection
    c. fearful—as if expecting a tragedy

_c_   7. <u>burned with the desire</u>
    a. felt a flash   b. smoldered to resist   c. desperately wanted

_b_   8. <u>frugal</u>
    a. selfish   b. thrifty   c. frantic

_c_   9. <u>blanched</u>
    a. blushed   b. bluffed   c. paled

_b_   10. <u>impoverished</u>
    a. incompetent—not able to perform
    b. poor—without any luxuries
    c. awkward—without grace and tact

_a_   11. <u>quay</u>
    a. wharf   b. country road   c. business street

_c_   12. <u>flat</u>
    a. boat   b. sanctuary   c. apartment

_b_   13. <u>vestibule</u>
    a. dressing room   b. entrance   c. food court

_c_   14. <u>prostrated</u>
    a. face down and weeping loudly
    b. relaxed and reminiscing
    c. stretched out in an exhausted manner

_a_   15. <u>enervated</u>
    a. weakened   b. vigorous   c. enduring

_b_   16. <u>racking</u>
    a. storing   b. searching   c. erasing

_c_   17. <u>promissory note</u>
    a. a note promising a promotion
    b. a note intended to harass
    c. a written promise to pay

___*a*___ 18. <u>loan sharks</u>
   a. persons who loan money at very high rates of interest
   b. persons who loan money to fishermen
   c. persons who collect money for loan companies

___*c*___ 19. <u>measly</u>
   a. meaningful   b. colossal   c. skimpy

___*b*___ 20. <u>moved</u>
   a. entertained   b. affected   c. inspired

COMPREHENSION

II. *Answer the following questions on the lines provided.*

1. As the story begins, why is Mathilde so unhappy?

   because she is poor and wants to be wealthy

2. Do you think she is justified in her feelings? Give reasons for your answer.

3. Contrast Mathilde and her husband.

   Mathilde is immature (immaginative) and ambitious while her husband was mature and realistic, practical, generous

4. Why is Mathilde unhappy when Mr. Loisel brings home the dinner invitation? What is the solution?

5. Do you consider Mr. Loisel blameless in regard to Mathilde's predicament? Give reasons for your answer.

_____

_____

_____

6. As the evening of the dinner approaches, why does Mathilde again become unhappy? What do the Loisels plan? Does the plan work?

_____

_____

_____

_____

7. Describe the dinner as it relates to Mathilde and her husband.

_____

_____

_____

8. When the Loisels return home from the dinner, what do they discover? What do they immediately do?

_____

_____

9. Describe in detail what they do to solve the problem. What does the solution cost?

_____

_____

_____

_____

10. The solution referred to in question Where do they get the money?

_____

_____

_____

11. When the item is delivered to Mrs. Forrestier, what is her reaction? How does her reaction affect Mathilde?

_____

_____

_____

12. Explain in detail what each of the Loisels do in order to repay the money that they have borrowed?

_____

_____

_____

_____

13. Describe the climax of the story.

_____

_____

_____

14. Why do you think the author chose to locate the Loisel home on the "Street of Martyrs"? (Look up the word *martyr* in your dictionary to aid you in answering this question.)

_____

_____

_____

15. What could Mathilde do early in the story to prevent the years of sacrifice?

_____

_____

_____

_____

One Good Turn

How machine-made screws brought the world together.

Witold Rybczynski

A common thread. Without the wood screw, the precision screw would have been unimaginable—and the Industrial Revolution might have been postponed indefinitely.

Some years ago my wife and I built a house. I mean really built it—ourselves, from the ground up. Electricity being unavailable, we used hand tools. I did not have a large toolbox. It contained different-size saws, a mallet and chisels, a plane, several hammers (for friends conscripted into our work force) and, for correcting major mistakes, a heavy sledge. In addition, I had a number of tools for measuring: a tape, a square, a spirit level and a plumb line. That was all we needed.

One of the rewards of building something yourself is the pleasure of using tools. Hand tools are really extensions of the human body, for they have evolved over centuries—millenniums—of trial and error. Power tools are more convenient, of course, but they lack precisely this sense of refinement. Using a clumsy nailing gun is work, but swinging a claw hammer is satisfying work.

Had a medieval carpenter come along—untutored neophyte, we could have used his help—he would have found most of my tools familiar. Indeed, even an ancient Roman carpenter would have found few surprises in my toolbox. He would recognize my plane, a version of his *plana;* he might admire my retractable tape measure, an improvement on his bronze folding *regula.* He would be puzzled by my brace and bit, a medieval invention, but being familiar with the Egyptian bow drill, he would readily infer its purpose. No doubt he would be impressed by my hard steel nails, so much superior to his hand-forged spikes.

Saws, hammers (and nails), chisels, drills and squares all date from the Bronze and early Iron Ages. Many types of modern tools originated even earlier, in the Neolithic period, about 8,000 years ago. In fact, there is only one tool in my toolbox that would puzzle a Roman and a medieval carpenter: my screwdriver. They would understand the principle of screws; after all, Archimedes invented the screw in the third century B.C. Ancient screws were large wood contraptions, used for raising water. One of the earliest devices that used a screw to apply pressure was a Roman clothes press; presses were also used to make olive oil and wine. The Middle Ages applied the same principle to the printing press and to that fiendish torturing device, the thumbscrew. Yet the ordinary screw as a small fixing device was unknown.

Wood screws originated sometime in the 16th century. The first screwdrivers were called turnscrews, flat-bladed bits that could be attached to a carpenter's brace. The inventor of the hand held screwdriver remains unknown, but the familiar tool does not appear in carpenters' toolboxes until after 1800. There was not a great call for screwdrivers, because screws were expensive. They had to be painstakingly made by hand and were used in luxury articles like clocks. It was only after 1850 that wood screws were available in large quantities.

Inexpensive screws are quintessentially modern. Their mass production requires a high degree of precision and standardization. The wood screw also represents an entirely new method of attachment, more durable than nails—which can pop out if the wood dries out or expands. (This makes screws particularly useful in shipbuilding.) The tapered, gimlet-pointed wood screw—like its cousin the bolt—squeezes the two joined pieces together. The more you tighten the screw—or the nut—the greater the squeeze. In modern steel buildings, for example, high-tension bolts are tightened so hard that it is the friction between the two pieces of steel—not the bolt itself—that gives strength to the joint. On a more mundane level, screws enable a vast array of convenient attachments in the home: door hinges, drawer pulls, shelf hangers, towel bars. Perhaps that is why if you rummage around most people's kitchen drawers you will most likely find at least one screwdriver.

Wood screws are stronger and more durable than nails, pegs or staples. But the aristocrat of screws is the precision screw. This was first made roughly—by hand—and later on screw-cutting lathes, which is a chicken-and-egg story, since it was the screw that made machine lathes possible. The machined screw represented a technological breakthrough of epic proportions. Screws enabled the minute adjustment of a variety of precision instruments like clocks, microscopes, telescopes, sextants, theodolites and marine chronometers.

It is not an exaggeration to say that accurately threaded screws changed the world. Without screws, entire fields of science would have languished, navigation would have remained primitive and naval warfare as well as routine maritime commerce in the 18th and 19th centuries would not have been possible. Without screws there would have been no machine tools, hence no industrial products and no Industrial Revolution. Think of that the next time you pick up a screwdriver to pry open a can of paint.

NAME _____ **DATE** _____

VOCABULARY

I. *Select the best definition for each of the following words and phrases as used in the selection. Indicate your choice on the line provided.*

_____ 1. <u>conscripted</u>
   a. commissioned   b. drafted   c. mandated

_____ 2. <u>evolved</u>
   a. evoked   b. multiplied   c. developed

_____ 3. <u>untutored neophyte</u>
   a. a young apprentice
   b. an uneducated beginner
   c. an ancient carpenter

_____ 4. <u>retractable</u>
   a. ability to draw back
   b. very reliable
   c. new and improved

_____ 5. <u>hand-forged</u>
   a. handpicked   b. hand-to-hand   c. handmade

_____ 6. <u>contraptions</u>
   a. conveniences   b. gadgets   c. spikes

_____ 7. <u>fiendish</u>
   a. cruel   b. old-fashion   c. tedious

_____ 8. <u>quintessentially modern</u>
   a. deceivingly necessary in present times
   b. increasingly common in present times
   c. an identifying trend in present times

_____ 9. <u>precision</u>
   a. pride   b. accuracy   c. planning

_____ 10. <u>standardization</u>
   a. uniformity   b. adjustments   c. skill

_____ 11. <u>attachment</u>
   a. construction   b. adjustment   c. fastening

_____ 12. <u>gimlet-pointed</u>
   a. pointed and smooth
   b. pointed and sharp
   c. pointed and spiraled

_____ 13. <u>friction</u>
   a. connecting point
   b. resistance to motion
   c. forward motion

_____ 14. <u>mundane</u>
   a. everyday   b. unusual   c. modern

_____ 15. <u>rummage</u>
   a. rumble   b. run   c. search

_____ 16. <u>aristocrat of screws</u>
   a. screws made in America
   b. screws of the highest quality
   c. screws made by machines

_____ 17. <u>epic</u>
   a. equal   b. grand   c. natural

_____ 18. <u>minute</u>
   a. fine   b. rapid   c. minimum

_____ 19. <u>languished</u>
   a. been prolonged   b. been impeded   c. been accelerated

_____ 20. <u>maritime</u>
   a. collective bargaining
   b. marine exploration
   c. shipping trade

COMPREHENSION

II. *Select the best answers for the following. Indicate your choice on the line provided.*

_____ 1. The author begins the passage with a personal experience of building a house. What was his purpose?

  a. To show that the quality of old-fashioined hand tools was superior to the quality of precision tools.

  b. To show that using simple hand tools often give more satisfaction in building than sophisticated power tools.

  c. To show that although it is possible to build a house without precision tools, it is best to have them handy.

_____ 2. In the third paragraph, the main idea is that

  a. the tools used today have no similarity to the tools used by an ancient Roman carpenter.

  b. since medieval carpenters were untutored, they would be puzzled by the tools we use today.

  c. although there are many new tools and they have improved in quality, the principle of use has not changed in centuries.

_____ 3. The author states that ancient Roman carpenters would understand the use of all his tools with the exception of the

  a. retractable tape measure.

  b. brace and bit.

  c. screwdriver.

_____ 4. Wood screws originated sometime in the _____ century, but they were not widely available until after _____.

  a. twentieth; 1910

  b. sixteenth; 1850

  c. nineteenth; 1800

_____ 5. Why were early screws so expensive?

  a. They had to be painstakingly made by hand.

  b. They were made from a scarce metal.

  c. They were seldom used by most carpenters.

_____ 6. Who invented the hand-held screwdriver?

    a. an ancient Roman

    b. Archimedes

    c. It is unknown.

_____ 7. Although the author does not give an exact date for the invention of the screwdriver, which of the following would be most probable?

    a. during the eighteenth century

    b. during the nineteenth century

    c. during the twentieth century

_____ 8. Why was it so long after the invention of the screw, that the screwdriver became widely used?

    a. Screws were of such poor quality.

    b. Screws were so expensive.

    c. Screws had so few uses.

_____ 9. Why would you likely find a screwdriver in the kitchen of most modern-day homes?

    a. A screwdriver is used to repair so many appliances and attachments in the home.

    b. A screwdriver is so easily misplaced, the kitchen is a common storing place.

    c. A screwdriver is seldom used in other places in the home.

_____ 10. What is the most technologically advanced screw?

    a. the wood screw

    b. the turn screw

    c. the precision screw

III. *The author believes that without precision screws the Industrial Revolution might not have taken place. Why could this be true?*

_____

_____

_____

_____

_____

_____

_____

_____

IV. Review the Industrial Revolution in your history book or in the library. Compare and contrast your life today to how it would be if there had not been an Industrial Revolution.

_____

_____

_____

_____

_____

_____

_____

_____

_____

_____

_____

_____

_____

_____

_____

_____

Selection Eleven

A Worn Path

EUDORA WELTY

It was December—a bright frozen day in the early morning. Far out in the country there was an old Negro woman with her head tied in a red rag, coming along a path through the pinewoods. Her name was Phoenix Jackson. She was very old and small and she walked slowly in the dark pine shadows, moving a little from side to side in her steps, with the balanced heaviness and lightness of a pendulum in a grandfather clock. She carried a thin, small cane made from an umbrella, and with this she kept tapping the frozen earth in front of her. This made a grave and persistent noise in the still air, that seemed <u>meditative</u> like the chirping of a solitary little bird.

She wore a dark striped dress reaching down to her shoe tops, and an equally long apron of bleached sugar sacks, with a full pocket, all neat and tidy, but every time she took a step she might have fallen over her shoelaces, which dragged from her unlaced shoes. She looked straight ahead. Her eyes were blue with age. Her skin had a pattern all its own of numberless branching wrinkles and as though a whole little tree stood in the middle of her forehead, but a golden color ran underneath, and the two knobs of her cheeks were <u>illumined</u> by a yellow burning under the dark. Under the red rag her hair came down on her neck in the frailest of ringlets, still black, and with an odor like copper.

Now and then there was a quivering in the thicket. Old Phoenix said, "Out of my way, all you foxes, owls, beetles, jack rabbits, coons, and wild animals! . . . Keep out from under these feet, little bobwhites. . . . Keep the big wild hogs out of my path. Don't let none of those come running my direction. I got a long way." Under her small black-freckled hand her cane, limber as a buggy whip, would switch at the brush as if to <u>rouse</u> up any hiding things.

On she went. The woods were deep and still. The sun made the pine needles almost too bright to look at, up where the wind rocked. The cones dropped as light as feathers. Down in the hollow was the mourning dove—it was not too late for him.

The path ran up a hill. "Seem like there is chains about my feet, time I get this far," she said, in the voice of argument old people keep to use with themselves. "Something always take a hold of me on this hill—pleads I should stay."

After she got to the top she turned and gave a full, severe look behind her where she had come. "Up through pines," she said at length. "Now down through oaks."

Her eyes opened their widest, and she started down gently. But before she got to the bottom of the hill a bush caught her dress.

Her fingers were busy and intent, but her skirts were full and long, so that before she could pull them free in one place they were caught in another. It was not possible to allow the dress to tear. "I in the thorny bush," she said. "Thorns, you doing your appointed work. Never want to let folks pass, no sir. Old eyes thought you was a pretty little *green* bush."

Finally, trembling all over, she stood free, and after a moment dared to stoop for her cane.

"Sun so high!" she cried, leaning back and looking, while the thick tears went over her eyes. "The time getting all gone here."

At the foot of this hill was a place where a log was laid across the creek.

"Now comes the <u>trial</u>," said Phoenix.

Putting her right foot out, she mounted the log and shut her eyes. Lifting her skirt, leveling her cane fiercely before her, like a festival figure in some parade, she began to march across. Then she opened her eyes and she was safe on the other side.

"I wasn't as old as I thought," she said.

But she sat down to rest. She spread her skirts on the bank around her and folded her hands over her knees. Up above her was a tree in a pearly cloud of mistletoe. She did not dare to close her eyes, and when a little boy brought her a plate with a slice of marblecake on it she spoke to him. "That would be acceptable," she said. But when she went to take it there was just her own hand in the air.

So she left that tree, and had to go through a barbed-wire fence. There she had to creep and crawl, spreading her knees and stretching her fingers like a baby trying to climb the steps. But she talked loudly to herself: she could not let her dress be torn now, so late in the day, and she could not pay for having her arm or her leg sawed off if she got caught <u>fast</u> where she was.

At last she was safe through the fence and risen up out in the clearing. Big dead trees, like black men with one arm, were standing in the purple stalks of the withered cotton field. There sat a buzzard.

"Who you watching?"

In the furrow she made her way along.

"Glad this not the season for bulls," she said, looking sideways, "and the good Lord made his snakes to curl up and sleep in the winter. A pleasure I don't see no two-headed snake coming around that tree, where it come once. It took a while to get by him, back in the summer."

She passed through the old cotton and went into a field of dead corn. It whispered and shook and was taller than her head. "Through the maze now," she said, for there was no path.

Then there was something tall, black, and skinny there, moving before her.

At first she took it for a man. It could have been a man dancing in the field. But she stood still and listened, and it did not make a sound. It was as silent as a ghost.

"Ghost," she said sharply, "who be you the ghost of? For I have heard of nary death close by."

But there was no answer—only the ragged dancing in the wind.

She shut her eyes, reached out her hand, and touched a sleeve. She found a coat and inside that an emptiness, cold as ice.

"You scarecrow," she said. Her face lighted. "I ought to be shut up for good," she said with laughter. "My senses is gone. I too old. I the oldest people I ever know. Dance, old scarecrow," she said, "while I dancing with you."

She kicked her foot over the furrow, and with mouth drawn down, shook her head once or twice in a little strutting way. Some husks blew down and whirled in streamers about her skirts.

Then she went on, parting her way from side to side with the cane, through the whispering field. At last she came to the end, to a wagon track where the silver grass blew between the red ruts. The quail were walking around like <u>pullets</u>, seeming all dainty and unseen.

"Walk pretty," she said. "This the easy place. This the easy going."

She followed the track, swaying through the quiet bare fields, through the little strings of trees silver in their dead leaves, past cabins silver from weather, with the doors and windows boarded shut, all like old women under a spell sitting there. "I walking in their sleep," she said, nodding her head vigorously.

In a <u>ravine</u> she went where a spring was silently flowing through a hollow log. Old Phoenix bent and drank. "Sweet-gum makes the water sweet," she said, and drank more. "Nobody know who make this well, for it was here when I was born."

The track crossed a swampy part where the moss hung as white as lace from every limb. "Sleep on, alligators, and blow your bubbles." Then the track went into the road.

Deep, deep the road went down between the high green-colored banks. Overhead the live-oaks met, and it was as dark as a cave.

A black dog with a <u>lolling tongue</u> came up out of the weeds by the ditch. She was <u>meditating</u>, and not ready, and when he came at her she only hit him a little with her cane. Over she went in the ditch, like a little puff of milkweed.

Down there, her senses drifted away. A dream visited her, and she reached her hand up, but nothing reached down and gave her a pull. So she lay there and presently went to talking. "Old woman," she said to herself, "that black dog come up out of the weeds <u>to stall you off</u>, and now there he sitting on his fine tail, smiling at you."

A white man finally came along and found her—a hunter, a young man, with his dog on a chain.

"Well, Granny!" he laughed. "What are you doing there?"

"Lying on my back like a June-bug waiting to be turned over, mister," she said, reaching up with her hand.

He lifted her up, gave her a swing in the air, and set her down. "Anything broken, Granny?"

"No sir, them old dead weeds is springy enough," said Phoenix, when she had got her breath. "I thank you for your trouble."

"Where do you live, Granny?" he asked, while the two dogs were growling at each other.

"Away back yonder, sir, behind the ridge. You can't even see it from here."

"On your way home?"

"No sir, I going to town."

"Why, that's too far! That's as far as I walk when I come out myself, and I get something for my trouble." He patted the stuffed bag he carried, and there hung down a little closed claw. It was one of the bobwhites, with it's beak hooked bitterly to show it was dead. "Now you go on home Granny!"

"I bound to go to town, mister," said Phoenix. "The time come around."

He gave another laugh, filling the whole landscape. "I know you old colored people! Wouldn't miss going to town to see Santa Claus!"

But something held old Phoenix very still. The deep lines in her face went into <u>a fierce and different radiation</u>. Without warning, she had seen with her own eyes a flashing nickel fall out of the man's pocket onto the ground.

"How old are you Granny?" he was saying.

"There is no telling, mister," she said, "no telling."

Then she gave a little cry and slapped her hands and said, "Git on away from here, dog! Look! Look at that dog!" She laughed as if in admiration. "He ain't scared of nobody. He a big black dog." She whispered, "Sic him!"

"Watch me get rid of that <u>cur</u>," said the man. "Sic him, Pete! Sic him!"

Phoenix heard the dogs fighting, and heard the man running and throwing sticks. She even heard a gunshot. But she was slowly bending forward by that time, further and further forward, the lids stretched down over her eyes, as if she were doing this in her sleep. Her chin was lowered almost to her knees. The yellow palm of her hand came out from the fold of her apron. Her fingers slid down and along the ground under the piece of money with the grace and care they would have in lifting an egg from under a <u>setting hen</u>. Then she slowly straightened up, she stood erect, and the nickel was in her pocket. A bird flew by. Her lips moved. "God watching me the whole time. I come to stealing." The man came back, and his own dog panted about them. "Well, I scared him off that time," he said, and then he laughed and lifted his gun and pointed it at Phoenix.

She stood straight and faced him.

"Doesn't the gun scare you?" he said, still pointing it.

"No, sir, I seen plenty go off closer by, in my day, and for less than what I done," she said, holding utterly still.

He smiled, and shouldered the gun. "Well, Granny," he said, "you must be a hundred years old, and scared of nothing. I'd give you a dime if I had any money with me. But take my advice and stay home, and nothing will happen to you."

"I bound to go on my way mister," said Phoenix. She inclined her head in the red rag. Then they went in different directions, but she could hear the gun shooting again and again over the hill.

She walked on. The shadows hung from the oak trees to the road like curtains. Then she smelled wood-smoke, and smelled the river, and she saw a steeple and the cabins on their steep steps. Dozens of little black children whirled around her. There ahead was Natchez shining. Bells were ringing. She walked on.

In the paved city it was Christmas time. There were red and green electric lights strung and crisscrossed everywhere, and all turned on in the daytime. Old Phoenix would have been lost if she had not distrusted her eyesight and depended on her feet to know where to take her.

She paused quietly on the sidewalk where people were passing by. A lady came along in the crowd, carrying an armful of red-, green-, and silver-wrapped presents; she gave off perfume like the red roses in hot summer, and Phoenix stopped her.

"Please, missy, will you lace up my shoe?" She held up her foot.

"What do you want, Grandma?"

"See my shoe," said Phoenix. "Do all right for out in the country, but wouldn't look right to go in a big building."

"Stand still then, Grandma," said the lady. She put her packages down on the sidewalk beside her and laced and tied both shoes tightly.

"Can't lace 'em with a cane," said Phoenix. "Thank you, missy. I doesn't mind asking a nice lady to tie up my shoe, when I gets out on the street."

Moving slowly and from side to side, she went into the big building, and into a tower of steps, where she walked up and around and around until her feet knew to stop.

She entered a door, and there she saw nailed up on the wall the document that had been stamped with the gold seal and framed in the gold frame, which matched the dream that was hung up in her head.

"Here I be," she said. There was a <u>fixed and ceremonial stiffness</u> over her body.

"A <u>charity</u> case, I suppose," said an attendant who sat at the desk before her.

But Phoenix only looked above her head. There was sweat on her face, the wrinkles in her skin shone like a bright net.

"Speak up, Grandma," the woman said. "What's your name?" We must have your history, you know. Have you been here before? What seems to be the trouble with you?"

Old Phoenix only gave a twitch to her face as if a fly were bothering her.

"Are you deaf?" cried the attendant.

But then the nurse came in.

"Oh, that's just old Aunt Phoenix," she said. "She doesn't come for herself—she has a little grandson. She makes these trips just as regular as clockwork. She lives away back off the Old Natchez Trace." She bent down. "Well, Aunt Phoenix, why don't you just take a seat? We won't keep you standing after your long trip." She pointed.

The old woman sat down, bolt upright in the chair.

"Now, how is the boy?" asked the nurse.

Old Phoenix did not speak.

"I said, how is the boy?"

But Phoenix only waited and stared straight ahead, her face very solemn and withdrawn into <u>rigidity</u>.

"Is his throat any better?" asked the nurse. "Aunt Phoenix, don't you hear me? Is your grandson's throat any better since the last time you came for the medicine?"

With her hands on her knees, the old woman waited, silent, erect and motionless, just as if she were in armor.

"You mustn't take up our time this way, Aunt Phoenix," the nurse said. "Tell us quickly about your grandson, and get it over. He isn't dead, is he?"

At last there came a <u>flicker and then a flame of comprehension</u> across her face, and she spoke.

"My grandson. It was my memory had left me. There I sat and forgot why I made my long trip."

"Forgot?" The nurse frowned. "After you came so far?"

Then Phoenix was like an old woman begging a dignified forgiveness for waking up frightened in the night. "I never did go to school, I was too old at the Surrender," she said in a soft voice. "I'm an old woman without an education. It was my memory fail me. My little grandson, he is just the same, and I forgot it in the coming."

"Throat never heals, does it?" said the nurse, speaking in a loud, sure voice to old Phoenix. By now she had a card with something written on it, a little list. "Yes. Swallowed lye. When was it?—January—two, three years ago—"

Phoenix spoke unasked now. "No missy, he not dead, he just the same. Every little while his throat begin to close up again, and he not able to swallow. He not get his breath. He not able to help himself. So the time come around, and I go on another trip for the soothing medicine."

"All right. The doctor said as long as you came to get it, you could have it," said the nurse. "But it's an <u>obstinate</u> case."

"My little grandson, he sit up there in the house all wrapped up, waiting by himself," Phoenix went on. "We is the only two left in the world. He suffer and it don't seem to put him back at all. He got a sweet look. He going to last. He wear a little patch quilt and peep out holding his mouth open like a little bird. I remembers so plain now. I not going to forget him again, no, the whole <u>enduring</u> time. I could tell him from all the others in creation."

"All right." The nurse was trying to hush her now. She brought her a bottle of medicine. "Charity," she said, making a check mark in a book.

Old Phoenix held the bottle close to her eyes, and then carefully put it into her pocket.

"I thank you," she said.

"It's Christmas time, Grandma," said the attendant. "Could I give you a few pennies out of my purse?"

"Five pennies is a nickel," said Phoenix stiffly.

"Here's a nickel," said the attendant.

Phoenix rose carefully and held out her hand. She received the nickel and then <u>fished</u> the other nickel out of her pocket and laid it beside the new one. She stared at her palm closely, with her head on one side.

Then she gave a tap with her cane on the floor.

"This is what come to me to do," she said. "I going to the store and buy my child a little windmill they sells, made out of paper. He going to find it hard to believe there such a thing in the world. I'll march myself back where he waiting, holding it straight up in this hand."

She lifted her free hand, gave a little nod, turned around, and walked out of the doctor's office. Then her slow step began on the stairs, going down.

NAME _____ **DATE** _____

VOCABULARY

I. Use context clues and your dictionary to determine the meaning of each of the following words and phrases as used in the selection.

1. meditative

   _____

2. illumined

   _____

3. rouse

   _____

4. trial

   _____

5. fast

   _____

6. pullets

   _____

7. ravine

   _____

8. lolling tongue

   _____

9. meditating

   _____

10. stall you off

11. a fierce and different radiation

_____

12. cur

_____

13. setting hen

_____

14. fixed and ceremonial

_____

15. charity

_____

16. rigidity

_____

17. a flicker and then a flame of comprehension

_____

18. obstinate

_____

19. enduring

_____

20. fished

_____

COMPREHENSION

II. *Answer the following questions on the lines provided.*

1. Why do you think the author titled the story "A Worn Path"?

_____

_____

2. In paragraph 1 the author states that the cane carried by Ms. Jackson was made from an umbrella. Why then, is it described as "limber as a buggy whip" in paragraph 3 on page 387?

_____

_____

_____

3. In paragraphs 2 on page 388, what does Phoenix mean when she says, "Thorns, you doing your appointed work?"

_____

_____

_____

_____

4. Explain the incident in paragraph 9 on page 388 concerning the little boy and the marble cake.

_____

_____

_____

5. How does the account in paragraph 14 on page 388 and the incident with the scarecrow relate to your answer of question 4?

_____

_____

_____

_____

6. In paragraph 14 on page 389, what is meant by the phrase "She was meditating and not ready. . . ." What happens to her then?

_____

_____

_____

_____

7. Relate the "trick" she pulls on the hunter so that she can pick up the nickel.

_____

_____

_____

_____

8. Do you think Phoenix thinks she has a right to pick up the nickel? Why?

_____

_____

_____

_____

9. The hunter points his gun at Phoenix after she picks up the nickel. What does she think is his reason? Is this true?

_____

_____

_____

10. Why is Phoenix going to the health clinic? Explain.

_____

_____

_____

_____

11. When the nurse asks her about her grandson, why does she wait so long to answer? How does she defend her delay in answering?

_____

_____

_____

_____

12. In addition to getting the medicine, Phoenix is given a nickel by the nurse's attendant. This makes a dime she has gotten on the trip. What does she plan to do with the money? Why do you approve or disapprove of how she plans to spend the dime?

_____

_____

_____

13. How does the author want you to see Phoenix?

_____

_____

_____

14. What tragic events could take place while Phoenix is on the trip for the medicine?

_____

_____

_____

15. Why do you think the author chooses Phoenix for Ms. Jackson's name? (Look up *phoenix* in your dictionary to aid you in answering this question.)

_____

_____

_____

_____

_____

_____

III. List at least four obstacles Phoenix encounters on her trip to the clinic and explain how she handles each one.

_____

_____

_____

_____

_____

_____

_____

_____

IV. Give an account of a person you know who has shown courage and steadfastness in the face of extreme hardships.

_____

_____

_____

_____

_____

_____

_____

_____

Selection Twelve

The Last Visit

James Baldwin

It was on the 28th of July, which I believe was a Wednesday, that I visited my father for the first time during his illness and for the last time in his life. The moment I saw him I knew why I had put off this visit so long. I had told my mother that I did not want to see him because I hated him. But this was not true. It was only that I had hated him and I wanted to hold on to this hatred. I did not want to look on him as a <u>ruin</u>: it was not a ruin I had hated. I imagine that one of the reasons people cling to their hates so stubbornly is because they sense, once hate is gone, that they will be forced to deal with pain.

We traveled out to him, his older sister and myself, to what seemed to be the very end of a very Long Island. It was hot and dusty and we <u>wrangled,</u> my aunt and I, all the way out, over the fact that I had recently begun to smoke and, as she said, to give <u>myself airs.</u> But I knew that she wrangled with me because she could not bear to face the fact of her brother's dying. Neither could I <u>endure</u> the reality of her despair, her unstated <u>bafflement</u> as to what had happened to her brother's life, and her own. So we wrangled and I smoked and from time to time she fell into a heavy <u>reverie.</u> <u>Covertly,</u> I watched her face, which was the face of an old woman; it had fallen in, the eyes were sunken and lightless; soon she would be dying, too.

In my childhood—it had not been so long ago—I had thought her beautiful. She had been quick-witted and quick-moving and very generous with all the children and each of her visits had been an event. At one time one of my brothers and myself had thought of running away to live with her. Now she could no longer produce out of her <u>handbag</u> some unexpected and yet familiar delight. She made me feel pity and <u>revulsion</u> and fear. It was awful to realize that she no longer caused me to feel affection. The closer we came to the hospital the more <u>querulous</u> she became and at the same time, naturally, grew more dependent on me. Between pity and guilt and fear I began to feel that there was another me trapped in my skull like a jack-in-the-box who might escape my control at any moment and fill the air with screaming.

She began to cry the moment we entered the room and she saw him lying there, all shriveled and still, like a little black monkey. The great, gleaming apparatus which fed him and would have compelled him to be still even if he had been able to move brought to mind, not beneficence, but torture; the tubes entering his arm made me think of pictures I had seen when a child, of Gulliver, tied down by the pygmies on that island. My aunt wept and wept, there was a whistling sound in my father's throat; nothing was said; he could not speak. I wanted to take his hand, to say something. But I do not know what I could have said, even if he could have heard me. He was not really in that room with us, he had at last really <u>embarked</u> on his journey; and though my aunt told me that he said he was going to meet Jesus, I did not hear anything except that whistling in his throat. The doctor came back and we left, into that unbearable train again, and home. In the morning came the telegram saying that he was dead. Then the house was suddenly full of relatives, friends, hysteria, and confusion and I quickly left my mother and the children to the care of those impressive women, who, in Negro communities at least, automatically appear at times of <u>bereavement</u> armed with lotions, proverbs, and patience, and an ability to cook. I went downtown. By the time I returned, later the same day, my mother had been carried to the hospital and the baby had been born.

EXERCISE 39: The Last Visit

NAME _____ **DATE** _____

VOCABULARY

I. *Select the best definition for the following words as used in the selection. Indicate your choice on the line provided.*

_____ 1. <u>ruin</u>
 a. damage   b. decay   c. wreck

_____ 2. <u>wrangled</u>
 a. argued   b. talked   c. thought

_____ 3. <u>endure</u>
 a. understand   b. prevent   c. bear

_____ 4. <u>bafflement</u>
 a. hindrance   b. confusion   c. satisfaction

_____ 5. <u>reverie</u>
 a. thoughtlessness   b. daydream   c. stupor

_____ 6. <u>covertly</u>
 a. cowardly   b. defiantly   c. secretly

_____ C   7. <u>revulsion</u>
         a. bitterness   b. shame   c. disgust

_____   8. <u>querulous</u>
         a. complaining   b. questioning   c. seeking

_____   9. <u>embarked</u>
         a. boarded   b. departed   c. engaged

_____   10. <u>bereavement</u>
         a. loneliness   b. disposition   c. mourning

COMPREHENSION

II. Select the best answer for each of the following. Indicate your choice on the line provided.

_____   1. The selection is mainly about
           a. how the narrator's father died.
           b. the inner feelings of the narrator as he visits his dying father.
           c. the narrator's childhood memories of his father.
           d. the narrator's relationship with his aunt.

_____   2. According to the selection, why are people slow to stop hating?
           a. The painful reality of the issue must then be faced.
           b. It is easier to hate than to love.
           c. It is embarrassing to admit that the hating is unnecessary.
           d. Most people are too stubborn to admit they are wrong.

_____   3. What did his aunt mean when she said the narrator had begun "to give himself airs"?
           a. He had recently started doing deep-breathing exercises.
           b. His smoking polluted the air around him.
           c. He was trying to act sophisticated beyond his years.
           d. He was not showing proper grief over his father's illness.

_____   4. According to the third paragraph, the narrator's feelings for his aunt had changed from
           a. love to pity.
           b. pity to love.
           c. love to hate.
           d. fear to pity.

_____ 5. What do you think the aunt felt toward the narrator's father?
   a. fear
   b. hate
   c. love
   d. indifference

_C_____ 6. You know the narrator understood his aunt's feelings because
   a. he had invited her to accompany him to see his father.
   b. he could see she was getting old.
   c. he had once loved her.
   d. he knew she quarreled with him to cover her feelings.

_____ 7. What were the aunt's emotions as described in the fourth paragraph?
   a. sadness and despair
   b. guilt and remorse
   c. fear and revulsion
   d. indifference and callousness

_____ 8. In contrast to his aunt's feelings, the narrator felt
   a. sad.
   b. indifferent.
   c. frustrated.
   d. relieved.

_____ 9. How did the narrator and his aunt travel to see his father?
   a. car
   b. bus
   c. airplane
   d. train

_____ 10. The day after the narrator's father died, new life came into the family when
   a. the narrator returned home to live.
   b. the neighborhood women came in to assist with the funeral.
   c. the narrator's mother had a new baby.
   d. the narrator's aunt moved in with them.

Selection Thirteen

The Attic of the Brain

LEWIS THOMAS

My parents' house had an attic, the darkest and strangest part of the building, reachable only by placing a stepladder beneath the trapdoor and filled with unidentifiable articles too important to be thrown out with the trash but no longer suitable to have at hand. This mysterious space was the memory of the place. After many years all the things deposited in it became, one by one, lost to consciousness. But they were still there, we knew, safely and comfortably stored in the tissues of the house.

These days most of us live in smaller, more modern houses or in apartments, and attics have vanished. Even the deep closets in which we used to pile things up for temporary forgetting are rarely designed into new homes.

Everything now is out in the open, openly acknowledged and displayed, and whenever we grow tired of a memory, an old chair, a trunkful of old letters, they are carted off to the dump for burning.

This has seemed a healthier way to live, except maybe for the smoke—everything out to be looked at, nothing strange hidden under the roof, nothing forgotten because of no place left in impenetrable darkness to forget. Openness is the new life-style, no undisclosed belongings, no private secrets. Candor is the rule in architecture. The house is a machine for living, and what kind of machine would hide away its worn-out, obsolescent parts?

But it is in our nature as human beings to clutter, and we hanker for places set aside, reserved for storage. We tend to accumulate and outgrow possessions at the same time, and it is an endlessly discomforting mental task to keep sorting out the ones to get rid of. We might, we think, remember them later and find a use for them, and if they are gone for good, off to the dump, this is a source of nervousness. I think it may be one of the reasons we drum our fingers so much these days.

We might take a lesson here from what has been learned about our brains in this century. We thought we discovered, first off, the attic, although its existence has been mentioned from time to time by all the people we used to call great writers. What we really found was the trapdoor and a stepladder, and off we clambered, shining flashlights into the corners, vacuuming the dust out of bureau drawers, puzzling over the names of objects, tossing them down to the floor below, and finally paying around fifty dollars an hour to have them carted off for burning.

After several generations of this new way of doing things we took up openness and candor with the <u>febrile</u> intensity of a new religion, everything laid out in full view, and as in the design of our new houses it seemed a healthier way to live, except maybe again for smoke.

And now, I think, we have a new kind of worry. There is no place for functionless, untidy, <u>inexplicable</u> notions, no dark comfortable parts of the mind to hide away the things we'd like to keep but at the same time forget. The attic is still there, but with the trapdoor always open and the stepladder in place we are always in and out of it, flashing lights around, naming everything, unmystified.

I have an earnest proposal for psychiatry, a novel set of therapeutic rules, although I know it means waiting in line.

Bring back the old attic. Give new instructions to the patients who are made nervous by our times, including me, to make a conscious effort to hide a reasonable proportion of thought. It would have to be a gradual process, considering how far we have come in the other direction talking, talking all the way. Perhaps only one or two thoughts should be repressed each day, at the outset. The easiest, gentlest way might be to start with dreams, first by forbidding the patient to mention any dream, much less to recount its details, then encouraging the outright forgetting that there was a dream at all, remembering nothing beyond the vague sense that during sleep there had been the familiar sound of something shifting and sliding, up under the roof.

We might, in this way, regain the kind of <u>spontaneity</u> and zest for ideas, things popping into the mind, uncontrollable and ungovernable thoughts, the feel that this notion is somehow connected unaccountably with that one. We could come again into possession of real memory, the kind of memory that can come only from jumbled forgotten furniture, old photographs, fragments of music.

It has been one of the great errors of our time to think that by thinking about thinking, and then talking about it, we could possibly straighten out and tidy up our minds. There is no <u>delusion</u> more damaging than to get the idea in your head that you understand the functioning of your own brain. Once you acquire such a notion, you run the danger of moving in to take charge, guiding your thoughts, shepherding your mind from place to place, *controlling* it, making lists of regulations. The human mind is not meant to be governed, certainly not by any book of rules yet written; it is supposed to run itself, and we are obliged to follow it along, trying to keep up with it as best we can. It is all very well to be aware of your awareness, even proud of it, but never try to operate it. You are not up to the job.

I leave it to the analysts to work out the techniques for doing what now needs doing. They are presumably the professionals most familiar with the route, and all they have to do is turn back and go the other way, session by session, step by step. It takes a certain amount of hard swallowing and a lot of revised jargon, and I have great sympathy for their <u>plight,</u> but it is time to reverse course.

If after all, as seems to be true, we are endowed with unconscious minds in our brains, these should be regarded as normal structures, installed wherever they are for a purpose. I am not sure what they are built to contain, but as a biologist, impressed by the usefulness of everything alive, I would take it for granted that they are useful, probably indispensable organs of thought. It cannot be a bad thing to own one, but I would no more think of meddling with it than trying to exorcise my liver, an equally mysterious apparatus. Until we know a lot more, it would be wise, as we have learned from other fields in medicine, to let them be, above all not to interfere. Maybe, even—and this is the notion I wish to suggest to my psychiatric friends—to stock them up, put more things into them, make *use* of them. Forget whatever you feel like forgetting. From time to time, practice *not* being open, discover new things *not* to talk about, learn reserve, hold the tongue. But above all, develop the human talent for forgetting words, phrases, whole unwelcome sentences, all experiences involving <u>wincing.</u> If we should ever lose the loss of memory, we might lose as well that most attractive of signals ever flashed from the human face, the blush. If we should give away the capacity for embarrassment, the touch of fingertips might be the next to go, and then the suddenness of laughter, the unaccountable sure sense of something gone wrong, and, finally, the marvelous conviction that being human is the best thing to be.

Attempting to operate one's own mind, powered by such a magical instrument as the human brain, strikes me as rather like using the world's biggest computer to add columns of figures, or towing a Rolls-Royce with a nylon rope.

I have tried to think of a name for the new professional activity, but each time I think of a good one I forget it before I can get it written down. <u>Psychorepression</u> is the only one I've hung on to, but I can't guess at the fee schedule.

NAME _____ **DATE** _____

VOCABULARY

I. *Use context clues and your dictionary to select the best definition for the following words as used in the passage. Indicate your choice on the line provided.*

_____ 1. <u>candor</u>
   a. intensity   b. purity   c. forthrightness

_____ 2. <u>obsolescent</u>
   a. out of date and useless   b. current and stylish
   c. large and hard to move

_____ 3. <u>hanker</u>
   a. travel   b. bargain   c. desire

_____ 4. <u>febrile</u>
   a. stylish   b. feverish   c. fiendish

_____ 5. <u>inexplicable</u>
   a. inexistant   b. inexpensive   c. inexplainable

_____ 6. <u>spontaneity</u>
   a. impulse   b. realism   c. obedience

_____ 7. <u>delusion</u>
   a. false belief   b. true insight   c. established fact

_____ 8. <u>plight</u>
   a. bad condition   b. poor technique   c. rapid flight

_____ 9. <u>wincing</u>
   a. distorting the facts   b. shrinking back involuntarily
   c. looking ahead

_____ 10. <u>psychorepression</u>
   a. exclusion from conscious thought
   b. treatment of a mental disorder
   c. study of the mind

COMPREHENSION

II. *Select the best answer for each of the following. Indicate your choice on the line provided.*

_____ 1. In this passage, the author is comparing the working of the unconscious mind to
   a. towing a Rolls-Royce.
   b. the functions of an attic.
   c. biological research.
   d. rules of good architecture.

_____ 2. The author makes his point through
   a. specific examples.
   b. critical analysis.
   c. analogy.
   d. explanation.

_____ 3. If you compared the kind of things that go into the attic with those things that might be stored in the unconscious mind, what would they have in common?
   a. All are possessions and memories we do not want to see or think about constantly, but do not want to totally forget.
   b. All are possessions and memories we want to store until we decide to discard them.

_____ 4. What, according to the author, is wrong with "spring cleaning" the brain periodically?
   a. It is too time-consuming and is easier to leave memories hidden away.
   b. Destroying anything makes us nervous and may lead to psychiatric problems.
   c. It is human nature to accumulate, outgrow, and then to store memories to be recalled at a later date.

_____ 5. What does the author mean, in the fifth paragraph, when he states that discovering that we have discarded something we wish we had kept is one of the reasons "we drum our fingers so much these days"?
   a. We are angry that we discarded the possession or memory.
   b. We are lonely when we discover an empty attic or a lack of memories.
   c. We are nervous because it is against human nature to discard possessions or memories.

6. The author is writing about the brain from the perspective of a
    a. psychiatrist.
    b. biologist.
    c. architect.

7. In accord with this perspective, the author believes that
    a. everything alive has usefulness.
    b. dreams are essential to well-being.
    c. smoke from burning things from the attic is harmful.

8. In paragraph 3 on page 406, what does the author imply by "I know it means waiting in line"?
    a. Psychiatrists are too busy to take suggestions.
    b. Psychiatrists are not interested in suggestions.
    c. There would be so many suggestions that not all of them could be heard.

9. With which of the following statements would the author probably *not* agree?
    a. Unconscious minds are normal structures and should be used.
    b. The mind, especially the unconscious, is mysterious and best left alone to function as intended.
    c. In our modern technological society, we have no need for comfortable memories and should be in total control of our unconscious, as well as conscious, mind at all times.

10. The therapeutic plan the author suggests would be to
    a. stock the unconscious mind with thoughts and then make total use of them.
    b. clean the mind of all useless memories periodically to make room for fresh new ideas.
    c. have a "sorting out" day periodically to discard the thoughts and memories that are no longer needed.

Selection Fourteen

The Pedestrian

RAY BRADBURY

To enter out into that silence that was the city at eight o'clock of a misty evening in November, to put your feet upon that buckling concrete walk, to step over grassy seams and make your way, hands in pockets, through the silences, that was what Mr. Leonard Mead most dearly loved to do. He would stand upon the corner of an intersection and peer down long moonlit avenues of sidewalk in four directions, deciding which way to go, but it really made no difference; he was alone in this world of 2053 A.D., or as good as alone, and with a final decision made, a path selected, he would stride off, sending patterns of frosty air before him like the smoke of a cigar.

Sometimes he would walk for hours and miles and return only at midnight to his house. And on his way he would see the cottages and homes with their dark windows, and it was not unequal to walking through a graveyard where only the faintest glimmers of firefly light appeared in flickers behind the windows. Sudden gray <u>phantoms</u> seemed to <u>mainfest</u> upon inner room walls where a curtain was still undrawn against the night, or there were whisperings and murmurs where a window in a tomb-like building was still open.

Mr. Leonard Mead would pause, cock his head, listen, look, and march on, his feet making no noise on the lumpy walk. For long ago he had wisely changed to sneakers when strolling at night, because the dogs in <u>intermittent squads</u> would parallel his journey with barkings if he wore hard heels, and lights might click on and faces appear and an entire street be startled by the passing of a lone figure, himself, in the early November evening.

On this particular evening he began his journey in a westerly direction, toward the hidden sea. There was a good crystal frost in the air, it cut the nose and made the lungs blaze like a Christmas tree inside; you could feel the cold light going on and off, all the branches filled with invisible snow. He listened to the faint push of his soft shoes through autumn leaves with satisfaction, and whistled a cold quiet whistle between his teeth, occasionally picking up a leaf as he passed, examining its skeletal pattern in the infrequent lamplights as he went on, smelling its rusty smell.

"Hello, in there," he whispered to every house on every side as he moved. "What's up tonight on Channel 4, Channel 7, Channel 9? Where are the cowboys rushing, and do I see the United States Cavalry over the next hill to the rescue?"

The street was silent and long and empty, with only his shadow moving like the shadow of a hawk in mid-country. If he closed his eyes and stood very still, frozen, he could imagine himself upon the center of a plain, a wintry, windless Arizona desert with no house in a thousand miles, and only dry river beds, the streets, for company.

"What is it now?" he asked the houses, noticing his wrist watch. "Eight-thirty P.M.? Time for a dozen assorted murders? A quiz? A revue? A comedian falling off the stage?"

Was that a murmur of laughter from within a moon-white house? He hesitated, but went on when nothing more happened. He stumbled over a particularly uneven section of sidewalk. The cement was vanishing under flowers and grass. In ten years of walking by night or day, for thousands of miles, he had never met another person walking, not one in all that time.

He came over to a cloverleaf intersection which stood silent where two main highways crossed the town. During the day it was a thunderous surge of cars, the gas station open, a great insect rustling and a ceaseless jockeying for position as the scarab-beetles, a faint incense puttering from their exhausts, skimmed homeward to the far directions. But now these highways, too, were like streams in a dry season, all stone and bed and moon radiance.

He turned back on a side street, circling around toward his home. He was within a block of his destination when the lone car turned a corner quite suddenly and flashed a fierce white cone of light upon him. He stood entranced, not unlike a night moth, stunned by the illumination, and then drawn toward it.

A metallic voice called to him:

"Stand still. Stay where you are! Don't move!"

He halted.

"Put up your hands!"

"But—" he said.

"Your hands up! Or we'll shoot!"

The police, of course, but what a rare, incredible thing; in a city of three million, there was only one police car left, wasn't that correct? Ever since a year ago, 2052, the election year, the force had been cut down from three cars to one. Crime was ebbing; there was no need now for the police, save for this one lone car wandering and wandering empty streets.

"Your name?" said the police car in a metallic whisper. He couldn't see the men in it for the bright light in his eyes.

"Leonard Mead," he said.

"Speak up!"

"Leonard Mead!"

"Business or profession?"

"I guess you'd call me a writer."

"No profession," said the police car, as if talking to itself. The light held him <u>fixed</u>, like a museum specimen, needle thrust through chest.

"You might say that," said Mr. Mead. He hadn't written in years. Magazines and books didn't sell any more. Everything went on in the tomb-like houses at night now, he thought, continuing his fancy. The tombs, ill-lit by television light, where the people sat like the dead, the gray or multi-colored lights touching their faces, but never really touching them.

"No profession," said the phonograph voice, hissing. "What are you doing out?"

"Walking," said Leonard Mead.

"Walking!"

"Just walking," he said simply, but his face felt cold.

"Walking, just walking, walking?"

"Yes, sir."

"Walking where? For what?"

"Walking for air. Walking to see."

"Your address!"

"Eleven South Saint James Street."

"And there is air in your house, you have an air conditioner, Mr. Mead?"

"Yes."

"And you have a viewing screen in your house to see with?"

"No."

"No?" There was a crackling quiet that in itself was an accusation.

"Are you married, Mr. Mead?"

"No."

"Not married," said the police voice behind the firey beam. The moon was high and clear among the stars and the houses were gray and silent.

"Nobody wanted me," said Leonard Mead with a smile.

"Don't speak unless you're spoken to!"

Leonard Mead waited in the cold night.

"Just walking, Mr. Mead?"

"Yes."

"But you haven't explained for what purpose."

"I explained; for air, and to see, and just to walk."

"Have you done this often?"

"Every night for years."

The police car sat in the center of the street with its radio throat faintly humming.

"Well, Mr. Mead," it said.

"Is that all?" he asked politely.

"Yes," said the voice. "Here." There was a sigh, a pop. The back door of the police car sprang wide. "Get in."

"Wait a minute, I haven't done anything!"

"Get in."

"I protest!"

"Mr. Mead."

He walked like a man suddenly drunk. As he passed the front window of the car he looked in. As he had expected, there was no one in the front seat, no one in the car at all.

"Get in."

He put his hand to the door and peered into the back seat, which was a little cell, a little black jail with bars. It smelled of riveted steel. It smelled of harsh antiseptic; it smelled too clean and hard and metallic. There was nothing soft there.

"Now if you had a wife to give you an alibi," said the iron voice. "But—"

"Where are you taking me?"

The car hesitated, or rather gave a faint whirring click, as if information, somewhere, was dropping card by punch-slotted card under electric eyes. "To the Psychiatric Center for Research on Regressive Tendencies."

He got in. The door shut with a soft thud. The police car rolled through the night avenues, flashing its dim lights ahead.

They passed one house on one street a moment later, one house in an entire city of houses that were dark, but this one particular house had all of its electric lights brightly lit, every window a loud yellow illumination, square and warm in the cool darkness.

"That's my house," said Leonard Mead.

No one answered him.

The car moved down empty river-bed streets and off away, leaving the empty streets with the empty sidewalks, and no sound and no motion all the rest of the chill November night.

NAME _____ **DATE** _____

VOCABULARY

I. *The words in column A are used in the selection. Match the definitions in column B to the appropriate word in column A.*

A	B
_____ 1. phantoms	a. maneuvering
_____ 2. manifest	b. motionless
_____ 3. intermittent	c. rush
_____ 4. squads	d. appear
_____ 5. surge	e. spellbound
_____ 6. jockeying	f. visions
_____ 7. entranced	g. excuse
_____ 8. ebbing	h. recurrent
_____ 9. fixed	i. packs
_____ 10. alibi	j. decreasing

COMPREHENSION

II. *Answer the following questions on the lines provided.*

1. When does the story take place? What is the population of the city?

   _____

   _____

2. Why do you think Mr. Mead always walks at night?

_____

_____

_____

3. In the first paragraph, what does the author mean when he says that "he was alone in this world of 2053 A.D., or as good as alone. . .?

_____

_____

_____

4. Why do you think the author uses "walking through a graveyard" to describe Mr. Mead's walk? Why does he use "tomb-like buildings" to describe what he sees along the way?

_____

_____

_____

_____

5. Mr. Mead whispers to the houses as he passed. What do you think this indicates?

_____

_____

_____

_____

6. What are all the people doing in the houses?

_____

_____

7. What is unusual about the police car that stops Mr. Mead on his walk?

_____

_____

8. Why do you think it is sufficient to have only one police car in the entire city? Explain.

_____

_____

_____

_____

_____

9. Describe the mood of the story.

_____

_____

10. Where is the police care taking Mr. Mead?

_____

11. How does Mr. Mead's house look compared with the others in the neighborhood?

_____

_____

_____

12. Do you think there is a possibility of this story being a reality in your lifetime? Give reasons for your answer.

_____

_____

_____

_____

_____

_____

_____

_____

III. Pretend that Mr. Mead runs from the police car rather than gets in it and then write a different ending for the story.

_____

_____

_____

_____

_____

_____

_____

_____

_____

_____

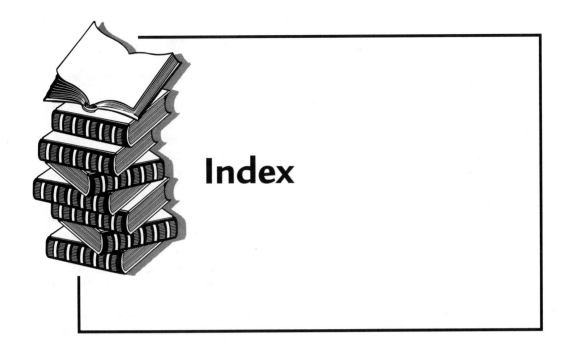

Index

Information Services Department (chart), 169

"In the Blink of an Eye" by Shawna Vogel, 341–43

L

Laboratories, as learning resources, 210
"Last Visit, The" by James Baldwin, 401–2
Learning resources, 209–13
"Legislative Obstacle Course, The," 178–79
Library, 210–13
Library of Congress classification system, 211
Literature, in content reading, 215–32
   general information, 215–16
   "Livvie" by Eudora Welty, 217–27
"Livvie" by Eudora Welty, 217–27

M

Main ideas, 53–78
   how to find main ideas, 54–55
Major Salesforce Management Decisions (chart), 170
Maps:
   Central American Rainforest, 186
   Ocmulgee National Monument, 173
   Projected Population Growth Rate, 172
"Market Usage Rate," 177
Maupassant, de Guy, "The Necklace," 367–73
"Measuring Intelligence," 271–77
Memory, in study, 203
Men and Women in the U.S. Labor Force (graph), 167

N

"Necklace, The" by Guy de Maupassant, 367–73

O

Objective tests, 206–7
"Ocmulgee National Monument," 19–20, (map), 173
On Line Public Access Catalog (OPAC), 212
"One Good Turn" by Witold Rybcznski, 379–80
"Open Window, The" by Saki (H. H. Munro), 335–37
Organizational patterns, 103–115
   cause and effect, 105–6
   comparison and contrast, 105
   definition, 106
   enumeration, 106–7
   example, 104
   explanation, 103–4

P

Parts of speech, in dictionary, 45
Payroll System (chart), 299
"Pedestrian, The" by Ray Bradbury, 411–14
"People and the Environment: Rainforest Removal," 184–85
Phrase reading, 192–93
Plan for vocabulary building, 2
Political science, in content reading, 249–67
   general information, 249–50
   "Presidency, The," 251–61
Popper, Adrienne, "I'm Going to Buy the Brooklyn Bridge," 317–19
"Postindustrial Sunbelt Cities," 182–83
Poverty Rate in the United States (graph), 167
Prefixes, 27–29
"Presidency, The," 251–61
Previewing, 205
Primary and Secondary Responses to Vaccinations (graph), 290
Priorities, establishing, 200–1